Andy Gill Terrance Sv

Practical Aspects of Declarative Languages

11th International Symposium, PADL 2009
Savannah, GA, USA, January 19-20, 2009
Proceedings

Volume Editors

Andy Gill
University of Kansas, 2001 Eaton Hall
1520 W. 15th St., Lawrence, KS 66045-7621, USA
E-mail: andygill@ku.edu

Terrance Swift
Universidade Nova de Lisboa, CENTRIA
PO Box 325, Sheperdstown, WV 25443, USA
E-mail: tswift@cs.sunysb.edu

Library of Congress Control Number: Applied for

CR Subject Classification (1998): D.3, D.1, F.3, D.2

LNCS Sublibrary: SL 2 – Programming and Software Engineering

ISSN 0302-9743
ISBN-10 3-540-92994-0 Springer Berlin Heidelberg New York
ISBN-13 978-3-540-92994-9 Springer Berlin Heidelberg New York

springer.com

Printed in Germany

Typesetting: Camera-ready by author, data conversion by Scientific Publishing Services, Chennai, India
Printed on acid-free paper SPIN: 12602995 06/3180 5 4 3 2 1 0

Preface

Declarative languages have long promised the ability to rapidly create easily maintainable software for complex applications. The International Symposium of Practical Aspects of Declarative Languages (PADL) provides a yearly forum for presenting results on the principles the implementations and especially the applications of declarative languages. The PADL symposium held January 19–20, 2009 in Savannah, Georgia was the 11th in this series.

This year 48 papers were submitted from authors in 17 countries. The Program Committee performed outstandingly to ensure that each of these papers submitted to PADL 2009 was thoroughly reviewed by at least three referees in a short period of time. The resulting symposium presented a microcosm of how the current generation of declarative languages are being used to address real applications, along with on-going work on the languages themselves. The program also included two invited talks, "Inspecting and Preferring Abductive Models" by Luis Moniz Pereira and "Applying Declarative Languages to Commercial Hardware Design" by Jeff Lewis. Regular papers presented a variety of applications, including distributed applications over networks, network verification, user interfaces, visualization in astrophysics, nucleotide sequence analysis and planning under incomplete information. PADL 2009 also included ongoing work on the declarative languages themselves. Multi-threaded and concurrent Prolog implementation was addressed in several papers, as were innovations for tabling in Prolog and functional arrays in Haskell. Recent applications have also sparked papers on meta-predicates in Prolog and a module system for ACL2. While the majority of this work was within the functional and logic programming paradigms, a paper also described improvements to PADS, a specialized language for processing data in ad hoc formats. Finally, the symposium also included papers whose contribution is mainly theoretical but whose practicality seems direct: these papers focussed on typed datalog and goal-directed querying of normal logic programs.

The PADL symposium was co-located with the ACM Symposium on Principles of Programming Languages (POPL 2009). We thank the University of Texas at Dallas, the University of Kansas, and the Centre for Research in Artificial Intelligence, Universidade Nova de Lisboa for their support. Finally, we would like to thank Gopal Gupta whose vision was instrumental in initiating the PADL symposia, and whose efforts have helped sustain them over more than a decade.

November 2008

Andy Gill
Terrance Swift

Organization

Conference Chair	Kevin Hamlen (University of Texas at Dallas)
Program Co-chair	Andy Gill (University of Kansas)
Program Co-chair	Terrance Swift (CENTRIA, Universidade Nova de Lisboa)

Program Committee

Lennart Augustsson	Standard Chartered Bank
Hasan Davulcu	Arizona State University
Inés Dutra	Universidade do Porto
John Gallagher	Roskilde University
Andy Gordon	Microsoft Research
Jeff Gray	University of Alabama at Birmingham
Fergus Henderson	Google
Gabriele Keller	University of New South Wales
Michael Kifer	SUNY Stony Brook
Ilkka Niemelä	Helsinki University of Technology
Johan Nordlander	Luleå University of Technology
Luís Pereira	Universidade Nova de Lisboa
Tom Schrijvers	Katholieke Universiteit Leuven
Lindsey Spratt	Ontology Works
Don Stewart	Galois, Inc
Walter Wilson	Systems Development and Analysis

Referees

José Alferes
Francisco Azevedo
Miguel Calejo
Manuel Chakravarty
Henning Christiansen
Vítor Santos Costa
Jorge Cruz
Iavor Diatchki
Paul Fodor
Louis-Julien Guillemette
Tomi Janhunen
Matti Järvisalo
Garrin Kimmell
Ludwig Krippahl
Roman Leshchinskiy
Senlin Liang
John Matthews
Paulo Moura
Manuel Ojeda-Aciego
Lee Pike
Alexandre Miguel Pinto
Morten Rhiger
Ricardo Rocha
Hui Wan
David S. Warren
Peter White

Table of Contents

Invited Talk

User Interfaces and Environments

Networks and Data

Multi-threading and Parallelism

Databases and Large Data Sets

Tabling and Optimization

Language Extensions and Implementation

On Preferring and Inspecting Abductive Models

Luís Moniz Pereira[1], Pierangelo Dell'Acqua[2], and Gonçalo Lopes[1]

[1] Departamento de Informática, Centro de Inteligência Artificial (CENTRIA), Universidade Nova de Lisboa 2829-516 Caparica, Portugal
lmp@di.fct.unl.pt, goncaloclopes@gmail.com

[2] Dept. of Science and Technology - ITN, Linköping University Norrköping, Sweden
pierangelo.dellacqua@itn.liu.se

Abstract. This work proposes the application of preferences over abductive logic programs as an appealing declarative formalism to model choice situations. In particular, both a priori and a posteriori handling of preferences between abductive extensions of a theory are addressed as complementary and essential mechanisms in a broader framework for abductive reasoning. Furthermore, both of these choice mechanisms are combined with other formalisms for decision making, like economic decision theory, resulting in theories containing the best advantages from both qualitative and quantitative formalisms. Several examples are presented throughout to illustrate the enounced methodologies. These have been tested in our implementation, which we explain in detail.

Keywords: Abduction, Preferences, Logic Programming, XSB-Prolog, Smodels.

1 Introduction

Much work in logic program semantics and procedures has focused on preferences between rules of a theory [5] and among theory literals [1,2], with or without updates. However, the exploration of the application of preferences to abductive extensions of a theory has still much to progress. An abductive extension is, by definition, a defeasible construct, and allows greater flexibility in enforcing preference relations. From our perspective, handling preferences over abductive logic programs has several advantages, and allows for easier and more concise translation into normal logic programs (NLP) than those prescribed by more general and complex rule preference frameworks.

In [5], a preliminary theory of revisable preferences between abducible literals was presented, and applied to theory revision, along with a formal semantics based on the definition of *abductive stable models*, illustrated in the paper with a number of applications and applied also to mutual preference revision in [15]. In [10] pre- and post-preferences on abducibles are employed to prospectively generate and filter likely agent preferred future scenarios. In [12], pre- and post-preferences on abducibles are applied to model and solve classic moral dilemmas.

Here we broaden the framework to account for more flexible and powerful means to express preferences between abducibles, over and above a priori relevancy rules embedded in a program's theory. We show there are many advantages as well to preferring a posteriori, i.e. to enact preferences on the computed models, after the consequences of

A. Gill and T. Swift (Eds.): PADL 2009, LNCS 5418, pp. 1–15, 2009.

opting for one or another abducible are known, by means of inspection points that examine specific side-effects of abduction. The advantages of so proceeding stem largely from avoiding combinatory explosions of abductive solutions, by filtering both irrelevant as well as less preferred abducibles. We combine these choice mechanisms with other formalisms for decision making, resulting in theories containing the best advantages from both qualitative and quantitative formalisms. Several examples are presented throughout to illustrate the enounced methodologies. These have been tested in our implementation, which we explain in detail.

2 Abductive Framework

2.1 Basic Abductive Language

Let $\mathcal{L}$ be a first order propositional language defined as follows. As usual, we study non-ground programs and their declarative semantics in terms of the set of all their ground instances, so that grounded literals can be envisaged as propositional constants. This does not preclude employing non-ground abductive programs for knowledge representation, though their practical use requires of course correct implementation techniques regarding non-ground abduction, an issue shared by constructive negation, so that the two are usefully combined. An inroad into these implementation techniques is to be found in [8].

Assume given an alphabet (set) of propositional atoms containing the reserved atom $\bot$ to denote falsity. A literal in $\mathcal{L}$ is an atom A or its default negation $not A$, the latter expressing that the atom is false by default (CWA).

Definition 1. *A rule in $\mathcal{L}$ takes the form $A \leftarrow L_1, \ldots, L_t$ where A is an atom and $L_1, \ldots, L_t$ $(t \geq 0)$ are literals.*

We follow the standard convention and call A the head of the rule, and the conjunction $L_1, \ldots, L_t$ its body. When $t = 0$ we write the rule simply as A, that is without '$\leftarrow$'. An integrity constraint is a rule whose head is $\bot$.

Definition 2. *A goal or query in $\mathcal{L}$ has the form $?{-}L_1, \ldots, L_t$, where $L_1, \ldots, L_t$ $(t \geq 1)$ are literals.*

A (logic) program P over $\mathcal{L}$ is a finite (countable) set of rules. We adopt the convention of using ';' to separate rules, thus we write a program P as $\{\text{rule}_1; \ldots; \text{rule}_n\}$.

Every program P is associated with a set of abducibles $\mathcal{A}$ consisting of literals which (without loss of generality) do not appear in any rule head of P. Abducibles may be thought of as hypotheses that can be used to extend the current theory in order to provide hypothetical solutions or possible explanations for given queries. Given an abductive solution, to test whether a certain abducible has been abduced, $\mathcal{L}$ contains the reserved abducible $abduced(a)$, for every abducible $a \neq abduced(.)$ in $\mathcal{L}$. Thus, $abduced(a)$ acts as a constraint that is satisfied in the solution if the abducible a is indeed assumed. It can be construed as meta-abduction in the form of abducing to check (or passively verify) that a certain abduction is adopted.

Example 1. Let $P = \{p \leftarrow abduced(a), a; q \leftarrow abduced(b)\}$ with set of abducibles $\mathcal{A}_P = \{a, b, abduced(a), abduced(b)\}$. Then, P has four intended models: $M = \{\}$,

$M_2 = \{p, a, abduced(a)\}$, $M_3 = \{q, b, abduced(b)\}$, and $M_4 = \{p, q, a, b, abduced(a), abduced(b)\}$. The set $\{q, abduced(b)\}$ is not an intended model since the assumption of $abduced(b)$ requires the assumption of b.

Given a set of abducibles $\mathcal{A}$, we write $\mathcal{A}^*$ to indicate the subset of $\mathcal{A}$ consisting of all the abducibles in $\mathcal{A}$ distinct from $abduced(.)$, that is:

$$\mathcal{A}^* = \{\ a\ :\ a \neq abduced(.) \text{ and } a \in \mathcal{A}\}.$$

Hypotheses Generation. The production of alternative explanations for a query is a central problem in abduction, because of the combinatorial explosion of possible explanations. In our approach, preferences among abducibles can be expressed in order to discard irrelevant assumptions. The notion of expectation is employed to express preconditions for enabling the assumption of an abducible. An abducible can be assumed only if there is an expectation for it, and there is not an expectation to the contrary. In this case, we say that the abducible is *considered*. These expectations are expressed by the following rules, for any given abducible $a \in \mathcal{A}^*$:

$$\begin{aligned} expect(a) &\leftarrow L_1, \ldots, L_t \\ expect\_not(a) &\leftarrow L_1, \ldots, L_t \end{aligned}$$

Note that $\mathcal{L}$ does not contain atoms of the form $expect(abduced(.))$ and of the form $expect\_not(abduced(.))$.

Example 2. Let $P = \{p \leftarrow a; q \leftarrow b; expect(a); expect(b); expect\_not(a) \leftarrow q\}$ with set of abducibles $\mathcal{A}_P = \{a, b, abduced(a), abduced(b)\}$. Then, P has three intended models: $M = \{expect(a), expect(b)\}$, $M_2 = \{p, a, abduced(a), expect(a), expect(b)\}$ and $M_3 = \{q, b, abduced(b), expect(a), expect(b)\}$. It is not possible to assume both a and b because the assumption of b makes q true which in turn makes $expect\_not(a)$ true preventing a to be assumed.

This notion of considered abducible allows to divide the abductive process into two distinct moments: the generation of hypotheses and the pruning of the unpreferred ones. Computation of preferences between models is problematic when both generation and comparison get mixed up, as mentioned in [2] which, however, does not introduce abductive preference and defeasibility also into generation like we do, but relegates all preference handling to posterior filtering. The two approaches could be conjoined.

Enforced Abduction. To express that the assumption of an abducible enforces the assumption of another abducible, $\mathcal{L}$ contains reserved atoms of the form $a \prec b$, for any abducibles $a, b \in \mathcal{A}^*$. The atom $a \prec b$ states that the assumption of b enforces the assumption of a, active abduction behavior. That is, if b is assumed, then $a \prec b$ forces a to be assumed provided that a can be considered. Note that the abducibles a, b are both required to be different from $abduced(.)$ since they belong to $\mathcal{A}^*$.

Example 3. Let $P = \{p \leftarrow a; a \prec b; b \prec a; expect(a); expect(b)\}$ with set of abducibles $\mathcal{A}_P = \{a, b, abduced(a), abduced(b)\}$. Then, P has two intended models for abduction: $M = \{a \prec b, b \prec a, expect(a), expect(b)\}$ and $M_2 = \{a \prec b, b \prec a, a, b, p, expect(a), expect(b), abduced(a), abduced(b)\}$ due to active abduction behavior of $a \prec b$ and $b \prec a$ preventing intended models containing either a or b alone.

Conditional Abduction. The assumption of an abducible a can be conditional on the assumption of another abducible b. The reserved atom $a \sqsubset b$ in $\mathcal{L}$, for any abducible $a, b \in \mathcal{A}^*$, states that a can be assumed only if b is (without assuming it for the purpose of having a), passive abduction behavior. That is, $a \sqsubset b$ acts as a check passively constraining the assumption of a to the assumption of b (passive abduction behavior). Note that the abducibles a, b are required to be different from $abduced(.)$.

Example 4. Let $P = \{p \leftarrow a; q \leftarrow b; a \sqsubset b; expect(a)\}$ with set of abducibles $\mathcal{A}_P = \{a, b, abduced(a), abduced(b)\}$. Then, there exists only one intended model of P: $M = \{a \sqsubset b, expect(a)\}$. Note that $M_2 = \{a \sqsubset b, b, q, expect(a), abduced(b)\}$ and $M_3 = \{a \sqsubset b, a, p, expect(a), abduced(a)\}$ are not intended models. In fact, M_2 is not a model since b cannot be assumed (there is no expectation for it). This fact also prevents the assumption of a (due to $a \sqsubset b$) and consequently M_3 is not a model.

Cardinality Constrained Abduction. To constrain the number of assumed abducibles, $\mathcal{L}$ contains reserved atoms of the form $L\ \{l_1, \ldots, l_n\}\ U$ where $n \geq 1$, every l_i is an abducible in $\mathcal{A}$, and L and U are natural numbers representing, respectively, the lower and upper bounds on the cardinality of abducibles. $L\ \{l_1, \ldots, l_n\}\ U$ states that at least L and at most U abducibles in $\{l_1, \ldots, l_n\}$ must be assumed (active abduction behavior). Since the abducibles l_i belong to $\mathcal{A}$, they can also take the form $abduced(.)$.

2.2 Declarative Semantics

The declarative semantics of programs over $\mathcal{L}$ is given in terms of abductive stable models. Let P be a program and $\mathcal{A}_P$ the abducibles in P. A 2-valued interpretation M of $\mathcal{L}$ is any set of literals from $\mathcal{L}$ that satisfies the condition that, for any atom A, precisely one of the literals A or $not\ A$ belongs to M. Interpretation M satisfies a conjunction of literals $L_1, \ldots, L_t$, if every literal L_i in the conjunction belongs to M. We need the notion of default assumptions of P with respect to an interpretation M, where a default literal $not\ A$ is considered an atom, and $not\ not\ A \equiv A$.

$$\begin{aligned}&Default(P, M) =\\ &\quad\{not\ A : \text{there exists no rule } A \leftarrow L_1, \ldots, L_t \text{ in } P \text{ such that } M \models L_1, \ldots, L_t\}\end{aligned}$$

Abducibles are false by default since we made the assumption that abducibles are not defined by any rule in P. An interpretation M is a stable model of P iff:

1. $M \not\models \bot$ and
2. $M = least(P \cup Default(P, M))$, where $least$ indicates the least model.

Let C be $L\,\{l_1, \ldots, l_n\}\,U$. Then, we let $W(C, M)$ be the number of abducibles in $\{l_1, \ldots, l_n\}$ satisfied by an interpretation M:

$$W(C, M) = |\,\{l : l \in \{l_1, \ldots, l_n\} \text{ and } M \models l\}\,|$$

Given a set of abducibles Δ, we write Δ^* to indicate :

$$\Delta^* = \{a\ :\ a \neq abduced(.) \text{ and } a \in \Delta\}$$

Definition 3. *Let $\Delta \subseteq \mathcal{A}_P$ be a set of abducibles. M is an abductive stable model with hypotheses Δ of P iff:*

1. $M \not\models \bot$
2. $M = least(Q \cup Default(Q, M))$, *where* $Q = P \cup \Delta$
3. $M \models expect(a)$ *and* $M \not\models expect\_not(a)$, *for every* $a \in \Delta^*$
4. *for every* $a \in \Delta^*$, *if* $M \models a$ *then* $M \models abduced(a)$
5. *for every atom* $a \prec b$, *if* $M \models a \prec b$, $M \models expect(a)$, $M \not\models expect\_not(a)$ *and* $M \models b$, *then* $M \models a$
6. *for every atom C of the form* $L\,\{l_1, \ldots, l_n\}\,U$, *if* $M \models C$ *then* $L \leq W(C, M) \leq U$
7. *for every* $a \in \Delta^*$, *if* $M \models abduced(a)$ *then* $M \models a$
8. *for every atom* $a \sqsubset b$, *if* $M \models a \sqsubset b$ *and* $M \models a$, *then* $M \models b$

Example 5. Let $P = \{p \leftarrow abduced(a); expect(a)\}$ and $\mathcal{A}_P = \{a, abduced(a)\}$. Then, $M = \{p, a, abduced(a), expect(a)\}$ is an abductive stable model with hypotheses $\Delta = \{a, abduced(a)\}$, while $M_2 = \{p, abduced(a), expect(a)\}$ is not since condition (7) of Def. 3 is not fulfilled.

Definition 4. *Δ is an abductive explanation for goal G in P iff there exists a model M such that M is an abductive stable model with hypotheses Δ of P and $M \models G$.*

Definition 5. *Δ is a strict abductive explanation for goal G in P iff there exists a model M such that:*

1. *Δ is a minimal set for which:*
   - $M \models G$
   - $M \not\models \bot$
   - $M = least(Q \cup Default(Q, M))$, *where* $Q = P \cup \Delta$
   - $M \models expect(a)$ *and* $M \not\models expect\_not(a)$, *for every* $a \in \Delta^*$
   - *for every* $a \in \Delta^*$, *if* $M \models a$ *then* $M \models abduced(a)$
   - *for every atom* $a \prec b$, *if* $M \models a \prec b$, $M \models expect(a)$, $M \not\models expect\_not(a)$ *and* $M \models b$, *then* $M \models a$
   - *for every atom C of the form* $L\,\{l_1, \ldots, l_n\}\,U$, *if* $M \models C$ *then* $L \leq W(C, M) \leq U$
2. *for every* $a \in \Delta^*$, *if* $M \models abduced(a)$ *then* $M \models a$
3. *for every atom* $a \sqsubset b$, *if* $M \models a \sqsubset b$ *and* $M \models a$, *then* $M \models b$

Note that in Def. 5 condition (2) is not subject to minimization. The reason for this is clarified by the next example.

Example 6. Reconsider P of Example 5. Suppose that the goal G is $?{-}p$. It holds that $\Delta = \{a, abduced(a)\}$ is an abductive explanation for G in P, but it is not strict since Δ is not a minimal set satisfying condition (1) of Def. 5. Indeed, the minimal set is $\Delta_2 = \{abduced(a)\}$. Hence, there exists no strict abductive explanation for G in P.

The following property relates abductive explanations to strict abductive explanations.

Proposition 1. *Let G be a goal and Δ a strict abductive explanation for G in P. Then, Δ is an abductive explanation for G in P.*

3 Pragmatics

3.1 Constraining Abduction

Quite often in domain problems it happens the assumption of abducibles is subject to the fulfillment of certain conditions, including other assumptions, which must be satisfied. This requirement is expressed by exploiting constrained abduction, $a \sqsubset b$.

Example 7. Consider a scenario where there is a pub that is open or closed. If the light is on in the pub then it is open or being cleaned. Late at night, one can assume the pub is open if there are people inside. The pub being located in an entertainment district, there is noise around if there are people in the pub or a party nearby. This scenario is described by the program P with $\mathcal{A}_P = \{open, cleaning, party, people, abduced(open),$ $abduced(cleaning), abduced(party), abduced(people)\}$.

$$
\begin{array}{l}
light \leftarrow open, not\ cleaning \\
light \leftarrow cleaning, not\ open, not\ abduced(people) \\
open \sqsubset people \leftarrow late\_night \\
noise \leftarrow party \\
noise \leftarrow people
\end{array}
$$

$$expect(open) \quad expect(cleaning) \quad expect(party) \quad expect(people)$$

Thus, in case it is night (but not late night) and one does observe lights in the pub, then one has two equally plausible explanations for it: $\{open\}$ or $\{cleaning\}$. Otherwise (late night is a given fact), there is a single explanation for the lights being on: $\{cleaning\}$. If instead it is late night and one hears noise too (i.e. the query is $?\!-light, noise$), then one will have three abductive explanations: $\{open, people\}$, $\{party, cleaning\}$ and $\{open, party, people\}$. The last one reflects that the pub may be open with late customers simultaneously with a party nearby, both events producing noise.

3.2 Preferring Abducibles

Now we illustrate how to express preferences between considered abducibles. We employ construct $L\,\langle l_1, \ldots, l_n \rangle\, U$ to constrain the number of abducibles possibly assumed. The construct has a passive abduction behavior and it is defined as:

$$L\,\langle l_1, \ldots, l_n \rangle\, U \equiv L\,\{abduce(l_1), \ldots, abduce(l_n)\}\, U$$

for any abducible $l_1, \ldots, l_n$ in $\mathcal{A}^*$. The next example illustrates the difference between $L\,\langle l_1, \ldots, l_n \rangle\, U$ and $L\,\{l_1, \ldots, l_n\}\, U$.

Example 8. Consider a situation where Claire drinks either tea or coffee (but not both). Suppose that Claire prefers coffee over tea when sleepy, and doesn't drink coffee when she has high blood pressure. This situation is described by program P over $\mathcal{L}$ with abducibles $\mathcal{A}_P = \{tea, coffee, abduced(tea), abduced(coffee)\}$:

$$drink \leftarrow tea \qquad expect(tea)$$
$$drink \leftarrow coffee \qquad expect(coffee)$$
$$expect\_not(coffee) \leftarrow blood\_pressure\_high$$

$$0\ \langle tea, coffee \rangle\ 1$$
$$coffee \prec tea \leftarrow sleepy$$

In the abductive stable model semantics, this program has two models, one with tea the other with coffee. Adding literal *sleepy*, enforced abduction comes into play, defeating the abductive stable model where only *tea* is present (due to the impossibility of simultaneously abducing coffee). If later we add *blood_pressure_high*, coffee is no longer expected, and the transformed preference rule no longer defeats the abduction of *tea* which then becomes the single abductive stable model, despite the presence of *sleepy*.

3.3 Abducible Sets

Often it is desirable not only to include rules about expectations for single abducibles, but also to express contextual information constraining the powerset of abducibles.

Example 9. Consider a situation where Claire is deciding what to have for a meal from a limited buffet. The menu has appetizers (which Claire doesn't mind skipping, unless she's very hungry), three main dishes, from which one can select a maximum of two, and drinks, from which she will have a single one. The situation, with all possible choices, can be modelled by program P over $\mathcal{L}$ with set of abducibles $\mathcal{A}_P$=$\{bread, salad, cheese, fish, meat, veggie, wine, juice, water, abduced(bread), abduced(salad), abduced(cheese), abduced(fish), abduced(meat), abduced(veggie), abduced(wine), abduced(juice), abduced(water)\}$:

$$0\ \{bread, salad, cheese\}\ 3 \leftarrow appetizers \qquad main\_dishes \prec appetizers$$
$$1\ \{fish, meat, veggie\}\ 2 \leftarrow main\_dishes \qquad drinks \prec appetizers$$
$$1\ \{wine, juice, water\}\ 1 \leftarrow drinks \qquad appetizers \leftarrow very\_hungry$$
$$2\ \{appetizers, main\_dishes, drinks\}\ 3$$

Here we model appetizers as the least preferred set from those available for the meal. It shows we can condition sets of abducibles based on the generation of literals from other cardinality constraints plus preferences among them.

3.4 Modeling Inspection Points

When finding an abductive solution for a query, one may want to check whether some other literals become true or false strictly within the abductive solution found, without performing additional abductions, and without having to produce a complete model to do so. Pereira and Pinto [11] argue this type of reasoning requires a new mechanism. To achieve it, they introduce the concept of inspection point, and show how to employ it to investigate side-effects of interest. Procedurally, inspection points are construed as a form of meta-abduction, by "meta-abducing" the specific abduction of checking (i.e. passively verifying) that a corresponding concrete abduction is indeed adopted. That is, one abduces the checking of some abducible A, and the check consists in confirming that A is part of the abductive solution by matching it with the object of the abduced check.

In their approach the side-effects of interest are explicitly indicated by the user wrapping the corresponding goals with a reserved construct $inspect/1$. Procedurally, $inspect$ goals must be solved without abducing regular abducibles, only "meta-abducibles" of the form $abduced/1$.

Example 10. Consider the following program taken from [11], where $tear\_gas$, $fire$, and $water\_cannon$ are abducibles.

$$\bot \leftarrow police, riot, not\, contain$$

$$contain \leftarrow tear\_gas \qquad contain \leftarrow water\_cannon$$

$$smoke \leftarrow fire \qquad smoke \leftarrow inspect(tear\_gas)$$

$$police \qquad riot$$

Note the two rules for $smoke$. The first states one explanation for smoke is fire, when assuming the hypothesis $fire$. The second states $tear\_gas$ is also a possible explanation for smoke. However, the presence of tear gas is a much more unlikely situation than the presence of fire; after all, tear gas is only used by police to contain riots and that is truly an exceptional situation. Fires are much more common and spontaneous than riots. For this reason, $fire$ is a much more plausible explanation for $smoke$ and, therefore, in order to let the explanation for $smoke$ be $tear\_gas$, there must be a plausible reason – imposed by some other likely phenomenon. This is represented by $inspect(tear\_gas)$ instead of simply $tear\_gas$. The $inspect$ construct disallows regular abduction – only meta-abduction – to be performed whilst trying to solve $tear\_gas$. I.e., if we take tear gas as an abductive solution for fire, this rule imposes that the step where we abduce $tear\_gas$ is performed elsewhere, not under the derivation tree for $smoke$. The integrity constraint, since there is $police$ and a $riot$, forces $contain$ to be true, and hence, $tear\_gas$ or $water\_cannon$ or both, must be abduced. $smoke$ is only explained if, at the end of the day, $tear\_gas$ is abduced to enact containment. Abductive solutions should be plausible, and $smoke$ is explained by $tear\_gas$ if there is a reason, a best explanation, that makes the presence of tear gas plausible; in this case the riot and the police. Plausibility is an important concept in science in lending credibility to hypotheses.

4 A Posteriori Preferences

A desirable result of encoding abduction semantics over models of a program is that we immediately obtain the consequences of committing to any one hypotheses set. Rules which contain abducibles in their bodies can account for the side-effect derivation of certain positive literals in some models, but not others, possibly triggering integrity constraints or indirectly deriving interesting consequences simply as a result of accepting a hypothesis.

Preferring a posteriori, only after model generation is achieved, is thus needed. However, cause and effect is not enough to draw conclusions and decide, due to the problem of imperfect information and uncertain conditions. To resolve these problems, combining causal models with probabilistic information about models is required.

4.1 Utility Theory

Abduction can be seen as a mechanism to enable the generation of the possible futures of an agent, with each abductive stable model representing a possibly reachable scenario of interest. Preferring over abducibles enacts preferences over the imagined future of the agent. In this context, it is unavoidable to deal with uncertainty, a problem decision theory is ready to address using probabilities coupled with utility functions.

Example 11. Suppose Claire is spending a day at the beach and she is deciding what means of transportation to adopt. She knows it is usually faster and more comfortable to go by car, but she also knows, because it is hot, there is possibility of a traffic jam. It is also possible to use public transportation (by train), but it will take longer, though it meets her wishes of being more environment friendly. The situation can be modeled by the abductive logic program:

$$\begin{array}{ll} go\_to(beach) \leftarrow car & expect(car) \\ go\_to(beach) \leftarrow train & expect(train) \\ hot & 1\ \{car, train\}\ 1 \end{array}$$

$$probability(traffic\_jam, 0.7) \leftarrow hot$$
$$probability(not\ traffic\_jam, 0.3) \leftarrow hot$$

$$utility(stuck\_in\_traffic, -8)$$
$$utility(wasting\_time, -4)$$

$$utility(comfort, 10)$$
$$utility(environment\_friendly, 3)$$

By assuming each of the abductive hypotheses, the general utility of going to the beach can be computed for each particular scenario:

Assume car
Probability of being stuck in traffic = 0.7
Probability of a comfortable ride = 0.3
Expected utility = 10 * 0.3 + 0.7 * -8 = -2.6

Assume train
Expected utility = -4 + 3 = -1

It should be clear that enacting preferential reasoning over the utilities computed for each model has to be performed after the scenarios are available, with an a posteriori meta-reasoning over the models and their respective utilities.

5 Implementation

The abductive framework described above has been implemented in the ACORDA [10] logic programming system, designed to accomodate abduction in evolving scenarios.

5.1 XSB-XASP Interface

Prolog is the most accepted means to codify and execute logic programs, and a useful tool for research and application development in logic programming. Several stable implementations were developed and refined over the years, with plenty of working solutions to pragmatic issues, ranging from efficiency and portability to explorations of language extensions. XSB-Prolog[1] is one of the most sophisticated, powerful, efficient and versatile, focusing on execution efficiency and interaction with external systems, implementing logic program evaluation following the Well-Founded Semantics (WFS).

The semantics of Stable Models is a cornerstone for the definition of some of the most important results in logic programming of the past decade, providing an increase in logic program declarativity and a new paradigm for program evaluation. However, the lack of some important properties of previous language semantics, like relevancy and cumulativity, somewhat reduces its applicability in practice, namely regarding abduction.

The XASP interface [3,4] (XSB Answer Set Programming), part of XSB-Prolog, is a practical programming interface to Smodels[9]. XASP allows to compute the models of a Normal LP, and also to effectively combine 3- with 2-valued reasoning.

This is gotten by using Smodels to compute the stable models of the residual program, one that results from a query evaluation in XSB using tabling[16]. The residual program is formed by delay lists, sets of undefined literals for which XSB could not find a complete proof, due to mutual loops over default negation in a set, as detected by the tabling mechanism. This method allows obtaining 2-valued models, by completion of the 3-valued ones of XSB. The integration maintains the relevance property for queries over our programs, something Stable Model semantics does not enjoy. In Stable Models, by its very definition, it is necessary to compute whole models of a given program. In the ACORDA implementation framework we sidestep this issue, using XASP to compute the query relevant residual program on demand, usually after some degree of transformation. Only the resulting residual program is sent to Smodels for computation of its abductive stable models. This is one of the main problems which abduction over stable models has been facing: it always needs to consider each abducible in a program, and then progressively defeat those irrelevant for the problem at hand. It is not so in our framework, since we can begin evaluation with a top-down derivation for a query, which immediately constrains the set of abducibles to those relevant to the satisfaction and proof of that query. Each query is conjoined with $not \perp$ to ensure Integrity Constraints satisfaction.

An important consideration in computing consequences, cf. Section 4, is not having to compute whole models of the program to obtain just a specific consequences subset, the one useful to enact a posteriori preferences. This is avoided by computing models just for the residual program corresponding to the consequences we wish to observe. Consequences which are significant for model preference are thus computed on the XSB side, and their residual program is then sent to Smodels. A posteriori preference rules are evaluated over the computed models, and are just consumers of considered

[1] Both the XSB Logic Programming system and Smodels are freely available at: `http://xsb.sourceforge.net` and `http://www.tcs.hut.fi/Software/smodels`

abducibles that have indeed been produced, meaning that any additional abductions are disallowed.

5.2 Top-Down Proof Procedure

In our implementation we aim for query-driven evaluation of abductive stable models, so that only the relevant part of the program is considered for computation. Computation of such models is performed in two stages. First XSB computes the Well-Founded Model (WFM) of the program w.r.t. the query, by supporting goal derivations on any considered expected abducibles, that are not otherwise being defeated; cf. Section 2.1. We aim to dynamically collect only those abducibles necessary to prove the query. We can assume them neither true nor false at this stage, so they end up undefined in the derivation tree. This is achieved by coding considered abducibles thus:

$$\begin{aligned} consider(A) &\leftarrow expect(A), not\ expect\_not(A), abduce(A) \\ abduce(A) &\leftarrow not\ abduce\_not(A) \\ abduce\_not(A) &\leftarrow not\ abduce(A) \end{aligned}$$

The latter two rules encode an abducible as an even-loop over default negation. They warrant any considered abducible is undefined in the WFM of the program, and hence contained in the residual program computed by the XSB Prolog meta-interpreter; cf. Section 5.1. In this way, any query which is supported on abductive literals will also have its entire derivation tree contained in the XSB's residual program. We can then use this tree as a partial program which is sent to Smodels for model computation. After the stable models of these partial programs are computed, all even-loops will be solved by either assuming the abduction, or assuming its negation.

5.3 Program Transformation

Now we consider a first-order propositional language $\mathcal{L}^{\#}$ containing rules as defined in Def. 1. Programs over $\mathcal{L}^{\#}$ are constrained to satisfy given properties.

Definition 6. *Let Γ and Σ be sets of rules over $\mathcal{L}^{\#}$. Then (Γ, Σ) is a restricted program.*

The basic idea is that Γ contains the rules formalizing the application domain while Σ formalizes the properties Γ must satisfy. Every restricted program is associated with a set of abducibles $\mathcal{A}_{(\Gamma,\Sigma)}$. In the sequel let $\Delta \subseteq \mathcal{A}_{(\Gamma,\Sigma)}$ be some subset.

Definition 7. *M is a valid stable model with hypotheses Δ of (Γ, Σ) iff $M \nvDash \bot$, $M = least(\Gamma^+ \cup Default(\Gamma^+, M))$, where $\Gamma^+ = \Gamma \cup \Delta$ and $M \vDash \Sigma$.*

A valid stable model is an abductive stable model (conditions (1) and (2)) satisfying the wffs in Σ (condition (3)).

Definition 8. *Δ is a valid explanation for goal G in (Γ, Σ) iff M is a valid stable model with hypotheses Δ of (Γ, Σ) and $M \vDash G$.*

Definition 9. *Δ is a strict valid explanation for goal G in (Γ, Σ) iff:*

1. *Δ is a minimal set for which:*
   - $M \not\models \bot$
   - $M = least(\Gamma^+ \cup Default(\Gamma^+, M))$, *where* $\Gamma^+ = \Gamma \cup \Delta$
   - $M \models G$
2. $M \models \Sigma$

We define transformation γ mapping programs over $\mathcal{L}$ to restricted ones over $\mathcal{L}^\#$.

Definition 10. *Let P be a program over $\mathcal{L}$ with set of abducibles $\mathcal{A}_P$. The restricted program $\gamma(P) = (\Gamma, \Sigma)$ over $\mathcal{L}^\#$ with set of abducibles $\mathcal{A}_{(\Gamma,\Sigma)} = \mathcal{A}_P$ is defined as follows.*

Γ consists of:

1. *all the rules in P*
2. $\bot \leftarrow a, not\ expect(a)$
   $\bot \leftarrow a, expect\_not(a)$
   for every abducible $a \in \mathcal{A}_P^*$
3. $\bot \leftarrow a, not\ abduced(a)$
   for every abducible $a \in \mathcal{A}_P^*$
4. $\bot \leftarrow a \prec b, expect(a), not\ expect\_not(a), b, not\ a$
   for every rule $a \prec b \leftarrow L_1, \ldots, L_t$ in P
5. $\bot \leftarrow L\,\{l_1, \ldots, l_n\}\,U, count([l_1, \ldots, l_n], N), N \leq L$
   $\bot \leftarrow L\,\{l_1, \ldots, l_n\}\,U, count([l_1, \ldots, l_n], N), N \geq U$
   for every rule $L\,\{l_1, \ldots, l_n\}\,U \leftarrow L_1, \ldots L_t$ in P

Σ consists of:

6. $\bot \leftarrow abduced(a), not\ a$
   for every abducible $a \in \mathcal{A}_P^*$
7. $\bot \leftarrow a \sqsubset b, a, not\ b$
   for every rule $a \sqsubset b \leftarrow L_1, \ldots, L_t$ in P

Remark 1. We assume given the atom $count([l_1, \ldots, l_n], m)$ that holds if m is the number of abducibles belonging to $[l_1, \ldots, l_n]$ that are assumed. That is, if C is the atom $L\,\{l_1, \ldots, l_n\}\,U$, then we have that $M \models count([l_1, \ldots, l_n], m)$ iff $W(C, M) = m$, for any interpretation M.

Remark 2. If P contains inspection points, then apply the transformation γ to $\Pi(P)$ (cf. Definition 6 of [11]) instead of to P directly.

Theorem 1. *Let P be a program over $\mathcal{L}$ with set of abducibles $\mathcal{A}_P$. M is an abductive stable model with hypotheses $\Delta \subseteq \mathcal{A}_P$ of P iff M is a valid stable model with hypotheses Δ of $\gamma(P)$.*

Theorem 2. *Let P be a program over $\mathcal{L}$. $\Delta \subseteq \mathcal{A}_P$ is a strict abductive explanation for goal G in P iff Δ is a strict valid explanation for G in $\gamma(P)$.*

5.4 Computation of Abductive Stable Models

In this second stage, Smodels will thus be used to compute abductive stable models from the residual program obtained from top-down goal derivation. Determination of relevant abducibles is performed by examining the residual program for ground literals which are arguments to *consider/1* clauses. Relevant preference rules are pre-evaluated at this stage as well, by querying for any such rules involving any pair of the relevant abducible set.

The XASP package [3] allows the programmer to collect rules in an XSB clause store. When the programmer has determined enough clauses were added to the store to form a semantically complete sub-program, it is then *committed.* This means information in the clauses is copied to Smodels, coded using Smodels data structures, so that stable models of those clauses can be computed and returned to XSB to be examined.

When both the relevant abducibles and preference rules are determined, a variation of transformation γ is applied, with every encoded clause being sent to the XASP store, reset beforehand in preparation for the stable models computation. Once the residual program, transformed to enact preferences, is actually committed to Smodels, we obtain through XASP the set of abductive stable models, and identify each one by their choice of abducibles, i.e. those *consider/1* literals collected beforehand in the residual program.

5.5 Inspection Points

Given the top-down proof procedure for abduction, implementing inspection points becomes just a matter of adapting the evaluation of derivation subtrees falling under $inspect/1$ literals at meta-interpreter level. Basically, considered abducibles evaluated under $inspect/1$ subtrees are codified thus:

$$\begin{aligned} consider(A) &\leftarrow abduced(A) \\ abduced(A) &\leftarrow not\ abduced\_not(A) \\ abduced\_not(A) &\leftarrow not\ abduced(A) \end{aligned}$$

All $abduced/1$ predicates are collected during computation of the residual program and later checked against the abductive stable models themselves. Every $abduced(a)$ predicate must pair with a corresponding abducible a for the model to be accepted; cf. transformation γ.

Let $\mathcal{L}^*$ be a first order propositional language defined as $\mathcal{L}$ except that $\mathcal{L}^*$ contains atoms of the form $inspect(.)$, $ea(.,.)$ and $ca(.,.)$, while it does not contain any atom of the form $a \prec b$, $a \sqsubset b$ and $abduced(.)$. The transformation below maps programs over $\mathcal{L}$ into programs over $\mathcal{L}^*$.

Definition 11. *Let P be a program over $\mathcal{L}$. Let Q be the set of all the rules obtained by the rules in P by replacing $abduced(a)$ with $inspect(a)$, $a \prec b$ with $ea(a,b)$ and $a \sqsubset b$ with $ca(a,b)$. Program $\Pi(P)$ over $\mathcal{L}^*$ consists of all rules in Q together with rules:*

$\bot \leftarrow not\ a, inspect(b), L_1, \ldots, L_t$ *for every* $ea(a,b) \leftarrow L_1, \ldots, L_t$ *in* Q,
$\bot \leftarrow inspect(a), not\ inspect(b), L_1, \ldots, L_t$ *for every* $ca(a,b) \leftarrow L_1, \ldots, L_t$ *in* Q.

5.6 A Posteriori Choice Mechanisms

If a single model emerges from computation of the abductive stable models, goal evaluation can terminate. When multiple models still remain, there is opportunity to introduce a posteriori choice mechanisms, which are domain-specific for a program. We account for this specificity by providing an implementation hook the user can adopt for introducing specific code for this final selection process, in addition to the a posteriori choice mechanisms in Section 4.

6 Conclusions

We have addressed issues of formalizing the combination of abduction with preferences, and its implementation, in an original way. Namely, we introduced the notion of expectable defeasible abducibles, enabled by the situation at hand and guided by the query, and catered for a priori preferences amongst abducibles; all mechanisms designed to cut down on the combinatory explosion of untoward abduction, that is relying only on a posteriori preferences to filter what should not have been generated in the first place. In regard to a posteriori preferences, we defined the notion of inspection points to cater for observing relevant side-effects of abductive solutions, and enable a posteriori choices without generating complete models which show all side-effects. In all, we showed how a combination of cardinality constraints, preferences and inspection points can be used to govern and constrain abduction, and how these mechanisms, coupled with a posteriori ones, are an important tool for knowledge representation in modeling choice situations where agents need to consider present and future contexts to decide about them. Finally, we showed the advantages of implementing our framework as a hybrid state-of-art declarative XSB-Prolog/Smodels system, to efficiently combine top-down query-oriented abductive backward chaining, and side-effect model generating forwards-chaining, respectively for constraining abducibles to preferred ones relevant for a goal, and to compute the consequences of assuming them in each scenario.

We cannot presume to survey and compare the present work with the by now formidable stock of separate works on abduction and on preferences in logic programming, though we have referred to some along the exposition. Our intent has been the rather original introduction of new features mentioned above, and their combination and implementation, and in that respect we know not of competitive similar attempts. However, regarding inspection points, in [14], a technical problem is detected with the IFF abductive proof procedure [7], in what concerns the treatment of negated abducibles in integrity constraints (e.g. their examples 2 and 3). They then specialize IFF to avoid such problems and prove correctness of the new procedure. The problems detected refer to the active use an IC of some not A, where A is an abducible, whereas the intended use should be a passive one, simply checking whether A is proved in the abductive solution found, as in our inspection points (though these more generally apply to any literal). To that effect they replace such occurrences of not A by not provable(A), in order to ensure that no new abductions are allowed during the checking.

In the way of future developments and application topics, in [13], arguments are given as to how epistemic entrenchment can be explicitly expressed as preferential reasoning. And, moreover, how preferences can be employed to determine believe revisions, or, conversely, how belief contractions can lead to the explicit expression of preferences. [6] provides a stimulating survey of opportunities and problems in the use of preferences, reliant on AI techniques.

On a more general note, it appears to us that the practical use and implementation of abduction in knowledge representation and reasoning, by means of declarative languages and systems, has reached a point of maturity, and of opportunity for development, worthy the calling of attention of a wider community of potential practitioners.

References

1. Brewka, G.: Logic programming with ordered disjunction. In: Kaufmann, M. (ed.) Proc. 18th National Conference on Artificial Intelligence, AAAI 2002 (2002)
2. Brewka, G., Niemelä, I., Truszczynski, M.: Answer set optimization. In: Proc. IJCAI 2003, pp. 867–872 (2003)
3. Castro, L., Swift, T., Warren, D.S.: XASP: Answer Set Programming with XSB and Smodels, `http://xsb.sourceforge.net/packages/xasp.pdf`
4. Castro, L.F., Warren, D.S.: An environment for the exploration of non monotonic logic programs. In: Kusalik, A. (ed.) Proc. of the 11th Intl. Workshop on Logic Programming Environments (WLPE 2001) (2001)
5. Dell'Acqua, P., Pereira, L.M.: Preferential theory revision. J. of Applied Logic 5(4), 586–601 (2007)
6. Doyle, J.: Prospects for preferences. Computational Intelligence 20(3), 111–136 (2004)
7. Fung, T.H., Kowalski, R.: The IFF Proof Procedure for Abductive Logic Programming. The J. of Logic Programming 33(2), 151–165 (1997)
8. Neg-Abdual. Constructive Negation with Abduction, `http://centria.di.fct.unl.pt/~lmp/software/contrNeg.rar`
9. Niemelä, I., Simons, P.: Smodels: An implementation of the stable model and well-founded semantics for normal logic programs. In: Fuhrbach, U., Dix, J., Nerode, A. (eds.) LPNMR 1997. LNCS (LNAI), vol. 1265, pp. 420–429. Springer, Heidelberg (1997)
10. Pereira, L.M., Lopes, G.: Prospective logic agents. In: Neves, J., Santos, M.F., Machado, J.M. (eds.) EPIA 2007. LNCS, vol. 4874, pp. 73–86. Springer, Heidelberg (2007)
11. Pereira, L.M., Pinto, A.M.: Notes on Inspection Points and Meta-Abduction in Logic Programs. Work in progress (2008), `http://centria.di.fct.unl.pt/~lmp/publications/online-papers/IP08.pdf`
12. Pereira, L.M., Saptawijaya, A.: Modelling morality with prospective logic. In: Neves, J., Santos, M.F., Machado, J.M. (eds.) EPIA 2007. LNCS (LNAI), vol. 4874, pp. 99–111. Springer, Heidelberg (2007)
13. Rott, H.: Change, Choice and Inference. Oxford University Press, Oxford (2001)
14. Sadri, F., Toni, F.: Abduction with Negation as Failure for Active and Reactive Rules. In: Lamma, E., Mello, P. (eds.) AI*IA 1999. LNCS (LNAI), vol. 1792, pp. 49–60. Springer, Heidelberg (2000)
15. Santana, P., Moniz Pereira, L.: Emergence of cooperation through mutual preference revision. In: Ali, M., Dapoigny, R. (eds.) IEA/AIE 2006. LNCS (LNAI), vol. 4031, pp. 81–90. Springer, Heidelberg (2006)
16. Swift, T.: Tabling for non-monotonic programming. Annals of Mathematics and Artificial Intelligence 25(3-4), 201–240 (1999)

Declarative Programming of User Interfaces*

Michael Hanus and Christof Kluß

Institut für Informatik, CAU Kiel, D-24098 Kiel, Germany
{mh,ckl}@informatik.uni-kiel.de

Abstract. This paper proposes a declarative description of user interfaces that abstracts from low-level implementation details. In particular, the user interfaces specified in our framework are executable as graphical user interfaces for desktop applications as well as web user interfaces via standard web browsers. Thus, our approach combines the advantages of existing user interface technologies in a flexible way without demands on the programmer's side. We sketch an implementation of this concept in the declarative multi-paradigm programming language Curry and show how the integrated functional and logic features of Curry are exploited to enable a high-level implementation of this concept.

1 Motivation

The implementation of a good user interface for application programs is a necessary but often non-trivial and tedious task. In order to support programmers in the implementation of user interfaces, one can find specific libraries that reflect different approaches to the construction of user interfaces. From a user's perspective, there are two kinds of user interfaces (UIs) that are currently the most important ones on conventional desktop computers:

Graphical User Interfaces (GUIs): These are user interfaces that followed the early textual user interfaces on single host computers. GUIs enabled non-expert users to easily interact with application programs. They provide a good reaction time (since they run on the local host) and are relatively easy to install as any other program, i.e., usually they are distributed with the executable of the application program. On the negative side, application programs with GUIs require some installation efforts if many users want to use them on their desktops, because one has to install them on all desktops that might have different configurations or operating systems. Moreover, they are difficult to maintain during their life time since updates must be performed on all existing installations.

Web User Interfaces (WUIs): These are user interfaces that became popular with the world-wide web and its opportunities for user interaction via dynamic web pages. In this case, the application runs on a web server and the user interacts with the application via a standard web browser. Thus, applications with WUIs are relatively easy to install for many users since every single user needs only a web browser on

* This work was partially supported by the German Research Council (DFG) under grant Ha 2457/5-2.

A. Gill and T. Swift (Eds.): PADL 2009, LNCS 5418, pp. 16–30, 2009.

his local host (which is usually already installed). Moreover, such applications are easy to maintain since one has to update the central installation on the web server only. On the negative side, WUIs have a moderate reaction time (since the web server is contacted for every state-changing interaction) and a complete application is more difficult to install on a single host (since one has to install and configure a web server).

A few years ago, there was also another important difference between GUIs and WUIs: the model of interaction. In application with GUIs, the user could immediately change the content of many widgets by mouse events, whereas with WUIs, each page containing user input has to be sent to the web server which returns a new web page with some modified content. However, this disadvantage of WUIs has been decreased or omitted by the development of the Ajax framework that supports an interaction with a web server without submitting and receiving complete new pages from the web server [7].

From these considerations, it is reasonable to combine the advantages of both kinds of user interfaces in a single framework so that the programmer has no additional burden to select between GUIs or WUIs (or both) for his application. This paper presents a concrete proposal of such a concept and its implementation in the declarative multi-paradigm language Curry.

In the following section, we review the main features of functional logic programming and Curry as required in this paper. Section 3 describes the concepts of our framework followed by a few examples shown in Section 4. Implementation issues and extensions are sketched in Sections 5 and 6 before we conclude in Section 7 with a discussion of related work.

2 Functional Logic Programming and Curry

In this section we review the basic concepts of functional logic programming with Curry that are relevant for this paper. More details can be found in a recent survey on functional logic programming [13] and in the definition of Curry [17].

Functional logic languages integrate the most important features of functional and logic languages to provide a variety of programming concepts to the programmer. Modern languages of this kind [8,17,19] combine the concepts of demand-driven evaluation and higher-order functions from functional programming with logic programming features like computing with partial information (logic variables), unification, and non-deterministic search for solutions. This combination, supported by optimal evaluation strategies [1] and new design patterns [2], leads to better abstractions in application programs, e.g., as shown for programming with databases [3,6] or web programming [10,12,14]. The declarative multi-paradigm language Curry [8,17] is a functional logic language extended by features for concurrent programming. In the following, we review the elements of Curry that are relevant to understand the contents of this paper. Further features (e.g., constraints, search strategies, concurrency, declarative I/O, modules), more details about Curry's computation model, and a complete description of the language can be found in [17].

From a syntactic point of view, a Curry program is a functional program extended by the possible inclusion of free (logic) variables in conditions and right-hand sides of defining rules. Curry has a Haskell-like syntax [22], i.e., (type) variables and function names usually start with lowercase letters and the names of type and data constructors start with an uppercase letter. The application of f to e is denoted by juxtaposition ("$f\ e$"). A Curry *program* consists of the definition of functions and data types on which the functions operate. Functions are first-class citizens and evaluated lazily. To provide the full power of logic programming, functions can be called with partially instantiated arguments and defined by conditional equations with constraints in the conditions. Function calls with free variables are evaluated by a possibly nondeterministic instantiation of demanded arguments (i.e., arguments whose values are necessary to decide the applicability of a rule) to the required values in order to apply a rule.

In general, functions are defined by *rules* of the form "$f\ t_1 \ldots t_n$ | c = e" with f being a function, $t_1, \ldots, t_n$ *patterns* (i.e., expressions without defined functions) without multiple occurrences of a variable, the (optional) *condition* c is a constraint (e.g., a conjunction of equations), and e is a well-formed *expression* which may also contain function calls, lambda abstractions etc. A rule can be applied if its left-hand side matches the current call and its condition, if present, is satisfiable.

The following Curry program defines the data types of Boolean values, possible values, and polymorphic lists, and functions to compute the concatenation of lists and the last element of a list:

```
data Bool     = True    | False
data Maybe a = Nothing | Just a
data List  a = []      | a : List a

(++) :: [a] -> [a] -> [a]
[]     ++ ys = ys
(x:xs) ++ ys = x : (xs ++ ys)

last :: [a] -> a
last xs | ys ++ [x] =:= xs    = x    where x,ys free
```

`[]` (empty list) and `:` (non-empty list) are the constructors for polymorphic lists (`a` is a type variable ranging over all types and the type "`List a`" is written as `[a]` for conformity with Haskell). The concatenation function "`++`" is written with the convenient infix notation. The (optional) type declaration ("`::`") of the function "`++`" specifies that "`++`" takes two lists as input and produces an output list, where all list elements are of the same (unspecified) type.[1]

As one can see in this example, logic programming is supported by admitting function calls with free variables (see "`ys ++ [x]`" above) and constraints in the condition of a defining rule. For instance, the equation "`ys ++ [x] =:= xs`" is solved by instantiating the first argument `ys` to the list `xs` without the last argument, i.e., the only solution to this equation satisfies that `x` is the last element of `xs`. In order to support some consistency checks, *extra variables*, i.e., variables of a rule not occurring in a pattern of the left-hand side, must be declared by "`where...free`" (see the rule defining `last`).

A *constraint* is any expression of the built-in type `Success`. For instance, an *equational constraint* e_1 `=:=` e_2 is satisfiable if both sides e_1 and e_2 are reducible to unifi-

[1] Curry uses curried function types where α`->`β denotes the type of all functions mapping elements of type α into elements of type β.

able constructor terms. Specific Curry systems also support more powerful constraint structures, like arithmetic constraints on real numbers or finite domain constraints (e.g., PAKCS [15]).

The operational semantics of Curry, described in detail in [8,17], is based on an optimal evaluation strategy [1] which is a conservative extension of lazy functional programming and (concurrent) logic programming. Curry also offers standard features of functional languages, like higher-order functions, modules, or monadic I/O (which is identical to Haskell's I/O concept [27]). Thus, "`IO` α" denotes the type of an I/O action that returns values of type α. For instance, the predefined I/O action `getChar` has the type "`IO Char`", i.e., it returns the next character from the keyboard when it is applied. Similarly, the predefined I/O action `readFile` has the type "`String -> IO String`", i.e., it takes a string (the name of a file) and returns the contents of the file when it is applied.

3 Specifying User Interfaces

In this section we describe our proposal for the declarative programming of user interfaces that can be executed either on a local host as a GUI (e.g., by the use of Tcl/Tk [21]) or as a WUI on a web server that is accessed by a standard web browser.

In order to develop appropriate abstractions for high-level UI programming, one has to analyze the essential components of these programming tasks. Based on earlier work on programming GUIs and WUIs with functional logic languages [9,10,12], one can distinguish the following ingredients of UI programming:

Structure: Each UI has a specific hierarchical structure which typically consists of basic elements (also called *widgets*), like text input fields or selection boxes, and composed elements, like rows or columns of widgets. Thus, UIs have a tree-like structure which can be easily specified by an algebraic data type in a declarative language.

Functionality: If the user interacts with UI elements by mouse or keyboard clicks, these UI elements emit some events on which the application program should react. A convenient way to connect the application program to such events is the concept of *event handlers*, i.e., functions that are associated to events of some widget and that are called whenever such an event occurs. Usually, the event handlers use the functionality of the application program to compute some data that is shown in the widgets of the UI. Thus, event handlers are associated to some widgets but need to refer to other widgets independently of the structural hierarchy. This means that UIs have not only a hierarchical (layout) structure but also a logical (graph-like) structure that connects the event handlers with various widgets of the UI structure. In previous works on GUI and WUI programming [9,10] it has been shown that free (logic) variables are an appropriate feature to describe this logical structure and to avoid many problems that occur if fixed strings are used as references to UI elements as in traditional GUI programming (e.g., [21,26]) or WUI programming (e.g., [4,20]).

Layout: In order to support a visually appealing appearance of a UI, it should be possible to influence the standard layout of a UI. Whereas in older approaches layout and structural information are often mixed (e.g., as in Tcl/Tk or older versions of HTML, and similarly in previous approaches to declarative GUI/WUI programming [9,10]), it has been realized that these issues should be distinguished in order to obtain clearer and reusable implementations. For instance, current versions of HTML recommend the use of cascading style sheets (CSS) to separate structure from layout.

The distinction between structure, functionality, and layout and their appropriate modelling in a declarative programming language are the key ingredients to our framework for UI programming. Although parts of these ideas can be found in our previous works [9,10,12], our current novel approach abstracts more from the underlying technology (Tcl/Tk, HTML/CGI) so that it enables a common method to specify user interfaces. In the following, we propose a concrete description of the structure, functionality, and layout of UIs in the language Curry by presenting appropriate data types and operations on them. In principle, one can transfer these ideas also to other declarative languages (where some restrictions might be necessary). However, we will see that the combined functional and logic programming features of Curry are exploited for our high-level and application-oriented description of UIs.

As already discussed, UIs have a hierarchical structure that can be appropriately described by the following data type:

```
data UIWidget = Widget WidgetKind        -- kind of widget
                       (Maybe String)    -- possible contents
                       (Maybe UIRef)     -- possible reference
                       [Handler]         -- event handlers
                       [StyleClass]      -- layout elements
                       [UIWidget]        -- subwidgets
```

In order to avoid unnecessary restrictions, the definition of a widget is quite general. In principle, one could also enumerate all kinds of widgets and distinguish between widgets having no structure (basic widgets) and widgets with structure (e.g., rows, columns). For the sake of generality, we have chosen one widget constructor where the concrete kind of widget is given as the first component (of type `WidgetKind`). The last two components are a list of layout elements (see below) and the widgets contained in this widget, respectively. The second component contains the possible contents of the widget (e.g., the entry string of a text input field, `Nothing` for widget combinators like row or column), the third component a possible reference to a widget used by other event handlers, and the fourth component a list of handlers for the various events that can occur in this widget. Concrete examples for widgets are shown below after we have discussed the other data types used in widgets.

Event handlers need to refer to other widgets independently of the widget hierarchy. Therefore, a widget can be equipped with an identity used as a reference by event handlers. Many approaches to user interface programming, like Tcl/Tk or HTML/CGI, use string constants as identifiers. Such approaches are error prone since a typo in a string constant causes a run-time error which is usually not detected at compile time. In order to provide a more reliable approach, we adapt the idea of previous works on declarative GUI and WUI programming [9,10] and make the type of widget references abstract. Thus, one cannot construct "wrong" identifiers but has to use free variables (whose declarations are checked at compile time) for this purpose. Therefore, our UI library contains a type declaration

```
data UIRef = ...
```

where only the type name UIRef but no data constructor is exported, i.e., UIRef is an abstract type. Since no constructor of this data type is available to the user of the UI library, the only reasonable way to use values of type UIRef is with a free variable (see below for a concrete example).

In general, event handlers are used for two main purposes. Either they should perform some calculations and show their results in some specific widgets of the UI, i.e., they influence the state of the UI, or they should change the state of the underlying application program, e.g., the execution of an event handler might change some application data that is stored in a file or database. In order to support the latter functionality, the result type of an event handler is always "IO ()", i.e., an event handler might have a side effect on the external world. Since there are also I/O actions to influence the state of the UI (see below), this result type of event handlers ensures that event handlers can influence the state of the UI as well as the state of the application program.

Furthermore, the calculations and actions performed by event handlers usually depend on the user inputs stored in the widgets of the interface, i.e., these input values must be passed as parameters to the event handlers. This can be adequately modelled by an *environment* parameter that is conceptually a mapping from widget references to the string values stored in the widgets. In order to abstract from the concrete implementation of such environments, our UI library contains the type declaration

```
data UIEnv = ...
```

where only the type name UIEnv is exported. Moreover, the UI library contains the type declarations

```
data Command = Cmd (UIEnv -> IO ())

data Handler = Handler Event Command
```

where Event is the type of possible events issued by user interfaces:

```
data Event = DefaultEvent | FocusIn | FocusOut
           | MouseButton1 | MouseButton2 | MouseButton3
           | KeyPress | Return | Change  | DoubleClick
```

Therefore, each element in the list of event handlers of a widget specifies a command (an I/O action depending on the value of some environment) that is executed whenever the associated event occurs.

The type WidgetKind specifies the different kinds of widgets supported by our library. Some constructors of this type are

```
data WidgetKind = Col | Row | Label | Button | Entry
                | TextEdit Int Int | ...
```

The constructors Col and Row specify combinations of widgets as columns and rows, respectively. Label is a widget containing a string not modifiable by the user, Button is a simple button, `Entry` is an entry field for a line of text, and `TextEdit` is a widget to edit larger text areas (the parameters are the height and width of the edit area).

Since it is tedious to define all widgets of a user interface by using the constructor `Widget` only, the library contains a number of useful abbreviations, like

```
col ws          = Widget Col    Nothing     Nothing     [] [] ws
row ws          = Widget Row    Nothing     Nothing     [] [] ws
label str       = Widget Label (Just str) Nothing       [] [] []
entry ref str = Widget Entry (Just str) (Just ref) [] [] []
button cmd label =
  Widget Button (Just label) Nothing
                   [Handler DefaultEvent (Cmd cmd)]) [] []
```

For instance, a simple UI showing the text "`Hello World!`" and a button to exit the UI can be specified as follows:

```
col [label "Hello World!",
     button exitUI "Stop"]
```

`exitUI` is a predefined event handler to terminate the UI. The environment passed to event handlers can be accessed and modified by the predefined I/O actions `getValue` and `setValue` that take a widget reference as their first argument. Thus, "`getValue r e`" returns the value of the widget referenced by `r` w.r.t. environment `e`, and "`setValue r v e`" updates the value of the widget referenced by `r` so that it becomes visible to the user.

In order to influence the layout of UIs, widgets can take a list of style parameters of type `StyleClass`. This type contains options to align the widget or the text contained in it, set the font and color of the widget's text, set the background color, and so on. The styles of a widget can be dynamically changed by predefined operations like `setStyles`, `addStyles`, etc.

4 Examples

In order to demonstrate the concrete application of our concept, we show a few programming examples in this section. As a first example, consider a simple counter UI shown in Fig. 1. Using our library, its structure and functionality is specified as follows:

```
counterUI = col [label "A simple counter:",
                 entry val "0",
                 row [button incr   "Increment",
                      button reset  "Reset",
                      button exitUI "Stop" ]]
 where
   val free
   reset env = setValue val "0" env
   incr  env = do v <- getValue val env
                  setValue val (show (readInt v + 1)) env
```

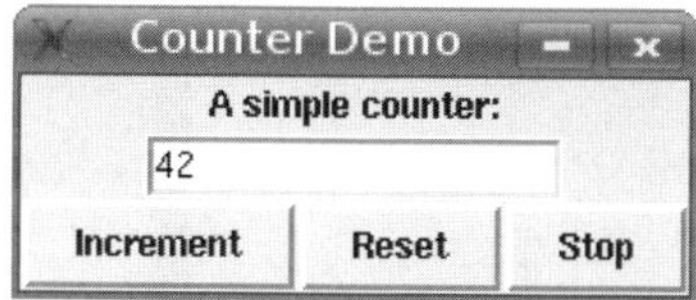

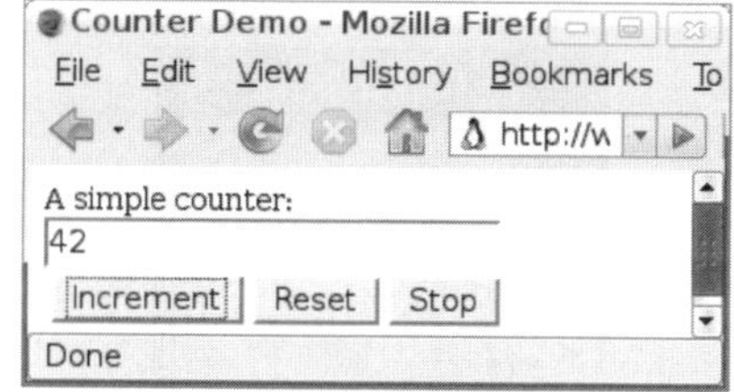

Fig. 1. A simple counter UI executed as a GUI (left) and as a WUI (right)

The free variable `val` (of type `UIRef`) denotes the reference to the entry field containing the string representation of the counter's value. It is used by the event handler `reset` to set the value of this entry widget to `"0"`. The event handler `incr` reads the current value of this widget (by "`getValue val env`") before replacing it by its incremented value (since the values in the widgets are strings, the string is transformed into an integer by "`readInt v`").

The UI specification can be executed by the predefined I/O action `runUI` that takes a string (usually shown as the label of the window containing the UI) and a UI specification as parameters. For instance, the counter UI shown above is executed by evaluating the main expression

```
runUI "Counter Demo" counterUI
```

Many interactive applications contain a state which is shown and modified by a UI. We want to demonstrate the implementation of such kinds of UIs with our concept by a simple desk calculator UI shown in Fig. 2. The implementation of this UI requires the access of the UI to some state that can be modified by the event handlers associated to the different buttons. In our application, the value of the state is a pair `(d,f)` containing the current operand `d` and an accumulator function `f` that is applied to `d` when the button "=" is pressed (this idea is due to [26]). In order to allow the change of the state's value by any event handler of the calculator UI, we model the calculator's state with `IORef`s, a concept from Haskell to deal with mutable state. `IORef`s are references to stateful objects, where their states can only be accessed and changed by the predefined I/O actions `readIORef` and `writeIORef` (in order to ensure referential transparency). Thus, the calculator UI can be implemented as follows (where the parameter `stref` of type `IORef (Int,Int->Int)` is an `IORef` to the calculator's state):

```
calcUI stref =
    col [entryS [Class [Bg Yellow]] display "0",
         row (map cbutton ['1','2','3','+']),
         row (map cbutton ['4','5','6','-']),
         row (map cbutton ['7','8','9','*']),
         row (map cbutton ['C','0','=','/'])]
  where
    display free
    cbutton c = button (buttonPressed c) [c]
```

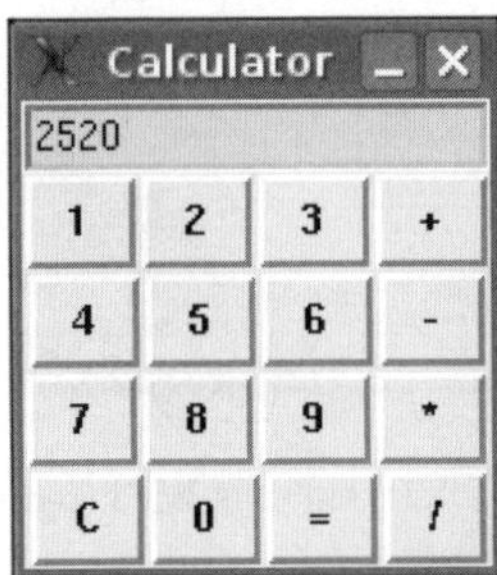

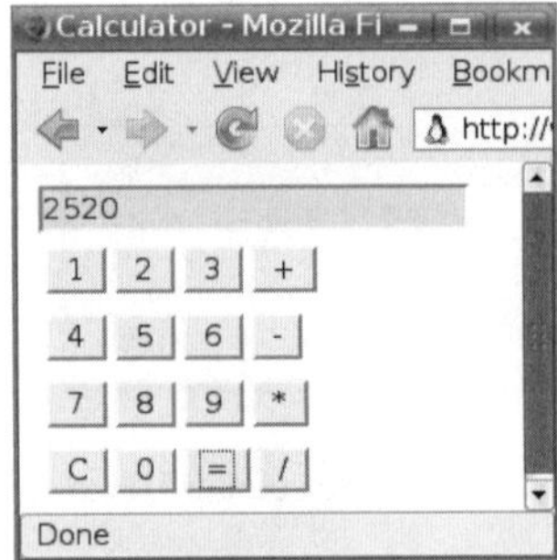

Fig. 2. A simple desk calculator UI executed as a GUI (left) and as a WUI (right)

```
buttonPressed c env = do
   state <- readIORef stref
   let (d,f) = processButton c state
   writeIORef stref (d,f)
   setValue display (show d) env
```

The operator `entryS` is similar to `entry` but has a further first argument to specify the initial layout of this widget (here: the background color). Note that we exploit the higher-order features of Curry to create the individual buttons by the generic function `cbutton` in a compact way. Each button has an associated event handler `buttonPressed` that reads the current state, modifies it, and shows the new operand in the entry widget referenced by the variable `display`. The actual update of the state depending on the selected button is computed by the operation `processButton`:

```
processButton :: Char -> (Int,Int->Int) -> (Int,Int->Int)
processButton b (d,f)
 | isDigit b = (10*d + ord b - ord '0', f)
 | b=='+'    = (0,((f d) +))
 | b=='-'    = (0,((f d) -))
 | b=='*'    = (0,((f d) *))
 | b=='/'    = (0,((f d) `div`))
 | b=='='    = (f d, id)
 | b=='C'    = (0, id)
```

Finally, the complete application is executed by evaluating the operation `main` that first creates a new `IORef` object and then runs the UI with this object:

```
main = do stref <- newIORef (0,id)
          runUI "Calculator" (calcUI stref)
```

We have already mentioned that the use of free variables as references to UI elements avoids the construction of wrong identifiers that might happen if strings are used as identifiers, as in scripting languages like Tcl/Tk, HTML/CGI, PHP, etc. Moreover, this also improves compositionality in the construction of UIs. For instance, if fixed strings are used as reference identifiers, there might be name clashes between different

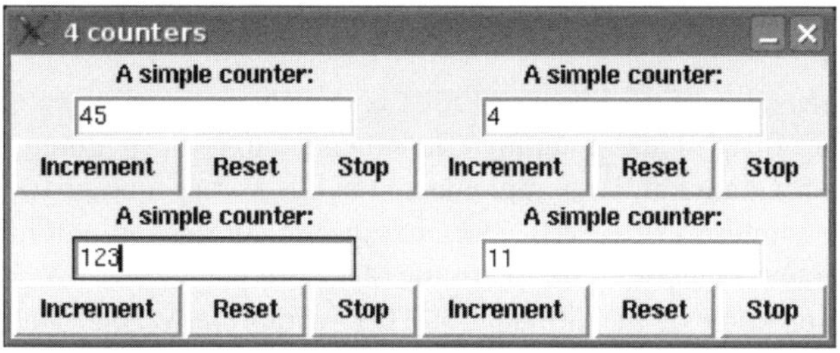

Fig. 3. A UI with four independent counters executed as a GUI

references when independent UIs are composed in a larger UI. Due to the use of free variables that represent fresh values every time they are introduced, such name clashes are avoided in our library. For instance, consider the simple counter UI above. Each use of `counterUI` introduces its own fresh local reference variable `val`. Thus, we can easily put four different counters in one UI by

```
counter4 = col [row [counterUI,counterUI],
                row [counterUI,counterUI]]
```

so that "`runUI "4 counters" counter4`" creates a UI with four independent counter UIs (see Fig. 3). This property of compositionality is particularly useful if one combines various UIs into complex web pages (see below).

The use of free variables for fresh references in data structures is a specific functional logic design pattern called "locally defined global identifier" [2]. An alternative would be a global counter to create unique references that is threaded through the construction of the user interface. Such an approach leads either to a monadic programming style with an imperative flavor [5,18] or puts some restrictions on the possible dependencies between input fields and buttons [25].

5 Implementation Issues

The definition of the components to specify a user interface, as discussed in Section 3, are contained in a library `UI` so that one has to import this library in order to define an interface. However, such an interface is not executable without specifying whether it should be run as a GUI or a WUI. For this purpose, our framework provides two implementations of the general UI concept by transforming UIs into GUIs or into WUIs. The necessary functionality is contained in the libraries `UI2GUI` and `UI2HTML`, respectively. In order to execute a UI as a GUI (as shown in the left-hand sides of Fig. 1 and 2), one has to import the library `UI2GUI` (which has the same interface as `UI`) instead of `UI`, i.e., one has to put the import declaration

```
import UI2GUI
```

at the beginning of the module containing the corresponding UI specification. In order to execute a UI as a WUI (as shown in the right-hand sides of Fig. 1 and 2), one has to replace `UI2GUI` by `UI2HTML` in the import declaration, and everything else is left unchanged (apart from the command to generate an executable from the corresponding Curry program).

The implementation of the library `UI2GUI` is straightforward by exploiting the existing Curry library `GUI` [9] and mapping UI elements into corresponding GUI elements. Thus, the main function `runUI` is implemented in this library by transforming the main term and all its subterms of type `UIWidget` into the corresponding GUI widgets and then calling the main function `runGUI` of the `GUI` library.

The implementation of the library `UI2HTML` is more advanced since the existing Curry library `HTML` [10] does not support server interaction inside a web page. Since this is possible by the Ajax framework [7], we have added extensions to the `HTML` library (based on Ajax) to support the interaction model implied by the `UI` library. Based on these extensions, the main function `runUI` is implemented in the library `UI2HTML` by transforming terms of type `UIWidget` into corresponding HTML expressions that are put into an HTML form that contains the HTML input elements and JavaScript code to implement the interaction with the web server.

In typical web applications, a user interface is not the single entity of a web page but often embedded in a larger web page (containing headers, navigation bars, other input elements, explaining text, etc). In order to put UIs as elements into larger web pages, our library `UI2HTML` also exports a function `ui2hexps` that maps a UI specification into an HTML expression that can be inserted into an HTML page constructed with the `HTML` library [10]. Since the references used in UIs (of type `UIRef` discussed above) and the references used in the `HTML` library to access the values of the input elements are of different type[2], there are also conversion functions between these kinds of references. Thus, the values set in a UI can be used to influence values or elements in the surrounding web page, and vice versa.

6 Extended UI Programming

The structure of UI specifications is a generalization compared to previous proposals for GUI or WUI programming. In this section, we discuss two possibilities to extend previous more specialized approaches to interface programming by exploiting our UI approach.

6.1 Transforming GUIs into WUIs

Since the structure of UI elements is very similar to the elements of the Curry library `GUI`, which has been already used for various applications (e.g., [11,16,23]), one can also use our concept of UIs to enable the execution of such GUI-based desktop applications as web applications. For this purpose, we have also implemented a library `GUI2HTML` that provides the same interface as the library `GUI` but executes a GUI as a WUI by exploiting the library `UI2HTML`. For instance, we have used this implementation to execute the Curry analysis environment CurryBrowser (its implementation

[2] This is necessary because UI references must be more general in order to support their mapping into GUIs or WUIs.

consists of almost 4000 lines of Curry code), which is written in Curry and has a quite advanced graphical user interface (see [11]), in a standard web browser. The only necessary change was the replacement of the import of the library `GUI` by the import of the library `GUI2HTML` in the source code of the CurryBrowser implementation.

6.2 Type-Safe UIs

[12] presented a technique to construct type-safe WUIs in a high-level manner. The basic idea is to provide a set of typed WUIs for basic data types, like `wInt` for integers or `wString` for strings, and a set of combinators for typed WUIs, like `wPair` for pairs, `wTriple` for triples, `wList` for lists, etc. For instance, the expression "`wlist (wPair wInt wString)`" specifies a WUI to manipulate values of type `[(Int,String)]`. One of the important properties of such typed WUIs is the fact that the user can only enter values of the correct type, i.e., if the user attempts to enter ill-typed values, an error message appears and the user has to correct the value. Thus, the application program need not check the values, provide error messages etc. A further important aspect is the possibility to constrain the type of allowed values by any computable predicate. For instance, if the predicate `correctDate` checks whether a triple of integers forms a legal date, one can specify by

```
wTriple wInt wInt wInt ‘withCondition‘ correctDate
```

a WUI where one can enter only legal dates.

We can apply the same idea to UIs in order to obtain type-safe WUIs (similarly to [12]) as well as type-safe GUIs (which have not been considered before). Therefore, we have implemented two libraries `TypedUI2HTML` and `TypedUI2GUI` that provide almost the same interface as [12] (i.e., it has all the entities, like `wInt`, `wString`, `wPair`, for specifying typed UIs) and an operation `typedui2ui` to map a typed UI specification together with an initial (type-correct) value into a standard UI widget that allows only the manipulation of type-correct data. In addition, `typedui2ui` also returns operations to access, set, and update the value shown in the typed UI. For instance, the following program defines a UI containing a list (`xs`) of integers that can be together incremented or reset, and a button to compute their sum:

```
counters :: [Int] -> UIWidget
counters xs =
  col [label "A list of counters:", widget,
       row [button (updval (map (+1))) "Increment all",
            button (setval (repeat 0)) "Reset all",
            button compute "Compute sum:", entry sval ""]]
 where
  sval free
  (widget,getval,setval,updval) = typedui2ui (wList wInt) xs
  compute env = do cs <- getval env
                   setValue sval (maybe "" (show . sum) cs) env
```

Note that the derived operations `getval`, `setval`, and `updval` access or manipulate values of type `[Int]`, i.e., the implementation checks whether all widgets contain only integer values (in contrast to the `counterUI` example in Section 4). As a consequence, `getval` returns a `Maybe` value, i.e., it returns `Nothing` if some of the current input fields contain illegal values. This is also the reason why the operation `compute` uses the standard function `maybe` in order to return the empty string as the sum value if the current content `cs` is `Nothing`. The result of this construction is a standard UI, i.e., we can create a type-safe GUI or WUI for a list of four integers by executing "`runUI "Counters" (counters [1..4])`".

7 Conclusions and Related Work

We described a framework to implement user interfaces in a high-level, declarative manner. Our approach is based on separating the structural, functional, and layout aspects of a user interface. We showed that the features available in functional logic languages can be exploited to provide appropriate specifications of these issues. The hierarchical structure of UIs can be easily specified as term structures. The associated functionality can be specified by attaching event handlers (i.e., functions) to the elements of these term structures. The connections of event handlers to the individual widgets of the UI can be described by logic variables. This avoids typical programming errors in untyped scripting languages and supports compositionality in the construction of complex UIs. Finally, the concrete layout is separated from the structural and functional aspects of the UI. This supports the use of the same UI specification in different contexts, i.e., one can create either graphical user interfaces for desktop applications or web-based user interfaces from such descriptions only by importing the appropriate libraries. This simplifies the programming efforts to combine the advantages of existing user interface technologies. Finally, our framework also enables the transformation of existing GUI applications into web applications, the embedding of UIs into arbitrary HTML pages, and the construction of type-safe UIs. Although this functionality is a distinctive feature of our approach based on declarative programming techniques, we discuss some related work in the following.

Approaches to construct UIs in a declarative manner have been intensively studied in the functional programming community, e.g., [5,18,20,24,25,26]. Although there are approaches to create GUIs for different platforms [18] from the same base code, none of them support the unified creation of GUIs and WUIs.

Adobe AIR[3] enables the use of the same base code to create applications that run in a web browser as well as on a desktop. In contrast to our approach, Adobe AIR is not based on standard features of web browsers but requires specific software to be installed on the client's side. Another related work is the Google Web Toolkit[4] (GWT). GWT is a framework to implement dynamic web pages for Java programs similarly to GUI programming in order to create highly interactive web applications with reasonable efforts. GWT does not support the use of the same program to generate both GUI and WUI applications in contrast to our approach where concrete implementations (GUIs or WUIs) are automatically inferred from a single UI description. Moreover, because of the applied declarative programming concepts, our concrete UI descriptions are more compact.

[3] `http://www.adobe.com/devnet/air/`

[4] `http://code.google.com/webtoolkit/`

Another popular method to construct UIs are graphical editors that support the construction of the UI's layout, e.g., Cocoa's Interface Builder[5]. Similarly to our approach, such UI editors also advocate the separation of layout and functionality by binding the graphical UI objects to the code of the base application. Although these graphical editors are useful to define the layout of appealing UIs in a simple manner, the connection of a constructed UI with the application code is less trivial than in our event handler model using a single implementation language. Moreover, a textual representation of UIs as program entities is precise and compact (all information about the UI is contained in the program), and it allows the application of standard programming techniques to construct complex UIs from application-oriented UI elements, e.g., as shown in [12] or Section 6.2 above. Another possibility is the generation of the textual UI specification from the data model of the application, e.g., one could generate the UIs to manipulate the application data from an entity-relationship model, as in the Ruby on Rails framework[6] (a similar framework for Curry is currently being developed).

The various features of the declarative base language Curry, in particular, algebraic data types, functions as first class citizens, logic variables, and polymorphic types, have shown to be useful to support the high-level, compact, and reliable specification of UIs that can be used in different contexts. The implementation of our concept as sketched in Section 5 is freely available with the latest distribution of PAKCS [15]. For future work it might be interesting to explore whether the same or a slightly modified concept can be also used to create user interfaces for other architectures, e.g., mobile devices.

References

1. Antoy, S., Echahed, R., Hanus, M.: A Needed Narrowing Strategy. Journal of the ACM 47(4), 776–822 (2000)
2. Antoy, S., Hanus, M.: Functional Logic Design Patterns. In: Hu, Z., Rodríguez-Artalejo, M. (eds.) FLOPS 2002. LNCS, vol. 2441, pp. 67–87. Springer, Heidelberg (2002)
3. Braßel, B., Hanus, M., Müller, M.: High-Level Database Programming in Curry. In: Hudak, P., Warren, D.S. (eds.) PADL 2008. LNCS, vol. 4902, pp. 316–332. Springer, Heidelberg (2008)
4. Cabeza, D., Hermenegildo, M.: Internet and WWW Programming using Computational Logic Systems. In: Workshop on Logic Programming and the Internet (1996), `http://clip.dia.fi.upm.es/Software/pillow/`
5. Claessen, K., Vullinghs, T., Meijer, E.: Structuring graphical paradigms in TkGofer. In: Proc. of the International Conference on Functional Programming (ICFP 1997), vol. 32(8), pp. 251–262. ACM SIGPLAN Notices (1997)
6. Fischer, S.: A Functional Logic Database Library. In: Proc. of the ACM SIGPLAN 2005 Workshop on Curry and Functional Logic Programming (WCFLP 2005), pp. 54–59. ACM Press, New York (2005)
7. Garrett, J.J.: Ajax: A New Approach to Web Applications (2005), `http://AdaptivePath.com`
8. Hanus, M.: A Unified Computation Model for Functional and Logic Programming. In: Proc. of the 24th ACM Symposium on Principles of Programming Languages, Paris, pp. 80–93 (1997)

[5] `http://developer.apple.com/tools/interfacebuilder.html`

[6] `http://www.rubyonrails.org/`

9. Hanus, M.: A Functional Logic Programming Approach to Graphical User Interfaces. In: Pontelli, E., Santos Costa, V. (eds.) PADL 2000. LNCS, vol. 1753, pp. 47–62. Springer, Heidelberg (2000)
10. Hanus, M.: High-level server side web scripting in curry. In: Ramakrishnan, I.V. (ed.) PADL 2001. LNCS, vol. 1990, pp. 76–92. Springer, Heidelberg (2001)
11. Hanus, M.: CurryBrowser: A Generic Analysis Environment for Curry Programs. In: Proc. of the 16th Workshop on Logic-based Methods in Programming Environments (WLPE 2006), pp. 61–74 (2006)
12. Hanus, M.: Type-Oriented Construction of Web User Interfaces. In: Proceedings of the 8th ACM SIGPLAN International Conference on Principles and Practice of Declarative Programming (PPDP 2006), pp. 27–38. ACM Press, New York (2006)
13. Hanus, M.: Multi-paradigm Declarative Languages. In: Dahl, V., Niemelä, I. (eds.) ICLP 2007. LNCS, vol. 4670, pp. 45–75. Springer, Heidelberg (2007)
14. Hanus, M.: Putting Declarative Programming into the Web: Translating Curry to JavaScript. In: Proceedings of the 9th ACM SIGPLAN International Conference on Principles and Practice of Declarative Programming (PPDP 2007), pp. 155–166. ACM Press, New York (2007)
15. Hanus, M., Antoy, S., Braßel, B., Engelke, M., Höppner, K., Koj, J., Niederau, P., Sadre, R., Steiner, F.: PAKCS: The Portland Aachen Kiel Curry System (2008), `http://www.informatik.uni-kiel.de/~pakcs/`
16. Hanus, M., Koj, J.: An Integrated Development Environment for Declarative Multi-Paradigm Programming. In: Proc. of the International Workshop on Logic Programming Environments (WLPE 2001), pp. 1–14, Paphos, Cyprus (2001); Computing Research Repository (CoRR), `http://arXiv.org/abs/cs.PL/0111039`
17. Hanus, M. (ed.): Curry: An Integrated Functional Logic Language (Vers. 0.8.2) (2006), `http://www.curry-language.org`
18. Leijen, D.: wxHaskell – A portable and concise GUI library for Haskell. In: Proceedings of the 2004 ACM SIGPLAN Workshop on Haskell, pp. 57–68. ACM Press, New York (2004)
19. López-Fraguas, F., Sánchez-Hernández, J.: TOY: A Multiparadigm Declarative System. In: Narendran, P., Rusinowitch, M. (eds.) RTA 1999. LNCS, vol. 1631, pp. 244–247. Springer, Heidelberg (1999)
20. Meijer, E.: Server Side Web Scripting in Haskell. Journal of Functional Programming 10(1), 1–18 (2000)
21. Ousterhout, J.K.: Tcl and the Tk toolkit. Addison-Wesley, Reading (1994)
22. Peyton Jones, S. (ed.): Haskell 98 Language and Libraries—The Revised Report. Cambridge University Press, Cambridge (2003)
23. Sadeghi, P.H., Huch, F.: The Interactive Curry Observation Debugger iCODE. Electronic Notes in Theoretical Computer Science, vol. 177, pp. 107–122 (2007)
24. Sage, M.: FranTk - a declarative GUI language for Haskell. In: Proceedings of the 5th ACM SIGPLAN International Conference on Functional Programming (ICFP 2000), pp. 106–117. ACM Press, New York (2000)
25. Thiemann, P.: WASH/CGI: Server-side Web Scripting with Sessions and Typed, Compositional Forms. In: Krishnamurthi, S., Ramakrishnan, C.R. (eds.) PADL 2002. LNCS, vol. 2257, pp. 192–208. Springer, Heidelberg (2002)
26. Vullinghs, T., Tuijnman, D., Schulte, W.: Lightweight GUIs for Functional Programming. In: Swierstra, S.D. (ed.) PLILP 1995. LNCS, vol. 982, pp. 341–356. Springer, Heidelberg (1995)
27. Wadler, P.: How to Declare an Imperative. ACM Computing Surveys 29(3), 240–263 (1997)

Huge Data But Small Programs: Visualization Design via Multiple Embedded DSLs

D.J. Duke[1], R. Borgo[1], M. Wallace[2], and C. Runciman[2]

[1] School of Computing, Uni. of Leeds, UK
{djd,rborgo}@comp.leeds.ac.uk
[2] Dept. of Computer Science, Uni. of York, UK
{malcolm,colin}@cs.york.ac.uk

Abstract. Although applications of functional programming are diverse, most examples deal with modest amounts of data – no more than a few megabytes. This paper describes how Haskell has been used to address a challenging astrophysics visualization problem, where the complete uncompressed dataset is nearly a terabyte. Our solution makes extensive use of three novel *domain-specific languages*: to specify data resources, to abstract over rendering operations, and most significantly, to design the desired visualization. The result is a powerful framework for time-varying multi-field visualization. This approach represents a significant departure from standard practices in the visualization field, and has application well beyond the original problem. That our solution consists of less than 4.5K lines of code is itself a notable result. This paper motivates and describes the overall architecture of our solution, and technical features of the DSLs that are used in place of the traditional visualization pipeline.

1 Introduction

Drawings, diagrams and graphs have a long history of use within scientific discovery, e.g. Snow's map correlating cholera cases with water pump location in London, 1854. Use of computer graphics for visualizing data is usually traced to an influential 1987 report produced for the National Science Foundation of the United States [1]. Data from instruments and supercomputer simulation was accumulating faster than it could be interpreted, and the report called for new methods to process these 'firehoses'. Visualization became established as a new research field within computing, and foundational work on data models, processing paradigms and depiction techniques for large-scale data led to rapid progress [2,3]. Much of this work concentrated on *scientific* visualization, where the data are located within some physical space. Data that has no 'natural' spatial component, for example metabolic networks, web sites, market trends, etc., is addressed by *information* visualization. The relationship between these two branches of visualization has been the subject of much debate [4]. Our concern is with scientific visualization.

A. Gill and T. Swift (Eds.): PADL 2009, LNCS 5418, pp. 31–45, 2009.

Huge dataset size is one of the defining characteristics of the field; other issues that arise include the need to design a new bespoke interactive tool for every new problem, typically by building a set of toolkit components into a so-called 'pipeline' (actually a directed graph). As an example, the widely-used open source VTK [3] toolkit has components written in C++, that can be plumbed together by Tcl scripts. This paper reports how we tackled these and other issues in a declarative way: through the creation of several *domain-specific languages* (DSLs), embedded in Haskell, to address a major design challenge problem, the 2008 IEEE Visualization Design Contest [5]. Three DSLs, respectively for large dataset management, for low-level rendering and interaction, and for high-level description of the desired picture, capture many of the interesting architectural aspects of the domain. The middle-level components for generating visual depictions are also implemented in Haskell [6,7]. In total, the code size is extremely small, especially given the range and flexibility of visualisations it can deal with. The use of the DSL strategy gave us a new and elegant way of *combining* visualization techniques, as well as an efficient way of managing large data resources.

Section 2 introduces the contest and explains its importance and relevance to practical applications of scientific visualization. Our solution utilises a two-stage pipeline, separating the management of datasets from the synthesis of pictures. The architecture is described in Section 3, with data management and picture synthesis forming sections 4 and 5. Section 6 sets out an evaluation of our work. We contrast our approach to the contest with entries from previous years, and reflect on the design decisions that were made. In the conclusion, Section 7, we pay particular attention to our use of domain-specific languages, and their further potential within visualization.

2 The IEEE Visualization Design Contest

Since its inception in 1990, IEEE Visualization has been the leading forum for research in the field. In 2004, the conference instituted a visualization contest, designed "to foster comparison of novel and established techniques, provide benchmarks for the community, and to create an exciting venue for discussion".

The logistical difficulties presented by the contest can be appreciated from an outline of the 2008 edition [5]. The dataset comprises 200 timesteps from an astrophysics simulation, modelling interaction between a radiation ionisation front and primordial gas within a $0.6 \times 0.25 \times 0.25$-parsec volume of space (sampled as a regular $600 \times 248 \times 248$-point grid). Understanding this interaction would provide new insight into structure formation in the early universe, and the contest itself sought answers to six specific questions relating to these interactions. At each point in the space, the simulation tracks ten scalars and one 3D vector, with the scalars recording temperature and density of the gas, and the relative densities of 8 chemical species. Data are stored using a 11-character ASCII representation of fixed-precision format numbers; uncompressed, the total size of the dataset would be $\approx$960GB.

Tackling the visualization design contest requires access to domain expertise, robust and scalable software, and significant time to explore the problem and solution space. Past entries have used mature off-the-shelf systems, either commercial products including the open-source VTK, or the output of long-running research initiatives.

In a series of papers [8,6,7] we have explored the use of a functional language such as Haskell to reconstruct visualization techniques, taking advantage of lazy evaluation to implement streaming of data, and the expressive type system to create new kinds of generic abstraction. This work provides a necessary foundation for our solution. However, it was not in itself sufficient. Central to the 2008 design contest is the problem of time-varying multi-field data, a challenge in many visualization applications. Although our previous implementations supported a combination of techniques, for the most part they only supported visualization of a single field within a single timestep.

3 Architecture of a Solution

Before designing a solution, we need first to unpack the problem. Visualization is used in three ways: to present known data, to confirm a known hypothesis, or to discover what might be present within unseen data. The six contest questions fall into the latter two categories. Five ask about interactions between specific fields. For example, here is question two:

> "Over 100 chemical reactions occur in primordial H and He (many of which are driven by radiation in the I-front) but what most interests those studying first structure formation in the universe is H_2. It allowed primeval gas clouds to collapse and form the first stars before galaxies later coalesced. Where is H_2 most prevalent in the simulation?" [5]

Although this question only mentions one field (H_2) explicitly, the answer has to be framed in terms of the relationship between H_2 concentrations and other features, e.g. the hottest regions, and the advancing I-front. This requires multiple fields. The final question is more open-ended and invites wholesale exploration:

> "Question 5 posed a very specific hypothesis about the cause of turbulence. The broader question of interest, and the one for which visualization offers the most promise of displaying something unexpected, is 'What is causing the turbulence?' Can you do an open-ended visualization of all variables to try and help answer this question? This is the 'seeing the unexpected' question that will hopefully provide new hypotheses." [5]

Putting aside the temporal element for now, there are two general strategies for dealing with multi-field data. (1) combine a number of standard techniques; for example, extracting an isosurface from one field and colouring it by probing into a second field, or by using multiple cutting planes. Or (2) use a visual technique designed specifically to expose relationships between fields. *Scatterplots* can be

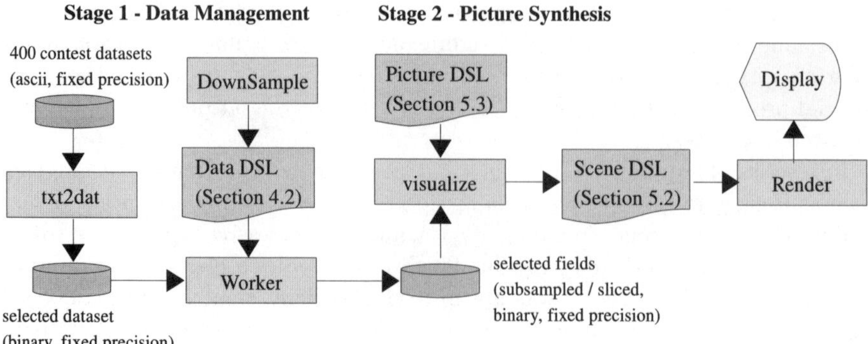

Fig. 1. System architecture

used for two or three fields, while *parallel coordinates* generalise to higher dimensions [9], but in both cases it is difficult to see correlation with 3D spatial locations, or features (e.g. the shockwave) mentioned in the contest questions. These needs could be addressed by *brushing* and other forms of interaction, but we took an early decision to focus our work on the first strategy, combining standard techniques within the physical space of the simulation.

For dealing with time, there are again two general strategies; either (1) represent it explicitly as a spatial dimension, for example plotting a graph with time as one axis, or (2) represent it implicitly, by using animation. Following a meeting with astrophysicists to obtain a better understanding of the problem, we were encouraged to explore animation. As we will see, our solution actually creates interesting possibilities for combining time and space within one representation. It consists of two stages:

Stage I: Data Management – conversion of datasets into a more compact binary representation, support for fixed-precision calculation, selection of fields, slicing, and downsampling.

Stage II: Picture Synthesis – specification of picture parameters, selection of files, synthesis and rendering of geometry, and interaction.

These stages are loosely coupled, driven by separate executables, and linked through the filesystem. Figure 1 shows the structure, and highlights the central role of three DSLs in mediating the transformation from data to rendered image. The architecture maps onto the remainder of the paper as follows: Section 4 is concerned with Stage I, including the DSL for managing transformation and downsampling of data. Section 5 addresses the design of Stage II. The visualization process (Section 5.1) constructs a graphical scene from the specification of a desired picture. Both the scene (Section 5.2) and the picture language (Section 5.3) are structured as DSLs, and it is this strategy that provides the expressive power to explore the complexity of multi-field data.

4 Stage I: Data Management

The contest data consists of 400 primary files, 200 holding the scalar field values for each timestep, and a further 200 carrying the vector (velocity) data. Within a scalar file, the value for each of the 10 fields is given for the first point, then the 10 values for the second point, and so on. Consequently the entire file must be traversed, even if only one or two fields are of interest. We decided to define our own storage model for this data, and at the same time to convert the ASCII encoding into a more compact binary form.

4.1 Fixed-Precision Values

Numeric computation in visualization and computer graphics often uses the 32 or 64-bit IEEE floating point representation, and it would have been straightforward to convert the given fixed-precision representation into this form. However, as part of the analysis we would need to carry out derivation of new fields from the existing data, for example computing the turbulence of the flow as the magnitude of the velocity field curl. The numerical ranges for some fields are large and, concerned about loss of precision, we decided to work as much as possible using our own fixed-precision representation. Each value was represented in mantissa-exponent format, with 15 bits for each value (plus a sign bit). Internally, this format was stored using a Haskell constructor with two 16-bit integer components, while externally values could be stored as 4 bytes in a binary file.

This representation required support from a small library of arithmetic operations, which we defined first in Haskell, as an instance of the *Num* type class. More importantly we utilised SmallCheck [10] to test expected properties of the system, for example commutativity:

$$
\begin{aligned}
&\mathit{prop\_plusCommutes} :: \mathit{FixedPrecision} \rightarrow \mathit{FixedPrecision} \rightarrow \mathit{Bool} \\
&\mathit{prop\_plusCommutes}\ x\ y = x + y \equiv y + x
\end{aligned}
$$

This was invaluable in quickly teasing out a number of bugs. Just as importantly, having established confidence in the Haskell ‘specification’, we were able to use it as a reference model for implementing the fixed precision library within C. Functions in the C implementation were exposed to Haskell via the FFI, and equivalence between C and Haskell representations was tested via commuting-diagram properties, e.g.

$$
\begin{aligned}
&\mathit{prop\_times} :: \mathit{FixedPrecision} \rightarrow \mathit{FixedPrecision} \rightarrow \mathit{Bool} \\
&\mathit{prop\_times}\ x\ y = (x * y) \equiv \mathit{fromCFP}\ (\mathit{toCFP}\ x * \mathit{toCFP}\ y)
\end{aligned}
$$

4.2 Downsampling DSL

We next addressed the resolution and bounds of the data. There are good reasons for *not* working directly from the full $600 \times 248 \times 248$-point grid at each timestep:

- A standard strategy in visualization is to first gain an overview of the data, and then descend into lower levels of detail, saving unnecessary computation.
- Our volume renderer has a very simple implementation, but one based on nested lists, and could not render the volume at full resolution.
- Our astrophysics colleagues suggested that for a number of the contest tasks, 2D slices might provide a more useful view (see Section 5.1).

So we needed a flexible mechanism for extracting subsets of the data, both by downsampling, and/or by restricting the range of one or more dimensions. Our implementation consisted of three components:

- a regular *naming scheme* for resources (files) that encodes information about the spatial bounds, sampling, and fields;
- a high-level *planner* that, given the specification of a required resource, computes the cheapest plan for generating that resource from the available files; and
- a *worker* program that implements a given plan.

The naming scheme forms a tiny DSL in its own right. Three examples of the resource naming conventions are:

```
x0-599y0-247z0-247t10.DGHH+HeHe+He++H-H2H2+.dat
x0-4-599y0-4-247z0-4-247t100.G.dat
x0-599y0-247z124t60.H2xD.dat
```

The first example specifies a full-resolution sampling of the entire grid, at time step 10, containing each of the 10 scalar attributes (D, G, H, H+, etc). In the second specification, the grid at time 100 has been downsampled, with every 4th sample selected in each spatial dimension, and only the G scalar component selected. The final example specifies a 2D slice at time step 60 corresponding to the plane $z = 124$, with full resolution along the remaining two axes, and carrying a derived field H_2xD, the product of H_2 and D.

The *planner*, implemented in Haskell, takes a resource specification as parameter, and then inspects the available files, deciding the cheapest method for generating the resource. Selection is implemented by defining a partial order over data files. This is an inclusion relation defined in terms of data files' bounds (spatial and temporal), granularity (spatial and temporal) and the set of fields present. After selecting the least dominator under the ordering, the planner invokes a *worker*. The worker, implemented in C for performance reasons, converts the plan into a tight set of nested for-loops that traverse the input and generate the output resource. It takes the worker around two minutes to downsample/slice from the largest resource file (1.48Gb), whilst starting from the least dominator can often reduce the time to a few seconds. In the case of *derived* fields, part of the worker traversal involves per-point numeric computation over selected samples from the input.

5 Stage II: Picture Synthesis

Before the announcement of the design contest, we had already implemented a modest library of *3D* visualization techniques, specifically:

- isosurface extraction;
- hedgehog rendering of a vector field;
- probing; and
- pseudo-volume rendering.

Experience gained in implementing these algorithms is reported in [7]. For addressing the contest tasks, three further techniques were implemented:

- slice visualization;
- 2D contouring; and
- 3D scatterplot.

Building on the Stage I work, we were easily able to adapt our infrastructure to process contest datasets, obtaining initial results such as the volume rendering of gas density, and isosurfaces of gas temperature, shown in Figure 2.

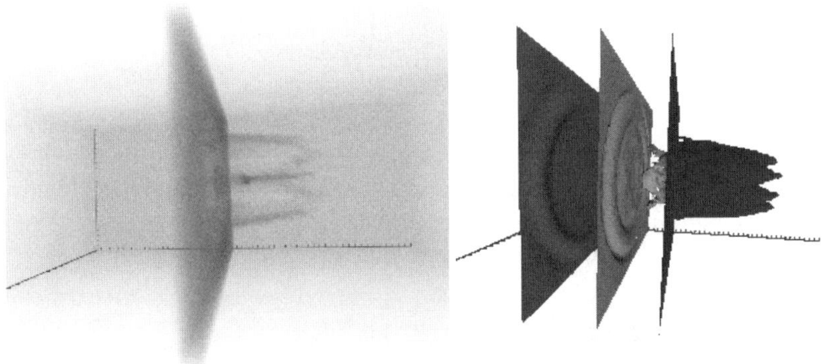

Fig. 2. Left: gas density as a volume rendering. Right: isosurfaces for gas temperature at 2.5K (blue), 16K (green) and 20K Kelvin (red). Both pictures are generated from time step 60, downsampled to a $150 \times 62 \times 62$ grid.

This figure highlights both the power of visualization to present data, and the limitations of standard 3D techniques for this particular challenge. The aim is to explore correlations between multiple fields. Superimposing 3D representations, even where they are known to be disjoint, creates problems of occlusion. This problem is avoided in Section 5.1 by utilising 2D techniques.

In Section 5.2 we introduce the rendering layer that mediates between specific visualization techniques and low-level graphical IO. Then Section 5.3 describes the high-level DSL for creating the compound images that enable effective exploration of the dataset.

5.1 Contours and Slices

Isosurfaces are a 3D generalisation of an older method for depicting scalar fields, the contour plot. Contour plots have the advantage that nesting of contours can be easily seen and interpreted. Contouring a field at regular intervals also highlights areas of high gradient, a feature that we found useful in addressing one of the contest questions. Similarly, a 2D slice through a dataset can also be rendered directly, by using a transfer function to associate a colour with each point, and then smooth-shading the resulting mesh. Figure 3 shows the same datasets as Figure 2, this time using slicing and contouring on a single plane. We found these images more useful in revealing details of the underlying field. In particular the contour plot reveals a region of hot gas embedded within the shell of the shockwave. As we shall see, these representations are also more amenable to composition.

The *implementation* of contouring provides a compelling example of the value of abstraction, and Haskell's type class system. Following our initial work on the 'marching cubes' algorithm [6], we generalised our dataset representation and implementation of the algorithm, to be independent of dimension, geometric organisation, and cell-shape. The signature of our isosurfacing algorithm now consists almost entirely of type variables and constraints:

$$\begin{aligned} \mathit{isosurface} :: (\mathit{Interp}\ a, \mathit{InvInterp}\ a, \mathit{Interp}\ g, \mathit{Cell}\ c\ v, \mathit{Enum}\ v) \Rightarrow \\ a \to [c\ v\ a] \to [c\ v\ g] \to [[g]] \end{aligned}$$

It requires three parameters: a threshold to be extracted (type a), a stream of sample values (also a), and a stream of the geometric locations g at which the samples were obtained. The two streams are structured into topological cells c defining local neighbourhoods within the grid. A cell c in turn is simply some instance of a type predicate that describes the capability to select a vertex v,

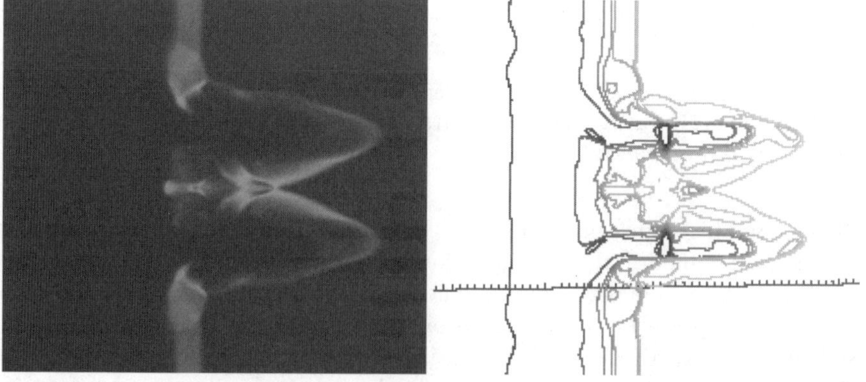

Fig. 3. Left: gas density as a slice. Right: contour lines for gas temperature, range 2K, 3K ... 21K Kelvin. Both pictures again from time step 60, now at full resolution within the plane $z = 124$.

and a case table that maps a *marking*, indicating which vertices of the cell are above a threshold, to the list of cell edges that are intersected by the surface. It took us less than one hour to implement *2D* contouring as a specific instance of this generalised algorithm. We had only to:

1. define a data constructor for 2D (square) cells;
2. implement the two *Cell* methods—the case table consisting of just 16 lines;
3. implement a function to turn a stream of values (samples or geometry) into a stream of square cells, a simpler instance of the technique described in [6]; and
4. wrap the output of the "isosurfacer" with the appropriate geometry for rendering at a set of line segments.

5.2 Rendering and Interaction DSL

The output of a single visualization algorithm, such as isosurfacing, contouring, or volume rendering, is a bag of primitives: coloured line segments, triangles, and surface normals. These must then be rendered to a display, in some fashion that allows for interactive exploration, e.g. rotation, translation and zooming of the "camera". Ultimately, the visualization front-end is implemented using the HOpenGL library that we have found to provide an excellent interface to OpenGL and GLUT [11]. However, rendering and event handling in OpenGL are handled through callbacks, which represent an unfortunately low-level intrusion into the functional environment of our visualization system. To mitigate this, we have implemented an intermediate layer, in the form of a *scene-graph* [12] abstraction for purely functional event handling. This provides a DSL for graphics, and serves as the target language into which the picture DSL, described in the next section, is compiled:

```
type HsHandler a = Maybe (Event → a → a)
type HsMovie     = (Bool, [HsScene], [HsScene])

data HsScene
   = Camera     (HsHandler HsView)        HsView HsScene
   | Geometry   (HsHandler [HsGeom])      PrimitiveMode [HsGeom]
   | Transform  (HsHandler HsTransform)   HsTransform
   | Group      (HsHandler [HsScene])     [HsScene]
   | Compiled   HsCompiledHandler         Extent DisplayList
   | Switch                               HsScene HsScene HsScene
   | Imposter                             HsScene HsScene
   | Animate    (HsHandler HsMovie)       HsMovie
   | Special                              (IO ())
```

There are expressions in this DSL for: scene geometry, transformations, groups of subtrees, compiled scenes (OpenGL display lists), and animations. Each animation is represented as a pair of lists along with a 'playing' flag. The lists hold the frames yet to be played, and the frames that have been played. The *Animate* event handler can be instantiated with a basic movie player supporting playback, pausing, and stepping through individual frames. Lazy evaluation means that one frame can be on the display while the next frame is still being generated.

In response to OpenGL's callback architecture, the rendering module uses a global IORef to store the root of the scene. Most scene expressions include an *event handler*, a pure function over the expression's substructure. When an OpenGL callback is invoked, for example due to a mouse or timer event, the scene graph is traversed: for each expression with a handler, a new expression is generated by evaluating the handler with the new event and previous expression as parameters. After the new scene description is computed, its value is written back to the IORef.

Although this solution hides some of the non-functional features of OpenGL's architecture, there is clearly room for further improvement. One possible direction is work on functional reactive programming; the Yampa library has for example been used to create interactive graphics applications [13], though it is unclear how well this would interface with the structured approach to rendering adopted here.

5.3 The Picture DSL

Slicing and contouring yielded simple static views of a single timeframe, but our greatest insights came from creating compound images and animations that exposed the relationship between fields over time. To achieve this, we wrote a small DSL of pictures that provides a task-oriented vocabulary, mediating between the rendering and data-management languages. A *picture* is either the output from one of our visualization techniques, or a compound of simpler pictures:

```
data Picture = Contour Colour (Range Float) DataExpr
             | Surface Colour (Range Float) DataExpr
             | Volume  Colour DataExpr
             | Slice   Colour DataExpr
             | Scatter DataExpr DataExpr DataExpr
             | Draw    [Picture]
             | Anim    [Picture]
```

There are two kinds of compound picture; *Draw* combines a list of subpictures within one display frame, while *Anim* creates an animation, rendering pictures into successive frames. Novel combinations of time and space are possible, e.g. by composing slices from multiple timesteps into one frame, or animating a plane moving through a single timestep. *Picture* uses a small number of supporting definitions. For example, the *Range* type provides a vocabulary for sampled intervals:

```
data Eq a ⇒ Range a = Single a
                    | Range a a
                    | Sampled a a a
```

It is used to specify the thresholds at which a scalar field is contoured or surfaced, and is also used to describe the spatial sampling of grids. The *Colour* data type specifies a number of schemes for mapping sample values onto colours, while *DataExpr* is used to select the time-volume-field to be visualized, including support for derived fields. (*DataExpr* compiles straightforwardly to the resource management scheme outlined in Section 4.2.) *Embedding* of the DSL within Haskell allows the use of host-language features such as comprehensions and let-sharing, to generate animations with an elegant specification:

```
overDensity =
    let slice t s = Use (From (Range 0 599) (Range 0 247) (Single 124) t s)
    in Anim [ Draw [Slice mblues        (slice t D)
                   , Contour mgreens (Sampled 200 400 1000) (slice t Mv)
                   , Contour reds     (Sampled 0 0.02 0.4)    (slice t H2xD)
                   ]
            | t ← [5, 10 .. 195]]
```

This example creates an animation showing correlation between the shockwave (as captured by overall gas density D), turbulence (Mv), and the absolute density of H_2, captured by the derived field $H2xD$. Figure 4 shows a snapshot from the animation, revealing that H_2 formation (white) is concentrated in regions bracketed by the shockwave (blue) and higher-turbulence regions (green).

Evaluation of a picture DSL expression is carried out in the context of an *environment* that carries the various data grids referenced from within the expression. A *Picture* expression is interpreted by a function *eval_picture* that pattern matches each of the *Picture* constructors, extracts appropriate grids from the environment, and constructs an expression in the scene graph DSL for

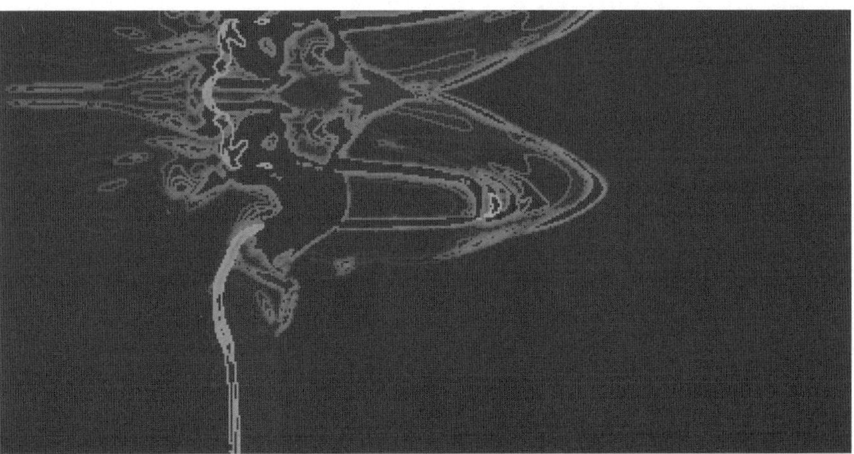

Fig. 4. Combination of gas density (slice), turbulence (green contours), and absolute H_2 concentration (white contours)

rendering the visualised geometry. Here, for example, are the cases for *Contour* and the two compound picture types:

$$
\begin{array}{l}
\textit{eval\_picture} :: \textit{Environment} \rightarrow \textit{Picture} \rightarrow \textit{HsScene} \\
\textit{eval\_picture env } (\textit{Contour pal thresholds dexpr}) \\
\quad = \textit{Group static geomlist} \\
\qquad \textbf{where} \\
\qquad\quad \begin{array}{lcl}
\textit{levels} & = & \textit{range\_to\_list thresholds} \\
\textit{nr\_levels} & = & \textit{float} \circ \textit{length} \; \$ \; \textit{levels} \\
\textit{field} & = & \textit{eval\_data env dexpr} \\
\textit{plane} & = & \textit{slice\_plane dexpr} \\
\textit{mkgrid} & = & \textit{squareGrid } (\textit{cell\_size\_2D field plane}) \\
\textit{points} & = & \textit{mkgrid} \; \$ \; \textit{plane\_points dexpr field} \\
\textit{values} & = & \textit{mkgrid} \; \$ \; \textit{samples field} \\
\textit{colour} & = & \textit{transfer pal } 1.0 \; 1.0 \; \textit{nr\_levels} \\
\textit{contours} & = & \textit{map } (\lambda t \rightarrow \textit{concat} \; \$ \; \textit{isosurface t values points}) \; \textit{levels} \\
\textit{colours} & = & \textit{map colour } [1.0 \,..\, \textit{nr\_levels}] \\
\textit{geomlist} & = & \textit{zipWith contour\_geom contours colours}
\end{array} \\
\textit{eval\_picture env } (\textit{Draw ps}) \\
\quad = \textit{Group static } (\textit{map } (\textit{eval\_picture env}) \; \textit{ps}) \\
\textit{eval\_picture env } (\textit{Anim ps}) \\
\quad = \textit{Animate anim\_control } (\textit{True}, \textit{map } (\textit{eval\_picture env}) \; \textit{ps}, [\,])
\end{array}
$$

The brevity of the compound cases, *Draw* and *Anim*, is particularly pleasing. Constructors for compound *pictures* are interpreted directly in terms of an analogous low-level *rendering* constructor acting on the interpretation of the sub-pictures. Composition of pictures is thus essentially an application of *map*. The only differences between the interpretations of *Contour* (2D) and *Surface* (3D) are (i) the *mkgrid* function for *Surface*s builds a cubic grid, and (ii) the geometry is constructed by *surface_geom* rather than *contour_geom*.

6 Comparisons with Other Approaches

Previous entries to the visualization contest have used large-scale visualization tools such as VTK and Amira, and/or specialised graphics hardware. We used a small, lightweight Haskell library running on a modest desktop PC. A direct comparison is difficult. Our solution consists of less than 4000 lines of Haskell and 630 lines of C, whilst for example VTK [3], a powerful toolkit for visualization developed over more than a decade, consists of nearly 1000 C++ classes, and 600K lines of code. Even comparing specific features such as isosurfacing is non-trivial; the VTK module has to deal with more complex data and execution models, but excludes the machinery for building and executing pipelines, which arguably should be counted. Despite these caveats, this overall comparison, along with the figures presented in [7] do highlight the brevity and expressive power that come with functional abstractions.

We found it necessary to use C to implement data conversion and selection. A Haskell utility for converting the input data files into our binary fixed-precision format required ≈45 minutes per file. The C utility runs in less than 2 minutes per file. When processing 200 files, this is a significant difference. Haskell's support for generating tight, fast loops is not yet ideal. Although it might have been possible to utilise recent work on ByteString fusion [14], our experience has been that, for very simple tasks over large data, the effort required to persuade a Haskell compiler to generate fast code is more time-consuming than simply writing it in a lower-level language. Any worries about the correctness of the low-level implementation were mitigated through initial specification and automated testing in Haskell.

Our major success was the high-level DSL for pictures, which gave us considerable freedom to explore the data. We are far from the first to realise the benefits of this approach in the context of graphics. 'Picture combinators' go back at least as far as Henderson's 1982 paper on functional geometry, recently revisited [15], and Arya's work on functional animation [16] provides a rich set of operators for constructing movies. More recently, Elliott has produced a series of papers showing the value of DSLs for image manipulation (Pan [17]) and graphical synthesis (Vertigo [18]).

7 Conclusions and Prospects

This paper is not *just* about the use of Haskell for one specific problem, however challenging. The rationale for the IEEE visualization contest is to explore new approaches to difficult visualization problems. The scenario explored here, with large volumes of multifield data, is one that is found widely in practice. Our contribution is to show how functional languages enable rapid exploration of new visualization techniques, and a particularly elegant way of describing novel *combinations* of technique.

Brevity is particularly valuable in the context of *exploratory* visualization. Although we started with a number of algorithms already implemented, the contest tasks required new infrastructure and techniques. These were developed on the fly within the four weeks in which the authors were working towards an entry. Isosurfacing and volume-rendering were reused, but slicing, contouring, animation, 3D scatterplots, and of course the fixed precision library and downsampling infrastructure were all new. Even so, we would estimate that less than 1000 lines of Haskell were written or modified specifically for the contest.

> *The practical implication is that, when faced with a novel visualization problem, it may well be easier to write a new bespoke technique in 20-30 lines of Haskell than to assemble a collection of coarse-grained modules within a large toolkit, let alone create a set of new modules.*

Our picture DSL was implemented only in the final week of the contest. Initially, we had concentrated on data management and visualization techniques. The driver for change was the need to include animation. At this point we finally appreciated how much our previous ad-hoc construction of pictures was a hindrance. With the picture DSL, we were able to make rapid progress. Significant insights emerged literally within the final hour before submission. Even then, we did not fully exploit our system. We had for example implemented a 3D scatterplot, to explore correlations between ion concentrations. Given our animation facilities, it would be interesting to create a time-varying scatterplot, showing how the relative concentrations evolve over time as the shock-front passes through space.

The primitives of our picture DSL can be seen as analogs to the modules of a pipelined architecture [3]. However, we are working towards a different strategy. The contour code in Section 5.1 uses stream-based operations that generalise our initial work [6]. We would like to exploit these, and possibly a similar library on array-like structures, to provide an *intermediate* language for visualization algorithms. We see a visualization system as a hierarchy of languages. At the top, a declarative result specification (the picture DSL) is interpreted within a language of stream/array operations, which are then mapped onto a language for dataset management (cf our 'Stage I' as described in Section 4), generating datasets on demand, before finally a rendering language constructs scenes for display and interaction. Stages I and II would then be coupled directly, with the downsampler invoked directly from the visualization engine to provide datasets on demand.

The work presented here addresses *scientific* visualization. There is another challenge where functional programming may provide profoundly new insights, namely providing new levels of abstraction for managing *information* visualization (aka *infovis*). A key challenge here is the diversity of both data organization and visual metaphor. As a result, tools tend to be specialised to limited types of data and/or applications, and it is difficult to identify generic, reusable abstractions. The first task in any infovis application is to impose some structure on the data, one that enables translation into a suitable visual representation, for example a tree or graph. Could the strategy of creating layers of DSLs help also to structure infovis applications? An equally interesting question is whether the richer type system of functional languages, possibly including ideas like polytypism, can be used to find unexplored regularities within both data and display techniques. Recent work [19] on using Haskell for *visual analytics*, a new synthesis of information visualization and statistical analysis, suggests that the conversation between functional programming and visualization has only just begun.

Source code for our implementation is available from the project web site, `www.comp.leeds.ac.uk/funvis/`

Acknowledgements

The work reported in this paper was funded by the UK Engineering and Physical Sciences Research Council.

References

1. McCormick, B.H., DeFanti, T.A., Brown, M.D.: Visualization in scientific computing. Computer Graphics 21(6) (1987)
2. Haber, R.B., Lucas, B., Collins, N.: A data model for scientific visualization with provision for regular and irregular grids. In: Proceedings of Visualization 1991. IEEE Computer Society Press, Los Alamitos (1991)
3. Schroeder, W., Martin, K., Lorensen, B.: The Visualization Toolkit: An Object-Oriented Approach to 3D Graphics, 2nd edn. Prentice-Hall, Englewood Cliffs (1998), http://www.vtk.org/
4. Rhyne, T.M., Tory, M., Munzner, T., Ward, M., Johnson, C., Laidlaw, D.W.: Information and scientific visualization: Separate but equal or happy together at last. In: Proc. Visualization. IEEE Computer Society Press, Los Alamitos (2003)
5. Whalen, D., Norman, M.L.: Competition data set and description. IEEE Visualization Design Contest (2008), http://vis.computer.org/VisWeek2008/vis/contests.html
6. Duke, D.J., Wallace, M., Borgo, R., Runciman, C.: Fine-grained visualization pipelines and lazy functional languages. Transactions on Visualization and Computer Graphics 12(5), 973–980 (2006)
7. Duke, D.J., Borgo, R., Runciman, C., Wallace, M.: Experience report: Visualizing data through functional pipelines. In: Proc. Intl.Conf. on Functional Programming. ACM Press, New York (2008)
8. Borgo, R., Duke, D.J., Wallace, M., Runciman, C.: Multi-cultural visualization: how functional programming can enrich visualization (and vice versa). In: Proc. Vision, Modeling, and Visualization. AKA Verlag - IOS Press (2006)
9. Spence, R.: Information Visualization. Addison-Wesley, Reading (2000)
10. Runciman, C., Naylor, M., Lindblad, F.: SmallCheck and Lazy SmallCheck: exhaustive testing for small values. In: Proc. of the ACM SIGPLAN Symposium on Haskell, pp. 37–48. ACM Press, New York (2008)
11. Khronos Group: OpenGL—the industry foundation for high-performance graphics, http://www.opengl.org/
12. Wernecke, J.: The Inventor Mentor: Programming Object-Oriented 3D Graphics with Open Inventor. Pearson, London (1994)
13. Courtney, A., Nilsson, H., Peterson, J.: The Yampa arcade. In: Proc. Haskell Workshop, pp. 7–18. ACM Press, New York (2003)
14. Coutts, D., Stewart, D., Leshchinskiy, R.: Rewriting Haskell strings. In: Practical Applications of Declarative Languages (January 2007)
15. Henderson, P.: Functional geometry. Higher-order and Symbolic Computation 15, 349–365 (2002)
16. Arya, K.: A functional approach to animation. Computer Graphics Forum 5(4), 297–311 (1986)
17. Elliott, C., Finne, S., de Moor, O.: Compiling embedded languages. Journal of Functional Programming 13(2) (2003)
18. Elliott, C.: Programming graphics processors functionally. In: Proc. of the Haskell Workshop. ACM Press, New York (2004)
19. Heard, J.: A gentle introduction to functional information visualization. ACM SIGPLAN Developers' Track on Functional Programming (DEFUN) (2008), http://bluheron.europa.renci.org/docs/BeautifulCode.pdf

Toward a Practical Module System for ACL2

Carl Eastlund and Matthias Felleisen

Northeastern University
Boston, Massachusetts, U.S.A.
{cce,matthias}@ccs.neu.edu

Abstract. Boyer and Moore's ACL2 theorem prover combines first-order applicative Common Lisp with a computational, first-order logic. While ACL2 has become popular and is being used for large programs, ACL2 forces programmers to rely on manually maintained protocols for managing modularity. In this paper, we present a prototype of Modular ACL2. The system extends ACL2 with a simple, but pragmatic functional module system. We provide an informal introduction, sketch a formal semantics, and report on our first experiences.

1 A Logic for Common Lisp, Modules for ACL2

In the early 1980s, the Boyer and Moore team decided to re-build their Nqthm theorem prover [1] for a first-order, functional sub-language of a standardized, industrial programming language: Common Lisp [2]. It was an attempt to piggy-back theorem proving on the expected success of Lisp and functional programming. Although Common Lisp didn't succeed, the ACL2 system became the most widely used theorem prover in industry. Over the past 20 years, numerous hardware companies and some software companies turned to ACL2 to verify critical pieces of their products [3]; by 2006, their contributions to the ACL2 regression test suite amounted to over one million lines of code. The ACL2 team received the 2005 ACM Systems Award for their achievement.[1]

During the same 20 years, programming language theory and practice have evolved, too. In particular, programming language designers have designed, implemented, and experimented with numerous module systems for managing large functional programs [4]. One major goal of these design efforts has been to help programmers reason locally about their code. That is, a module should express its expectations about imports, and all verification efforts for definitions in a module should be conducted with respect to these expectations. Common Lisp and thus ACL2, however, lack a proper module system. Instead, ACL2 programmers emulate modular programming with Common Lisp's namespace management mechanisms, or by hiding certain program fragments from the theorem prover. Naturally, the manual maintenance of abstraction boundaries is difficult and error prone. Worse, it forces the programmer to choose between local reasoning and end-to-end execution, as functions hidden from the theorem prover cannot be run.

[1] `campus.acm.org/public/pressroom/press_releases/3_2006/software.cfm`

A. Gill and T. Swift (Eds.): PADL 2009, LNCS 5418, pp. 46–60, 2009.

Over the past year, we have investigated the design of a module system for ACL2. Specifically, we have extended ACL2's language with modules and produced two translations for modular programs: a compiler to ACL2 executables and a logic translator to ACL2 proof obligations. With the latter, programmers can now reason locally about individual modules. One goal is to empower ACL2 programmers with large code bases to gradually migrate their monolithic program into a modular world. Another goal is to expand Rex Page's [5] use of this industrial-strength theorem prover in software engineering courses to teach theorem proving in a modular setting. Without modules, such a software engineering course simply isn't convincing enough.

This paper is our first report on bringing this module technology to ACL2. In section 2, we demonstrate our module system and its prototype implementation. In section 3, we present our formal model of the module system. We have also implemented several projects as modules; in section 4 we describe the positive and negative outcomes of these experiments. Section 5 presents related work, and the last section sketches our future challenges.

2 Reasoning with Modules

ACL2. The ACL2 theorem prover is similar to a LISP read-eval-print loop; it accepts *events* such as function definitions or logical conjectures from the user, verifies each in turn, and updates the logical state for the next event. Its interface is purely text-based; the system comes with an Emacs mode as the preferred interface for professional ACL2 users.

Four years ago, Rex Page (Oklahoma University) started the ambitious effort of teaching a senior-level course sequence on software engineering in ACL2 [5]. Students reported difficulty with the text-based interface to ACL2; in response, Felleisen and Vaillancourt produced Dracula [6] as a graphical user interface for ACL2. Dracula has since been used in courses on software engineering and symbolic logic [7].

Dracula. Dracula is a language level in the DrScheme integrated development environment. It provides a simulation of Applicative Common Lisp (ACL), the executable component of ACL2. Dracula incorporates DrScheme's usual programming tools, including a syntax checker, stack traces, unit testing, and a functional, graphical toolkit geared toward novice programmers. It provides an interface to the ACL2 theorem prover for the logical component.

Figure 1 shows a screenshot of Dracula in action. The left-hand side of the Dracula interface provides two windows for formulating and executing programs: the definitions window, where users edit their programs, and the interactions window, where users may try out their functions.

The right-hand side of the display is Dracula's interface to the ACL2 theorem prover. It provides buttons to invoke ACL2 and to send each term from the definitions window to the theorem prover. Dracula paints the terms green when ACL2 proves them sound and red when it fails. Green terms are locked from further editing to faithfully represent ACL2's logical state; users may edit red

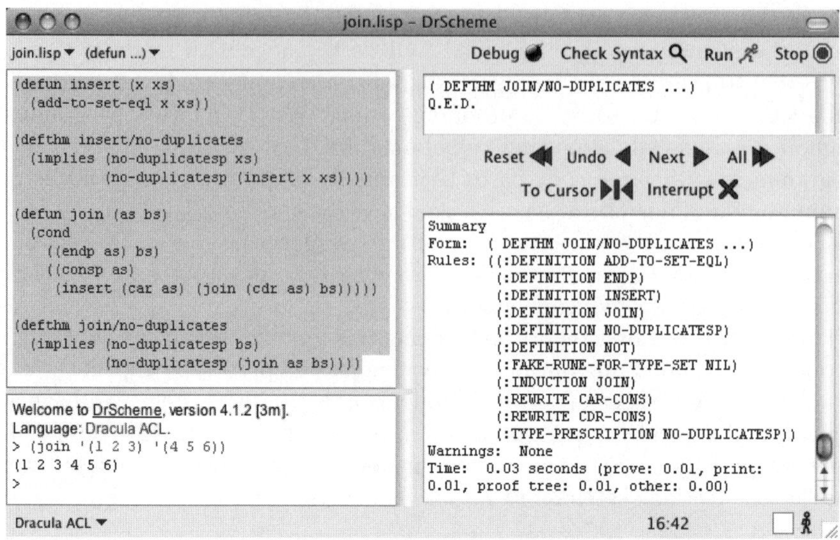

Fig. 1. The Dracula graphical user interface

terms or undo the admission of green terms to edit those. Below the control buttons, Dracula shows the theorem prover's output; above them, it shows a proof tree, naming key checkpoints for quick diagnosis of a failed attempt.

Figure 1 shows a program with two functions and two theorems. The functions are *insert*, which adds a single element to a set, and *join*, which adds multiple elements. The theorems *insert/no-duplicates* and *join/no-duplicates* state that the functions preserve the the uniqueness of set elements.

Dracula's simulation of ACL ignores the theorems, as they are logical rather than executable, and compiles the rest. As we can see in the interactions window, *join* produces the expected output when given '(1 2 3) and '(4 5 6) as input.

In contrast, the ACL2 theorem prover attempts to verify the logical soundness of each term successively. First it checks *insert*, which it must prove terminating for all inputs—a requirement of all functions in ACL2's logic. Next ACL2 checks *insert/no-duplicates*, for which it must prove that the conjecture expression produces a true value (non-**nil**). Free variables in **defthm** conjectures (such as x and xs) are implicitly universally quantified over all ACL2 values. ACL2 repeats the verification process for *join* and *join/no-duplicates*.

ACL2 successfully admits all these terms. The ACL2 output window displays a list of rules used in the proof of *join/no-duplicates*. The list includes the definitions of *insert* and *add-to-set-eql*, but not *insert/no-duplicates*. Rather than using the lemma proved above to reason about *join*, ACL2 re-examined the definition of *insert* to prove the uniqueness of its elements. The theorem prover's search strategies often prefer to delve into a function definition rather than use an existing lemma, resulting in duplicated proofs that span several functions.

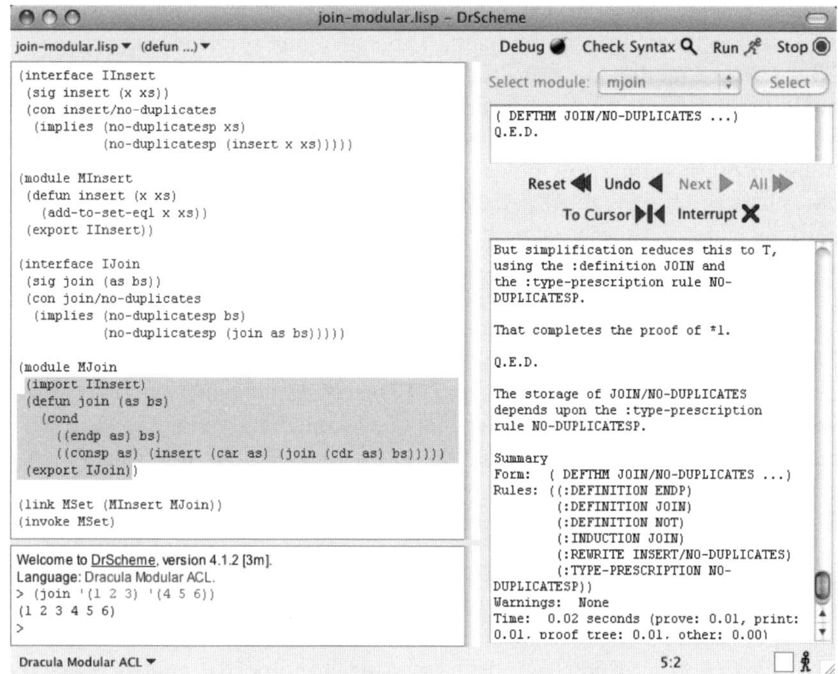

Fig. 2. A modular program in Dracula

Modular ACL2. Figure 2 shows a version of the *join* program in our new language, Modular ACL2. The definitions window contains two **interface**s, two **module**s, a **link** clause, and an **invoke** clause.

Interfaces contain **sig**natures and **con**tracts. A signature declares a function, providing its name and argument list. A contract declares a logical property that may refer to the signatures. Interfaces may also **include** other interfaces. This allows them to refer to other signatures in their contracts, extending them with new properties or stating relationships between multiple interfaces. The *IInsert* interface contains a signature *insert* and a contract *insert/no-duplicates*. They have the same arity and state the same property as the previous *insert* and *insert/no-duplicates*, but the interface does not provide a definition for *insert*. The *IJoin* interface similarly contains a signature and the *join/no-duplicates* contract for *join*.

Modules contain definitions, **import** clauses, and **export** clauses. The **import** and **export** clauses each name an interface. Definitions form the body of the module; they may refer to functions from imported interfaces, and rely on the properties declared by imported contracts. Conversely, the body of the module must define all functions declared in exported modules in a way that satisfies the associated contracts. A **link** clause constructs a new module from two existing modules. The exports of all the modules are combined, and the imports of each module are connected to the matching exports of any prior module.[2]

The *MInsert* module contains the same definition of *insert* we saw before and exports *IInsert*. This obligates *insert* to satisfy *insert/no-duplicates*. The *MJoin* module imports *IInsert*. This allows it to call the binary function *insert* and assume *insert/no-duplicates* holds. It then defines *join* as before, and exports *IJoin*. Once again, *join* must satisfy *join/no-duplicates*. This time, however, its soundness is not with respect to a concrete definition of *insert*, but rather with respect to the imported signature and its associated contract.

The *MSet* module in our example provides *IInsert* from *MInsert* and *IJoin* from *MJoin*; the reference to *insert* in *MJoin* is resolved to the definition in *MInsert*. Linking is applicative; the original *MJoin* is unchanged and may later be linked to a different implementation of *IInsert*. Finally, our example program **invoke**s *MSet*, making its exported functions available outside the module.

As with standard ACL, Dracula compiles the modular program to an executable form and disregards the logical aspects. It compiles *insert* and *join*, links them together, and provides them for use in the interactions window.

Reasoning locally. The ACL2 GUI allows the user to verify each module separately using the theorem prover. Once the user selects a module, Dracula provides ACL2 with *stubs* (abstract functions) representing its imported signatures and *axioms* (unproven logical rules) asserting its imported contracts. Dracula then passes the body of the module to ACL2. Once that is admitted, it sends ACL2 a theorem corresponding to each exported contract. If ACL2 admits all three stages—stubs and axioms for imports, body definitions, and theorems for exports—the module is guaranteed to satisfy its export interface for any sound implementation of its import interface.

The presence of stubs and axioms may seem troubling; these are unverified assumptions added to ACL2's logical state. Using them is sound with respect to a fully linked program, however. The interface imported by one module must be linked to an export from another, so contracts assumed as axioms in one module must be proved as theorems in another before the whole program is verified.

Dracula only admits *primitive* modules, such as *MInsert* and *MJoin*, via ACL2. It safely disregards *linked* modules, such as *MSet*; once *MInsert* and *MJoin* have been verified separately, they can be linked to any module with a matching interface without need for re-verification.

In figure 2, we see that ACL2 has admitted *MJoin*. This time the proof of *join/no-duplicates* does not refer to the definitions of *insert* or *add-to-set-eql*; instead, it uses the imported contract *insert/no-duplicates*.

Manual modularization in ACL2. ACL2 has mechanisms for abstract reasoning and proof reuse. Certain definitions in a book (separate file) or **encapsulate** block (lexical scope) may be declared **local**, which hides some or all of their definition from the remaining proof, but renders them unexecutable as well.

[2] As ACL2 does not allow forward references, neither do linked modules; this prevents cyclic definitions and preserves each module's termination proofs.

These abstract proofs may later be applied to concrete functions, but the rules must be applied on a theorem-by-theorem basis, and no executable content is reused. Logical rules may be selectively disabled in the global theory, but they may be re-enabled later, defeating abstraction boundaries.

Worse, these mechanisms require the programmer to maintain the invariants of an abstraction boundary *manually*, setting up a "negative interface" by declaring which logical entities are not available for reasoning rather than which are. ACL2 can simulate a normal, "positive interface" by layering these mechanisms, but not a reusable, externally stated one.

3 The Dual Semantics of Modules

The purpose of our module system is to enable programmers to develop units of code in isolation and to reason about them independently. This informal specification implies the need for two additions to core ACL2: modules and interfaces. For an untyped language such as ACL2, a module consists of definitions and manages the scope of names. An interface describes the functions that a module provides in terms of signatures and contracts, which play the role of both obligations on the exporting module and promises for the importing one.

Naturally a module can use the services of another module, i.e., it can import functions and rely on the contracts that hold for them. Using just those contracts and the definitions in the module, a programmer must be able to verify the module's export interface. That is, it is the task of the module system to reformulate the imported contracts and the module body so that the ACL2 theorem prover can verify the exported contracts from these premises.

Another design choice concerns the connection between modules. One alternative is to used fixed links between modules, specified via interfaces. The other one is to think of modules as relations from interfaces to interfaces and to link modules separately. Based on our experience with Scheme units [8,9] and ML functors [4], we have chosen the second alternative. Finally, we also decided to separate module invocation from module linking. The rest of the section presents a model of Modular ACL2, its syntax and two semantic mappings.

Syntax. Figure 3 shows the core syntax of ACL2 and Modular ACL2. ACL2 has two variable namespaces: function parameters and local variables (v), and functions and theorems (n). Modular ACL2 introduces a third namespace for modules and interfaces (N).

An ACL2 program consists of of a sequence of *def*initions and *expr*essions. Definitions give names to functions, stubs, theorems, or axioms, or may in turn be a sequence of other definitions. Expressions include variables, literal constants, function application, conditionals, and variable bindings.

Modular programs consist of a sequence of top-level forms including interface definitions, primitive module definitions, linking specifications, module invocations, and expressions from the core language. An **interface** contains *Spec*ifications, including **sig**natures, **con**tracts, and other **include**d interfaces, as described in section 2. A primitive **module** contains a sequence of *Def*initions,

prog = *top* ...
top = *def* | *expr*
def = (**defun** *n* (*v* ...) *expr*)
| (**defstub** *n* (*v* ...) **t**)
| (**defthm** *n* *expr*)
| (**defaxiom** *n* *expr*)
| (**progn** *def* ...)
expr = *v* | *const*
| (*n* *expr* ...)
| (**cond** (*expr* *expr*) ...)
| (**let** ((*v* *expr*) ...) *expr*)
const = **t** | **nil** | *number* | *string*

Prog = *Top* ...
Top = *Ifc* | *Mod* | *Link* | *Inv* | *expr*
Ifc = (**interface** *N* *Spec* ...)
Mod = (**module** *N* *Def* ...)
Link = (**link** *N* (*N* *N*))
Inv = (**invoke** *N*)
Spec = (**sig** *n* (*v* ...))
| (**con** *n* *expr*)
| (**include** *N*)
Def = *Imp* | *Exp* | *def*
Imp = (**import** *N*)
Exp = (**export** *N* (*n* *n*) ...)

Fig. 3. The core grammars of ACL2 (left) and Modular ACL2 (right)

extended from ACL2 to allow **import**s and **export**s via interfaces. Exported interfaces allow renaming, in case the internal and external names of a function differ. A compound module **link**s together two other modules.[3] Fully-linked modules—those whose imports have all been resolved—may be **invoke**d, making their declared exports available to top level expressions.

Dual Semantics. Modular ACL2 programs can be verified logically, and they can be executed. For this reason, modules in a program are either translated into ACL2 proof obligations, or linked together and run as an ACL2 program.

The two semantics are closely related, so that verification has meaning with respect to execution. Specifically, once a module is verified, its exports are guaranteed to satisfy their contracts whenever the implementations of their imports satisfy theirs as well. Put another way, once every module in a program has been verified, every contract must hold true at run-time.

We do not present the straightforward description of a static semantics for determining the syntactic well-formedness of programs. In order for a Modular ACL2 program to translate to well-formed ACL2, it must avoid forward references, name clashes within interfaces and modules, modules that import one interface without importing another that it includes, and a few other errors.

Logical Semantics. A Modular ACL2 program is verified by tranforming each primitive module into an ACL2 proof obligation stating that its definitions satisfy its exported contracts, predicated on the correctness of its imports. We represent this transformation as the function L (for "Logical") that consumes a Modular ACL2 program and produces a sequence of ACL2 programs, one for each module. Figure 4 shows the definition of L and its auxiliary functions.

The L function transforms a program by invoking LT with two accumulators: a list of interfaces and a list of obligations. This function traverses the top-level definitions of a modular program. Each interface LT encounters is added to Γ. Each primitive module is transformed into a proof obligation; the proof

[3] In our full implementation, imported interfaces allow renaming as well, and compound modules may link any number of modules.

$$L : \mathit{Prog} \rightarrow \mathit{prog} \ldots$$

$$L(\mathit{Prog}) = LT(\epsilon, \mathit{Prog}, \epsilon)$$

$$LT : (\mathit{Ifc} \ldots, \mathit{Top} \ldots, \mathit{prog} \ldots) \rightarrow \mathit{prog} \ldots$$

$$\begin{aligned}
LT(\Gamma, \epsilon, \Phi) &= \Phi \\
LT(\Gamma, \mathit{Ifc}\ \mathit{Top} \ldots, \Phi) &= LT(\Gamma\ \mathit{Ifc}, \mathit{Top} \ldots, \Phi) \\
LT(\Gamma, \mathit{Mod}\ \mathit{Top} \ldots, \Phi) &= LT(\Gamma, \mathit{Top} \ldots, \Phi\ LM(\Gamma, \mathit{Mod})) \\
LT(\Gamma, \mathit{Top}_0\ \mathit{Top} \ldots, \Phi) &= LT(\Gamma, \mathit{Top} \ldots, \Phi) \text{ where } \mathit{Top}_0 = \mathit{Link} \mid \mathit{Inv} \mid \mathit{expr}
\end{aligned}$$

$$LM : (\mathit{Ifc} \ldots, \mathit{Mod}) \rightarrow \mathit{prog}$$

$$LM(\Gamma, (\textbf{module}\ N\ \mathit{Def} \ldots)) = LD(\Gamma, \epsilon, \mathit{Def} \ldots, \epsilon)$$

$$LD : (\mathit{Ifc} \ldots, n \rightarrow n, \mathit{Def} \ldots, \mathit{def} \ldots) \rightarrow \mathit{prog}$$

$$\begin{aligned}
LD(\Gamma, \rho, \epsilon, \Delta) &= \Delta \\
LD(\Gamma, \rho, \mathit{def}\ \mathit{Def} \ldots, \Delta) &= LD(\Gamma, \rho, \mathit{Def} \ldots, \Delta\ \mathit{def}) \\
LD(\Gamma, \rho, (\textbf{import}\ N)\ \mathit{Def} \ldots, \Delta) &= LD(\Gamma, \rho, \mathit{Def} \ldots, \Delta\ LI(\mathit{Spec} \ldots, \epsilon)) \\
&\quad \text{where } \Gamma(N) = (\textbf{interface}\ N\ \mathit{Spec} \ldots) \\
LD(\Gamma, \rho, (\textbf{export}\ N\ (n_1\ n_2) \ldots)\ \mathit{Def} \ldots, \Delta) &= LD(\Gamma, \rho[n_2/n_1 \ldots], \mathit{Def} \ldots, \Delta\ \Delta') \\
&\quad \text{where } \Gamma(N) = (\textbf{interface}\ N\ \mathit{Spec} \ldots) \\
&\quad \text{and } LE(\rho', \mathit{Spec} \ldots, \epsilon) = \Delta'
\end{aligned}$$

$$LI : (\mathit{Spec} \ldots, \mathit{def} \ldots) \rightarrow \mathit{def} \ldots$$

$$\begin{aligned}
LI(\epsilon, \Delta) &= \Delta \\
LI((\textbf{include}\ N)\ \mathit{Spec} \ldots, \Delta) &= LI(\mathit{Spec} \ldots, \Delta) \\
LI((\textbf{sig}\ n\ (v \ldots))\ \mathit{Spec} \ldots, \Delta) &= LI(\mathit{Spec} \ldots, \Delta\ (\textbf{defstub}\ n\ (v \ldots)\ \textbf{t})) \\
LI((\textbf{con}\ n\ e)\ \mathit{Spec} \ldots, \Delta) &= LI(\mathit{Spec} \ldots, \Delta\ (\textbf{defaxiom}\ n\ e))
\end{aligned}$$

$$LE : (n \rightarrow n, \mathit{Spec} \ldots, \mathit{def} \ldots) \rightarrow \mathit{def} \ldots$$

$$\begin{aligned}
LE(\rho, \epsilon, \Delta) &= \Delta \\
LE((\textbf{include}\ N)\ \mathit{Spec} \ldots, \Delta) &= LE(\rho, \mathit{Spec} \ldots, \Delta) \\
LE(\rho, (\textbf{sig}\ n\ (v \ldots))\ \mathit{Spec} \ldots, \Delta) &= LE(\rho, \mathit{Spec} \ldots, \Delta) \\
LE(\rho, (\textbf{con}\ n\ e)\ \mathit{Spec} \ldots, \Delta) &= LE(\rho, \mathit{Spec} \ldots, \Delta\ (\textbf{defthm}\ \rho[\![n]\!]\ \rho[\![e]\!]))
\end{aligned}$$

Fig. 4. Translation from Modular ACL2 to one proof obligation per module

obligation is added to Φ. Link clauses, invocations, and expressions are ignored, as they carry no additional logical obligations.

Within the definition of L and its helpers, Γ is treated as an environment. The notation $\Gamma(N)$ represents looking up an interface by name.

The LM function converts a module to a proof obligation by calling LD on its internal definitions. The LD function traverses the module's definitions, accruing a substitution that associates external names with internal names as declared by **export** clauses, and a list Δ of resulting definitions. The function converts imported signatures and contracts to stubs and axioms with LI and exported contracts to conjectures (**defthm**) with LE respectively. Regular ACL2 definitions are left as-is.

Executable Semantics. In addition to a logical meaning, we also need a regular run-time semantics for modular programs. Modular ACL2 programs are translated to executable form by two main processes. One is the successive

$E : \mathit{Prog} \rightarrow \mathit{prog}$

$E(\mathit{Prog}) = ET(\epsilon, \epsilon, \mathit{Prog}, \epsilon)$

$ET : (\mathit{Top} \ldots, n \rightarrow n, \mathit{Top} \ldots, \mathit{def} \ldots) \rightarrow \mathit{prog}$

$$\begin{aligned}
&ET(\Gamma, \rho, \epsilon, \Delta) &&= \Delta \\
&ET(\Gamma, \rho, \mathit{Ifc}\ \mathit{Top} \ldots, \Delta) &&= ET(\Gamma\ \mathit{Ifc}, \rho, \mathit{Top} \ldots, \Delta) \\
&ET(\Gamma, \rho, \mathit{Mod}\ \mathit{Top} \ldots, \Delta) &&= ET(\Gamma\ EM(\Gamma, \mathit{Mod}), \rho, \mathit{Top} \ldots, \Delta) \\
&ET(\Gamma, \rho, \mathit{Link}\ \mathit{Top} \ldots, \Delta) &&= ET(\Gamma\ EL(\Gamma, \mathit{Link}), \rho, \mathit{Top} \ldots, \Delta) \\
&ET(\Gamma, \rho, \mathit{Inv}\ \mathit{Top} \ldots, \Delta) &&= ET(\Gamma, \rho\ \rho', \mathit{Top} \ldots, \Delta\ \Delta') \text{ where } EI(\Gamma, \mathit{Inv}) = (\rho', \Delta') \\
&ET(\Gamma, \rho, \mathit{expr}\ \mathit{Top} \ldots, \Delta) &&= ET(\Gamma, \rho, \mathit{Top} \ldots, \Delta\ \rho[\![\mathit{expr}]\!])
\end{aligned}$$

$EM : (\mathit{Top} \ldots, \mathit{Mod}) \rightarrow \mathit{Mod}$

$EM(\Gamma, (\mathbf{module}\ N\ \mathit{Def}\ \ldots)) = (\mathbf{module}\ N\ \mathit{Imp}\ \ldots\ \mathit{def}\ \mathit{Exp}\ \ldots)$
where $\mathit{sort}(\mathit{Def} \ldots) = \mathit{Imp}\ \ldots\ \mathit{def}\ \ldots\ (\mathbf{export}\ N_1\ (n_1\ n_2)\ \ldots)\ \ldots$
and $(n_3\ \ldots)\ \ldots = \mathit{names}(\Gamma(N_1)) \ldots$
and $\mathit{Exp}\ \ldots = (\mathbf{export}\ N_1\ (n_3\ [n_2/n_1 \ldots][\![n_3]\!])\ \ldots)\ \ldots$

$EL : (\mathit{Top} \ldots, \mathit{Link}) \rightarrow \mathit{Mod}$

$EL(\Gamma, (\mathbf{link}\ N\ (N_1\ N_2))) = (\mathbf{module}\ N\ \mathit{Imp}\ \ldots\ \mathit{def}\ \ldots\ \mathit{Exp}\ \ldots)$
where $\Gamma(N_1) =$
$(\mathbf{module}\ N_1\ (\mathbf{import}\ A_1)\ \ldots\ \mathit{def}_1\ \ldots\ (\mathbf{export}\ B_1\ (b_1\ a_1)\ \ldots)\ \ldots)$
and $\Gamma(N_2) =$
$(\mathbf{module}\ N_2\ (\mathbf{import}\ A_2)\ \ldots\ \mathit{def}_2\ \ldots\ (\mathbf{export}\ B_2\ (b_2\ a_2)\ \ldots)\ \ldots)$
and $A_3 \ldots = (A_2 \ldots) - (A_1 \ldots B_1 \ldots)$
and $b_3 \ldots = \mathit{names}(\Gamma((A_2 \ldots) \cap (B_1 \ldots)) \ldots)$
and $\rho_1 = \mathit{freshen}(\mathit{def}_1 \ldots)$
and $\rho_2 = \mathit{freshen}(\mathit{def}_2 \ldots)$
and $\rho_3 = [\rho_1[\![[a_1/b_1 \ldots][\![b_3]\!]]\!]/b_3 \ldots]$
and $\mathit{Imp} \ldots = (\mathbf{import}\ A_1)\ \ldots\ (\mathbf{import}\ A_3)\ \ldots$
and $\mathit{def} \ldots = \rho_1[\![\mathit{def}_1]\!] \ldots\ \rho_2[\![\rho_3[\![\mathit{def}_2]\!]]\!] \ldots$
and $\mathit{Exp} \ldots = (\mathbf{export}\ B_1\ (b_1\ \rho_1[\![a_1]\!])\ \ldots)\ \ldots$
$(\mathbf{export}\ B_2\ (b_2\ \rho_2[\![\rho_3[\![a_2]\!]]\!])\ \ldots)\ \ldots$

$EI : (\mathit{Top} \ldots, \mathit{Inv}) \rightarrow (n \rightarrow n, \mathit{def} \ldots)$

$EI(\Gamma, (\mathbf{invoke}\ N)) = ([\rho[\![n_2]\!]/n_1 \ldots], \rho[\![\mathit{def}]\!] \ldots)$
where $\Gamma(N) = (\mathbf{module}\ N\ \mathit{def}\ \ldots\ (\mathbf{export}\ N'\ (n_1\ n_2)\ \ldots)\ \ldots)$
and $\rho = \mathit{freshen}(\mathit{def} \ldots)$

$\mathit{sort}(\mathit{Def} \ldots)$: Sort module body into imports, definitions, and exports.
$\mathit{names}(\mathit{Ifc} \ldots)$: Extract the names of signatures from interfaces.
$\mathit{freshen}(\mathit{def} \ldots)$: Produce a substitution giving fresh names to definitions.

Fig. 5. Translation from Modular ACL2 to an executable program

linking of each compound module into a primitive one. The other is the extraction of definitions from each invoked primitive module; these are concatenated with top-level expressions. We perform this transformation with the function E (for "Executable"), shown in figure 5 along with some auxiliary translation functions. To simplify the presentation, we introduce a and b for function and theorem names, and A and B for interface and module names. We use Γ as an environment again, this time for both interfaces and modules.

This E function invokes ET with an empty environment, substitution, and sequence of result terms. The ET function adds interfaces to the environment, as well as primitive modules reduced to canonical form by EM. All modules in the environment contain imports first, then internal definitions, and finally exports with fully explicit external/internal name associations. Compound modules are converted to primitive modules by EL and stored in the environment. The EI function extracts definitions and a substitution from a module in the environment, which ET uses to splice the module's body into the top level and link top-level expressions to it.

The EL function combines two primitive modules into one. It looks up their definitions in the environment, then extracts their imports, exports, and internal definitions. The definitions are given fresh names and linked together by substituting names exported (from N_1) and imported (to N_2) across a shared interface. Finally, EL concatenates both sets of source imports (except any resolved by linking), definitions, and exports.

4 Experience with Modules

Designing a new language is insufficient; one must program in it to determine its merit. We have therefore added a prototype of Modular ACL2 to Dracula and have used it to convert a number of ACL2 programs into modular shape. In this section, we present our experience writing, verifying, and executing three illustrative examples. We then demonstrate the advantages of modules for ACL2 and explain the most serious problem encountered.

Illustrative Experiments. The *Worm game* is illustrative of the projects assigned to freshmen at Northeastern University and the courses at Oklahoma.

The top-left box in figure 6 displays a concise description of the game. The implementation consists of three main modules implementing the food, the worm, and the game itself. These are supported by three other modules, defining a pseudorandom number generator, basic point geometry, and the game grid. We implemented the game and verified two nontrivial properties: the worm's tail stays within the grid during the game, and it never crosses itself. Figure 6 shows portions of the game and point interfaces.

Graph traversal is the first canonical ACL2 case study [3]. The task is to represent directed graphs, implement an algorithm to find a path from one node to another, and prove the algorithm always produces a valid path.[4]

We designed our graph traversal program around two interfaces: one for representing a graph, the other for the search algorithm. See figure 7 for details. A successful *find-path* is guaranteed to produce a path, specified by *pathp* in *IGraph* as a list of adjacent nodes. We produced four modules in total: neighbors list and edge list representations of graphs, and depth-first and breadth-first search. The modules are interchangeable; either graph representation may be linked with either search algorithm.

[4] The original case study also proves that it finds a path so long as one exists.

Game Description:
The player directs a constantly-moving worm on a grid. The grid has walls and, somewhere, a piece of food. If the worm eats the food, the worm grows in length and a new piece of food appears. If the worm runs into a wall or its own tail, the game ends.

```
(interface IPoint
 (sig points-uniquep (pt pts))
 (sig points-uniquep (pts))
 (con points-uniquep/nil
  (points-uniquep nil))
 (con points-uniquep/cons
  (implies
   (and (pointp pt)
        (point-listp pts)
        (point-uniquep pt pts)
        (points-uniquep pts))
   (points-uniquep (cons pt pts)))))
```

```
(interface IGame
 (include IPoint)
 (sig live-gamep (v))
 (sig uncrossedp (v))
 (sig worm-tail (g))
 (sig game-tick (g))
 (con uncrossedp/worm-tail
  (implies (uncrossedp g)
           (points-uniquep (worm-tail g))))
 (con initial-game/uncrossedp
  (uncrossedp (initial-game)))
 (con game-tick/uncrossedp
  (implies (and (uncrossedp g)
                (live-gamep g))
           (uncrossedp (game-tick g))))
 (con game-key/uncrossedp
  (implies (and (uncrossedp g)
                (live-gamep g)
                (stringp k))
           (uncrossedp (game-key g k)))))
```

Fig. 6. Interface excerpts from the Worm game

```
(interface IGraph
 (sig graphp (v))
 (sig nodep (g n))
 (sig edgep (g a b))
 (sig pathp (g x y p))
 (con pathp/one
  (iff (pathp g x y (list a))
       (and (equal x a) (equal y a) (nodep g a))))
 (con pathp/append
  (implies
   (and (edgep g b c) (pathp g a b p) (pathp g c d q))
   (pathp g a d (append p q)))))
```

```
(interface IFindPath
 (include IGraph)
 (sig find-path (g x y))
 (con find-path/pathp
  (implies
   (and (graphp g)
        (nodep g x)
        (nodep g y)
        (find-path g x y))
   (pathp
    g x y
    (find-path g x y)))))
```

Fig. 7. Interface excerpts from the graph search program

Different strategies for implementing *language interpreters* suggest natural exercises in proving equivalence of two recursive algorithms. In our interpreters, an expression is either an integer or a binary operator $+$, $-$, or $*$ applied to two expressions. Our small-step interpreter reduces the leftmost redex in an expression, producing a new expression until no reductions remain. Our alternative interpreter uses a big-step strategy. We specified the program in four interfaces: expressions, big-step evaluation, small-step reductions, and equivalence between the two. Figure 8 shows some representative excerpts.

```
(interface ILanguage ;; datatypes
 (sig exprp (v))
 (sig calcp (v))
 (sig calc (f a b)))
```

```
(interface IBigStep
 (include ILanguage)
 (sig eval (e))
 (con eval/plus
  (equal (eval (calc '+ a b))
         (+ (eval a) (eval b)))))
```

```
(interface IEquivalence
 (include ILanguage)
 (include IBigStep)
 (include ISmallStep)
 (con eval=last-reduction
  (implies (exprp e)
           (equal (last (reduce-all e))
                  (list (eval e))))))
```

```
(interface ISmallStep
 (include ILanguage)
 (sig reduce (e))
 (sig reduce-all (e))
 (con reduce/plus
  (implies
   (and (integerp a) (integerp b))
   (equal (reduce (calc '+ a b)) (+ a b))))
 (con reduce/left
  (implies (calcp a)
           (equal (reduce (calc f a b))
                  (calc f (reduce a) b))))
 (con reduce-all/calcp
  (implies
   (and (exprp e) (calcp e))
   (equal (reduce-all e)
          (cons e (reduce-all (reduce e)))))))
```

Fig. 8. Interface excerpts from the interpreter program

Theorem	Mono.	Mod.	Theorem	Mono.	Mod.
game-tick/uncrossedp	845.95	0.06	*game-mouse/uncrossedp*	8.82	0.01
game-tick/gamep	387.12	0.03	*connected-wormp/wormp*	3.00	0.06
game-tick/in-bounds	362.97	0.03	*worm-turn/uncrossed-wormp*	0.48	0.10
connected-gamep/gamep	173.55	0.03	*worm-move/uncrossed-wormp*	0.38	0.05
game-key/uncrossedp	148.65	0.05	*worm-grow/uncrossed-wormp*	0.25	0.04
game-key/in-bounds	64.58	0.03	*worm-turn/in-bounds-wormp*	0.23	0.06
game-key/gamep	64.24	0.02	*random-nat/range*	0.10	0.10
uncrossedp/gamep	10.75	0.01	*modulo/range*	0.08	0.08

Fig. 9. Time (in seconds) to verify theorems from two versions of the Worm game

Performance Improvements. Programming in a modular style naturally reduces the scope of ACL2's proof search space and improves the engine's efficiency. Plain ACL2 typically requires "hints"—e.g., restrictions of the global theory—to complete or speed up a proof. Modules restrict theories by design and in a disciplined manner; it is often unnecessary to guide the search.

Our modular verification of the Worm game required no hints at all; the verification takes just a few seconds per module. We compared this to a naïve translation into a monolithic ACL2 proof. We concatenated the contents of the modules and inserted the contracts of each module's exports as theorems. ACL2 was able to verify the monolithic version as well, but took several orders of magnitude longer.

Figure 9 shows the CPU time (in seconds) used to prove the slowest nine theorems from each version of the Worm game. The modular version never takes over a tenth of a second, while the monolithic proof peaks at several minutes. Near the end of the monolithic program, proof attempts had the entirety of the game to inspect, while the modular proof started with a clean slate per module. The slow performance measured here does not reflect the professional ACL2 user's experience; rather, such ACL2 users refine their proofs by manually maintaining abstraction boundaries that occur naturally with modules.

Conciseness and Reuse. Modular design also promotes abstraction and code reuse. Standard ACL2 programs cannot, in general, change their implementation strategy without adjusting the accompanying theorems. Put differently, separating implementations and specifications imposes a serious cost of manual coding and, because of that, prevents common patterns of code reuse and refactoring.

In contrast, Modular ACL2 encourages and simplifies reuse. Clients of our graph modules may swap representations or search algorithms freely in a **link** clause without changing a single **defthm**. Even undergraduates can now program for reuse in ACL2.

Limitations. Unfortunately, our gains in terms of local reasoning come with a serious loss, best illustrated with our interpreter example. In this example, our final equivalence proof imports *ILanguage*, *IBigStep*, and *ISmallStep* (fig. 8), representing respectively the grammar and two interpreters. Sadly, while a natural modularization calls for this organization, doing so prevents ACL2's search engine from finding an inductive proof.

The key problem is that, on one hand, ACL2 associates induction schemes with function definitions, and that, on the other hand, Modular ACL2's interfaces hide function definitions. For the specific case of our interpreters, the main theorem must perform induction on the structure of expressions and of the two interpreter algorithms. Because these definitions are hidden behind module barriers, ACL2's proof engine can't possibly find a proof. The only way to expose the induction schemes to ACL2 is to provide a concrete function definition, but exposing *eval* and *reduce-all* defeats the abstraction boundaries of *ISmallStep* and *IBigStep*.

From a high level perspective, we have traded improved local reasoning for a loss in global reasoning. Naturally we consider this a major limitation of our current approach. Induction is a critical aspect of ACL2, and inductive proofs should not be limited to individual modules. Hence, our next step in designing Modular ACL2 is to add a linguistic mechanism for specifying induction principles across interfaces and verifying their correct implementation as exports.

5 Related Work

The design of the module system derives from PLT Scheme's unit system [8,9], with linking semantics based on mixins [10,11]. More precisely, Modular ACL2 contributes contracts to the unit model, but inherits the idea of linking primitive and compound modules in hierarchical shape. It subtracts recursive linking as this would complicate ACL2's termination proofs.

Coq [12,13], Twelf [14], and similar proof assistants adopt an ML-like module system for encapsulating proofs about metatheory. Our modules and interfaces correspond closely to ML's functors and signatures. Modular ACL2 can express type specifications via contracts and sharing constraints via interface inclusion; it cannot currently express nested modules. However, we face different challenges, having chosen to work with a first-order functional language and an automated theorem prover with idiosyncratic limitations. We must deal with the lack of abstract induction schemes, the inexpressibility of higher-order logical statements such as a module's proof obligation, and the lack of execution-preserving proof abstraction mechanisms.

Extended ML (EML) [15] equips SML [16] with logical properties and a verification semantics. The language is designed around the methodology of beginning with an abstract specification and refining it step-by-step to a concrete implementation. EML offers signatures, structures, and functors, any of which may contain axioms, analogous to our modules and interfaces with contracts. EML also offers the abstract term "**?**" for specified but unimplemented types, values, or structures; Modular ACL2's stubs and axioms serve a similar purpose. EML has the benefit of SML's powerful type system, but lacks a theorem prover. In contrast, Modular ACL2 is based on the industry's leading, general-purpose, automated theorem prover.

Some theorem proving languages also provide named scopes, such as Isabelle's locales [17], Coq's sections [18], and the "little theories" of IMPS [19]. These scopes allow local and global definitions, and export the global ones by translating or abstracting over the local ones. They provide a lightweight approach to abstraction and namespace management, but do not support explicit interfaces or introduce abstraction beyond that of the underlying language.

6 Conclusion

While Boyer and Moore took an existing functional language and constructed a theorem prover for it, we have chosen to take an existing theorem prover and to equip it with a pragmatic module system. Thus far, we have designed a series of models and prototypes. In this paper, we present the first version that makes modular programming truly practical. Our examples in this paper illustrate how Modular ACL2 introduces and encourages information hiding and code reuse. As a result, Modular ACL2 naturally improves the performance of the proof search engine. Novices to the system now easily succeed with complex proofs where before professionals would have had to manually encode search strategies.

Unsurprisingly, the development of Modular ACL2 pinpoints the major problem with modularization of ACL2 programs: the hiding of inductive structures. We intend to tackle this challenging problem over the next year and expect to report progress on Modular ACL2 then. In the meantime, we will deploy and maintain our implementation to get feedback through classroom experience.

References

1. Boyer, R.S., Moore, J.S.: Mechanized reasoning about programs and computing machines. In: Veroff, R. (ed.) Automated Reasoning and Its Applications: Essays in Honor of Larry Wos, pp. 146–176. MIT Press, Cambridge (1996)
2. Steele Jr., G.L.: Common Lisp—The Language. Digital Press (1984)
3. Kaufmann, M., Manolios, P., Moore, J.S.: Computer-Aided Reasoning: ACL2 Case Studies. Kluwer Academic Publishers, Dordrecht (2000)
4. Harper, R., Pierce, B.C.: Design considerations for ML-style module systems. In: Advanced Topics in Types and Prog. Languages, pp. 293–345. MIT Press, Cambridge (2004)
5. Page, R.: Engineering software correctness. J. of Func. Prog. 17(6), 675–686 (2007)
6. Vaillancourt, D., Page, R., Felleisen, M.: ACL2 in DrScheme. In: Proc. 6th Intern. Works. ACL2 Theorem Prover and its Applications, pp. 107–116. ACM Press, New York (2006)
7. Eastlund, C., Vaillancourt, D., Felleisen, M.: ACL2 for freshmen: First experiences. In: Proc. 7th Intern. ACL2 Workshop, pp. 200–211. ACM Press, New York (2007)
8. Flatt, M., Felleisen, M.: Units: Cool modules for HOT languages. In: ACM SIGPLAN Conference on Prog. Language Design and Implementation, pp. 236–248 (June 1998)
9. Owens, S., Flatt, M.: From structures and functors to modules and units. In: ACM SIGPLAN Intern. Conference on Func. Prog., pp. 87–98. ACM Press, New York (2006)
10. Bracha, G., Lindstrom, G.: Modularity meets inheritance. In: Proceedings of the International Conference on Computer Languages, pp. 282–290. IEEE, Los Alamitos (1992)
11. Dreyer, D., Rossberg, A.: Mixin' up the ML module system. In: Proceedings of the 13th ACM SIGPLAN International Conference on Functional Programming, pp. 307–320. ACM, New York (2008)
12. Chrzaszcz, J.: Implementing modules in the Coq system. In: Basin, D., Wolff, B. (eds.) TPHOLs 2003. LNCS, vol. 2758, pp. 270–286. Springer, Heidelberg (2003)
13. Courant, J.: $\mathcal{MC}_2$: A Module Calculus for Pure Type Systems. J. of Func. Prog. 17, 287–352 (2006)
14. Harper, R., Pfenning, F.: A module system for a programming language based on the LF logical framework. Journal of Logic and Computation 8(1), 5–31 (1998)
15. Sannella, D.: Formal program development in Extended ML for the working programmer. In: Proc. 3rd BCS/FACS Workshop on Refinement, pp. 99–130 (1991)
16. Milner, R., Tofte, M., Harper, R., MacQueen, D.: The Definition of Standard ML (2e). MIT Press, Cambridge (1990)
17. Kammüller, F., Wenzel, M., Paulson, L.C.: Locales: A sectioning concept for Isabelle. In: Bertot, Y., Dowek, G., Hirschowitz, A., Paulin, C., Théry, L. (eds.) TPHOLs 1999. LNCS, vol. 1690, pp. 149–166. Springer, Heidelberg (1999)
18. The Coq Development Team: The Coq Proof Assistant Reference Manual (2006), `http://coq.inria.fr/V8.1pl3/refman/index.html`
19. Farmer, W.M., Guttman, J.D., Thayer, F.J.: IMPS: An interactive mathematical proof system. Journal of Automated Reasoning 11, 213–248 (1993)

Declarative Network Verification

Anduo Wang[1], Prithwish Basu[2], Boon Thau Loo[1], and Oleg Sokolsky[1]

[1] Computer and Information Sciences Department, University of Pennsylvania,
3330 Walnut Street, Philadelphia, PA 19104-6389
[2] Network Research Group, BBN Technologies,
10 Moulton Street, Cambridge, MA 02138
{anduo,boonloo,sokolsky}@seas.upenn.edu, pbasu@bbn.com

Abstract. In this paper, we present our initial design and implementation of a *declarative network verifier* (*DNV*). *DNV* utilizes *theorem proving*, a well established verification technique where logic-based *axioms* that automatically capture network semantics are generated, and a user-driven proof process is used to establish network correctness properties. *DNV* takes as input declarative networking specifications written in the Network Datalog (*NDlog*) query language, and maps that automatically into logical *axioms* that can be directly used in existing theorem provers to validate protocol correctness. *DNV* is a significant improvement compared to existing use case of theorem proving which typically require several man-months to construct the system specifications. Moreover, *NDlog*, a high-level specification, whose semantics are precisely compiled into *DNV* without loss, can be directly executed as implementations, hence bridging specifications, verification, and implementation. To validate the use of *DNV*, we present case studies using *DNV* in conjunction with the PVS theorem prover to verify routing protocols, including eventual properties of protocols in dynamic settings.

Keywords: Declarative networking, network protocol verification, domain-specific languages, theorem proving.

1 Introduction

In recent years, we have witnessed a proliferation of new overlay networks [24] that use the existing Internet to enable deployable network evolution and introduce new services. Concurrently, as sophisticated, bandwidth-intensive, and even mission-critical services are being deployed over heterogeneous network infrastructure, there is increased demand for new network routing protocols that can flexibly adapt to a wide range of variability in network connectivity and data traffic patterns. This has cummulated into recent efforts at clean-slate efforts aimed at redesigning the Internet.

Given the proliferation of new architectures and protocols, there is a growing consensus on the need for formal software tools and programming frameworks that can facilitate the design, implementation, and verification of new protocols. This has lead to several recent proposals broadly classified as: (1) *algebraic and*

A. Gill and T. Swift (Eds.): PADL 2009, LNCS 5418, pp. 61–75, 2009.

logic frameworks [11,9] that enable protocol correctness in the design phase; (2) *testing platforms* [16,27] that provide mechanisms for runtime verification and distributed replay, and (3) *programming toolkits* [8,14] that enable network protocols to be specified, implemented, and model-checked.

In this paper, we present our initial design and implementation of a *declarative network verifier* (*DNV*). Our work is a significant step towards *bridging* network specifications, protocol verification, and implementation within a common language and system. *DNV* achieves this unified capability via the use of *declarative networking* [20,19,18], a declarative domain-specific approach for specifying and implementing network protocols, and *theorem proving*, a well established verification technique based on logical reasoning.

In declarative networking, network protocols are specified using a declarative logic-based query language called *Network Datalog* (*NDlog*). In prior work, it has been shown that traditional routing protocols can be specified in a few lines of declarative code [20], and complex protocols such as Chord DHT [31] in orders of magnitude less code [19] compared to traditional imperative implementations. This compact and high-level specifications enables rapid prototype development, ease of customization, optimizability, and the potentiality for protocol verification. When executed, these declarative networks result in efficient implementations, as demonstrated by the *P2* declarative networking system [1].

Recent significant advances in model checking of network protocol implementations include *MaceMC* [13] and *CMC* [7]. Compared to these proposals, *DNV* has the advantage that it achieves complete verification for networks of arbitrary size, a long-standing challenge in any practical network verification system. Incomplete verification is a common limitation in *MaceMC* and *CMC* due to the the state-explosion problem, particularly when used to verify large networks with complex protocol behavior. In addition, since *DNV* directly verifies declarative networking specifications, an explicit model extraction step via execution exploration is not required.

This paper makes the following two contributions. First, we propose *DNV*, a declarative network verifier that leverages declarative networking's connection to logic programming to automatically compile high-level *NDlog* program into formal specifications as *axioms* without semantics loss, which can be further used in a theorem prover to validate protocols. A semi-automated proof guided by the user is then carried out and mechanically checked in a general-purpose theorem prover to establish the protocol correctness properties. High-level *NDlog* programs that have been verified in *DNV* can be directly executed as implementations, hence bridging specifications and implementations within a unified declarative framework.

Second, we demonstrate that *DNV* enables the verification of network protocols in *dynamic settings*, where protocols continuously update network state based on incoming network events. *DNV* achieves this via its use of declarative networking which incorporates the notion of periodic *soft-state* [26] maintenance of network state into its query language and semantics. Soft state is central and critical in networking implementations because in a very simple manner it provides eventually correct semantics in the face of reordered messages, node disconnection, and other unpredictable occurrences.

DNV aims to provide a practical solution towards network protocol verification, one that achieves a unifying framework that combines specifications, verification, and implementation. Our work is a significant improvement over existing usage of theorem proving [12,10] which typically require several man-months to develop the system specifications, a step that *DNV* reduces to a few hours through the use of declarative networking. To our best knowledge, *DNV* is also one of the first attempts at using theorem proving to verify eventual semantics of protocols in dynamic settings.

2 Background: Declarative Networking

In this section, we will provide a brief overview of declarative networking. Interested readers are referred to references [20,19,18,17] for more details.

2.1 Datalog Language

Declarative networks are specified using *Network Datalog (NDlog)*, a distributed logic-based recursive query language first introduced in the database community for querying network graphs. *NDlog* is primarily a distributed variant of Datalog. We first provide a short review of Datalog, following the conventions in Ramakrishnan and Ullman's survey [25]. A Datalog program consists of a set of declarative *rules*. Each rule has the form `p :- q1, q2, ..., qn.`, which can be read informally as "`q1` and `q2` and ... and `qn` implies `p`". Here, `p` is the *head* of the rule, and `q1`, `q2`,...,`qn` is a list of *literals* that constitutes the *body* of the rule. Literals are either *predicates* with *attributes* (which are bound to variables or constants by the query), or boolean expressions that involve function symbols (including arithmetic) applied to attributes. In Datalog, rule predicates can be defined with other predicates in a cyclic fashion to express recursion. The order in which the rules are presented in a program is semantically immaterial; likewise, the order predicates appear in a rule is not semantically meaningful. Commas are interpreted as logical conjunctions (`AND`). The names of predicates, function symbols, and variable names begin with an upper letter, while constants names begin with an lowercase letter. An optional `Query` rule specifies the output of interest (i.e. result tuples).

2.2 Path-Vector Protocol

We present an example *NDlog* program that implements the *path-vector* protocol [23], a standard textbook route protocol used for computing paths between any two nodes in the network.

```
p1 path(@S,D,P,C):- link(@S,D,C),P=f_init(S,D).
p2 path(@S,D,P,C):- link(@S,Z,C1), path(@Z,D,P2,C2),C=C1+C2,
                    P=f_concatPath(Z,P2), f_inPath(P2,S)=false.
p3 bestPathCost(@S,D,min<C>):-path(@S,D,P,C).
p4 bestPath(@S,D,P,C):- bestPathCost(@S,D,C), path(@S,D,P,C).
Query bestPath(@S,D,P,C).
```

The program takes as input `link(@S,D,C)` tuples, where each tuple corresponds to a copy of an entry in the neighbor table, and represents an edge from the node itself (`S`) to one of its neighbors (`D`) of cost `c`. *NDlog* supports a *location specifier* in each predicate, expressed with `@` symbol followed by an attribute. This attribute is used to denote the source location of each corresponding tuple. For example, `link` tuples are stored based on the value of the `S` field.

Rules `p1-p2` recursively derive `path(@S,D,P,C)` tuples, where each tuple represents the fact that the path from `S` to `D` is via the path `P` with a cost of `C`. Rule `p1` computes one-hop reachability trivially given the neighbor set of `S` stored in `link(@S,D,C)`. Rule `P2` computes transitive reachability as follows: if there exists a link from `S` to `Z` with cost `C1`, and `Z` knows about a shortest path `P2` to `D` with cost `C2`, then transitively, `S` can reach `D` via the path `f_concatPath(Z,P2)` with cost `C1+C2`. Note that `p1-p2` also utilizes two list manipulation functions to maintain path vector `p`: `f_init(S,D)` initializes a path vector with two elements `S` and `D`, while `f_concatPath(Z,P2)` prepends `Z` to path vector `P2`.

Rules `p3-p4` take as input `hop` tuples generated by rules `p1-p2`, and then derive the hop along the path with the minimal cost for each source/destination pair. The output of the program is the set of `bestPathHop(@S,D,Z,C)` tuples, where each tuple stores the next hop `Z` along the shortest path from `S` to `D`. To prevent computing paths with cycles, an extra predicate $f\_inPath(P, S) = false$ is used in rule `p2`, where the function $f\_inPath(P, S)$ returns true if node S is in the path vector P.

The execution model of declarative networks is based on a distributed variant of the standard evaluation technique for Datalog programs that is commonly known as *semi-naïve* (SN) evaluation [18], with modifications to enable pipelined asynchronous evaluation suited to a distributed setting. Reference [18] provides details on the implementation and execution model of declarative networking.

For the purposes of formal verification, we do not consider the location specifiers within the proof. This does not affect the program in terms of the set of eventual facts being generated but does affect the notion of data distribution. Our extended technical report [32] elaborate this issue in greater detail.

3 Overview of DNV

Figure 1 provides an overview of *DNV*'s basic approach towards unifying specifications, verification, and implementation within a common declarative framework. *DNV* takes as input *NDlog* program specifications of the declarative protocol (see Section 2 for an example). Since most theorem provers leverage type information, *DNV* further includes a *Type Schema* with the *NDlog* program specifications. This is not unlike a database-like schema storing the attribute types of all network state being used.

In order to carry out the formal verification process, the *NDlog* programs and schema information are automatically compiled into formal specifications recognizable by a standard theorem prover (e.g. PVS [21], Coq [3]) using the *axiom generator*. As depicted in the left-part of Figure 1, At the same time, the protocol designer specifies high-level invariant properties of the protocol to be checked via two mechanisms: invariants can be written directly as theorems into

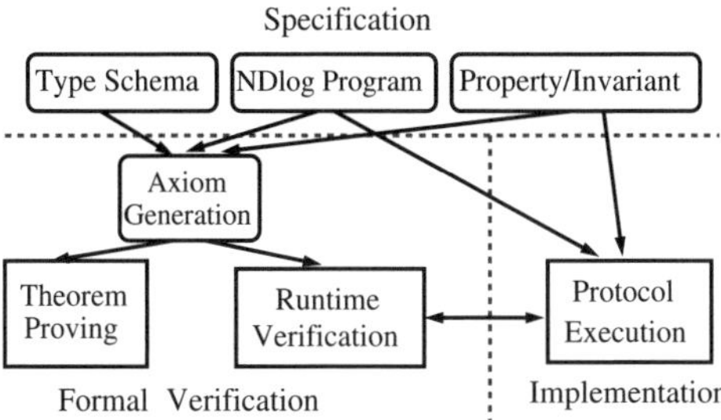

Fig. 1. DNV overview block diagram. Arrows denote flow of information.

the theorem prover, or expressed as *NDlog* rules which are then automatically translated into theorems using the axiom generator. The first approach increases the expressiveness of invariant properties, where one can reason with invariants that can be only expressible in higher order logic. The second approach has restricted expressiveness based on *NDlog*'s use of Datalog, but has the added advantage that the same properties expressed in *NDlog* can be verified by both theorem prover and at runtime.

From the perspective of network designers, as depicted in the left part of Figure 1, they reason about their protocols using the high-level protocol specifications and invariant properties. The *NDlog* high-level specifications are directly executed and also proved within the theorem prover. Any errors detected in the theorem prover can be corrected by changing the *NDlog* specifications. Our initial *DNV* prototype uses the PVS theorem prover, due to its substantial support for proof strategies which significantly reduce the time required in the actual proof process. However, the techniques describe in this paper are agnostic to other theorem provers. We have also validated some of the verification presented in this paper using the Coq [3] prover.

To illustrate the verification process, we step through the path-vector protocol example, shown in Section 2. For ease of exposition, we defer the treatment of soft-state derivations and events to Section 4, focusing instead on traditional *hard-state* data (with infinite lifetimes) that are valid until explicitly deleted.

3.1 Axiom Generation: From *NDlog* Rules to PVS Axioms

The first step in *DNV* involves the *automatic* generation of PVS *formalization* (or axioms) directly from *NDlog* rules. Based on the proof-theoretic semantics of Datalog [30], there is a natural and automatic mapping from *NDlog* rules to PVS axioms.[1] Before showing the actual PVS encoding for the path-vector protocol, it is informative to understand the proof-theoretic semantics of `p1` and `p2` as inference rules used in proof system:

The inference rule `p1` expresses the logical statement $\forall(S, D, P, C).link(S, D, C) \wedge P = f_{init}(S, D) \implies path(S, D, P, C)$.

[1] The equivalence of *NDlog*'s proof-theoretic semantics and operational semantics guarantees that *DNV* is sound in the sense that, the correctness property established by *DNV* corresponds precisely to the operational semantics of *NDlog* execution.

Rule p2 is slightly more complex as some attribute variables do not appear in the resulting head. The general technique to express these variables is in terms of existential quantification. Accordingly, rule p2 expresses the logical statement that $\forall(S, D, P, C).\exists(C_1, C_2, Z, P_2).link(S, Z, C_1) \wedge bestPath(Z, D, P_2, C_2) \wedge C = C_1 + C_2 \wedge P = f_{concatPath}(Z, P_2) \implies path(S, D, P, C)$.

From the above logical statements, *DNV* generates the following axioms:

```
path_generate: AXIOM
FORALL (S,D,Z:Node)(C:Metric)(P:Path):(link(S,D,C) AND P=f_init(S,D)) OR
  ((EXISTS (P2:Path)(C1,C2:Metric):(link(S,Z,C1) AND bestPath(Z,D,P2,C2)
    AND C=C1+C2 AND P=f_concatPath(Z,P2))) =>path(S,D,P,C)
path_close: AXIOM
 FORALL (S,D,Z:Node)(C:Metric)(P):path(S,D,P,C)=>
   ((link(S,D,C) AND P=f_init(S,D)) OR (EXISTS (Z:Node)(P,P2:Path)
     (C1,C2:Metric): (link(S,Z,C1) AND bestPath(Z,D,P2,C2) AND C=C1+C2
      AND P=f_concatPath(Z,P2))))
```

The first `path_generate` axiom is generated in a straightforward manner from rules `p1` and `p2`, where the logical `OR` indicates that `path` facts can be generated from either rule. The `path_close` axiom indicates that the `path` tuple is the smallest set derived by the two rules, ensuring that these axioms automatically generated in *DNV* correctly reflected the minimal model of *NDlog* semantics. The list manipulation functions `f_concatPath` and `f_init` are predefined from PVS primitive types. We omit this discussion due to space constraints.

PVS provides *inductive definitions* that allows the two axioms above to be written in a more concise and logically equivalent form:

```
path(S,D,(P: Path),C): INDUCTIVE bool =
  (link(S,D,C) AND P=f_init(S,D) AND Z=D) OR (EXISTS (C1,C2:Metric)
  (Z2:Node) (P2:Path): link(S,Z,C1) AND path(Z,D,P2,C2) AND
  C=C1+C2 AND P=f_concatPath(S,P2) AND f_inPath(S,P2)=FALSE)
```

The universal quantifiers over the attributes to `path` (i.e. `S,D,Z...`) are implicitly embedding and existential quantifiers such as `C1` and `C2` are explicitly stated. *DNV* axiom generator always produces this inductive definition, and employs the axiom form only in the presence of mutual dependencies among the head predicates which makes PVS inductive definition impossible. Also note that the use of `f_inPath(S,P2)=FALSE` constraint prevents loops in `path`.

Accordingly, *NDlog* rules `p3-p4` are automatically compiled into PVS formalization in a similar way:

```
bestPathCost(S,D,min_C): INDUCTIVE bool =
  (EXISTS (P:Path): path(S,D,P,min_C)) AND (FORALL (C2:Metric):
    (EXISTS (P2:Path): path(S,D,P2,C2)) => min_C<=C2)
bestPath(S,D,P,C):INDUCTIVE bool =
  bestPathCost(S,D,C) AND path(S,D,P,C)
```

In addition to the above PVS encoding for *NDlog* rules, type definitions are produced automatically from the database schema information. For instance, given a database schema definition for `link(src:string, dst:string, metric:integer)` the corresponding PVS type declaration is `link: [Node,Node,Metric -> bool]` where `Node` is declared as a string type and `Metric` as an integer type.

3.2 Proving Route Optimality in the Path-Vector Protocol

The next step involves proving actual properties in PVS. Properties are expressed as PVS *theorems* and serve as *starting points* (or *goals*) in the proof construction process. We illustrate this process by verifying the *route optimality* property in the path-vector protocol expressed in the following PVS `bestPathStrong` theorem:

```
bestPathStrong: THEOREM
  FORALL (S,D:Node) (C:Metric) (P:Path): bestPath(S,D,P,C) =>
    NOT (EXISTS (C2:Metric) (P2:Path): path(S,D,P2,C2) AND C2<C)
```

The above theorem specifies that for a given `bestPath(S,D,P,C)` from `S` to `D`, `P` is the *optimal* path, i.e. there does not exist another path `P2` from `S` to `D` with lower cost `C2`.

Given the above theorem, one can then utilize PVS to carry out the proof process. PVS performs the proof in a *goal-directed* fashion, in this case, starting from the `bestPathStrong` goal, and then recursively reducing it to subgoals until all subgoals are trivially true. PVS has approximately 100 built-in proof strategies, of which 20 are usually sufficient to automate a majority of the proof effort. We display the strawman proof process that does not utilize any user-defined proof strategies specific to declarative network beyond PVS's built-in proof commands:

```
("" (skosimp*) (expand bestPath) (prop) (expand bestPathCost)
(prop) (skosimp*) (inst -2 C2!1) (grind))
```

The proof script reflects the interactive proof process in PVS directed by the user, where PVS takes care of all low level proof details and allows the user to concentrate on high-level proof strategies. Without going into details of each PVS command, we provide a high-level intuition of each step. The first command `skosimp*` performs repeated skolemization that removes universal quantifiers `S,D,C` and `P` in the theorem. Skolemization is generally the first proof step to try in proving any universal quantified theorems. The subsequent two `expand` commands are used to unfold the earlier inductive definition shown in 3.1, each followed by `prop` that performs proportional simplification. Then `skosimp*` is employed to remove universal quantifiers and `inst` to instantiate the existential quantified variable with proper instance (`C2!1`). The rest of the proof is complete by using PVS's `grind` command which performs skolemization, heuristic instantiation, propositional simplification and decision procedures for linear arithmetic and equality.

Once the above proof script is supplied, PVS requires only fraction of a second to carry out the actual proof. When the proof is completed, it covers *all* instances of the network. This is in contrast to model checking, which explores only specific network instances. In addition to proving the route optimality property of the declarative path-vector protocol, we have proven properties such as the potential cycles in the protocol if the cycle check (enforced using the `f_inPath` function) is removed.

The strawman proof process here is restricted to PVS's built-in proof commands, and does not utilize any user-defined proof strategies that exploits domain-specific information. As a result, the proof requires an expert in declarative network and theorem proving. Given that our target users are network designers, the proof process should ideally be automated. In reference [32], we discuss the potential of using domain-specific PVS strategies tailored to declarative networking to support the proof construction.

4 Soft-State, Events and Network Dynamics

Up to this point, we have limited our verification to a subset of the complete *NDlog* language by omitting the treatment of *soft-state tuples (i.e. predicates)*. This simplification enables us to generate axioms recognizable by a theorem prover directly from *NDlog* programs without having to worry about the semantics of time and data expiration. In practice, soft-state data and events are central in network protocols, and adopted in many declarative network implementations. In the rest of this section, we will introduce the soft-state model in declarative networking, describe how rules with soft-state predicates (referred as *soft-state rules*) can be verified in a similar fashion as shown in Section 3, by first rewriting soft-state rules into logically equivalent rules with only hard-state predicates (i.e.*hard-state rules*).

4.1 Soft-State Model in Declarative Networking

Declarative networking incorporates support for *soft-state* [26] derivations commonly used in networks. In the soft state storage model, all data (input and derivations) has an explicit "time to live" (TTL) or lifetime, and all expired tuples must be explicitly reinserted with their latest values and a new TTL or they are deleted.

To support soft-state, an additional language feature is added to the *NDlog* language, in the form of a `materialize` [19] declaration at the beginning of each *NDlog* program that specifies the TTL of predicates. For example, the expression `materialized(link,10,keys(1,2))` specifies that the `link` tuple is stored at a table with primary key set to the first and second attributes (denoted by `keys(1,2)` and that each `link` tuple has a lifetime of 10 seconds[2]. If the TTL is set to infinity, the predicate will be treated as *hard-state*.

The soft-state storage semantics are as follows. When a tuple is derived, if there exists another tuple with the same primary key but differs on other attributes, an *update* occurs, in which the new tuple replaces the previous one. On the other hand, if the two tuples are identical, a *refresh* occurs, in which the existing tuple is extended by its TTL.

For a given predicate, in the absence of any `materialize` declaration, it is treated as an *event* predicate with lifetime set to zero. Since events are not stored, they are primarily used to trigger other rules or in response to network events. Reference [17] provides more details on how soft-state storage model and events are implemented within a declarative networking engine.

---

[2] Following the conventions of the *P2* declarative networking system, attribute 0 is reserved for the predicate name.

4.2 Soft-State to Hard-State Rewrite in *DNV*

The rule rewrite consists of two steps. First, all soft-state predicates of the form `p(...)` where "..." refer to predicate arguments, are translated into an equivalent hard-state predicate of the form `p(...,Tc,Tl)`, where the additional attributes `Tc` and `Tl` denote the creation time and lifetime of each tuple `p` respectively. This initial rewrite step makes explicit the creation time and lifetime by adopting `Tc`, `Tl` in each soft-state predicate. Event predicates are rewritten in a similar fashion. However, `Tl` is omitted since events have zero lifetime by definition.

After the first step, additional constraints reflecting soft-state semantics are added to ensure that all soft-state facts only process with other facts valid within the same window period of time, as expressed in terms of constraints over `Tc` and `Tl`. Consider soft-state rules of the form, $e : -e_1, s_1, s_2, ..., s_n$. This rule triggered by input event e_1 with creation time Tc_{e1}, takes as input both the triggering event and several soft-state predicates $s_1, s_2, ..., s_n$, and generates a event. The rewritten equivalent hard-state rules is of the form:

$$e(..., Tc_{e1}) : -e_1(..., Tc_{e1}), s_1(..., Tc_{s1}, Tl_{s1}), s_2(..., Tc_{s2}, Tl_{s2}), ..., s_n(..., Tc_{sn}, Tl_{sn}),$$
$$Tc_{s1} < Tc_{e1} \leq Tc_{s1} + tl_{s1}, ..., Tc_{sn} < Tc_{e1} \leq Tc_{sn} + Tl_{sn}.$$

Since the event e_1 directly triggers the derivation of e, the creation time of the derived event e is set to be the same as that of the input e_1 (i.e. Tc_{e1}). An additional n constraints $Tc_{si} < Tc_{e1} \leq Tc_{si} + Tl_{si}$ are added to ensure that only soft-states s_i with valid time interval $[Tc_{si}, Tc_{si} + Tl_{si}]$ that always overlaps with Tc_{e1} are used to generate e.

Another possible class of soft-state rules are of the form, $e : -s_1, s_2, ..., s_n$, where an event e is generated by sets of soft-states. The main difference compared to the previous soft-state rule is the lack of a triggering event. The rewritten hard-state rule is of the form:

$$e(..., Tc) : -s_1(..., Tc_{s1}, Tl_{s1}), s_2(..., Tc_{s2}, Tl_{s2}), ..., s_n(..., Tc_{sn}, Tl_{sn}), Tc = max < Tc_{s1},$$
$$Tc_{s2}, ..., Tc_{sn} >, Tc_{s1} < Tc \leq Tc_{s1} + tl_{s1}, ..., Tc_{sn} < Tc \leq Tc_{sn} + Tl_{sn}.$$

Note that Tc is set to the max of all possible creation times of the input soft-state predicates (since the derived fact is true only when all the input facts are present).

The same rewrite process applies to rules that derive soft-state predicates s instead of events e. The main difference is an additional `Tl` attribute to s in the rewritten rule. This `Tl` attribute is set to the to the declared lifetime in corresponding table for s (indicated in the `materialize` statement). We omit the presentation due to space constraints.

5 Case Study: Distance-Vector in a Dynamic Network

In this section, we illustrate the capability of *DNV* in reasoning about eventual semantics of protocols in dynamic networks. We base our illustration on the verification of the *distance-vector* protocol, commonly used for computing shortest routes in a network. Due to space constraints, we are not able to show exhaustively all the PVS specifications and proofs. The interested reader is referred to reference [6] for the complete PVS axioms, theorems, and proofs.

5.1 Distance Vector Protocol Specification in *NDlog*

The following soft-state *NDlog* program implements the distance-vector protocol, computing best paths with least cost:

```
materialize(hop,10,keys(1,2,3)).
materialize(bestHop,10,keys(1,2)).
materialize(bestHopCost,10,keys(1,2)).
dv1 hop(@S,D,D,C) :- link(@S,D,C).
dv2 hop(@S,D,Z,C) :- hopMsg(@S,D,Z,C).
dv3 bestHopCost(@S,D,min<C>) :- hop(@S,D,Z,C).
dv4 bestHop(@S,D,Z,C) :- bestHopCost(@S,D,C), hop(@S,D,Z,C).
dv5 hopMsg(@N,D,S,C1+C2):-periodic(@S,5),bestHop(@S,D,Z,C1),link(@S,N,C2).
Query bestHop(@S,D,Z,C)
```

This program derives soft-state predicates `hop`, `bestHop`, and `bestHopCost` with TTL of 10 seconds, and an event predicate `hopMsg`, and takes as input `link` tuples which represents dynamic network topology and is implemented by some periodic neighbor maintenance mechanism [6].

First, rules `dv1-dv2` derive `hop(@S,D,Z,C)` tuples, where `Z` denotes the next hop (instead of the entire path) along the path from `S` to `D`. Second, the protocol is driven by the periodic generation of `hopMsg(@S,D,Z,C)` in rule `dv5`, where each node `S` advertises its knowledge of all possible best hops table (`bestHop`) to all its neighbors. Note that bidirectional connectivity and cost is assumed. Each node receives the advertisements as `hopMsg` events (rule `dv2`) which it then stores locally in its `hop` table. Finally, Rules `dv3-dv4` compute the best hop for each source/destination pair in a similar fashion as the earlier path-vector protocol.

Unlike the path-vector protocol presented in Section 2.2, the distance-vector protocol computes only the *next hop* along the best path, and hence does not store the entire path between any two nodes.

5.2 Soft-State Rewrite and Automated Axiom Generation

The following *NDlog* rules `dv1-dv6` shows the equivalent hard-state rules after applying the soft-state rewrite process described in Section 4.2.

```
dv1 hop(@S,D,D,C,Tc,10) :- link(@S,D,C,Tc,10).
dv2 hop(@S,D,Z,C,Tc,10) :- hopMsg(@Z,D,W,C2,Tc2), Tc=Tc2+5, C=C2+1.
dv3 bestHopCost(@S,D,min<C>,Tc,10) :- hop(@S,D,D,C,Tc,10).
dv4 bestHop(@S,D,Z,C,Tc,10) :- bestHopCost(@S,D,C,Tc,10),
                               hop(@S,D,Z,C,Tc1,10), Tc1<Tc<=Tc1+10.
dv5 hopMsg(@N,D,Z,C,Tc) :- periodic_dv(@S,5,Tc), bestHop(@S,D,Z,C,Tc1,10),
                    link(@S,N,C,Tc2,10), Tc2<Tc<=Tc2+10, Tc1<Tc<=Tc1+10.
dv6 periodic_dv(@S,5,Tc) :- periodic_dv(@S,5,Tc2), Tc=Tc2+5
Query bestHop(@S,D,Z,C,Tc,Tl)
```

Rules `dv1-dv5` are the corresponding hard-state rewrites, and `dv6` emulates the behavior of `periodic` streams employed in `dv5`, as described in Section 4.2. We introduce an extra constraint `Tc=Tc2+5` in rule `dv2`. This condition is required so that causality of rule execution is preserved within one interval: resulting `hopMsg` events generated within one periodic interval derives `hop` facts used in the next period internal and not vice versa. We note that this addition constraint is automatically added: required only in cases when rules depend on each other in a cyclical fashion (e.g. `hop` derived in `dv1-dv2`, `hopMsg` in `dv5`, and `bestHop` in `dv4`), a dependency that can be detected via static check.

Based on this rewritten program, the automatically generated PVS axioms are as follows:

```
hopMsg(S,D,Z,C,Tc): INDUCTIVE bool =
  (EXISTS (Tc2,T3:Time): bestHop (S,D,Z,C,Tc2,10) AND periodic(S,5,Tc)
    AND link(S,D,Tc3,10) AND Tc2<Tc<=Tc2+10 AND Tc3<Tc<=Tc3+10 AND C=1)
hop(S,D,Z,C,Tc,Tl): INDUCTIVE bool =
  (link(S,D,Tc,10) AND Z=D AND Tl=10 AND C=1) OR (EXISTS (C2:Metric)
    hopMsg(S,D,Z,C2,Tc2) AND C=C2+1 AND Tl=10 AND Tc=Tc2+5)
bestHopCost(S,D,MIN_C,Tc,Tl): INDUCTIVE bool =
  (EXISTS (Z:Node): hop(S,D,Z,MIN_C,Tc) AND Tl=10) AND
    (FORALL (C:Metric): (EXISTS (Z:Node): hop(S,D,Z,C,Tc,10))=>MIN_C<=C)
bestHop_refresh: AXIOM
  FORALL (S,D,Z:Node) (C:Metric) (Tc:Time): bestHopCost(S,D,C,Tc,10)
    AND hop(S,D,Z,C,Tc,10)=>bestHop(S,D,Z,C,Tc,10)
bestHop_close: AXIOM
  FORALL (S,D,Z:Node) (C:Metric) (Tc:Time): bestHop(S,D,Z,C,Tc,10)
    => (bestHopCost(S,D,C,Tc,10) AND hop(S,D,Z,C,Tc,10))
periodic_dv(S,I,Tc): INDUCTIVE bool =
  EXISTS (Tc2:Time): periodic_dv(S,I,Tc2) AND Tc=Tc2+5 AND I=5
```

Recall automatic axiom generation process in Section 3.1, PVS axioms would be explicitly used in face of mutual dependencies between rules (that derive `bestHop`, `hop`, and `hopMsg`). To break the dependency, we therefore specify `dv4` with two axioms `bestHop_refresh` and `bestHop_close`.

5.3 Eventual Convergence Proof in a Stable Network

The lack of knowledge of the entire path in the distance-vector protocol comes at the expense of potential update loops in the presence of link updates. This is a well-known limitation of the distance-vector protocol, commonly known as the *count-to-infinity* problem.

Our verification is performed on a 4-node network instance as shown in Figure 2. Note that this instance represents a loop consisting of three nodes (`a`, `b`, and `c`) that can reach the rest part of the network via a fourth node `d`, and the results of this verification apply to any *arbitrary* network that contains such a loop. For ease of exposition we do not consider computation of `link` tuple here and supply this network instance using the following PVS inductive definition, where each clause connected by logical operator `OR` represents a link between two nodes:

```
link(S,D,C,Tc,Tl): INDUCTIVE bool =
((S=a AND D=b AND C=1 AND Tl=10 AND (EXISTS (i:posnat): Tc=5*i)) OR
((S=b AND D=c AND C=1 AND Tl=10 AND (EXISTS (i:posnat): Tc=5*i)) OR
...
((S=a AND D=d AND C=1 AND Tl=10 AND (EXISTS (i:posnat): Tc=5*i))
```

Network convergence is expressed using the following theorem:

```
bestHopCost_converge: THEOREM
EXISTS (j:posnat): FORALL (S,D:Node)(C:Metric)(i:posnat): (i>j)
  => bestHopCost(S,D,C,5*i,10) = bestHopCost(S,D,C,5*j,10)
```

Given an input network, the distance-vector protocol requires a number of rounds of communication among all nodes, for route advertisements (in the form of `hopMsg`) to be propagated in the network. In the above theorem, the existential quantified variable `j` denotes the initial number of periodic intervals (set to be at least the network diameter) required to propagate all route advertisements. The theorem states that for any arbitrary time `i` after `j`, the value of `bestHopCost` always converges (i.e. no longer changes).

5.4 Count-to-Infinity Analysis in a Dynamic Network

In the final *DNV* example, we demonstrate the capability of *DNV* to prove the presence of the *count-to-infinity* problem in the distance-vector protocol. This is a well-studied limitation where the protocol potentially *diverges* (i.e. not reach steady state) in the presence of link failures.

Before showing the actual proofs, we provide a textbook example [23] that clearly demonstrates the problem intuitively. Revisiting the network in Figure 2, when `link(a,d)` fails, node `a` would advertises this information to its immediate neighbors `b` and `c`. However, despite the fact that `d` is no longer reachable from either `a` `b` or `c`, based on information that `c` can reach `d` in two hops, `b` would conclude that it can reach `d` in three hops. Node `c` makes a similar conclusion. In the next round of updates, node `a` learns that `b` and `c` can reach `d` in three hops, and updates its distance to `d` as four accordingly. This cycle continues indefinitely, resulting in the count-to-infinity problem.

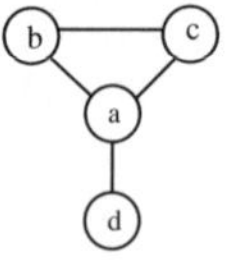

Fig. 2. Network Dynamics

The proof requires a network scenario that results in a count-to-infinity problem. Using the example described above, we supply this network dynamics using the following PVS inductive definition:

```
link (S,D,C,Tc): INDUCTIVE bool =
((S=a AND D=b AND C=1 AND (EXISTS (i:posnat): Tc=5*i) AND Tc<100)) OR
((S=b AND D=a AND C=1 AND (EXISTS (i:posnat): Tc=5*i) AND Tc<100)) OR
...
((S=a AND D=d AND C=1 AND (EXISTS (i:posnat): Tc=5*i) AND Tc<100)) OR
((S=d AND D=a AND C=1 AND (EXISTS (i:posnat): Tc=5*i) AND Tc<100)) OR
((S=a AND D=b AND C=1 AND (EXISTS (i:posnat): Tc=5*i) AND Tc>=100)) OR
((S=b AND D=a AND C=1 AND (EXISTS (i:posnat): Tc=5*i) AND Tc>=100)) OR
```

```
...
((S=c AND D=b AND C=1 AND (EXISTS (i:posnat): Tc=5*i) AND Tc>=100)) OR
((S=b AND D=c AND C=1 AND (EXISTS (i:posnat): Tc=5*i) AND Tc>=100))
```

The definition indicates that the `link(a,d)` and `link(d,a)` facts are only present before time `100`, denoting that a link failure between nodes `a` and `d` happens at time `100`. The count-to-infinity theorem is expressed as follows:

```
bestHop_increase_to_infinity: THEOREM
FORALL (a,b,d:Node)(t:Time)(c:Metric):(t>100 AND bestHop(a,d,b,c,t,10))=>
(EXISTS (t':Time)(c':Metric):(t'>t AND c'>c AND bestHop(a,d,b,c',t',10)))
```

The theorem above states that if the distance vector protocol diverges, the best hop from `a` to `d` will increase indefinitely over time, a symptom of the count-to-infinity problem. In reference [6], we have the complete proof of this theorem, as well as addition theorems that further verify the presence of the count-to-infinity problem. Interestingly, we have been able to prove a *stronger* PVS theorem specific to a three-node network cycle: $\forall b,d,a,c,t.(\exists i.t = i \times 5 \wedge t > 100) \implies (bestHop(b,d,a,c,t,10) \implies bestHop(b,d,a,c+2,t+10,10))$, which expresses the precise pattern that the value of `cost` argument increases by 2 at every two update intervals of 10 seconds.

We further verify that a well-known solution to this problem, known as the *split-horizon* solution can avoid any two-node cycle, and show that this solution is insufficient for fixing the count-to-infinity problem in a three-node cycle. Refer to our extended technical report [32] for more details.

6 Related Work

We briefly survey existing work on network protocol verification.

Classical theorem proving has been used in the past few decades for verification of network protocols [29,5,10,4]. Despite extensive work, this approach is generally restricted to protocol design and standards, and cannot be directly applied to protocol implementation. A high initial investment based on domain expert knowledge is often required to develop the system specifications acceptable by some theorem prover (up to several man-months). Therefore, even after successful proofs in the theorem prover, the actual implementation is not guaranteed to be error-free. *DNV* avoids this problem by using a common executable declarative networking language that can be directly verified in a theorem prover.

Runtime verification techniques (e.g. [15,16,27]) is a mechanism for checking at runtime that a system does not violate expected properties. Since declarative networks utilize a distributed query engine to execute its protocols, these checks can be expressed as *monitoring queries* in *NDlog*. However, any runtime verification scheme will incur additional runtime overheads, and subtle bugs may require a long time to be encountered. Moreover, the properties can be checked in this case are restricted to those can be expressed in *NDlog*. In particular, any universal quantified properties, such as `bestPathStrong` we demonstrated in Section 3.2 is not checkable in runtime verification based on *NDlog* query engine.

Model checking is a collection of algorithmic techniques for checking temporal properties of system instances based on exhaustive state space exploration.

Recent significant advances in model checking network protocol implementations include *MaceMC* [13] and *CMC* [7]. Compared to *DNV*, these approaches are *sound* as well, but not *complete* in the sense that the large state space persistent in network protocols often prevents complete exploration of the huge system states. While the heuristics used in exploration maximize the chances of detecting property violations, they are typically inconclusive and restricted to small network instances and temporal properties.

By adopting a theorem-proving based approach in this paper, *DNV* is more expressive and flexible compared to *MaceMC* and *CMC*, since higher-order logics can be used to specify network properties. In addition, since *DNV* directly verifies declarative networking specifications, an explicit model extraction step via execution exploration is not required.

7 Future Work

We are in the process of applying *DNV* to more complex overlay networks, and reasoning about routing protocols, particularly when integrated with policies [11,9]. Our initial experiences suggest that *DNV* is a promising approach towards a unified framework that integrates specification, implementation, and verification. Moving forward, we have identified a few areas of future work, in the areas of domain specific proof strategies [22,2], proof automation [33,34,28]. We further plan to leverage PVS's support for CTL (variant of temporal logic) model-checking [21] to integrate model checking into *DNV*. Our extended report [32] details our ongoing and future work.

Acknowledgments

This work was partially sponsored by NSF CNS-0721845 and DARPA through Air Force Research Laboratory (AFRL) Contract FA8750-07-C-0169. The views and conclusions contained in this document are those of the authors and should not be interpreted as representing the official policies, either expressed or implied, of the Defense Advanced Research Projects Agency or the U.S. Government.

References

1. P2: Declarative Networking, `http://p2.cs.berkeley.edu`
2. Archer, M., Vito, B.D., Muñoz, C.: Developing user strategies in PVS: A tutorial. In: STRATA 2003, NASA/CP-2003-212448 (2003)
3. Bertot, Y., Castéran, P.: Interactive theorem proving and program development. coq'art: The calculus of inductive constructions (2004)
4. Bhargavan, K., Obradovic, D., Gunter, C.A.: Formal verification of standards for distance vector routing protocols. J. ACM 49(4), 538–576 (2002)
5. Cardell-Oliver, R.: On the use of the hol system for protocol verification. In: TPHOLs, pp. 59–62 (1991)
6. DNV use cases for protocol verification, `http://www.seas.upenn.edu/~anduo/dnv.html`
7. Engler, D., Musuvathi, M.: Model-checking large network protocol implementations. In: NSDI (2004)

8. Rodriguez, A., et al.: MACEDON: Methodology for Automatically Creating, Evaluating, and Designing Overlay Networks. In: NSDI (2004)
9. Feamster, N., Balakrishnan, H.: Correctness Properties for Internet Routing. In: Allerton Conference on Communication, Control, and Computing (2005)
10. Felty, A.P., Howe, D.J., Stomp, F.A.: Protocol verification in nuprl. In: Y. Vardi, M. (ed.) CAV 1998. LNCS, vol. 1427. Springer, Heidelberg (1998)
11. Griffin, T.G., Sobrinho, J.L.: Metarouting. In: ACM SIGCOMM (2005)
12. Havelund, K., Shankar, N.: Experiments in theorem proving and model checking for protocol verification. In: Gaudel, M.-C., Woodcock, J.C.P. (eds.) FME 1996. LNCS, vol. 1051. Springer, Heidelberg (1996)
13. Killian, C., Anderson, J., Jhala, R., Vahdat, A.: Life, death, and the critical transition: Finding liveness bugs in systems code. In: NSDI (2007)
14. Killian, C.E., Anderson, J.W., Braud, R., Jhala, R., Vahdat, A.M.: Mace: language support for building distributed systems. In: PLDI (2007)
15. Lee, I., Kannan, S., Kim, M., Sokolsky, O., Viswanathan, M.: Runtime assurance based on formal specifications. In: PDPTA (1999)
16. Liu, X., Guo, Z., Wang, X., Chen, F., Tang, X.L.J., Wu, M., Kaashoek, M.F., Zhang, Z.: D3S: Debugging Deployed Distributed Systems. In: NSDI (2008)
17. Loo, B.T.: The Design and Implementation of Declarative Networks (Ph.D. Dissertation). Technical Report UCB/EECS-2006-177, UC Berkeley (2006)
18. Loo, B.T., Condie, T., Garofalakis, M., Gay, D.E., Hellerstein, J.M., Maniatis, P., Ramakrishnan, R., Roscoe, T., Stoica, I.: Declarative Networking: Language, Execution and Optimization. In: ACM SIGMOD (2006)
19. Loo, B.T., Condie, T., Hellerstein, J.M., Maniatis, P., Roscoe, T., Stoica, I.: Implementing Declarative Overlays. In: ACM SOSP (2005)
20. Loo, B.T., Hellerstein, J.M., Stoica, I., Ramakrishnan, R.: Declarative Routing: Extensible Routing with Declarative Queries. In: ACM SIGCOMM (2005)
21. Owre, S., Rajan, S., Rushby, J.M., Shankar, N., Srivas, M.K.: PVS: Combining Specification, Proof Checking, and Model Checking. In: Alur, R., Henzinger, T.A. (eds.) CAV 1996. LNCS, vol. 1102. Springer, Heidelberg (1996)
22. Owre, S., Shankar, N.: Writing PVS proof strategies. In: STRATA 2003 (2003)
23. Peterson, L., Davie, B.: Computer Networks: A Systems Approach, 4th edn. Morgan Kaufmann, San Francisco (2007)
24. Peterson, L., Shenker, S., Turner, J.: Overcoming the Internet Impasse Through Virtualization. In: HotNets-III (2004)
25. Ramakrishnan, R., Ullman, J.D.: A Survey of Research on Deductive Database Systems. Journal of Logic Programming 23(2), 125–149 (1993)
26. Raman, S., McCanne, S.: A model, analysis, and protocol framework for soft state-based communication. In: SIGCOMM, pp. 15–25 (1999)
27. Reynolds, P., Killian, C., Wiener, J.L., Mogul, J.C., Shah, M.A., Vahdat, A.: Pip: Detecting the Unexpected in Distributed Systems. In: NSDI (2006)
28. Riazanov, A., Voronkov, A.: The design and implementation of vampire. AI Commun. 15(2), 91–110 (2002)
29. Rushby, J.: Specification, proof checking, and model checking for protocols and distributed systems with PVS. In: Tutorial FORTE X/PSTV XVII 1997 (1997)
30. Abiteboul, S., et al.: Foundations of Databases. Addison-Wesley, Reading (1995)
31. Stoica, I., Morris, R., Karger, D., Kaashoek, M.F., Balakrishnan, H.: Chord: A Scalable P2P Lookup Service for Internet Applications. In: SIGCOMM (2001)
32. Wang, A., Basu, P., Loo, B.T., Sokolsky, O.: Declarative Network Verification. University of Pennsylvania Department of Computer and Information Science Technical Report No. MS-CIS-08-34 (2008)
33. Yices, `http://yices.csl.sri.com`
34. Z3, `http://research.microsoft.com/projects/Z3/`

Operational Semantics for Declarative Networking

Juan A. Navarro and Andrey Rybalchenko

Max Planck Institute for Software Systems

Abstract. Declarative Networking has been recently promoted as a high-level programming paradigm to more conveniently describe and implement systems that run in a distributed fashion over a computer network. It has already been used to implement various networked systems, e.g., network overlays, Byzantine fault tolerance protocols, and distributed hash tables. Declarative Networking relies upon a rule-based programming language that resembles Datalog and allows one to declaratively specify the flow of networking events. However, the presence of asynchronous communication, distribution, and imperative modification of the program state in Declarative Networking applications have been an obstacle for defining its semantics. Currently, the reference semantics is determined by the runtime environment only, which hinders further application development and makes any efforts to develop program analysis and verification tools impossible. In this paper, we propose an operational semantics for Declarative Networking that addresses these problems. The semantics is parameterized to keep open a design space required at the current stage of the language development. We also report on our first experience with an interpreter for Declarative Networking applications that implements the proposed semantics.

Keywords: Declarative networking, programming language semantics, distributed systems.

1 Introduction

Design and implementation of distributed systems is a challenging task that requires research efforts from various perspectives. In addition to improvements achieved by applying more sophisticated communication protocols, novel system designs, and more efficient algorithms, programming languages can make a significant impact on the implementation process by supporting the programmer with adequate constructs and primitives, e.g., control statements, type systems, and libraries [1,2,3,4,5,6]. In this line of research, Declarative Networking stands out as a high-level programming paradigm to more conveniently describe and implement distributed applications that run over computer networks [5].

The leading thought behind the Declarative Networking approach is to carry over declarative programming techniques inspired by Datalog to the domain of systems and networking applications. It builds upon a rule-based programming

A. Gill and T. Swift (Eds.): PADL 2009, LNCS 5418, pp. 76–90, 2009.

language called P2 that allows the programmer to declaratively specify the flow of networking events. Compared to the traditional approaches that use general purpose imperative languages, e.g., C++ [7] and Java [8], the implementations written in P2 reduce the code base size by several orders of magnitude, while improving its clarity and succinctness.

The distinctive features offered by Declarative Networking attracted interest in the networking and distributed systems community, in both academia and industry. A growing number of implementation efforts have chosen P2 as the programming language. The main applications are various network protocols, including sensor networks, Byzantine fault tolerance, and distributed hash tables, see e.g. [9,4,10,11]. The literature describing the resulting systems attributes their success, to a large extent, to the Declarative Networking paradigm.

The initial success and increasing adoption of Declarative Networking encourages the development of program analysis and verification tools for applications written in P2. These tools require a program semantics as a starting point, e.g., in order to simulate the execution of P2 programs on symbolic inputs, or to trace the flow of communication events through a sequence of rule invocations.

Unfortunately, a well-defined semantics for P2 has not been identified yet. Asynchronous communication, distribution, and presence of imperative modifications of the program state have been an obstacle. An additional source of complexity comes from its database-oriented setting that uses distributed query processing machinery as a basic vocabulary to define semantics. The existing specifications are incomplete and represented in an informal style that allows contradicting interpretations, as we show by examples in Section 3. Currently, P2 semantics is implicitly determined by the runtime environment [12], which in turn deviates from the descriptions in the literature [13,5]. This state of affairs hinders further development of Declarative Networking applications and makes any efforts to provide program analysis and verification tools for P2 impossible.

In this paper, we propose a parameterized operational semantics for Declarative Networking, which addresses the open questions about the semantics of P2 programs. The semantics is given by a state transition system and is represented by an algorithm that defines the transition relation of a given P2 program. The algorithm contains a collection of parameters that determine the main characteristics of P2 computations, e.g., when the effect of rule application is propagated to the program state. We avoided a presentation of the algorithm with some fixed valuation of the parameters, since any commitment to a particular set of design choices might be premature at this stage of the language's development.

In order to show the applicability of our approach we have also developed a P2 interpreter which simulates the execution of the parametrized semantics presented in this paper. This allows one to experiment with different choices of semantics and have a better understanding on the impact that these parameters have. This implementation, moreover, is a first stepping stone towards the development of verification and symbolic execution tools. Moreover, after coupling it with a networking back-end, it will also provide a full-fledged P2 interpreter.

In summary, our proposed semantics generalizes and unifies both specifications as presented in the literature and determined by the runtime environment. This can be used as a starting point for the development of new interpreters, verification and analysis tools built on top of a formally defined semantics.

Related Work. The challenges of distributed programming are addressed by active efforts in development of adequate programming languages and extensions. The recent developments include Acute [6], Alice [14], Curry [3], Erlang [1], JoCaml [2], Mace [4], and P2 [5]. The recurrent theme is to provide high-level programming abstractions for dealing with distributed computation and communication. Most of these languages follow functional and logic programming paradigms and their combinations. Mace is an exception that provides means for the specification of distributed protocols as transition systems that are compiled to C++. Statically typed functional languages Acute, Alice, and JoCaml extend the type discipline to values that are communicated over the network [2,15,6]. Curry, which is based on multiple paradigms, strives for a seamless integration of distribution in the context of logical variables, non-determinism, and search.

Many of the above efforts provide experimental platforms for studying distributed programming languages. Moreover, the languages Erlang, Mace, and P2 have been proven successful from the application development perspective. Erlang is widely used to develop telecommunication software, while Mace and P2 have gained increasing interest in the systems and networking community. The main applications are network protocols, including overlays, sensor networks, Byzantine fault tolerance, and distributed hash tables, see e.g. [9,4,10,11].

In comparison with the above languages, P2 stands out due to its simplicity and declarative foundations, while providing sufficient capabilities to develop state-of-the-art networking applications. Its increasing adoption by systems and networking researchers motivates our interest in its semantics, which provides a foundation for the development of program analysis tools for P2.

We note that besides P2, Datalog has been the basis for the development of other successful domain specific languages, e.g., for mining software artefacts using relational queries [16] and pointer alias analysis for imperative programs [17]. Tuples, which are atomic pieces of data in Datalog, are successfully applied as a communication primitive for distributed programming, as pioneered by the Linda system [18].

Our work can be seen as a parallel to what SLD resolution does for logic programming systems such as Prolog. Although any implementation may follow a particular strategy for the rule evaluation, any such strategy must conform to SLD resolution, which serves as the reference semantics of Prolog systems. Similarly, we wish to provide such a semantics foundation for declarative networking programming languages.

2 P2 by Example

In this section, we briefly present the P2 language used for Declarative Networking. Our description follows [10].

Program states. P2 programs manipulate tables, i.e., sets of tuples, as in relational databases. We distinguish between *materialized* tuples that are stored in a distributed fashion among nodes in the network, and *event* tuples that carry data between nodes and signal the occurrence of a particular event at a node.

A P2 program starts with a declaration of materialized tables. It lists the materialized tables, and specifies the primary keys for each of them. We consider as events all tuples in tables that are not declared as materialized. For example, the declarations

```
materialize(neighbor, keys(1,2)).
materialize(sequence, keys(1)).
```

specify that whenever a *neighbor* or *sequence* tuple is produced by a node, it should also be stored in a table with the corresponding name. The *keys* declaration specifies the fields that define the primary key of each table. At any time during execution, the runtime system ensures that there is at most one tuple stored for any valuation of the tuple positions appearing in the key declaration. In our example, the declaration requires that there is at most one *sequence* tuple for each value of the first position.

The declaration of materialization can also constrain the lifetime and quantity of tuples that a table can store [10]. Since these constraints are seldom in the existing P2 code base and can be simulated within the P2 language, we choose to omit them for clarity of presentation.

Program rules. Rules are the main component specifying computations of a P2 program. They are represented by constructs of the form '*head* :– *body*.' where *body* is a list of *predicates* applied to variables and constants, and *head* is a predicate applied to a subset of variables that appear in the body of the rule. The order of appearance of predicates in the rule, and of rules in the program text is irrelevant.

For example, we consider the following rule.

```
refresh(@X) :- periodic(@X, E, 3).
```

The *periodic* predicate in the body of the rule is a special built-in event predicate. It is automatically generated every 3 seconds by the P2 runtime environment at the node with the address X, and is instantiated with a unique value E. An optional fourth parameter can be used in the *periodic* predicate to indicate how many times should the event be generated. With respect to the declaration above, both *refresh* and *periodic* are events (i.e. they are not materialized). An intuitively reading of this rule is "generate a *refresh* event tuple at node X whenever there is a *periodic* event tuple at node X with the values E and 3." Note a convention that the first field of predicates appearing in the rule denotes the address of the node where the corresponding tuple resides. It is additionally marked by the '@' symbol.

As another example, consider the following two rules.

```
sequence(@X, NewSeq) :- refresh(@X), sequence(@X, CurSeq),
    NewSeq := CurSeq + 1.
send_updates(@X) :- refresh(@X).
```

The first rule specifies that every time that a *refresh* event is seen at the node X, the current value stored at the materialized *sequence* table is read, incremented, and a tuple with the new value is inserted into the *sequence* table at the same node. Since the primary key of the sequence table includes only the address field, each node can store at most one tuple in this table. The insertion of the new tuple into the table will implicitly remove the previous tuple with the old value. The second rule in the example produces a new *send_updates* event tuple every time there is a *refresh* event tuple at the node X.

So far, we have only seen rules that are evaluated at a single network node. The following rule illustrates how distributed computation is performed in P2.

```
update(@Y, X, S) :- send_updates(@X), neighbor(@X, Y),
    sequence(@X, S).
```

Intuitively, this rule can be read as "every time there is a *send_updates* at a node X, for every *neighbor* tuple stored at X with value Y and every *sequence* tuple stored at X with value S send an *update* event tuple to the node Y with the values X and S." In a networked system, an execution of this rule at a node X notifies its neighbors about the current sequence number of X.

Finally, we introduce a few more features of P2.

```
delete neighbor(@X, Y) :- purge(@X),
    last_update(@X, Y, LastTime), f_now(@X) - LastTime > 20.
```

The keyword *delete* appears in the head of the rule. It is used in P2 to request deletion of tuples from a table whenever the body of the rule is satisfied. The built-in function *f_now* returns the current wall-clock time of a node. In order to execute this rule, assume that *purge* is an event that is periodically generated at the node X and that *last_update* is another materialized table storing the time stamp of the last update event received from a node Y. Then, this rule will remove Y from the set of X's neighbors if it has not received an update from Y within an interval of 20 seconds.

3 From Declaration to Execution

The P2 language can greatly simplify network protocol development, however the ease with which a P2 program can be turned into a working implementation is often overstated in previous work on Declarative Networking. In many situations, the existing description of the language is not precise enough to determine how a P2 should be interpreted. In this section, we illustrate such cases by examples.

Event creation vs. effect. First, we consider the program given in Figure 1. It consists of the rules presented in the previous section. As described above, every time that a *refresh* event is generated the node's sequence number is incremented and a *send_updates* event tuple is generated. Then, the *update* event will forward the current sequence number to all neighbor nodes. Though, at this point we need to decide what should be the value of the *current* sequence number. Should it be the value before or after executing the increment?

```
materialize(neighbor, keys(1,2)).
materialize(sequence, keys(1)).

refresh(@X) :- periodic(@X, E, 3).

sequence(@X, NewSeq) :- refresh(@X), sequence(@X, CurSeq),
    NewSeq := CurSeq + 1.
send_updates(@X) :- refresh(@X).

update(@Y, X, S) :- send_updates(@X), neighbor(@X, Y),
    sequence(@X, S).
```

Fig. 1. An example P2 program in which a node increments and sends its sequence number to all of its neighbors. Various event processing schemes are conceivable where the sequence number value either before or after the increment is sent by the last rule.

There might exist reasons to prefer one choice over the other, or even to declare that the P2 runtime environment can make an arbitrary choice among the two options. Unfortunately, the existing work on the P2 language does not address such corner cases. The documentation of the P2 runtime [12] does not go beyond an informal introduction to the language, leaving open ambiguities such as the one presented here. A recent work [5] gives a formal definition of both the syntax and semantics of a subset of the P2 language that does not deal with event tuples, i.e. all tables are materialized. Thus, it does not clarify how interactions between event processing and table updates should be handled.

Algorithms 5.1 and 5.3 in [13] implicitly suggest that updates are immediately applied after evaluating each individual rule. In our example this means that the sequence number is incremented before sending the update. An experimental evaluation using the current implementation of P2 exhibits the opposite semantics in which events that are addressed to the same node that generated it, so-called *internal events*, are propagated and evaluated before any updates are applied to the materialized store.[1] This means that we observed an update event that contains the old sequence number.

Internal vs. external events. Under-specified semantics can lead to other significant deviation between possible outcomes. See the example shown in Figure 2. The presented program maintains three materialized tables that are initialized after the declaration. Besides a *neighbor* table, every node contains ten *store* tuples and a sequence number that is initialized to zero.

The first rule specifies that a node will increment its sequence number each time that it receives a *ping* event. The second rule causes a node, upon receiving a *broadcast* event, to send ten *ping* events to each neighbor node. Finally, the last rule causes the node *node1* to generate a *broadcast* event after five seconds

[1] We used `runStagedOverlog` executable from the P2 distribution that is compiled from the revision 2114 of the publicly available code from the anonymous SVN server `https://svn.declarativity.net/p2/trunk/`

```
materialize(neighbor, keys(1,2)).
materialize(store, keys(1,2)).
materialize(sequence, keys(1)).

neighbor(@X, "node1").
neighbor(@X, "node2").
neighbor(@X, "node3").

store(@X, 1).
store(@X, 2).
...
store(@X, 10).

sequence(@X, 0).

sequence(@X, New) :- ping(@X), sequence(@X, Old),
    New := Old + 1.

ping(@Y) :- broadcast(@X), neighbor(@X, Y), store(@X, _).

broadcast(@X) :- periodic(@X, E, 5, 1), X = "node1".
```

Fig. 2. In this example, a node *node1* sends ten ping messages to each neighbor. Upon receiving a ping message, each node increments own sequence number.

of activity. After all events have been sent, received, and processed by the corresponding nodes, one would expect that the program reaches a state in which every node stores the sequence number ten. However, this is not the case for the current P2 implementation.

The reason for a different outcome is rooted in the fact that *node1* sends ten *ping* events to itself, whereas other nodes receive them from *node1*. At the node *node1*, events will be processed simultaneously. They will refer to the current sequence value zero, and each rule invocation will result in updating it to one. Meanwhile, all other nodes will receive and process the incoming ping events one after another, and iteratively increment their respective sequence numbers, as we would expect, from zero to ten.

We argue that the observed behavior of the P2 program is unexpected, since the first two rules do not contain any predicates that should be evaluated differently on different nodes.

4 P2 Programs

In this section, we present a definition of P2 programs, which is used to define their operational semantics in Section 5.

A distributed P2 program $P = \langle \mathcal{L}, \mathcal{D}, \mathcal{K}, \mathcal{R}, S_0 \rangle$ consists of

- $\mathcal{L}$: a set of predicate symbols,
- $\mathcal{D}$: a set of data elements,

- $\mathcal{K}$: a keys-declaration,
- $\mathcal{R}$: a set of declarative rules,
- S_0: an initial state.

Predicates and tuples. Each predicate symbol in $p \in \mathcal{L}$ is associated with an arity n that is strictly greater than zero. A *predicate* is an expression of the form $p(v_1, \ldots, v_n)$, where $p \in \mathcal{L}$ is a predicate symbol of arity n and $v_1, \ldots, v_n$ are variables from a set of variables $\mathcal{V}$. We will also often use the notation $p(\boldsymbol{v})$, where $\boldsymbol{v}$ is a sequence of variables of the appropriate length. A *tuple* is obtained by, given a predicate $p(\boldsymbol{v})$, applying a substitution $\sigma\colon \mathcal{V} \to \mathcal{D}$ to maps all the variables in the predicate to values from the data domain. The assumption that the arity of each predicate is strictly greater than zero is due to the convention that the first argument of a predicate as well as the first position of a corresponding tuple represent its *address*. Henceforth, we shall omit the '@' symbol.

The set of predicate symbols is partitioned into two disjoint sets of materialized and event predicate symbols $\mathcal{M}$ and $\mathcal{E}$, respectively. We have

$$\mathcal{L} = \mathcal{M} \uplus \mathcal{E} .$$

Tuples obtained from materialized predicates are called materialized tuples. Similarly, we obtain event tuples by applying substitutions to event predicates.

Key declarations. A *keys-declaration* is a function $\mathcal{K}$ that maps each materialized predicate symbol $p \in \mathcal{M}$ of arity n to a subset $\mathcal{K}(p) \subseteq \{1, \ldots, n\}$ of indices of its fields. We assume that $1 \in \mathcal{K}(p)$ for all materialized predicates, i.e., the address of a predicate is always an element of its key. Given a materialized tuple $m = p(c_1, \ldots, c_n)$, we write $\mathcal{K}{\downarrow}m$ to denote the tuple obtained by removing all fields that are not included into the set $\mathcal{K}(p)$. For example, given $m = p(c_1, c_2, c_3, c_4)$ and $\mathcal{K}(p) = \{1, 3\}$, we obtain $\mathcal{K}{\downarrow}m = p(c_1, c_3)$.

We say that a set of materialized tuples M is *keys-inconsistent* if M contains a pair of tuples m and m' such that $m \neq m'$ but $\mathcal{K}{\downarrow}m = \mathcal{K}{\downarrow}m'$, i.e., it contains two tuples with the same key but different values. Otherwise, we say that the set of materialized tuples is *keys-consistent*.

Rules. In order to avoid some of the concerns with the interpretation of P2 programs discussed in the previous section, we include an action specification as part of the rule declaration. Formally, an *action* is a keyword in the set $\mathcal{A} = \{\mathsf{add}, \mathsf{delete}, \mathsf{send}, \mathsf{exec}\}$. These keywords correspond to adding and deleting materialized tuples from tables, as well as sending external events and executing internal events. A *rule* in a P2 program

$$\underbrace{\alpha\ h(\boldsymbol{v})}_{\text{head}}\ :-\ \underbrace{\overbrace{t(\boldsymbol{v}_0)}^{\text{optional}}, m_1(\boldsymbol{v}_1), \ldots, m_n(\boldsymbol{v}_n).}_{\text{body}}$$

consists of a head and a body separated by the ':–' symbol such that

- $\alpha \in \mathcal{A}$ is an action and $h(\boldsymbol{v})$ is a predicate,
- the body may contain an event predicate $t(\boldsymbol{v}_0)$ called *trigger*,
- the rest of the body consists of materialized predicates $m_i(\boldsymbol{v}_i)$, for $1 \leq i \leq n$,
- all variables in the head must appear in the body of the rule.

We require the following correspondence between the action and head predicate:

- if the rule action is add or delete then $h(\boldsymbol{v})$ must be a materialized predicate, and otherwise $h(\boldsymbol{v})$ must be an event predicate,
- if the rule action is exec then all predicates appearing in the rule must have the same address, i.e., either the same variable or the same constant at the first position.

If a trigger is present in the rule then we call it a *soft-rule*. Otherwise we say that the rule is a *materialized-rule*. Intuitively, triggers are used to control which rules have to be evaluated and when, i.e. a soft-rule is not evaluated until an event that matches its trigger is seen by a node. Materialized rules (without triggers) are evaluated whenever an update is made to any of the predicates on its body.

Note that a rule can contain predicates referring to different addresses (except for exec rules). We need to make an additional assumption on the interplay between addresses appearing in the rule to ensure the possibility of its execution in a distributed setting, as formalized by the following definitions.

Given a rule r, let x and y be the addresses of two predicates in the body of r. We say that x is *linked* to y, denoted $x \rightsquigarrow y$, if there is a predicate $p(x, \boldsymbol{v})$ in the body of r such that y occurs among the set of parameters $\boldsymbol{v}$. x is *connected* to y if $x \rightsquigarrow^* y$, where $\rightsquigarrow^*$ is the reflexive and transitive closure of $\rightsquigarrow$. An address x is a *source* in the body of r, if $x \rightsquigarrow^* y$ for all addresses y that also appear in the body of r. Finally, we say that a rule is *well-connected* if its body has at least one source. From now on, we shall only consider P2 programs whose rules are well-connected.

Local and basic rules. Execution in distributed setting requires a further distinction of P2 rules. We say that a rule is *local* if all predicates in its body have the same address and i) either the rule action is send, or ii) the address of the head is equal to the address of the predicates in the body. In particular, exec rules are always local. Finally, a *basic* rule is both soft and local. We say that a P2 program is *local* (resp. *basic*) if it only contains local (resp. basic) rules.

We illustrate different rule kinds on the following example. Here, we assume materialized predicates m, n, and p together with event predicates e and t.

r1: send $e(x, y) :- m(x, z), m(y, z)$.

r2: delete $m(w, v) :- e(x, y, v), n(y, v, z), m(z, w)$.

r3: send $t(y) :- m(x, v), n(x, v, y)$.

r4: add $m(x, w) :- m(x, u), m(x, v), p(x, u, v, w)$.

r5: add $m(x, w) :- t(x), m(x, u), m(x, v), n(x, u, v, w)$.

The rule *r1* is invalid since x and y are disconnected in its body. All other rules are well-connected. Rules *r3*–*r5* are local. Soft rules are *r2* and *r5*, while all other rules are materialized. The only basic rule *r5*, i.e., it is soft and local.

States. We define a *state* of a P2 program to be a pair $S = \langle M, E \rangle$ that consists of a *materialized store* M and an *external event queue* E. The store M is a keys-consistent set of materialized tuple. The queue E is a multi-set of event tuples. The *initial* state S_0 shall be used to start the program execution, as described in the next section.

5 Semantics of Basic P2

We present the operational semantics for P2 programs, i.e., we show how program rules are evaluated with respect to the current state of the program and define the resulting state. In this section, we only consider P2 programs that contain only basic rules. Section 6 presents a transformation from an arbitrary program to a basic one. Such incremental approach simplifies the exposition and separates the rule localization from rule execution.

Figure 3 shows a procedure EVALUATE for the execution of basic P2 programs. It consists of two nested loops. We refer to an iteration of the outer and inner loops as *step* and *round*, respectively. The state of the program under execution is maintained by the pair $S = \langle M, E \rangle$, which contains the materialized store and the external event queue. We use an auxiliary function UPDATE that updates the materialized store. Note that this function is non-deterministic, since a P2 program can attempt to simultaneously add several tuples that are not keys-consistent. In such case, the resulting materialized store depends on the choice of tuples in line 2 of UPDATE.

At each step, some events are selected from the external event queue, and then several rounds are executed to compute the effects of applying the program rules triggered by the selected events. We leave several choices open as parameters of the execution procedure, e.g., how many events are selected for processing at each step and when updates are actually applied to the materialized store.

It is important to note is that although EVALUATE is described from the global perspective on the state of the program, its adaption to the distributed perspective is straightforward. In the distributed perspective, each node executes the same procedure EVALUATE. Since rules are basic, they can be executed locally without requiring any information about the tuples stored at other nodes. The only change required in the exposition of the procedure is at line 10, where events may be sent over the network using an appropriate transport mechanism instead of being added directly to the local event queue E.

The following are the design choices left open in the EVALUATE procedure:

- **External selection:** We do not specify which events and how many of them are selected at line 3 from the external event queue to be processed at each step. Two possible choices are: (1) to non-deterministically select **one** event from the queue, or (2) to select **all** current events in the queue.
- **Internal selection:** Similarly, we do not specify which events to select from the internal event queue I at line 6. Again, we could select either (1) **one** non-deterministically chosen, or (2) **all** events in the queue.

```
procedure EVALUATE
input
    P = ⟨L, D, K, R, S0⟩ : a basic program
vars
    M : materialized store
    E : external event queue
    △,▽ : set of tuples to add and delete
    I, J : internal event queues
begin
    ⟨M, E⟩ := S0
    while E ≠ ∅ do                                              ▷ step loop
        I := select and remove elements from E
        ⟨△,▽⟩ := ⟨∅, ∅⟩
        while I ≠ ∅ do                                          ▷ round loop
            J := select and remove elements from I
            for each rule α h(v) :− t(v0), m1(v1), ..., mn(vn) ∈ R
                and subst. σ such that t(v0)σ ∈ J and mi(vi)σ ∈ M
do
                    case a of
                        send: E := E ∪ {h(v)σ}
                        exec: I := I ∪ {h(v)σ}
                        add: △ := △ ∪ {h(v)σ}
                        delete: ▽ := ▽ ∪ {h(v)σ}
                    end case
            if update after each round then
                M := UPDATE(M, K, △,▽)
                ⟨△,▽⟩ := ⟨∅, ∅⟩
            if
            if use only one cycle then break while
        done                                                    ▷ end round loop
        E := E ∪ I
        if update after each step then M := UPDATE(M, K, △,▽)
    done                                                        ▷ end step loop
end.

function UPDATE
input
    M : a set of materialized tuples
    K : a keys-declaration
    △,▽ : sets of tuples to add and delete
begin
    M := M \ ▽
    for each m ∈ △ do
        M := (M \ {m′ | K↓m = K↓m′}) ∪ {m}
end.
```

Fig. 3. Parametrized procedure for evaluating basic P2 rules, and its auxiliary function to update the materialized store

- **Update:** As the execution proceeds, the procedure uses the pair of sets of tuples $\langle \triangle, \nabla \rangle$ to record the updates that have to be applied to the materialized store. These updates can be atomically applied either: (1) at the end of every **round** in line 15, or (2) at the end of every **step** in line 22.
- **Number of cycles:** EVALUATE processes events using **two** cycles, viz., the round and the step cycles. By breaking the internal loop at line number 19, we achieve an execution behavior with only **one** evaluation cycle.

These design choices are independent, although some combinations of parameters are not viable. For example, if considering only **one cycle**, then the choice when to apply the materialized updates becomes irrelevant. Moreover, only the cumulative effect of both selection functions is important, i.e., if they select in conjunction either **one** or **all** events to process at each iteration.

If the variant with **two cycles** is used with **step updates**, then the internal selection function becomes irrelevant. As no changes to the materialized store are performed within the evaluation of rounds, the sets E and $\triangle, \nabla$ do not depend, when exiting the inner loop, on the particular choice of internal selection.

Emulating P2 implementation. To the best of our knowledge, the set of parameters required to emulate the semantics currently implemented in P2 corresponds to the version with **two** evaluation cycles, selecting **one** external event for processing each step, fully propagating the internal events in rounds until fix-point, and updating only after the end of the **step**.

Recall that the original definition of P2 rules, see [10], does not specify the actions, except for rules whose action is delete. If the head of the rule contains a materialized predicate then the rule is implicitly assumed to have a add action. We observe that in our formalization a basic rule of the form

$$h(x, \boldsymbol{v}) :- t(y, \boldsymbol{v}_0), m_1(\boldsymbol{v}_1), \ldots, m_n(\boldsymbol{v}_n).$$

where $h(x, \boldsymbol{v})$ is an event predicate corresponds to the pair of rules below.

$$\begin{aligned} &\mathsf{send}\ h(x, \boldsymbol{v}) :- t(y, \boldsymbol{v}_0), m_1(\boldsymbol{v}_1), \ldots, m_n(\boldsymbol{v}_n), x \neq y. \\ &\mathsf{exec}\ h(x, \boldsymbol{v}) :- t(y, \boldsymbol{v}_0), m_1(\boldsymbol{v}_1), \ldots, m_n(\boldsymbol{v}_n), x = y. \end{aligned}$$

The explicit treatment of rule actions makes visible whether the effect of evaluating these rules is different depending on whether x and y are equal addresses. Furthermore, if we would like a node to send a message to itself, but behave as if the message was received from the network, we have now the possibility to write a rule

$$\mathsf{send}\ h(x, \boldsymbol{v}) :- t(y, \boldsymbol{v}_0), m_1(\boldsymbol{v}_1), \ldots, m_n(\boldsymbol{v}_n).$$

This scheme can be used to modify the program given in Figure 2 such that all nodes exhibit the same behavior, i.e., count up to ten.

6 Reduction to Basic Rules

The procedure EVALUATE for the execution of P2 program, as presented in the previous section, assumed that the input program consists of basic rules. In this section, we relax this assumption and show how any program with well-connected rule can be transformed into a basic one. The transformation proceeds in two steps by first making the rules local, and then turning materialized rules into soft rules. Since these transformation can be automatically performed by the P2 runtime environment, they liberate the programmer from the burden of ensuring the local availability of tuples necessary to rule execution and event handling to signal updates to the materialized store.

Rule localization. Let r be a well connected rule of the form

$$\alpha\ h(\boldsymbol{v}) :- p_1(x, \boldsymbol{v}_1), \dots, p_{k-1}(x, \boldsymbol{v}_{k-1}), p_k(y_k, \boldsymbol{v}_k), \dots, p_n(y_n, \boldsymbol{v}_n).$$

such that $x \neq y_i$ for each $k \leq i \leq n$, and $x \rightsquigarrow y_k$. Let $\boldsymbol{v}'$ be a sequence of the variables that appear in the set $\{\boldsymbol{v}_0, \dots, \boldsymbol{v}_{i-1}\}$, and let $|\boldsymbol{v}'|$ denote its length. In particular, we have that y_k occurs in $\boldsymbol{v}'$, and there is at most one event predicates among $p_1, \dots, p_{k-1}$ (recall that a rule can have at most one trigger). If all these predicates are materialized we define β to be add action and q be a fresh materialized predicate of arity $|\boldsymbol{v}'| + 2$ with keys-declaration $\mathcal{K}(q)$ that contains all predicate fields, i.e., $\mathcal{K}(q) = \{1, \dots, |\boldsymbol{v}'| + 2\}$. Otherwise, we have $\beta = \mathsf{send}$ and q is a fresh event predicate symbol of arity $|\boldsymbol{v}'| + 2$.

Now the original rule r is replaced by the pair of rules

$$\beta\ q(y_k, x, \boldsymbol{v}') :- p_1(x, \boldsymbol{v}_1), \dots, p_{k-1}(x, \boldsymbol{v}_{k-1}).$$
$$\alpha\ h(\boldsymbol{v}) :- q(y_k, x, \boldsymbol{v}'), p_k(y_k, \boldsymbol{v}_k), \dots, p_n(y_n, \boldsymbol{v}_n).$$

Note that the first rule has a local body, and the second rule is a well-connected rule with exactly one address variable less than the original rule r. By iteratively applying the above transformation to the non-local rules in the program, we obtain a P2 program whose rules have local bodies.

After applying this transformation some rules may still not be local, since the address in the head of a materialized update may not be equal to the address in the rule body. Such rules have the form

$$\alpha\ h(y, \boldsymbol{v}) :- p_1(x, \boldsymbol{v}_1), \dots, p_n(x, \boldsymbol{v}_n).$$

where $x \neq y$ and α is either add or delete action. We replace each of these rules by the pair below

$$\mathsf{send}\ u(y, \boldsymbol{v}) :- p_1(x, \boldsymbol{v}_1), \dots, p_n(x, \boldsymbol{v}_n).$$
$$\alpha\ h(y, \boldsymbol{v}) :- u(y, \boldsymbol{v}).$$

where u is a fresh event predicate symbol of arity $|\boldsymbol{v}| + 1$. Now all rules are local.

Rule softening. We replace all materialized rules in the program, after rule localization procedure was applied, by soft rules as follows. First, for each materialized predicate m we create a fresh event predicate $\hat{m}$ of the same arity. Then, we replace each materialized rule of the form

$$\alpha\ h(\boldsymbol{v}) :- m_1(\boldsymbol{v}_1), \ldots, m_n(\boldsymbol{v}_n).$$

by n soft rules such that for each $1 \leq i \leq n$ we insert

$$\alpha\ h(\boldsymbol{v}) :- \hat{m}_i(\boldsymbol{v}_i), m_1(\boldsymbol{v}_1), \ldots, m_n(\boldsymbol{v}_n).$$

where the new update event $\hat{m}_i$ serves as the rule trigger.

Finally, we create rules that generate update events whenever a new tuple is inserted to a table. For this purpose for each add rule of the form

$$\mathsf{add}\ m(\boldsymbol{v}) :- t(\boldsymbol{v}_0), m_1(\boldsymbol{v}_1), \ldots, m_n(\boldsymbol{v}_n).$$

we create a fresh event predicate u of the same arity as m, and replace the rule by the three basic rules below.

$$\begin{aligned} \mathsf{exec}\ u(\boldsymbol{v}) &:- t(\boldsymbol{v}_0), m_1(\boldsymbol{v}_1), \ldots, m_n(\boldsymbol{v}_n). \\ \mathsf{add}\ m(\boldsymbol{v}) &:- u(\boldsymbol{v}). \\ \mathsf{send}\ \hat{m}(\boldsymbol{v}) &:- u(\boldsymbol{v}). \end{aligned}$$

We note that more sophisticated methods can be defined to localize and soften a set of well connected rules. For example, such methods may seek for opportunities to distribute the evaluation of the body among different nodes. We leave the development of optimized localization and softening methods for future work, since this paper focuses on a definition of semantics for basic rules. Our localization method can be viewed as a generalization of the *rule localization rewrite* procedure defined by Loo et al. [5] for rules containing at most two different addresses.

Moreover, similar to the treatment of localization in [5] our semantics together with the transformations is *eventually consistent* under the *bursty update* network model for P2 programs that contains only materialized rules with add actions. (Such rules define almost-Datalog programs, since they still contain function symbols.) This kind of consistency means that if after a burst of updates the network eventually quiesces then the models defined by our semantics correspond to those of the standard semantics of Datalog.

7 Conclusions

We presented a definition and operational semantics for the P2 programming language, which provides a programming foundation for Declarative Networking. Our work addresses questions that were left open by the existing literature on Declarative Networking. The main contribution of our semantics is in its utility as a starting point for the development of program analysis and verification tools for Declarative Networking, as well as advancing the evolution of the P2 language, its interpreters and runtime environments.

References

1. Armstrong, J.: Making reliable distributed systems in the presence of software errors. PhD thesis, KTH (2003)
2. Fournet, C., Fessant, F.L., Maranget, L., Schmitt, A.: JoCaml: A language for concurrent distributed and mobile programming. In: Advanced Func. Prog. Springer, Heidelberg (2002)
3. Hanus, M.: Distributed programming in a multi-paradigm declarative language. In: Nadathur, G. (ed.) PPDP 1999. LNCS, vol. 1702. Springer, Heidelberg (1999)
4. Killian, C.E., Anderson, J.W., Braud, R., Jhala, R., Vahdat, A.: Mace: language support for building distributed systems. In: PLDI. ACM, New York (2007)
5. Loo, B.T., Condie, T., Garofalakis, M., Gay, D.E., Hellerstein, J.M., Maniatis, P., Ramakrishnan, R., Roscoe, T., Stoica, I.: Declarative networking: Language, execution and optimization. In: SIGMOD, pp. 97–108. ACM, New York (2006)
6. Sewell, P., Leifer, J.J., Wansbrough, K., Nardelli, F.Z., Allen-Williams, M., Habouzit, P., Vafeiadis, V.: Acute: High-level programming language design for distributed computation. J. Funct. Program. 17(4–5), 547–612 (2007)
7. Stoica, I., Morris, R., Liben-Nowell, D., Karger, D.R., Kaashoek, M.F., Dabek, F., Balakrishnan, H.: Chord: A scalable peer-to-peer lookup protocol for Internet applications. IEEE/ACM Trans. Netw. 11(1), 17–32 (2003)
8. Rowstron, A., Druschel, P.: Pastry: Scalable, decentralized object location, and routing for large-scale peer-to-peer systems. In: Guerraoui, R. (ed.) Middleware 2001. LNCS, vol. 2218, p. 329. Springer, Heidelberg (2001)
9. Chu, D., Popa, L., Tavakoli, A., Hellerstein, J.M., Levis, P., Shenker, S., Stoica, I.: The design and implementation of a declarative sensor network system. In: SenSys. ACM, New York (2007)
10. Loo, B.T., Condie, T., Hellerstein, J.M., Maniatis, P., Roscoe, T., Stoica, I.: Implementing declarative overlays. In: SIGOPS, pp. 75–90. ACM, New York (2005)
11. Singh, A., Das, T., Maniatis, P., Druschel, P., Roscoe, T.: BFT protocols under fire. In: NSDI, USENIX (2008)
12. Condie, T., Gay, D.E., Loo, B.T., et al.: P2: Declarative networking website (2008)
13. Loo, B.T.: The Design and Implementation of Declarative Networks. PhD thesis, UC Berkeley (2006)
14. Rossberg, A., Botlan, D.L., Tack, G., Brunklaus, T., Smolka, G.: Alice through the looking glass. In: Trends in Func. Prog., Intellect. (2004)
15. Rossberg, A., Tack, G., Kornstaedt, L.: Status report: HOT pickles, and how to serve them. In: Workshop on ML, pp. 25–36. ACM, New York (2007)
16. Beyer, D., Noack, A., Lewerentz, C.: Efficient relational calculation for software analysis. Trans. on Soft. Eng. 31(2), 137–149 (2005)
17. Whaley, J., Lam, M.S.: Cloning-based context-sensitive pointer alias analysis using binary decision diagrams. In: PLDI. ACM, New York (2004)
18. Carriero, N., Gelernter, D.: Linda in context. Commun. ACM 32(4) (1989)

Ad Hoc Data and the Token Ambiguity Problem

Qian Xi[1], Kathleen Fisher[2], David Walker[1], and Kenny Q. Zhu[1]

[1] Princeton University
[2] AT&T Research

Abstract. PADS is a declarative language used to describe the syntax and semantic properties of *ad hoc data sources* such as financial transactions, server logs and scientific data sets. The PADS compiler reads these descriptions and generates a suite of useful data processing tools such as format translators, parsers, printers and even a query engine, all customized to the ad hoc data format in question. Recently, however, to further improve the productivity of programmers that manage ad hoc data sources, we have turned to using PADS as an *intermediate language* in a system that first infers a PADS description directly from example data and then passes that description to the original compiler for tool generation. A key subproblem in the inference engine is the *token ambiguity problem* — the problem of determining which substrings in the example data correspond to complex tokens such as dates, URLs, or comments. In order to solve the token ambiguity problem, the paper studies the relative effectiveness of three different statistical models for tokenizing ad hoc data. It also shows how to incorporate these models into a general and effective format inference algorithm. In addition to using a declarative language (PADS) as a key intermediate form, we have implemented the system as a whole in ML.

1 Introduction

An *ad hoc data format* is any data format for which useful data processing tools do not exist. Examples of ad hoc data formats include web server logs, genomic data sets, astronomical readings, financial transaction reports, agricultural data and more.

PADS [7,20] is a declarative language that describes the syntax and semantics of ad hoc data formats. The PADS compiler, developed in ML, reads these declarative descriptions and produces a series of programming libraries (parser, printer, validator and visitor) and end-to-end tools (XML translator, query engine, reformatter, error monitor, *etc.*). Consequently, PADS can dramatically improve the productivity of data analysts who work with ad hoc data. However, PADS is not (yet) a silver bullet. It takes time for new users to learn the language syntax and even experienced users can take hours or days to develop descriptions for complex formats. Hence, to further improve programmer productivity, we have developed a system called LEARNPADS that automatically generates end-to-end data processing tools directly from example data [9,8]. It uses machine learning techniques to infer a PADS description and then it passes that description on to the PADS compiler. The compiler will in turn produce its suite of custom data processing tools. Hence PADS now serves as a declarative intermediate language in the tool generation process.

A. Gill and T. Swift (Eds.): PADL 2009, LNCS 5418, pp. 91–106, 2009.

Our past experiments [9] have shown that LEARNPADS is highly effective when the set of tokens it uses matches the tokens used in the unknown data set. For instance, when the unknown data set contains URLs, dates and messages the inference system will work very well when its tokenizer contains the correct corresponding definitions for URLs, dates and messages used in the file. If the tokenizer does not contain these elements, inference is still possible, but the inferred descriptions are generally much more complex than they would be otherwise.

The challenge then is to develop a general-purpose tokenizer containing a wide variety of abstractions like URLs, dates, messages, phone numbers, file paths and more. The key problem is that when using the conventional approach to building a tokenizer (*i.e.,* regular expressions), as we did in our previous work, the definitions of basic tokens overlap tremendously. For example, "`January 24, 2008`" includes a word made up of letters, a couple of numbers, some spaces and English-like punctuation such as the "`,`". Does that mean this string should be treated as an arbitrary text fragment or is it a date? Perhaps "`January`" an element of an string-based enumeration unconnected to integers `24` and `2008`? Perhaps the entire phrase should be merged with surrounding characters rather than treated in isolation? Doing a good job of format inference involves identifying that the string of characters `J-a-n-...-0-8` should be treated as an indivisible token and that it is in fact a date. More generally, an effective format inference engine for ad hoc data solves the *Token Ambiguity Problem* – the problem of determining which substrings of a data file correspond to which token definitions in the presence of syntactic ambiguity.

In this paper, we describe our attempts to solve the token ambiguity problem. In particular, we make the following contributions:

- We redesign our format inference algorithm [9] to take advantage of information generated from an arbitrary statistical token model. This advance allows the algorithm to process a set of ambiguous parses, selecting the most likely parses that match global criteria.
- We instantiate the arbitrary statistical token model with Hidden Markov Models (HMMs), Hierarchical Maximum Entropy Models (HMEMs) and Support Vector Machines (SVMs) and evaluate their relative effectiveness empirically. We also compare the effectiveness of these models to our previous approach, which used regular expressions and conventional prioritized, longest match for disambiguation.
- We augment our algorithm with an additional phase to analyze the complexity of inferred descriptions and to simplify them when description complexity exceeds a threshold relative to the underlying data complexity.

2 The Token Ambiguity Problem

Consider the log files generated by `yum`, a common software package manager. These log files consist of a series of lines, each of which is broken into several distinct fields: date, time, action taken, package name and version. Single spaces separate the fields. For instance:

```
Penum action {
  install Pfrom("Installed");
  update Pfrom("Updated");
  erase Pfrom("Erased");
};
Pstruct version_hdr {
  Pint major; ':';
}
Pstruct sp_version {
  ' ';
  Popt version_hdr h_opt;
  Pid version;
}
```

```
Precord Pstruct entry_t {
          Pdate date;
    ' ';  Ptime time;
    ' ';  action m;
   ": ";  Pid package;
          Popt sp_version sv;
};
Psource Parray yum {
          entry_t[];
};
```

Fig. 1. Ideal PADS description of `yum.txt` format

```
May 02 06:19:57 Updated: openssl.i686 0.9.7a-43.8
Jul 16 12:37:13 Erased: dhcp-devel
Dec 10 04:07:51 Updated: openldap.x86_64 2.2.13-4
...
```

Figure 1 shows an *ideal* PADS description of `yum.txt` written by a human expert. The description is structured as a series of C-like type declarations. There are *base types* like `Pdate` (a date), `Ptime` (a time) and `Pint` (an integer). There are also *structured types* such as `Penum` (one of several strings), `Pstruct` (a sequence of items with different types, separated by punctuation symbols), `Popt` (an optional type) and `Parray` (a sequence of items with the same type). PADS descriptions are often easiest read from bottom to top, so the best place to start examining the figure is the last declaration in the right-hand column. There, the declaration says that the entire source file (as indicated by the `Psource` annotation) is an array type called `yum`. The elements of the array are items with type `entry_t`. Next, we can examine the type `entry_t` and observe that it is a new-line terminated record (as indicated by the `Precord` annotation) and it contains a series of fields including a date, followed by a space, followed by a time, followed by an action (which is another user-defined type), followed by a colon and a space, *etc.* We leave the reader to peruse the rest of the figure.

Unfortunately, when we ran our original format inference algorithm [9] on this data source, rather than inferring a compact 23-line description, our algorithm returned a verbose 179-line description that was difficult to understand and even harder to work with. After investigation, we discovered the problem. The data can be tokenized in many ways, and the inference system was using a set of regular expressions to do the tokenization that was a poor match for this data set. More concretely, consider the string "`2.2.13-4`." This string may be parsed by any of the following token sequences:

```
Option 1: [int] [.] [int] [.] [int] [-] [int]
Option 2: [float] [.] [int] [-] [int]
Option 3: [int] [.] [float] [-] [int]
Option 4: [id]
```

The best choice for this format is Option 4, `id`, because `id` can be used to parse the data found at this point in all lines of the `yum` format. Unfortunately, the simplistic disambiguation rules for the original system chose Option 2. Moreover, other lines are tokenized in different ways. For instance, `dhcp-devel`, which also could have been an `id` is tokenized as `[word]` and `0.9.7a-43.8` is tokenized as `[float] [.] [int] [char] [-] [float]`. As each distinct tokenization of similar data regions is introduced, the inference engine attempts to find common patterns and unify them. However, in this case, unification was unsuccessful and the result was an overly complex format.

The original inference algorithm disambiguates between overlapping tokens by using the same strategy as common lexer-generators: It tries each token in a predefined order and picks the first, longest token that matches. While effective for some data sources, this simple policy makes fixed tokenization decisions up front, does not take contextual information into account, and restricts the use of complex tokens like `id`, `url` and `message` that *shadow* simpler ones.

3 The Format Inference Algorithm

Our new format inference algorithm consists of four stages: (1) building a statistical token model from labeled training data; (2) dividing the text into newline-separated *chunks* of data and finding all possible tokenizations of each chunk; (3) inferring a *candidate structure* using the statistical model and the tokenizations; and (4) applying rewriting rules to improve the candidate structure. Because this algorithm shares the general structure of our earlier work [9], we focus on the salient differences here.

Training the statistical models. To speed up the training cycle, we created a tool capable of reading any PADS description and labelling the described data with the tokens specified in the description. This way, all data for which we have PADS descriptions can serve as a training suite. As we add more descriptions, our training data improves. Currently, the training suite is biased towards systems data, and includes tokens for integers, floats, times, dates, IP addresses, hostnames, file paths, URLs, words, ids and punctuation. Parsing of tokens continues to use longest match semantics and hence the string "43.8" can be parsed by sequences such as `[int] [.] [int]` or `[int] [.] [float]` or `[float]`, but not by `[float] [.] [int]` or `[float] [.] [float]`. We have experimented with a number of statistical models for tokenization, which we discuss in Section 4.

Tokenization. When inferring a description, the algorithm computes the set of all possible tokenizations of each data chunk. Because these sequences share subsequences, we organize them into a directed acyclic graph called a SEQSET. For example, Figure 2 shows the SEQSET for the substring "2.2.13-4".

Each edge in the SEQSET represents an occurrence of a token in the data, while each vertex marks a location in the input. If a token edge ends at a vertex v, then v indicates the position immediately after the last character in the token. The first vertex in a SEQSET marks the position before the first character in its outgoing edges.

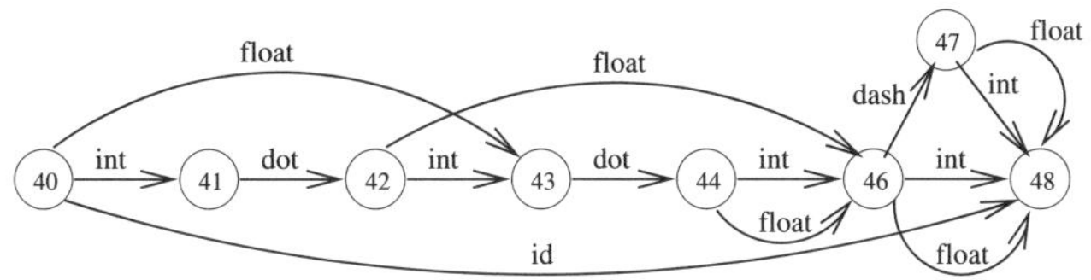

Fig. 2. SEQSET from parsing string "2.2.13-4"

```
type description  (* abstract syntax of pads description *)
type seqset       (* the seqset data structure *)
type seqsets = seqset list

(* A top-level description guess *)
datatype prophecy =
   BaseProphecy   of description
 | StructProphecy of seqsets list
 | ArrayProphecy  of seqsets * seqsets * seqsets
 | UnionProphecy  of seqsets list

(* Guesses the best top-level description *)
fun oracle : seqsets -> prophecy

(* Implements a generic inference algorithm *)
fun discover (sqs:seqsets) : description =
 case (oracle sqs) of
   BaseProphecy b => b

 | StructProphecy sqss =>
     let Ts = map discover sqss in
     struct { Ts }

 | ArrayProphecy (sqsfirst,sqsbody,sqslast) =>
     let Tfirst = discover sqsfirst in
     let Tbody  = discover sqsbody  in
     let Tlast  = discover sqslast  in
     struct { Tfirst; array { Tbody }; Tlast; }

 | UnionProphecy sqss =>
     let Ts = map discover sqss in
     union { Ts }
```

Fig. 3. A generic structure-discovery algorithm in Pseudo-ML

Structure discovery. The structure discovery phase uses a *top-down, divide-and-conquer* algorithm outlined in Figure 3 in the pseudo-ML function `discover`. Each invocation of `discover` calls the `oracle` function to guess the structure of the data represented by the current set of SEQSETs. The oracle can prophesy either a *base type*, a *struct*, an *array* or a *union*. The `oracle` function also partitions the input SEQSETs into sets

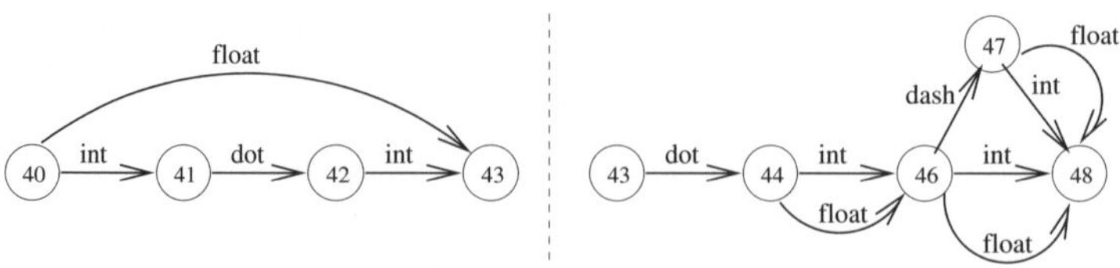

Fig. 4. Cutting SEQSET for "2.2.13-4" after the first float token

of sub-SEQSETs, each of which corresponds to a component in the guessed structure. The `discover` function then recursively constructs the structure of each set of sub-SEQSETs.

How does the `oracle` produce its prophecy? First, it uses the trained statistical model to assign probabilities to the edges in the input SEQSETs. Next, it computes for each SEQSET the *most probable token sequence* (MPTS) among all the possible paths using a modified *Viterbi* algorithm [22], which we discuss in Section 4. Then, based on the statistics of the tokens in the MPTSs, the oracle predicts the structure of the current collection of SEQSETs using the heuristics designed for our earlier algorithm [9].

As an example, consider applying the oracle to determine the top-level structure of the first line in `yum.txt`. It would predict the following:

```
struct {date;  ' '; time; ' '; word; ':'; ' '; id; TBD}
```

i.e., a `struct` containing nine sub-structures including `TBD`, which is a sub-structure whose form will be determined recursively. At this point, the `oracle` partitions every SEQSET in the input into nine parts, corresponding to sub-structure boundaries, *i.e.*, at the vertices after tokens `date`, `space`, `time`, *etc.* During partitioning, the oracle removes SEQSET edges that cross partition boundaries because such edges are irrelevant for the next round of structure discovery. For example, if the oracle cuts after the first `float` token in the SEQSET in Figure 2, then it removes the `id` edge and the `float` edge between vertices 42 and 46, creating the two new SEQSETs in Figure 4. Finally, the `oracle` function returns the predicted structure as a "prophecy" along with the partitioned SEQSETs.

Format refinement with blob-finding. The refinement phase, which follows structure discovery, tries to improve the initial rough structure by applying a series of rewriting rules. We have modified the earlier algorithm to use a "blob-finding" rule. This rule tries to identify data segments with highly complex, structured descriptions where none of the individual pieces of the description describe much of the data. Intuitively, such occurrences correspond to places where the data contained a high degree of variation, and the inference algorithm built a description that enumerated all the possible variations in painstaking detail. The blob rule replaces such complexity with a single *blob* token. A typical example of this kind of data is free-form text comments that sometimes appear at the end of each line in a log file. The blob-finding rule reduces the overall complexity of the resulting description and hence makes it more readable.

The format refinement algorithm applies the blob-finding rule in a bottom-up fashion. It converts into a blob each sub-structure that it deems overly complex and for which it can find a terminating pattern. The PADS parser uses the terminating pattern to find the extent of the blob. The algorithm merges adjacent blobs.

To decide whether a given structure is a blob, the algorithm computes the *variance* of the structure, which measures the total number of union/switch/enum branches and different array lengths in the structure. When the ratio between the variance and the amount of the data described by the structure exceeds a threshold, the algorithm decides to convert the structure to a blob if it can find a terminating sequence.

4 Statistical Models

A key component of the format inference algorithm described in the previous section is a selection of the best token sequence from each SEQSET. To prioritize sequences, the algorithm assigns probabilities using a statistical token model. This section describes three such models that we have experimented with.

Character-by-character Hidden Markov Model (HMM). The first model we investigate is the classic first-order, character-by-character Hidden Markov Model (HMM) [22]. An HMM is a statistical model that includes one set of states whose values we can observe and a second set whose values are *hidden* and we wish to infer. The hidden states determine, with some probability, the values of the observable states. In our case, we can observe the sequence of characters in the input string and wish to infer the token that is associated with each character. The model assumes the probability that we see a particular character depends upon its associated token and moreover, since the HMM is first-order, the probability of observing a particular token depends upon the previous token but no other earlier tokens. The picture below illustrates the process of generating the character sequence "2.2.13-4" from a token sequence. Hidden HMM states are white and observables are shaded. Notice particularly that the adjacent digits "1" and "3" are generated from two consecutive instances of the token `int`, when in a true token sequence, both characters are generated from a single `int` token. A postpass will clean this up, but such situations are dealt with more effectively by the HMEMs described in the following subsection.

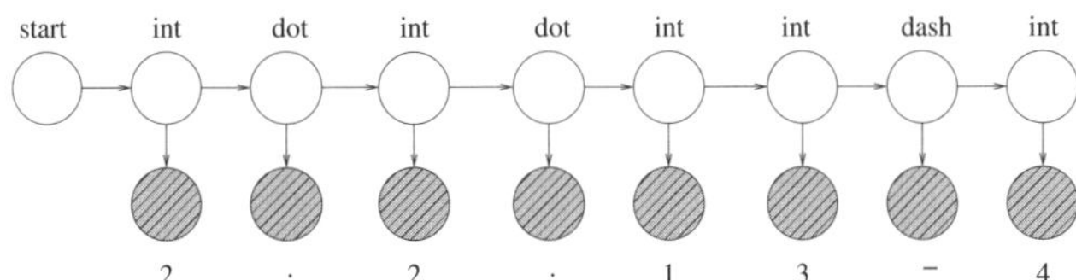

Finally, since our training data is limited, we employ one further approximation in our model. Instead of modelling every individual character separately, we classify characters using a set of boolean features including features for whether the character is (a) a digit, (b) an upper-case alphabetic letter, (c) white space, or (d) a particular punctuation character such as a period. We call the feature vectors involving (a)-(d) *observations.*

Let $\mathbf{T}_i$ denote the ith hidden state; its value ranges over the set of all token names. Let $\mathbf{C}_i$ denote the observation emitted by hidden state $\mathbf{T}_i$. Three parameters determine the model: the transition matrix $\mathbf{P}(T_i|T_{i-1})$, the sensor matrix $\mathbf{P}(C_i|T_i)$ and the initial probabilities $\mathbf{P}(T_i|begin)$. We compute these parameters from the training data as follows:

$$\mathbf{P}(T_i|T_{i-1}) = \frac{\text{occurrences where } T_i \text{ follows } T_{i-1}}{\text{occurrences of } T_{i-1}} \tag{1}$$

$$\mathbf{P}(C_i|T_i) = \frac{\text{occurrences of } C_i \text{ annotated with } T_i}{\text{occurrences of } T_i} \tag{2}$$

$$\mathbf{P}(T_1|begin) = \frac{\text{occurrences of } T_1 \text{ being first token}}{\text{number of training chunks}} \tag{3}$$

Given these parameters and a fixed input, we want to find the token sequence with the highest probability, *i.e.*, from the input sequence $C_1, C_2, ..., C_n$, we want to find the token sequence $T_1, T_2, ..., T_n$ that maximizes the conditional probability $\mathbf{P}(T_1, T_2, ..., T_n| C_1, C_2, ..., C_n)$. This probability is defined as usual:

$$\begin{aligned}\mathbf{P}(T_1, T_2, ..., T_n|C_1, C_2, ..., C_n) &\propto \mathbf{P}(T_1, T_2, ..., T_n, C_1, C_2, ..., C_n) \\ &= \mathbf{P}(T_1|begin) \cdot \prod_{i=2}^{n} \mathbf{P}(T_i|T_{i-1}) \end{aligned} \tag{4}$$

To calculate the highest probability token sequence from this model, we run a slightly modified variant of the Viterbi algorithm over the SEQSET.

Because the character-by-character HMM is first-order and employs only single character features, it cannot capture complex features in the data such as a substring "`http://`" which indicates a strong likelihood of being part of a URL. One obvious solution is increasing the order of the HMM. However, since the token length is variable in our application, it is not clear what the order should be. In addition, increasing the order also increases the complexity exponentially. Instead, in the next sections, we pursue two hybrid methods that incorporate existing classification techniques into the HMM framework.

Hierarchical Maximum Entropy Model (HMEM). The character-by-character HMM extracts a set of features from each character to create an observation and then runs a standard HMM over these observations. In contrast, the Hierarchical Maximum Entropy Model (HMEM), which we will explore next, extracts a set of features from each substring, uses the Maximum Entropy (ME) procedure [24,19] to produce an observation and runs a standard HMM over these new kinds of observations. Using the sequence "2.2.13-4" as our example again, the corresponding HMEM may be drawn as follows:

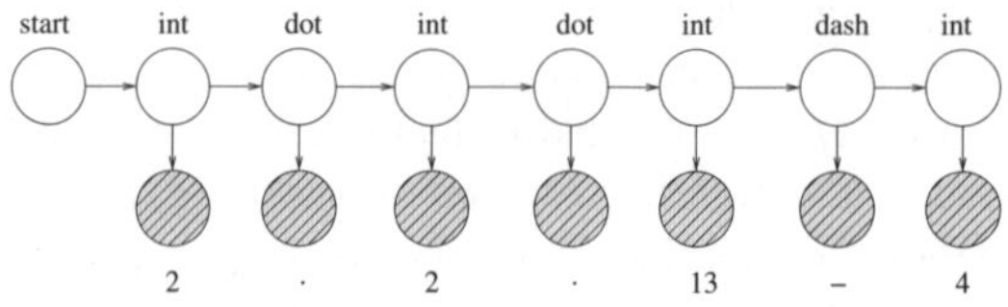

Formally, let $\mathbf{T}_i$ be the ith hidden state or token in the sequence (denoted by a white node in picture above) and let $\mathbf{S}_i$ be the substring annotated by $\mathbf{T}_i$. Suppose the number of tokens in the chunk is l; then the target probability is as follows.

$$\mathbf{P}(T_1, T_2, ..., T_n | S_1, S_2, ..., S_l) \propto \mathbf{P}(T_1 | begin) \cdot \prod_{i=2}^{l} \mathbf{P}(T_i | T_{i-1}) \cdot \prod_{i=1}^{l} \mathbf{P}(S_i | T_i) \quad (5)$$

Equations (1) and (3) allow us to calculate the transition matrix and the initial probability. We can compute $\mathbf{P}(S_i|T_i)$ using Bayes Rule,

$$\mathbf{P}(S_i|T_i) = \frac{\mathbf{P}(T_i|S_i) \cdot \mathbf{P}(S_i)}{\mathbf{P}(T_i)} \quad (6)$$

Finally, since obtaining accurate estimates of $\mathbf{P}(S_i)$ and $\mathbf{P}(T_i)$ appears to require more training data than we currently have, we have further approximated by simply using $\mathbf{P}(T_i|S_i)$ to estimate $\mathbf{P}(S_i|T_i)$. Estimation of $P(T_i|S_i)$ through the ME procedure involves using the following features (among others): (a) total number of characters in the string, (b) the number of occurrences of certain punctuation characters, (c) the total number of punctuation characters in the string, (d) the presence of certain substrings such as "`am`", "`pm`", "`January`", "`Jan`", "`january`", and (e) the presence of digit sequences. When we substitute $\mathbf{P}(T_i|S_i)$ for $\mathbf{P}(S_i|T_i)$ in equation (5), we obtain the following:

$$\mathbf{P}(T_1, T_2, ..., T_n | S_1, S_2, ..., S_l) \propto \mathbf{P}(T_1 | begin) \cdot \prod_{i=2}^{l} \mathbf{P}(T_i | T_{i-1}) \cdot \prod_{i=1}^{l} \mathbf{P}(T_i | S_i) \quad (7)$$

Finally, notice that in equation (7), the number of tokens in a sequence will determine the number of terms in the product. Consequently, a sequence with more tokens will produce more terms, which our experiments have shown produces a significant bias towards shorter token sequences. To avoid such bias, we modify Equation (7) to use the average log likelihood.

$$\begin{aligned} &\log \mathbf{P}(T_1, T_2, ..., T_n | S_1, S_2, ..., S_l) \\ &\propto \frac{\log \mathbf{P}(T_1|begin) + \sum_{i=2}^{l} \log \mathbf{P}(T_i|T_{i-1}) + \sum_{i=1}^{l} \log \mathbf{P}(T_i|S_i)}{l} \end{aligned} \quad (8)$$

Using average log likelihood guarantees that the algorithm will not select shorter token sequences unless the average value of all conditional probabilities $\mathbf{P}(T_i|S_i)$ exceeds a threshold.

To find the highest probability sequence for a chunk under this model, we implemented a modified Viterbi algorithm that takes into account the number of tokens in the sequence. In what follows, let the number of characters in the chunk be n and the number of tokens be l. Let C_i be the character at position i, and PT_i be the partial token that emits the character C_i. Then $\mathbf{P}(PT_1, PT_2, ..., PT_i | C_1, C_2, ..., C_i, k)$ is the probability of a partial token sequence $PT_1, PT_2, ..., PT_i$ conditioned on a substring of characters $C_1, C_2, ..., C_i$, collectively emitted by a sequence of k tokens. Now, let T_i be a token that ends at position i and let S_i be the corresponding substring. The probability of the most likely partial token sequence up to position i is

$$\max_{PT_1,\ldots,PT_i} \log \mathbf{P}(PT_1, PT_2, ..., PT_i, PT_{i+1}|C_1, C_2, ..., C_{i+1}, k+1) \propto$$

$$\begin{cases} \log \mathbf{P}(S_{i+1}|T_{i+1}) + \max\limits_{T_{i+1-\delta}} (\log \mathbf{P}(T_{i+1}|T_{i+1-\delta}) + \\ \quad \max\limits_{PT_1,\ldots,PT_{i-1}} \log \mathbf{P}(PT_1, ..., PT_i|C_1, ..., C_i, k)), \\ \quad \text{if } i+1 \text{ is the end of an edge in SEQSET, } \delta \text{ is the length of token } T_{i+1}; \\ \\ \max\limits_{PT1,\ldots,PT_i} \log \mathbf{P}(PT_1, ..., PT_i|C1, ..., C_i, k+1) \\ \quad \text{otherwise.} \end{cases} \tag{9}$$

The left-hand-side of (9), known as a *forward message*, contains the token sequence up to a position i in the chunk as well as the lengths of the tokens. At the last position n, we compute l from

$$\max_{l} \log \frac{\mathbf{P}(TP_1, TP_2, ..., TP_n|C_1, C_2, ..., C_n, l)}{l} \tag{10}$$

and select the last token in the most likely token sequences. After tracing backwards through the chain of messages, we obtain the most likely token sequences. The modified Viterbi algorithm is linear to the number of characters n in the chunk.

We saw there were some problems with the basic HMM model that motivated the use of the HMEM model. What further problems plague the HMEMs? The most worrisome problem is that the HMEM is a generative model that simulates the procedure of generating the data, and estimates the target conditional probability by a joint probability. Therefore, it is biased towards tokens with more occurrences in the training data. In practice, we found that when particular tokens appear infrequently in our training data, the algorithm would never identify them, even when they had clear distinguishing features. These difficulties motivated us to explore the effectiveness of Hierarchical Support Vector Machines (HSVM), which use a discriminative model as opposed to a generative one.

4.1 Hierarchical Support Vector Machines (HSVM)

An HSVM is exactly the same as an HMEM except it uses a Support Vector Machine (SVM) [5] as opposed to Maximum Entropy to classify tokens. Basically, an SVM measures the target conditional probability $\mathbf{P}(T_i|S_i)$ by generating hyperplanes that divide the feature vector space according to the positions of training data points. The hyperplanes are positioned so that the data points (feature vectors in our case) are separated into classes with the maximum margin between any two classes. The data points that lie on the margins (or boundaries) of each class are called *support vectors.*

5 Evaluation

We use sample files from twenty different ad hoc data sources to evaluate our overall inference algorithm and the different approaches to probabilistic tokenization. These data sources, many of which are published on the web [20], are mostly system-generated log files of various kinds and a few ASCII spreadsheets describing business transactions. These files range in size from a few dozen lines to a few thousand.

To test a given tokenization approach on a particular sample file, we first construct a statistical model from the other nineteen sample files using the given approach. We then use the resulting model to infer a description for the selected file. We repeat this process for all three tokenization approaches (HMM, HMEM, and HSVM) and all twenty sample files. We use three metrics described in the following sections to evaluate the results: *token accuracy*, *quality of description* and *execution time*.

Token accuracy. To evaluate tokenization accuracy for a model M on a given sample file, we compare the most likely sequence of tokens predicted by M, denoted S_m, with the ideal token sequence, denoted S. We define S to be the sequence of tokens generated by the hand-written PADS description of the file. We define three kinds of error rates, all normalized by $|S|$, the total number of tokens in S:

$$\text{token error} = \frac{\text{number of misidentified tokens in } S_m}{|S|}$$

$$\text{token group error} = \frac{\text{number of misidentified groups in } S_m}{|S|}$$

$$\text{token boundary error} = \frac{\text{number of misidentified boundaries in } S_m}{|S|}$$

The token error rate measures the number of times a token appears in S but the same token does not appear in the same place in S_m. A *token group* is a set of token types that have similar feature vectors and hence are hard to distinguish, *e.g.*, `hex string` and `id`, which both consist of alpha-numeric characters. The token group error rate measures the number of times a token from a particular token group appears in S but no token from the same group appears in the same location in S_m. Intuitively, if the algorithm mistakes a token for another token in the same token group, it is doing better than choosing a completely unrelated token type. The *token boundary* error rate measures the number of times there is a boundary between tokens in S but no corresponding boundary in S_m. This relatively coarse measure is interesting because boundaries are important to structure discovery. Even if the tokens are incorrectly identified, if the boundaries are correct, the correct structure can be still discovered.

Table 1 lists the token error, token group error, and token boundary error rates of the twenty benchmarks. The results from the original LEARNPADS system are presented in columns marked by `lex`. The original system produces high error rates for many files because the lexer is unable to resolve overlapping tokens effectively. HMM relies heavily on transition probabilities, which require a lot of data to compute to a useful precision. Because we currently have insufficient data, HMM generally does not perform as well as HMEM and HSVM. In the case of `asl.log`, `corald.log` and `coralwebsrv.log`, HMM's failure to detect some punctuation characters causes the entire token sequences to be misaligned and hence gives very high error rates.

Table 1. Tokenization errors

Data source	Token Error (%)				Token Group Error (%)				Token Boundary Error (%)			
	lex	HMM	HMEM	HSVM	lex	HMM	HMEM	HSVM	lex	HMM	HMEM	HSVM
1967Transactions	30	30	18.93	18.93	11.07	11.07	0	0	11.07	11.07	0	0
ai.3000	70.23	15.79	18.98	11.20	70.23	14.68	17.26	10.27	53.53	12.34	4.79	4.00
yum.txt	19.44	13.33	21.80	0	19.17	11.73	21.80	0	19.17	11.49	21.80	0
rpmpkgs.txt	99.66	2.71	15.01	0.34	99.66	2.14	14.67	0	99.66	0.23	14.67	0
railroad.txt	51.94	9.47	6.48	5.58	51.94	9.36	5.93	5.58	46.08	8.77	5.41	5.58
dibbler.1000	15.72	43.40	11.91	0.00	15.72	36.78	11.91	0.00	4.54	13.33	13.15	0.00
asl.log	89.92	98.91	8.94	5.83	89.63	98.91	8.94	5.83	83.28	98.54	6.27	3.29
scrollkeeper.log	18.58	28.48	18.67	9.86	18.58	18.77	8.96	0.12	18.58	17.83	8.96	0.12
page_log	77.72	15.29	0	7.52	72.76	15.29	0	7.52	64.70	5.64	0	5.64
MER_T01_01.csv	84.56	23.09	31.32	15.40	84.56	23.09	31.22	15.40	84.56	7.71	13.20	0.02
crashreporter	51.89	7.91	4.99	0.19	51.85	7.91	4.96	0.14	51.34	7.91	4.92	0.14
ls-l.txt	33.73	18.70	19.96	6.65	33.73	18.23	19.96	6.65	19.70	7.45	19.76	6.45
windowserver_last	73.31	14.98	10.16	3.24	71.50	14.98	10.07	3.15	69.18	11.16	8.05	3.14
netstat-an	13.89	17.83	9.61	9.01	12.51	15.44	5.95	5.95	12.51	14.90	5.80	5.20
boot.txt	10.67	25.40	9.37	2.77	3.99	25.10	9.14	2.43	3.34	14.48	8.27	1.69
quarterlyincome	82.99	5.52	1.98	1.98	82.99	4.22	1.53	1.54	77.53	1.54	1.53	1.54
corald.log	84.86	100	5.67	3.02	83.11	98.25	3.93	1.27	81.76	97.80	1.27	1.27
coraldnssrv.log	91.04	18.17	10.64	5.23	91.04	18.17	9.33	5.22	83.07	14.37	4.11	3.92
probed.log	1.74	27.99	16.50	16.50	1.74	27.99	16.50	16.50	1.75	27.98	16.42	16.42
coralwebsrv.log	86.67	100	8.75	23.99	86.67	100	8.75	23.99	81.90	98.33	8.75	23.81

Quality of description. To assess description quality quantitatively, we use the *Minimum Description Length Principle* (MDL) [13], which postulates that a useful measure of description quality is the sum of the cost in bits of transmitting the description (the type cost) and the cost in bits of transmitting the data *given the description* (the data cost). In general, the type cost measures the complexity of the description, while the data cost measures how loosely a given description explains the data. Increasing the type cost generally reduces the data cost, and *vice versa*. The objective is to minimize both. Table 2 shows the percentage change in the type and data costs of the descriptions produced by the new algorithm using each of the three tokenization schemes when compared to the same costs produced by the original LEARNPADS system. In both cases, the measurements were taken before the refinement case.

For most of the data sources, the probabilistic tokenization scheme improved the quality of the description by reducing both the type and the data costs. In the files `dibbler.1000`, `netstat-an` and `coralwebsrv.log`, a few misidentified tokens cause the resulting descriptions to differ significantly from the ones produced by the original system.

In another experiment, a human expert judged how each description compared to the original LEARNPADS results, focusing on the readability of the descriptions, *i.e.*, whether the descriptions present the structure of the data sources clearly. In this experiment, the judge rated the descriptions one by one, on a scale from -2 (meaning the description is too concise and it loses much useful information) to 2 (meaning the description is too precise and the structure is unclear). The score of a good description is therefore close to 0, which means the description provides sufficient information for

Table 2. Increase (+%) or decrease (-%) in type cost and data cost before refinement

Data source	Type Cost			Data Cost		
	HMM	HMEM	HSVM	HMM	HMEM	HSVM
1967Transactions	-39.661	-27.03	-27.03	-2.80	-2.80	-2.80
ai.3000	-26.27	+4.44	-19.27	-3.16	-6.85	-12.68
yum.txt	-57.60	+50.93	-76.27	-1.55	-7.93	-1.05
rpmpkgs.txt	-92.03	-76.29	-91.86	+1.47	-0.00	+1.47
railroad.txt	-31.86	-20.88	-22.93	-29.54	-29.22	-29.16
dibbler.1000	+611.22	+17.83	+7.03	-19.88	-22.11	-22.10
asl.log	-75.71	-22.33	-25.54	+8.57	-15.13	-17.53
scrollkeeper.log	-14.55	-58.86	-21.18	-7.77	-9.98	-11.36
page_log	0	0	0	-11.46	-11.67	-11.67
MER_T01_01.csv	-8.59	-12.74	-12.74	-25.59	-24.15	-24.14
crashreporter	+4.03	-8.66	-12.73	-9.38	-9.41	-12.45
ls-l.txt	-74.61	-51.32	-39.30	+0.10	-7.26	-2.18
windowserver_last	-62.84	-33.29	-56.18	+6.93	-11.12	-9.87
netstat-an	+147.07	-12.00	-21.63	+14.18	+6.74	+7.65
boot.txt	-72.60	-38.95	-71.29	+5.26	-6.54	-5.03
quarterlyincome	-18.36	-18.36	-18.36	-32.04	-32.51	-32.51
corald.log	-4.75	-5.53	-5.53	-27.28	-29.81	-29.81
coraldnssrv.log	-1.86	-2.03	-5.86	+59.53	+59.53	+59.53
probed.log	-14.61	-33.48	-33.48	+59.53	+63.18	+63.18
coralwebsrv.log	-8.75	+94.58	-71.55	-49.30	-15.91	+13.36

Table 3. Qualitative comparison of descriptions learned using probabilistic tokenization to descriptions learned by original LEARNPADS algorithm

Data source	lex	HMM	HMEM	HSVM	Data source	lex	HMM	HMEM	HSVM
1967Transactions	0	0	0	0	crashreporter	2	0	1	1
ai.3000	1	1	1	0	ls-l.txt	2	0	1	1
yum.txt	2	-1	1	0	windowserver_last	2	0	1	1
rpmpkgs.txt	2	-1	-2	0	netstat-an	2	-2	0	0
railroad.txt	2	1	1	1	boot.txt	2	-1	1	1
dibbler.1000	0	2	0	0	quarterlyincome	1	1	1	1
asl.log	2	-2	2	2	corald.log	0	1	1	0
scrollkeeper.log	1	2	1	1	coraldnssrv.log	0	1	1	-1
page_log	0	0	0	0	probed.log	0	0	0	0
MER_T01_01.csv	0	1	0	0	coralwebsrv.log	0	1	1	-1

the user to understand the data source and the user can easily understand the structure from the description. Table 3 shows that on average, HMEM and HSVM outperform the original system denoted by `lex`.

Execution time. Compared to the original system, statistical inference requires extra time to construct SEQSETs and compute probabilities. We measured the execution times on a 2.2 GHz Intel Xeon processor with 5 GB of memory. The original algorithm takes anywhere from under 10 seconds to 25 minutes to infer a description, while the new system requires a few seconds to several hours, depending on the amount of test data and the statistical model used. In general, the character-by-character HMM model is the fastest, while HSVM is most time-consuming.

We have performed a number of experiments (not shown due to space constraints) that demonstrate that execution time is proportional to the number of lines in the data source. Moreover, we have found that for most descriptions, a relatively small representative sample of the data is sufficient for learning its structure with high accuracy. For instance, out of the twenty benchmarks we have, seven data sources have more than 500 records. Preliminary results show that for these seven data sources, we can generate descriptions from just 10% of the data that can parse 95% of records correctly.

6 Related Work

In the last two decades, there has been extensive work on classic grammar induction problems [25,11,3,1,6], XML schema inference [3,10], information extraction [17,15,2], and other related areas such as natural language processing [4,14] and bioinformatics [16]. Machine learning techniques have played a very important role in these areas. Our earlier paper [9] contains an extensive comparison of our basic format inference algorithm to others that have appeared in the literature.

One of the most closely related pieces of work to this paper is Soderland's WHISK system [23], which extracts useful information from semi-structured text such as stylized advertisements from an online community service called Craig's List [12]. In the WHISK system, the user is presented with a few online ads as training data and is asked to label which bits of information to extract. Then the system learns extraction rules from labeled data and uses them to retrieve more wanted information from a much larger collection of data. The WHISK system differs from our system in several ways. First, WHISK, as well as other information extraction systems, have a clear and fixed token set, defined by words, numbers, punctuations, HTML tags and user pre-specified semantic classes, etc. Second, WHISK only focuses on certain bits of information, namely, single or multiple fields in records, whereas we not only identify useful fields, but also obtain the organization and relations of these fields by generating the complete description of the entire data file. Last, in WHISK, the extraction rules learned from a particular domain can only be used on data from the same domain. For example, rules learned from sample on-line rental ads are only relevant to other rental ads, and cannot be applied to software job postings. But the statistical token models we learned in our system can be applied to many different types of data, as shown in the experiments we have done in Section 5.

Also closely related is the work on text table extraction by Pinto and others [21]. Text tables can be viewed as special ad hoc data with a tabular layout. There are often clear delimiters between columns in the table, and table rows are well defined with new line characters as their boundaries. Because of its tabular nature, the data studied has less variation in general. The goal of their work is to identify tables embedded in free text and the types of table rows such as header, sub-header and data row, etc, whereas we are learning the entire structure of the data. To this end, Pinto et al. use Conditional Random

Fields (CRFs) [18], a statistical model that is useful in learning from sequence data with overlapping features. Their system extracts features from white space characters, text between white spaces and punctuations. Although not explicitly stated, words, numbers and punctuations are used as fixed set of tokens.

To summarize, problems studied by previous efforts in grammar induction and information extraction do not typically suffer from token ambiguities that we see in ad hoc data, because tags cleanly divide XML and web-based data, while spaces and known punctuation symbols separate natural language text. In contrast, the separators and token types found in ad hoc data sources such as web logs and financial records are far more variable and ambiguous.

7 Conclusion

Ad hoc data is unpredictable, poorly documented, filled with errors, and yet ubiquitous. It poses tremendous challenges to the data analysts that must analyze, vet and transform it into useful information. Our goal is to alleviate the burden, risk and confusion associated with ad hoc data by using the declarative PADS language and system.

In this paper, we describe our continuing efforts to develop a format inference engine for the PADS language. In particular, we show how to redesign our format inference algorithm so that it can take advantage of information generated from an arbitrary statistical token model and we study the effectiveness of three candidate models: Hidden Markov Models (HMMs), Hierarchical Maximum Entropy Models (HMEMs) and Support Vector Machines (SVMs). We show that each model in succession is generally more accurate than the last, but at an increased performance cost.

Acknowledgement. This material is based upon work supported by the NSF under grants 0612147 and 0615062. Any opinions, findings, and conclusions or recommendations expressed in this material are those of the authors and do not necessarily reflect the views of the NSF.

References

1. Angluin, D.: Inference of reversible languages. Journal of the ACM 29(3), 741–765 (1982)
2. Arasu, A., Garcia-Molina, H.: Extracting structured data from web pages. In: SIGMOD, pp. 337–348 (2003)
3. Bex, G.J., Neven, F., Schwentick, T., Tuyls, K.: Inference of concise DTDs from XML data. In: VLDB, pp. 115–126 (2006)
4. Borkar, V., Deshmukh, K., Sarawagi, S.: Automatic segmentation of text into structured records. In: SIGMOD, New York, NY, USA, pp. 175–186 (2001)
5. Chang, C.-C., Lin, C.-J.: LIBSVM: a library for support vector machines. Software (2001), `http://www.csie.ntu.edu.tw/~cjlin/libsvm`
6. Chen, S.F.: Bayesian grammar induction for language modeling. In: Proceedings of the 33rd Annual Meeting of the ACL, pp. 228–235 (1995)
7. Fisher, K., Gruber, R.: PADS: A domain specific language for processing ad hoc data. In: PLDI, pp. 295–304 (June 2005)

8. Fisher, K., Walker, D., Zhu, K.Q.: LearnPADS: Automatic tool generation from ad hoc data. In: SIGMOD (June 2008)
9. Fisher, K., Walker, D., Zhu, K.Q., White, P.: From dirt to shovels: Fully automatic tool generation from ad hoc data. In: POPL (January 2008)
10. Garofalakis, M.N., Gionis, A., Rastogi, R., Seshadri, S., Shim, K.: XTRACT: A system for extracting document type descriptors from XML documents. In: SIGMOD, pp. 165–176 (2000)
11. Gold, E.M.: Language identification in the limit. Information and Control 10(5), 447–474 (1967)
12. Craig's List (2008), `http://www.craigslist.org/`
13. Grünwald, P.D.: The Minimum Description Length Principle. MIT Press, Cambridge (2007)
14. Heeman, P.A., Allen, J.F.: Speech repairs, intonational phrases and discourse markers: Modeling speakers' utterances in spoken dialog. Computational Linguistics 25(4), 527–571 (1999)
15. Hong, T.W.: Grammatical Inference for Information Extraction and Visualisation on the Web. Ph.D. Thesis, Imperial College, London (2002)
16. Kulp, D., Haussler, D., Reese, M.G., Eeckman, F.H.: A generalized hidden markov model for the recognition of human genes in DNA. In: Proceedings of the Fourth International Conference on Intelligent Systems for Molecular Biology, pp. 134–141 (1996)
17. Kushmerick, N.: Wrapper induction for information extraction. PhD thesis, University of Washington, Department of Computer Science and Engineering (1997)
18. Lafferty, J.D., McCallum, A., Pereira, F.C.N.: Conditional random fields: Probabilistic models for segmenting and labeling sequence data. In: ICML, pp. 282–289 (2001)
19. MEGA model optimization package (2007), `http://www.cs.utah.edu/~hal/megam/`
20. PADS project (2007), `http://www.padsproj.org/`
21. Pinto, D., McCallum, A., Wei, X., Croft, W.B.: Table extraction using conditional random fields. In: SIGIR, New York, NY, USA, pp. 235–242 (2003)
22. Rabiner, L.R.: A tutorial on hidden markov models and selected applications in speech recognition. Proceedings of the IEEE 77(2) (February 1989)
23. Soderland, S.: Learning information extraction rules for semi-structured and free text. Machine Learning 34(1-3), 233–272 (1999)
24. Adam, L., Berger, T., Vincent, J., Della Pietra, Stephen, A.: A maximum entropy approach to natural language processing. Computational Linguistics 22(1) (March 1996)
25. Vidal, E.: Grammatical inference: An introduction survey. In: ICGI, pp. 1–4 (1994)

High Level Thread-Based Competitive Or-Parallelism in Logtalk*

Paulo Moura[1,3], Ricardo Rocha[2,3], and Sara C. Madeira[1,4]

[1] Dep. of Computer Science, University of Beira Interior, Portugal
{pmoura,smadeira}@di.ubi.pt
[2] Dep. of Computer Science, University of Porto, Portugal
ricroc@dcc.fc.up.pt
[3] Center for Research in Advanced Computing Systems, INESC–Porto, Portugal
[4] Knowledge Discovery and Bioinformatics Group, INESC–ID, Portugal

Abstract. This paper presents the logic programming concept of *thread-based competitive or-parallelism*, which combines the original idea of competitive or-parallelism with committed-choice nondeterminism and speculative threading. In thread-based competitive or-parallelism, an explicit disjunction of subgoals is interpreted as a set of concurrent alternatives, each running in its own thread. The individual subgoals usually correspond to predicates implementing different procedures that, depending on the problem specifics, are expected to either fail or succeed with different performance levels. The subgoals compete for providing an answer and the first successful subgoal leads to the termination of the remaining ones. We discuss the implementation of thread-based competitive or-parallelism in the context of Logtalk, an object-oriented logic programming language, and present experimental results.

Keywords: Or-parallelism, speculative threading, implementation.

1 Introduction

Or-parallelism is a simple form of parallelism in logic programs [1], where the bodies of alternative clauses for the same goal are executed concurrently. Or-parallelism is often explored *implicitly*, possibly with hints from the programmer to guide the system. Common uses include search-oriented applications, such as parsing, database querying, and data mining. In this paper, we introduce a different, explicit form of or-parallelism, *thread-based competitive or-parallelism*, that combines the original idea of competitive or-parallelism [2] with committed-choice nondeterminism [3] and speculative threading [4]. Committed-choice nondeterminism, also known as *don't-care* nondeterminism, means that once an alternative is taken, the computation is committed to it and cannot backtrack or explore in parallel other alternatives. Committed-choice nondeterminism is useful whenever a single solution is sought among a set of potential alternatives.

* This work has been partially supported by the FCT research projects STAMPA (PTDC/EIA/67738/2006) and MOGGY (PTDC/EIA/70830/2006).

A. Gill and T. Swift (Eds.): PADL 2009, LNCS 5418, pp. 107–121, 2009.

Speculative threading allows the exploration of different alternatives, which can be interpreted as competing to provide an answer for the original problem. The key idea is that multiple threads can be started without knowing *a priori* which of them, if any, will perform useful work. In competitive or-parallelism, different alternatives are interpreted as competing for providing an answer. The first successful alternative leads to the termination of the remaining ones. From a declarative programming perspective, thread-based competitive or-parallelism allows the programmer to specify alternative procedures to solve a problem without caring about the details of speculative execution and thread handling. Another key point of thread-based competitive or-parallelism is its simplicity and implementation portability when compared with classical or-parallelism implementations. The ISO Prolog multi-threading standardization proposal [5] is currently implemented in several systems including SWI-Prolog, Yap and XSB, providing a highly portable solution given the number of operating systems supported by these Prolog systems. In contrast, most or-parallelism systems described in the literature [1] are no longer available, due to the complexity of maintaining and porting their implementations.

Our research is driven by the increasing availability of multi-core computing systems. These systems are turning into a viable high-performance, affordable and standardized alternative to the traditional (and often expensive) parallel architectures. The number of cores per processor is expected to continue to increase, further expanding the areas of application of competitive or-parallelism.

The remainder of the paper is organized as follows. First, we present in more detail the concept of competitive or-parallelism. Second, we discuss the implementation of competitive or-parallelism in the context of Logtalk [6], an object-oriented logic programming language, and compare it with classical or-parallelism. Next we present experimental results. Follows a discussion on how tabling can be used to take advantage of partial results gathered by speculative computations. We then identify further potential application areas where competitive or-parallelism can be useful. Finally, we outline some conclusions and describe further work. In the remaining of the paper, the expression *competitive or-parallelism* will be used interchangeably with the expression *thread-based competitive or-parallelism*.

2 Thread-Based Competitive Or-Parallelism

The concept of thread-based competitive or-parallelism is based on the interpretation of an *explicit disjunction of subgoals* as a set of concurrent alternatives, each running in its own thread. Each individual alternative is assumed to implement a different procedure that, depending on the problem specifics, is expected to either fail or succeed with different performance results. For example, one alternative may converge quickly to a solution, other may get trapped into a local, suboptimal solution, while a third may simply diverge. The subgoals are interpreted as competing for providing an answer and the first subgoal to complete leads to the termination of the threads running the remaining subgoals. The semantics of a competitive or-parallelism call are simple. Given a disjunction of subgoals, a competitive or-parallelism call blocks until one of the following situations occurs: one of the subgoals succeeds; all the subgoals fail; or one of the subgoals generates an exception. All the remaining threads are terminated once one of the subgoals succeeds or an exception is thrown during the execution of one of the running threads. The competitive or-parallelism call succeeds if and only if one of the subgoals succeeds. When one of the subgoals generates an exception, the competitive or-parallelism call terminates with the same exception.[1] When two or more subgoals generate exceptions, the competitive or-parallelism call terminates with one of the generated exceptions.

For example, assume that we have implemented several methods for calculating the roots of real functions.[2] In Logtalk, we may then write:

```
find_root(F, A, B, Error, Zero, Method) :-
    threaded((
        bisection::find_root(F, A, B, Error, Zero), Method = bisection
    ;   newton::find_root(F, A, B, Error, Zero), Method = newton
    ;   muller::find_root(F, A, B, Error, Zero), Method = muller
    )).
```

In this example, the competitive or-parallelism call (implemented by the Logtalk built-in meta-predicate `threaded/1`) returns both the identifier of the fastest successful method and its result. Depending on the function and on the initial interval, one method may converge quickly to the root of the function while the others may simply diverge. Thus, by avoiding committing to a specific method that might fail for some functions, the competitive or-parallelism call allows a solution to be found corresponding to the fastest, successful method.

Consider now a different example, the *generalized water jugs* problem. In this problem, we have several jugs of different capacities and we want to measure a certain amount of water. We may *fill* a jug, *empty* it, or *transfer* its contents to another jug. As in our previous example, we may apply several methods to solve this problem. The water jugs state-space can be explored using e.g. breadth-first, depth-first, or hill-climbing search strategies. We could write:

```
solve(WaterJug, Liters, Jug1, Jug2, Steps) :-
    threaded((
        depth_first::solve(WaterJug, Liters, Jug1, Jug2, Steps)
    ;   hill_climbing::solve(WaterJug, Liters, Jug1, Jug2, Steps)
    ;   breadth_first::solve(WaterJug, Liters, Jug1, Jug2, Steps)
    )).
```

Different heuristics could also be explored in parallel. As before, without knowing *a priori* the amount of water to be measured, we have no way of telling which method or heuristic will be faster. This example is used later in this paper to provide experimental results.

[1] If we want the computation to proceed despite the exception generated, we can convert exceptions into failures by wrapping the thread subgoal in a `catch/3` call.

[2] The full source code of this example is included in the current Logtalk distribution.

These examples illustrate how thread-based competitive or-parallelism distinguish itself from existing or-parallel systems by allowing fine-grained control at the goal level using an explicit parallelism construct. As in most implementations of or-parallelism, the effectiveness of competitive or-parallelism relies on several factors. These factors are discussed in detail next.

3 Implementation

In this section we discuss the implementation of competitive or-parallelism in the context of Logtalk, given the core predicates found on the ISO standardization proposal for Prolog threads [5].

3.1 Logtalk Support

Logtalk is an open source object-oriented logic programming language that can use most Prolog implementations as a back-end compiler. Logtalk takes advantage of modern multi-processor and multi-core computers to support high level multi-threading programming, allowing objects to support both synchronous and asynchronous messages without bothering with the details of creating and destroying threads, implement thread communication, or synchronizing threads.

Competitive or-parallelism is implemented in Logtalk using the built-in meta-predicate `threaded/1`, which supports both competitive or-parallelism and independent (and quasi-independent) and-parallelism.

The `threaded/1` predicate proves a conjunction or disjunction of subgoals running each subgoal in its own thread.[3] When the argument is a conjunction of goals, a call to this predicate implements independent and-parallelism semantics. When the argument is a disjunction of subgoals, a call to this predicate implements the semantics of competitive or-parallelism, as detailed in the previous section. The `threaded/1` predicate is deterministic and opaque to cuts and, thus, there is no backtracking over completed calls.

The choice of using Prolog core multi-threading predicates to implement competitive or-parallelism provides several advantages in terms of simplicity and portability when compared with traditional, low-level or-parallelism implementation solutions. Nevertheless, three problems must be addressed when exploiting or-parallelism: (i) multiple binding representation, (ii) work scheduling, and (iii) predicate side-effects. These problems are addressed in the sections below.

3.2 Multiple Binding Representation

The multiple binding representation is a crucial problem for the efficiency of classical or-parallel systems. The concurrent execution of alternative branches

[3] The predicate argument is not flattened; parallelism is only applied to the outermost conjunction or disjunction. When the predicate argument is neither a conjunction nor a disjunction of subgoals, no threads are used. In this case, the predicate call is equivalent to a call to the ISO Prolog standard predicate `once/1`.

of the search tree can result in several conflicting bindings for shared variables. The main problem is that of efficiently representing and accessing *conditional bindings*.[4] The environments of alternative branches have to be organized in such a way that conflicting conditional bindings can be easily discernible.

The multiple binding representation problem can be solved by devising a mechanism where each branch has some private area where it stores its conditional bindings. A number of approaches have been proposed to tackle this problem (see e.g [1]). Arguably, the two most successful ones are *environment copying*, as implemented in the Muse [7] and YapOr [8] systems, and *binding arrays*, as implemented in the Aurora system [9]. In the environment copying model, each worker maintains its own copy of the environment (stack, heap, trail, etc) in which it can write without causing binding conflicts. In this model, even unconditional bindings are not shared. In the binding arrays model, each worker maintains a private array data structure, called the *binding array*, where it stores its conditional bindings. Each variable along a branch is assigned to a unique number that identifies its offset entry in the binding array.

In a competitive or-parallelism call, only the first successful subgoal in the disjunction of subgoals can lead to the instantiation of variables in the original call. This simplifies our implementation as the Prolog core support for multi-threading programming can be used straightforward. In particular, we can take advantage of the Prolog thread creation predicate `thread_create/3`. Each new Prolog thread created by this predicate runs a *copy* of the goal argument using its own set of data areas (stack, heap, trail, etc). Its implementation is similar to the environment copying approach but simpler as only the goal is copied. As each thread runs a copy of the goal, no variables are shared across threads. Thus, the bindings of shared variables occurring within a thread are independent of bindings occurring in other threads. This operational semantics simplifies the problem of multiple binding representation in competitive or-parallelism, which results in a simple implementation with only a small number of lines of Prolog source code. Nevertheless, because each thread is running a copy of the original goal, thus breaking variable bindings, we need a solution for retrieving the bindings of the successful thread; our implementation solution is presented later. Copying a goal into a thread and copying the successful bindings back to the following computations may result in significant overhead for goals with large data structures arguments. Thus, we sacrifice some performance in order to provide users with an high-level, portable implementation.

3.3 Work Scheduling

Even though the cost of managing multiple environments cannot be completely avoided, it may be minimized if the *operating-system's scheduler* is able to divide efficiently the available work between the available computational units during execution. In classical or-parallelism, the or-parallel system usually knows the

[4] A binding of a variable is said to be *conditional* if the variable was created before the last choice point, otherwise it is said to be *unconditional*.

number of computational units (processors or cores) that are available in the supporting architecture. A high-level scheduler then uses this number to create an equal number of workers (processes or threads) to process work. The scheduler's task of load balancing and work dispatching, from the user's point-of-view, is completely *implicit*, i.e., the user cannot interfere in the way work is scheduled for execution. This is a nice property as load balancing and work dispatching are usually complex tasks due to the dynamic nature of work.[5]

In competitive or-parallelism, the problem of work scheduling differs from classical or-parallelism due to the use of explicit parallelism. The system can also know the number of computational units that are available in the supporting architecture, but the user has *explicit* control over the process of work dispatching. This explicit control can lead to more complex load balancing problems, as the number of running workers (threads) can easily exceed the number of available computational units (processors or cores). Our current implementation delegates load balancing to the operating-system thread scheduler. However, we can explicitly control the number of running threads using parametric objects with a parameter for the maximum number of running threads. This is a simple programming solution, used in most of the Logtalk multi-threading examples.

In classical or-parallelism, another major problem for scheduling is the presence of pruning operators like the cut predicate. When a cut predicate is executed, all alternatives to the right of the cut are pruned, therefore never being executed in a sequential system. However, in a parallel system, the work corresponding to these alternatives can be picked for parallel execution before the cut is executed, therefore resulting in wasted computational effort when pruning takes place. This form of work is known as *speculative work* [14]. An advanced scheduler must be able to reduce to a minimum the speculative computations and at the same time maintain the granularity of the work scheduled for execution [15,16].

In competitive or-parallelism, the concept of speculative work is part of its operational semantics, not because of the cut's semantics as the `threaded/1` predicate is deterministic and opaque to cuts, but because of the way subgoals in a competitive or-parallelism call are terminated once one of the subgoals succeeds. In this case, the speculative work results from the computational effort done by the unsuccessful or slower threads when pruning takes place. We can view the `threaded/1` predicate as an high-level *green cut* predicate that prunes all the alternatives to the left and to the right of the successful subgoal. For now, we have postponed working on an advanced, high-level scheduler.

3.4 Thread Results and Cancellation Issues

Logtalk multi-threading support uses message queues to collect thread results. This allows execution to be suspended while waiting for a thread result to be posted to a message queue, avoiding polling, which would hurt performance.

[5] A number of different scheduling strategies have been proposed to efficiently deal with this problem on classical or-parallelism; see e.g. [10,11,12,13].

Each thread posts its result to the message queue of the parent thread within the context of which the competitive or-parallelism call is taking place. The results posted by each thread are tagged with the identifiers of the remaining threads of the competitive or-parallelism call. This allows the cancellation of the remaining threads once a successful result (or an exception) is posted. In Logtalk, a template with the thread tags and the original disjunction subgoals is constructed when compiling a competitive or-parallelism call. The template thread tags are instantiated at run-time using the identifiers of the threads created when executing the competitive or-parallelism call. The first successful thread unifies its result with the corresponding disjunction goal in the template, thus retrieving any variable bindings resulting from proving the competitive or-parallelism call.[6]

The effectiveness of competitive or-parallelism relies on the ability to cancel the slower threads once a winning thread completes (or throws an exception), as they would no longer be performing useful work. But canceling a thread may not be possible and, when possible, may not be as fast as desired if a thread is in a state where no interrupts are accepted. In the worst case scenario, some slower threads may run up to completion. Canceling a thread is tricky in most low-level multi-threading APIs, including POSIX threads. Thread cancellation usually implies clean-up operations, such as deallocating memory, releasing mutexes, flushing and possibly closing of opened streams.

In Prolog, thread cancellation must occur only at safe points of the underlying virtual machine. In the case of the ISO Prolog multi-threading standardization proposal, the specified safe points are blocking operations such as reading a term from a stream, waiting for a message to be posted to a message queue, or thread sleeping. These blocking operations allow interrupt vectors to be checked and signals, such as thread cancellation, to be processed. Therefore, the frequency of blocking operations determines how fast a thread can be canceled. Fortunately, to these minimal set of cancellation safe points, the compilers currently implementing the proposal often add a few more, e.g., whenever a predicate enters its *call port* in the traditional box model of Prolog execution. In practical terms this means that, although tricky in its low-level implementation details, it is possible to cancel a thread whenever necessary. The standardization proposal specifies a predicate, `thread_signal/2`, that allows signaling a thread to execute a goal as an interrupt. Logtalk uses this predicate for thread cancellation. Some current implementations of this predicate fail to protect the processing of a signal from interruption by other signals. Without a solution for suspending further signals while processing an interrupt, there is the danger in corner cases of leaving dangling, zombie threads when canceling a thread whose goal recursively creates other threads. This problem is expected to be solved in the short term.

3.5 Side-Effects and Dynamic Predicates

The subgoals in a competitive or-parallelism call may have side-effects that may clash if not accounted for. Two common examples are input/output operations

[6] For actual implementation details and programming examples, the reader is invited to consult the sources of the Logtalk compiler, which are freely available online [17].

and asserting and retracting clauses for dynamic predicates. To prevent conflicts, Logtalk and the Prolog compilers implementing the ISO Prolog multi-threading standardization proposal allow predicates to be declared synchronized, thread shared (the default), or thread local. Synchronized predicates are internally protected by a mutex, thus allowing for easy thread synchronization. Thread private dynamic predicates may be used to implement thread local dynamic state.

In Logtalk, predicates with side-effects can be declared as synchronized by using the `synchronized/1` directive. Calls to synchronized predicates are protected by a mutex, thus allowing for easy thread synchronization. For example:

```
:- synchronized(db_update/1).    % ensure thread synchronization
db_update(Update) :- ...         % predicate with side-effects
```

A dynamic predicate, however, cannot be declared as synchronized. In order to ensure atomic updates of a dynamic predicate, we need to declare as synchronized the predicate performing the update.

The standardization proposal specifies that, by default, dynamic predicates are shared by all threads. Thus, any thread may call and may assert and retract clauses for the dynamic predicate. The Prolog compilers that implement the standardization proposal allow dynamic predicates to be instead declared thread local.[7] Thread-local dynamic predicates are intended for maintaining thread-specific state or intermediate results of a computation. A thread local predicate directive tells the system that the predicate may be modified using the built-in assert and retract predicates during execution of the program but, unlike normal shared dynamic data, each thread has its own clause list for the predicate (this clause list is empty when a thread starts). Any existing predicate clauses are automatically reclaimed by the system when the thread terminates.

4 Experimental Results

We chose the *generalized water jug* problem to provide the reader with some experimental results for competitive or-parallelism. In this problem, two water jugs with p and q capacities are used to measure a certain amount of water. A third jug is used as an accumulator. When p and q are relatively prime, it is possible to measure any amount of water between 1 and $p + q$ [18]. This is a classical state-space search problem, which we can try to solve using blind or heuristic search methods. In this experiment, we used competitive or-parallelism (COP) to simultaneously explore depth-first (DF), breadth-first (BF), and hill-climbing (HC) search strategies. Depending on the values of p and q, the required number of steps to measure a given amount of water can range from two steps (in trivial cases) to several dozens of steps.[8] Moreover, the number of potential nodes to explore can range from a few nodes to hundreds of thousands of nodes.

[7] Due to syntactic differences between these Prolog compilers, directives for specifying both thread local and thread shared dynamic predicates are not yet specified in the standardization proposal.

[8] There is an upper bound to the number of steps necessary for measuring a certain amount of water [19]. In this simple experiment we ignored this upper bound.

Our experimental setup used Logtalk 2.33.0 with SWI-Prolog 5.6.59 64 bits as the back-end compiler on an Intel-based computer with four cores and 8 GB of RAM running Fedora Core 8 64 bits.[9] Table 1 shows the running times, in seconds, when 5-liter and 9-liter jugs were used to measure from 1 to 14 liters of water. It allows us to compare the running times of single-threaded DF, HC, and BF search strategies with the COP multi-threaded call where one thread is used for each individual search strategy. The results show the average of thirty runs. We highlight the fastest method for each measure. The last column shows the number of steps of the solution found by the competitive or-parallelism call. The maximum solution length was set to 14 steps for all strategies. The time taken to solve the problem ranges from 0.000907 to 8.324970 seconds. Hill climbing is the fastest search method in six of the experiments. Breadth-first comes next as the fastest search method in five experiments. Depth-first search is the fastest search method only in three experiments. Repeating these experiments with other capacities for the water jugs yields similar results.

Table 1. Measuring from 1 to 14 liters with 5-liter and 9-liter jugs

Liters	DF	HC	BF	COP	Overhead	Steps
1	26.373951	0.020089	**0.007044**	0.011005	0.003961	5
2	26.596118	12.907172	**8.036822**	8.324970	0.288148	11
3	20.522287	**0.000788**	1.412355	0.009158	0.008370	9
4	20.081001	**0.000241**	0.001437	0.002624	0.002383	3
5	**0.000040**	0.000240	0.000484	0.000907	0.000867	2
6	3.020864	0.216004	**0.064097**	0.098883	0.034786	7
7	3.048878	**0.001188**	68.249278	0.008507	0.007319	13
8	2.176739	**0.000598**	0.127328	0.007720	0.007122	7
9	2.096855	**0.000142**	0.000255	0.003799	0.003657	2
10	**0.000067**	0.009916	0.004774	0.001326	0.001295	4
11	**0.346695**	5.139203	0.587316	0.404988	0.058293	9
12	14.647219	**0.002118**	10.987607	0.010785	0.008667	14
13	0.880068	0.019464	**0.014308**	0.029652	0.015344	5
14	0.240348	0.003415	**0.002391**	0.010367	0.007976	4

These results show that the use of competitive or-parallelism allows us to quickly find a sequence of steps of acceptable length to solve different configurations of the water jug problem. Moreover, given that we do not know *a priori* which search method will be the fastest for a specific measuring problem, competitive or-parallelism is a better solution than any of the individual search methods.

The overhead of the competitive or-parallelism calls is due to the implicit thread and memory management, plus low-level Prolog synchronization tasks.

The asynchronous nature of thread cancellation implies a delay between the successful termination of a thread and the cancellation of the other competing threads. Moreover, the current Logtalk implementation only returns the result

[9] The experiments can be easily reproduced by the reader by running the query `logtalk_load(mtbatch(loader)), mtbatch(swi)::run(search, 30).`

of a competitive or-parallelism call after all spawned threads are terminated. An alternative implementation where cancelled threads are detached in order to avoid waiting for them to terminate and being joined proved tricky and unreliable due to the reuse of thread identifiers by the back-end Prolog compilers.

The initial thread data area sizes and the amount of memory that must be reclaimed when a thread terminates can play a significant role on observed overheads, depending on the Prolog compiler memory model and on the host operating system. Memory allocation and release is a possible contention point at the operating-system level, as testified by past and current work on optimized, multi-threading aware memory allocators. (see e.g. [20]).

Low-level SWI-Prolog synchronization tasks also contribute to the observed overheads. In the current SWI-Prolog version, dynamic predicates are mutex locked even when they are declared thread local (in this case collisions occur when accessing the shared data structures used by SWI-Prolog to find and update local predicate definitions). Logtalk uses dynamic predicates to represent the method lookup caches associated with dynamic binding. While in previous versions the lookup caches are thread shared, the current Logtalk release uses thread local lookup caches. This change had a small impact on performance in Linux but provided a noticeable performance boost on MacOS X. Table 2 shows the results for the dynamic predicate used for the main lookup cache when running the query `mtbatch(swi)::run(search, 20)` in both Linux and MacOS.

Table 2. Mutex locks and collisions

	Linux		**MacOS X**	
	Locks	Collisions	Locks	Collisions
Thread shared	1022796427	3470000	907725567	17045455
Thread local	512935818	846213	458574690	814574

Thus, by simply making the lookup caches thread local, we reduced the number of collisions by 75% in Linux and 94% in MacOS X. Although different hardware is used in each case, is worth noting that, with a thread shared lookup cache, the number of collisions in MacOS X is five times the number of collisions in Linux. This is in accordance with our experience with other multi-threading tests where the Linux implementation of POSIX threads consistently outperforms that of MacOS X (and also the emulation of POSIX threads in Windows).

We are optimizing our implementation in order to minimize the thread management overhead. There is also room for further optimizations on the Prolog implementations of core multi-threading support. Nevertheless, even with the current implementations, our experimental results are promising.

5 The Role of Tabling

In complex problems, such as the ones discussed in the previous section, some of the competing threads, even if not successful, may generate intermediate results useful to other threads. Thus, dynamic programming in general, and tabling [21,22] in particular, is expected to play an important role in effective problem solving when using competitive or-parallelism.

In multi-threading Prolog systems supporting tabling, tables may be either private or shared between threads. In the latter case, a table may be shared once completed or two or more threads may collaborate in filling it. For applications using competitive or-parallelism, the most interesting uses of tabling will likely require the use of shared tables.

While thread-private tables are relatively easy to implement, all other cases imply sharing a dynamic data structure between threads, with all the associated issues of locking, synchronization, and potential deadlock cases. Thus, despite the availability of both threads and tabling in Prolog compilers such as XSB, Yap, and recently Ciao [23], the implementation of these two features such that they work together seamlessly implies complex ties to one another and to the underlying Prolog virtual machine. Nevertheless, promising results are described in a recent PhD thesis [24] and currently implemented in XSB [25]. In the current Yap version, tabling and threads are incompatible features; users must chose one or the other when building Yap. Work is planned to make Yap threads and tabling compatible. Ciao features a higher-level implementation of tabling when compared with XSB and Yap, which requires minimal modifications to the compiler and the abstract machine. This tabling support, however, is not yet available in the current Ciao stable release [26]. It will be interesting to see if this higher-level implementation makes the use of tabled predicates and thread-shared tables easier to implement in a multi-threading environment. These Prolog implementations are expected to eventually provide robust integration of these two key features. Together with the expected increase on the number of cores per processor, we can foresee a programming environment that provides all the building blocks for taking full advantage of competitive or-parallelism.

6 Potential Application Areas

Competitive or-parallelism support is useful when we have several algorithms to perform some computation and we do not know *a priori* which algorithm will be successful or will provide the best performance. This pattern is common to several classes of problems in different application areas. Problems where optimal solutions are sought may also be targeted when optimality conditions or quality thresholds can be incorporated in the individual algorithms.[10]

Interesting applications usually involve solving problems whose computational complexity implies using heuristic approaches with suboptimal solutions. In these cases, each thread in a competitive or-parallelism call can tackle a different starting point, or apply a different heuristic, in order to find a solution that, even if not optimal, is considered good enough for practical purposes.

A good example are biclustering applications (see e.g [27,28]), which provide multiple opportunities for applying speculative threading approaches, such as

[10] The cost or quality of the solutions being constructed by each algorithm may also be shared between threads.

competitive or-parallelism. Most instances of the biclustering problem are NP-hard. As such, most algorithmic approaches presented to date are heuristic and thus not guaranteed to find optimal solutions [27]. Common application areas include biological data analysis, information retrieval and text mining, collaborative filtering, recommendation systems, target marketing and database research. Given the complexity of the biclustering problem, the most promising algorithmic approaches are *greedy iterative search* and *distribution parameter identification* [27]. Both are amenable to speculative threading formulations.

Greedy iterative search methods are characterized by aggressively looking for a solution by making locally optimal choices, hoping to quickly converge to a globally good solution [29]. These methods may make wrong decisions and miss good biclusters when trapped in suboptimal solutions. Finding a solution satisfying a quality threshold often implies several runs using different starting points and possibly different greedy search strategies. Therefore, we may speculatively try the same or several greedy algorithms, with the same or different starting points, hopefully leading to different solutions satisfying a given quality threshold. In this case, the returned solution will be the first solution found that satisfies the quality metric and not necessarily the best solution. Note that this is a characteristic of greedy search, irrespective of the use of speculative threading.

Distribution parameter identification approaches assume that biclusters were generated from an underlying statistical model. Models are assumed to be defined by a fixed statistical distribution, whose set of parameters may be inferred from data. Different learning algorithms can be used to identify the parameters more likely to have generated the data [30]. This may be accomplished by iteratively minimizing a certain criterion. In this context, we can speculatively try different algorithms to infer the statistical model given the same initialization parameters, try different initialization parameters for the same distribution (using the same or different algorithms), or even assume different statistical models.

With the increasing availability of powerful multi-core systems, the parallel use of both greedy search and distribution parameter identification in biclustering applications is a promising alternative to current biclustering algorithms. In this context, high-level concepts, such as competitive or-parallelism, can play an important role in making speculative threading applications common place.

7 Conclusions and Future Work

We presented the logic programming concept of thread-based competitive or-parallelism, resulting from combining key ideas of competitive or-parallelism, committed-choice nondeterminism, speculative threading, and declarative programming. This concept is fully supported by an implementation in Logtalk, an open-source object-oriented logic programing language. We provided a description of our implementation and discussed its semantic properties, complemented with a discussion on thread cancellation and computational performance issues. This concept is orthogonal to the object-oriented features of Logtalk and can be implemented in plain Prolog and in non-declarative programming languages supporting the necessary threading primitives.

Competitive and classical or-parallelism target different classes of problems. Both forms of or-parallelism can be useful in non-trivial problems and can be supported in the same programming language. Competitive or-parallelism provides fine-grained, explicit control at the goal level of the tasks that should be executed in parallel, while classical parallel systems make use of implicit parallelism with possible parallelization hints at the predicate level.

For small problems, the benefits of competitive or-parallelism may not outweigh its inherent overhead. For computationally hard problems, this overhead is expected to be negligible. Interesting problems are characterized by the existence of several algorithms and heuristics, operating in a large search-space. In this context, we discussed potential applications where competitive or-parallelism can be a useful tool for problem solving.

Meaningful experimental results, following from the application of competitive or-parallelism to real-world problems, require hardware that is becoming common place. Consumer and server-level computers containing from two to sixteen cores, running mainstream operating-systems, are readily available. Each processor generation is expected to increase the number of cores, broadening the class of problems that can be handled using speculative threading in general, and competitive or-parallelism in particular.

Most research on speculative threading focus on low-level support, such as processor architectures and compiler support for automatic parallelization. In contrast, competitive or-parallelism is a high-level concept, targeted to programmers of high-level languages. In the case of Logtalk, thread-based competitive or-parallelism is supported by a single and simple to use built-in meta-predicate.

We found that core Prolog support for multi-threading programming provides all the necessary support for implementing Logtalk parallelism features. From a pragmatic perspective, this is an important result as (i) it leads to a simple, high-level implementation of both competitive or-parallelism and independent and-parallelism [31] that translates to only a few hundred lines of Prolog source code; (ii) it ensures wide portability of our implementation (the programmer can choose between SWI-Prolog, XSB, or Yap as the back-end compiler for exploring Logtalk multi-threading features on POSIX and Windows operating-systems).

Ongoing work focuses on improving and expanding the Logtalk support for multi-threading programming. In particular, we are fine-tuning the Logtalk implementation and working closely with the Prolog developers in the specification and implementation of the ISO standardization proposal for Prolog multi-threading programming. Major goals are minimizing the implicit overhead of thread management and testing our implementation for robustness in corner cases such as exhaustion of virtual memory address space in 32 bits systems. Future work will include exploring the role of tabling in competitive or-parallelism, implementing a load-balancing mechanism, and applying competitive or-parallelism to field problems.

Authors' Contributions. PM is the developer of the Logtalk language; he implemented the thread-based competitive or-parallelism concept, wrote the original draft of this paper and worked on the experimental results. RR contributed with its knowledge on classical or-parallelism and tabling, helped with the comparison between the two concepts of or-parallelism, and made several contributions to the remaining sections of this paper. SM wrote the section on potential application areas; her current research on bioinformatics is one of the main motivations for this work. All authors read and approved the final manuscript.

Acknowledgments. We are grateful to Jan Wielemaker, Vítor Costa, Terrance Swift and Rui Marques for their groundwork implementing Prolog multi-threading core support and for helpful discussions on the subject of this paper.

A preliminary version of this work was published as a short paper in [32]. This paper provides additional implementation details, a detailed discussion of the experimental results, and additional sections on potential application areas and on the role of tabling on thread-based competitive or-parallelism. We thank the anonymous reviewers of our previous work for their helpful comments.

References

1. Gupta, G., Pontelli, E., Ali, K., Carlsson, M., Hermenegildo, M.V.: Parallel Execution of Prolog Programs: A Survey. ACM Transactions on Programming Languages and Systems 23, 472–602 (2001)
2. Ertel, W.: Performance Analysis of Competitive Or-Parallel Theorem Proving. Technical report fki-162-91, Technische Universität München (1991)
3. Shapiro, E.: The Family of Concurrent Logic Programming Languages. ACM Computing Surveys 21, 413–510 (1989)
4. González, A.: Speculative Threading: Creating New Methods of Thread-Level Parallelization. Technology@Intel Magazine (2005)
5. Moura, P.: (ISO/IEC DTR 13211–5:2007 Prolog Multi-threading Support), `http://logtalk.org/plstd/threads.pdf`
6. Moura, P.: Logtalk – Design of an Object-Oriented Logic Programming Language. PhD thesis, Department of Computer Science, University of Beira Interior (2003)
7. Ali, K., Karlsson, R.: The Muse Approach to OR-Parallel Prolog. International Journal of Parallel Programming 19, 129–162 (1990)
8. Rocha, R., Silva, F., Santos Costa, V.: YapOr: an Or-Parallel Prolog System Based on Environment Copying. In: Barahona, P., Alferes, J.J. (eds.) EPIA 1999. LNCS (LNAI), vol. 1695, pp. 178–192. Springer, Heidelberg (1999)
9. Lusk, E., Butler, R., Disz, T., Olson, R., Overbeek, R., Stevens, R., Warren, D.H.D., Calderwood, A., Szeredi, P., Haridi, S., Brand, P., Carlsson, M., Ciepielewski, A., Hausman, B.: The Aurora Or-Parallel Prolog System. In: International Conference on Fifth Generation Computer Systems, Institute for New Generation Computer Technology, pp. 819–830 (1988)
10. Calderwood, A., Szeredi, P.: Scheduling Or-parallelism in Aurora – the Manchester Scheduler. In: International Conference on Logic Programming, pp. 419–435. MIT Press, Cambridge (1989)
11. Ali, K., Karlsson, R.: Full Prolog and Scheduling OR-Parallelism in Muse. International Journal of Parallel Programming 19, 445–475 (1990)
12. Beaumont, A., Raman, S., Szeredi, P., Warren, D.H.D.: Flexible Scheduling of OR-Parallelism in Aurora: The Bristol Scheduler. In: Aarts, E.H.L., van Leeuwen, J., Rem, M. (eds.) PARLE 1991. LNCS, vol. 506, pp. 403–420. Springer, Heidelberg (1991)

13. Sindaha, R.: Branch-Level Scheduling in Aurora: The Dharma Scheduler. In: International Logic Programming Symposium, pp. 403–419. MIT Press, Cambridge (1993)
14. Ciepielewski, A.: Scheduling in Or-parallel Prolog Systems: Survey and Open Problems. International Journal of Parallel Programming 20, 421–451 (1991)
15. Ali, K., Karlsson, R.: Scheduling Speculative Work in MUSE and Performance Results. International Journal of Parallel Programming 21, 449–476 (1992)
16. Beaumont, A., Warren, D.H.D.: Scheduling Speculative Work in Or-Parallel Prolog Systems. In: International Conference on Logic Programming, pp. 135–149. MIT Press, Cambridge (1993)
17. Moura, P.: (Logtalk), `http://logtalk.org`
18. Pfaff, T.J., Tran, M.M.: The generalized jug problem. Journal of Recreational Mathematics 31, 100–103 (2003)
19. Boldi, P., Santini, M., Vigna, S.: Measuring with jugs. Theoretical Computer Science 282, 259–270 (2002)
20. Berger, E.D., Mckinley, K.S., Blumofe, R.D., Wilson, P.R.: Hoard: A scalable memory allocator for multithreaded applications. In: International Conference on Architectural Support for Programming Languages and Operating Systems, pp. 117–128 (2000)
21. Tamaki, H., Sato, T.: OLDT Resolution with Tabulation. In: Shapiro, E. (ed.) ICLP 1986. LNCS, vol. 225, pp. 84–98. Springer, Heidelberg (1986)
22. Chen, W., Warren, D.S.: Tabled Evaluation with Delaying for General Logic Programs. Journal of the ACM 43, 20–74 (1996)
23. Chico de Guzmán, P., Carro, M., Hermenegildo, M.V., Silva, C., Rocha, R.: An Improved Continuation Call-Based Implementation of Tabling. In: Hudak, P., Warren, D.S. (eds.) PADL 2008. LNCS, vol. 4902, pp. 197–213. Springer, Heidelberg (2008)
24. Marques, R.: Concurrent Tabling: Algorithms and Implementation. PhD thesis, Department of Computer Science, New University of Lisbon (2007)
25. Marques, R., Swift, T., Cunha, J.: Extending tabled logic programming with multithreading: A systems perspective (2008), `http://www.cs.sunysb.edu/~tswift`
26. Bueno, F., Cabeza, D., Carro, M., Hermenegildo, M.V., López, P., Puebla, G.: (Ciao Prolog System Manual), `http://clip.dia.fi.upm.es/Software/Ciao`
27. Madeira, S.C., Oliveira, A.L.: Biclustering algorithms for biological data analysis: a survey. IEEE/ACM Transactions on Computational Biology and Bioinformatics 1, 24–45 (2004)
28. Mechelen, I.V., Bock, H.H., Boeck, P.D.: Two-mode clustering methods: a structured overview. Statistical Methods in Medical Research 13, 979–981 (2004)
29. Cormen, T.H., Leiserson, C.E., Rivest, R.L., Stein, C.: Introduction to Algorithms, 2nd edn. The MIT Electrical Engineering and Computer Science Series. MIT Press, Cambridge (2001)
30. Hastie, T., Tibshirani, R., Friedman, J.: The Elements of Statistical Learning. Data Mining, Inference and Prediction. Springer Series in Statistics (2001)
31. Moura, P., Crocker, P., Nunes, P.: High-Level Multi-threading Programming in Logtalk. In: Hudak, P., Warren, D.S. (eds.) PADL 2008. LNCS, vol. 4902, pp. 265–281. Springer, Heidelberg (2008)
32. Moura, P., Rocha, R., Madeira, S.C.: Thread-Based Competitive Or-Parallelism. In: Garcia de la Banda, M., Pontelli, E. (eds.) ICLP 2008. LNCS, vol. 5366, pp. 713–717. Springer, Heidelberg (2008)

Implementing Thread Cancellation in Multithreaded Prolog Systems

Atef Suleiman and John Miller

School of Electrical Engineering and Computer Science
Washington State University (Tri-Cities)
West 201B, Richland, WA 99354-2125, USA
{asuleiman,jhmiller}@tricity.wsu.edu

Abstract. The Prolog primitive `thread_cancel/1`, which simply cancels a thread as recommended in ISO/IEC DTR 13211-5:2007, is conspicuously absent in well-maintained, widely used multithreaded Prolog systems. The ability to cancel a thread is useful for application development and is critical to Prolog embeddability. The difficulty of cancelling a thread is due to the instant mapping of Prolog multithreading primitives to the native-machine thread methods. This paper reports on an attempt to implement thread cancellation using self-blocking threads. A thread blocks at the same safe execution point where the state of the underlying virtual machine is defined. A blocked thread awaits a notification to resume or terminate. A resumed thread may be redirected to self-block by a blocking primitive. Experimental results based on a prototype implementation show that using self-blocking threads not only simplifies the implementation of thread cancellation but also improves the performance of message-passing primitives.

Keywords: Prolog, concurrency, threads.

1 Introduction

Explicit expressions of concurrency advance Prolog's standing as a practical programming language capable of exploiting modern multiprocessor computers. Prolog programs consist largely of static code, knowledge expressed as facts and rules, accessible to any number of execution threads running concurrently, in parallel or otherwise. Additionally, due to their declarative and high-level nature, Prolog programs retain and expose opportunities for parallel execution unparalleled in conventional programming languages. To facilitate expressions of concurrency, a thread model is proposed in ISO/IEC DTR 13211-5:2007 [1], variants of which are implemented in well-maintained, widely used Prolog systems, such as Ciao [2], SWI-Prolog [3], XSB [4], Yap [5] and others. The model includes a set of low-level primitives for thread creation, synchronization and communication. In addition to sharing the static database on a read-only basis,

A. Gill and T. Swift (Eds.): PADL 2009, LNCS 5418, pp. 122–136, 2009.

Prolog threads may modify and share the dynamic database in a mutually exclusive manner. Recent research in definition and implementation of high-level parallelism primitives shows that a relevant speedup is obtainable by exploiting parallelism expressly at the source-language level [6,7]. As this research activity illustrates, there are situations in which a need to cancel a thread arises after the thread has already started.

The need for cancelling a thread is illustrated by the high-level primitive `threaded/1` defined in [6]. Given a conjunction of well-formed goals, this primitive simulates an and-parallel operator executing the goals concurrently using a dedicated thread for each goal. The primitive succeeds if all goals succeed; otherwise, if a goal fails or raises an exception, it fails. Hence, once a thread at some point returns a failure result for a goal it has executed, the remaining threads should be cancelled since they serve no purpose at that point. A similar need for cancelling a thread arises when a threaded goal executes successfully as part of a deterministic disjunction executing concurrently. These and other practical examples, such as an asynchronously generated cancel condition initiated by a user request to exit a running program, show that thread cancellability is a desirable method of Prolog threads.

The option of cancelling a Prolog thread is provided by the primitive `thread_cancel/1`, described in [1] as follows:

> *`thread_cancel/1` cancels a thread. Any mutexes held by the thread shall be automatically released. The main Prolog thread cannot be cancelled. Other than this, any thread can cancel any other thread. It is expected that all the resources consumed by the thread be released upon thread cancellation.*

Prolog systems, however, implement `thread_cancel/1` in a variable way. XSB shares the responsibility for cancelling a thread with the programmer, whereas SWI-Prolog defers the implementation of `thread_cancel/1` altogether to the programmer, with the insight that the primitive is best implemented depending on the thread model of the problem at hand. In Ciao, the outcome of cancelling a thread is partly defined and depends wholly on the state of the target thread. The implementation of `thread_cancel/1` in these and other otherwise-compliant Prolog systems suggests that the above description for `thread_cancel/1` may be easier said than done.

The difficulty of cancelling a thread is due to blocking functions. Standard library functions, such as `read`, `accept`, `wait`, are subject to blocking as they are dependent on external events, e.g., the availability of input, establishment of a network connection, occurrence of a specified event. A thread attempting to cancel a blocked thread must be able to interact with the function inside which the target thread is blocked. The interaction may be initiated by either the cancelling thread, by means of signalling, or the cancelled thread, by means of polling. The latter method is adapted by POSIX threads [8], on which the majority of Prolog systems is based.

Also referred to as *Pthreads*, POSIX threads is a set of C functions for managing threads, mutual exclusion and condition variables.[1] A Prolog thread is directly mapped to a POSIX thread, running a Prolog engine within a multi-engined Prolog virtual machine. Cancelling a Prolog thread in the context of POSIX threads is a well-defined process insofar as the semantics of the latter is concerned.

POSIX specifies a subset of blocking functions as *cancellation points*. A blocking function designated as cancellation-point is expected to call an internal or external Pthreads function, e.g., `pthread_testcancel`, at sufficient intervals and be prepared for the possibility that the function may not return due to the thread being cancelled. Consequently, any function calling a cancellation-point function must be equally prepared to give up control without further notice. A function prepares for the possible loss of control by registering thread-specific cleanup functions to be executed in the event of thread cancellation. The process of cancelling a Prolog thread may, thus, proceed as follows. Given a proper accounting of consumed resources using `pthread_cleanup_push` and `pthread_cleanup_pop` within every lexical scope containing a cancellation point, a thread cancels another thread asynchronously by calling `pthread_cancel`, which flags the target thread as cancelled and returns immediately. If the target thread is active, the Prolog engine traps the thread at a safe execution point and destroys it by exiting the thread startup function. Otherwise, if the target thread is blocked or is to block, Pthreads takes over control at the next cancellation point and begins the actual cancellation process by calling the thread cleanup functions in a last-in-first-out order. Apart from excluding certain blocking functions, most notably `pthread_mutex_lock`, from the standard list of cancellation points, the process of cancelling a POSIX thread seems transparent enough to support an orderly cancellation of the adjoining Prolog thread.

However, as evident by the lack of support for `thread_cancel/1` in well-maintained Prolog systems, the direct mapping approach to thread cancellation faces implementation issues related, in part, to Prolog signals and garbage collection. As recommended in [1], a Prolog thread should be able to signal another thread to execute a goal as a soft interrupt at safe points, including, for example, the point at which a Prolog thread is suspended waiting for a message from a message queue. At that point, neither POSIX signals nor Pthreads cancellation points provide a mechanism for processing Prolog signals. While a Prolog thread can process a POSIX signal, thus receive a Prolog signal, it can not execute the signal, while the thread is blocked by a cancellation-point function. Similarly, memory and atom garbage collection algorithms require a high level of cooperation among Prolog threads incompatible with low-level mapping of Prolog threads to Pthreads. For example, when an active Prolog thread triggers atom garbage-collection, all other threads must suspend and produce their list of atoms. Here, again, a Prolog thread blocked by a cancellation-point function can not be guaranteed to heed a garbage-collection interrupt in any specifiable

[1] Condition variables are synchronization objects that allow threads to wait for certain events (conditions) to occur.

manner. In order to effect a working level of cooperation among Prolog threads, a high-level mapping of Prolog threads to Pthreads is required.

This paper reports on an attempt to implement thread cancellation using self-blocking threads. A self-blocking thread blocks at the same safe execution point where the state of the underlying Prolog engine is defined. A blocked thread awaits a notification to resume or terminate. A resumed thread may be reinstructed to self-block by a blocking primitive. Experimental results based on a proof-of-concept implementation show that using self-blocking threads is a viable approach for creating Prolog threads with the provision of facilitating their cancellation at any point during execution.

Section 2 presents the approach of self-blocking threads in the context of enabling synchronous cancellation of active and blocked threads. Section 3 includes implementation notes related to select blocking primitives. Section 4 presents the results of a performance comparison between self-blocking and directly-mapped threads. Section 5 briefly describes existing implementations of `thread_cancel/1`. Section 6 concludes with a summary of the cost-benefits of self-blocking threads.

2 An Execution Engine and Self-block

Cancelling an active thread is a straightforward task. The thread is simply tagged as cancelled and the actual cancellation takes place upon the thread reaching a safe execution point. Cancelling a blocked thread, on the other hand, is a complex task requiring the consent and cooperation of the blocking function. Figure 1(a) shows a conceptual depiction of active and blocked threads inside the execution engine of a Prolog virtual machine. The difficulty of cancelling a thread lies with those threads that are blocked as a result of calling blocking functions. Figure 1(b) depicts the same threads in a new formation: active threads continue to be active; blocked threads are blocked on their own accord, using a self-blocking mechanism. The blocking functions are replaced by their cooperative counterparts, which are asynchronous, persistent and capable of instructing threads to block (suspend) or unblock (resume) as it may be warranted during execution. The task of cancelling a blocked thread is specifiable independent of the cancel method of the underlying native thread.

A blocking function directs a calling thread to self-block by returning a code indicating a *pending result*, based on which the thread self-blocks (suspends) waiting to be resumed or cancelled. A blocked thread is resumed by notifying the thread to continue execution from the point at which it was suspended, and is cancelled by notifying the thread to exit using the same control path used by an active thread exiting normally. A blocked thread may also be notified to perform atom-garbage collection or execute a goal as an interrupt. Multiple notifications are serialized using mutual exclusion. A notifying thread acquires exclusive control of the target thread prior to notification, with the caveat that control is granted only if the thread is suspended. A thread is suspended using the interrupt-vector mechanism commonly used in single-threaded systems to break into the top-level loop.

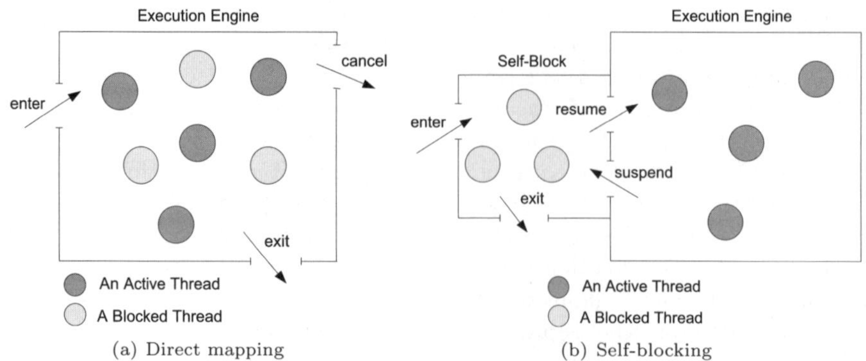

(a) Direct mapping (b) Self-blocking

Fig. 1. Graphical depiction of active and blocked threads

2.1 Implementing the Self-block

The self-block is implemented using a standard synchronization composite of a *mutex*, *condition variable* and *counter*. Each thread is associated with a composite instance, which is initialized upon thread creation *in sync* with the creating thread. A blocking thread atomically unlocks the mutex and waits for the condition variable to be signalled by another thread. A signalling thread locks the mutex momentarily and signals the condition variable of the target thread. A blocked thread whose condition variable has been signalled re-locks its mutex, increments the counter and resumes execution. In addition to its standard role of preventing a race condition, the mutex is used to query the status of a thread. A thread queries the status of another thread by attempting to lock its mutex. If the attempt is successful, the thread is idle; otherwise, it is running. The counter is intended to be used in a test-yield loop to compel a signalled thread to assume ownership of its mutex.

The start-up algorithm for self-blocking threads is outlined in Figure 2. The algorithm takes a Prolog engine as input and proceeds as follows. First, it initializes a synchronization composite and swaps a reference to it with that of the temporary composite initialized by the creating thread for synchronizing with the current, newly created, thread (Lines 1-3). Second, it momentarily locks the mutex and signals the condition variable of the creating thread so that the latter may proceed (Line 4). Third, the algorithm iteratively suspends and resumes calling the execution engine for as often as the latter indicates a pending result (Lines 6-10). Lastly, the synchronization composite is destroyed and the native thread of control exits detaching from the adjoining Prolog engine.

2.2 Implementing `thread_cancel/1`

Cancelling a thread involves first suspending the thread, then destroying it. Since suspending and destroying a thread are well-defined tasks, they are implemented by the predicates `thread_suspend/1` and `thread_destroy/1`. With a negligible risk of raising an unintended exception, `thread_cancel/1` is defined as follows:

```
thread_cancel(Thread) :-
    thread_suspend(Thread),
    thread_destroy(Thread).
```

The algorithms for implementing *thread_suspend* and *thread_destroy* are listed in Figure 3 and 4, respectively. Both algorithms begin by decoding the target thread *thread* from the current actual arguments of the calling thread *self*. It is assumed that access to shared resources, such as the list of existing threads *list_of_threads*, is serialized using a locking mechanism.

```
Input : A Prolog engine self
initialize (composite = {mutex,condition,counter})
lock (mutex)
swap (self.composite, composite)
lock (mutex), signal (condition), unlock (mutex)
composite ← self.composite
do
  | wait (condition, mutex)
  | counter ← counter + 1
  | execution_engine (self)
while self.result is a pending result
terminate (composite)
```

Fig. 2. Start-up algorithm of self-blocking threads

```
thread ← decode (self,1)
lock (thread_resource)
if thread ∉ list_of_threads then
    unlock (thread_resource)
    throw existence_error
end
if thread.reference > 0 then
    unlock (thread_resource)
    throw permission_error
end
if thread = self then
    unlock (thread_resource)
    thread.signal ← thread.signal ∨
    suspend_signal
    return signal_result
end
thread.reference ← thread.reference + 1
unlock (thread_resource)
thread.signal ← thread.signal ∨
suspend_signal
lock (thread.mutex)
if thread.result ≠ signal_result then
    thread.signal ← thread.signal ∧
    ¬suspend_signal
end
unlock (thread.mutex)
lock (thread_resource)
thread.reference ← thread.reference − 1
unlock (thread_resource)
goto next_instruction
```

Fig. 3. *thread_suspend* algorithm

```
thread ← decode (self,1)
lock (thread_resource)
if thread ∉ list_of_threads then
    unlock (thread_resource)
    throw existence_error
end
if thread = self ∨ thread.reference ≠ 0
∨ ¬ trylock(thread.mutex) then
    unlock (thread_resource)
    throw permission_error
end
destroy (thread)
unlock (thread_resource)
goto next_instruction
```

Fig. 4. *thread_destroy* algorithm

The algorithm for *thread_suspend* starts by locking the list of existing threads and performing a series of tests, including whether the target thread is non-existent (Lines 3-6), referenced by other threads (Lines 7-10) or itself the calling thread (Lines 11-14), in which cases it throws an appropriate error-term or returns a pending result; otherwise, it increments the reference counter of the target thread and unlocks the list of existing threads (Lines 15-16). Next, the algorithm suspends the target thread by first setting its interrupt vector, then locking its mutex momentarily (Lines 17-22). Since it is possible that the target thread suspends for a reason other than having been interrupted, the thread interrupt vector is reset based on the return result. Lastly, the algorithm decrements the reference counter of the target thread and continues execution with the following instruction (Lines 23-26). Chances are that the next instruction to be executed corresponds to *thread_destroy*. In a like manner, *thread_destroy* algorithm destroys a target thread, provided the thread exists, is idle, different from the calling thread and unreferenced by any other threads.

3 Implementing Thread-Blocking Predicates

Blocking predicates, be they built-in or user-defined, i.e., foreign, block by instructing the calling thread to self-block. For Prolog systems that provide a foreign-language interface, blocking foreign code communicates its blocking instructions by calling an appropriate interface function. The following are implementation notes related to select blocking predicates.

`get_code(+Stream, ?Code)` gets the character code of a single character from the (non-standard) input stream *Stream* and unifies it with the term *Code*. The predicate behaves like the standard built-in `get_code/2`, except that if the stream position of *Stream* is *end-of-stream* and *eof_action(suspend)* is a property of *Stream*, then the calling thread suspends, with the expectation that the foreign module that created *Stream* (e.g., an embedding application or shared library) will call an appropriate interface function to resume the calling thread when new characters become available.

`thread_get_message(+Queue, ?Term)` searches the message queue *Queue* for a term unifiable with the term *Term*. If a term is found, the term is unified with *Term* and deleted from *Queue*. Otherwise, if a term is not found, the calling thread is added to a waiting list associated with *Queue* and instructed to block (suspend). The search, deletion and addition are performed in a mutually exclusive manner.

`thread_send_message(+Queue, @Term)` searches the waiting list of the message queue *Queue* for a thread whose receiving term is unifiable with the term *Term*. If a thread is found, then the thread is deleted from the waiting list, the receiving term is unified with *Term*, and the thread is instructed to unblock (resume). Otherwise, if a receiving thread is not found, *Term* is added to *Queue*. The search, deletion and addition are performed in a mutually exclusive manner.

`mutex_lock(+Mutex)` acquires the Prolog mutex *Mutex* blocking if necessary. If *Mutex* is already acquired by a thread other than the calling thread, then the calling thread is added to a waiting list associated with *Mutex* and instructed to suspend. If Mutex is previously acquired by the calling thread, then the recursion counter of *Mutex* is incremented. Otherwise, if *Mutex* is free, the calling thread acquires *Mutex*. The conditionals and corresponding actions are performed in a mutually exclusive manner.

`mutex_unlock(+Mutex)` releases the Prolog mutex *Mutex*. If *Mutex* is acquired by the calling thread and the recursion counter of *Mutex* is greater than zero, then the recursion counter is decremented. If *Mutex* is acquired by the calling thread and the recursion counter of *Mutex* is zero, then *Mutex* is first released, then acquired by the first thread, if any, on the waiting list of *Mutex* and the thread is instructed to resume. The conditionals and corresponding actions are performed in a mutually exclusive manner.

`sleep(+Interval)` suspends execution of the calling thread for the interval *Interval*. If *Interval* is an integer greater than zero, then the calling thread *Self* is suspended immediately and resumed after *Interval* is elapsed as follows. If an alarm is already set for a thread *Thread* and is expected to set off after interval $Interval_{thread}$ is elapsed, and $Interval > Interval_{thread}$, then the pair ($Self$, $Interval$ - $Interval_{thread}$) is inserted into list *List*, containing ordered pairs of alarms to be set and threads to be resumed. Otherwise, if $Interval < Interval_{thread}$, then the alarm is cancelled, a new alarm is created to set off after *Interval* is elapsed, and the pair ($Thread$, $Interval_{thread}$ - $Interval$) is inserted into *List*. The insertion and cancellation are performed in a mutually exclusive manner. The alarm is a special thread that sleeps synchronously for and on behalf of the intervals and threads in *List*.

4 Performance Evaluation

A prototype Prolog implementation was developed to assess the performance of self-blocking threads on two popular operating systems: Linux and Windows. The prototype is a simple compiler and emulator comparable in performance to SWI-Prolog [3]. A select number of multithreading primitives were implemented using the self-blocking method, as described in Section 3, and the direct mapping method, as implemented in SWI-Prolog. The method in effect is determined at build time using conditional compilation. Three performance parameters were measured: thread-creation time, message-passing time and synchronization time. The latter parameters were also measured using SWI-Prolog. All measurements were obtained by averaging ten runs per input per program. The computing environment is comprised of a single computer, equipped with Intel Core 2 Quad processor (2.5GHz), 3GB RAM (800MHz), dual-bootable with Linux Debian version 4.0 and Windows Vista (32-bit).

It should be noted that although both Linux and Windows use one-to-one mapping between user threads and kernel threads, Linux threads appear to be considerably more lightweight than Windows threads, possibly due in part to the Windowing system of Windows being an integral part of Windows kernel. The objective of this evaluation is to compare the performance of self-blocking threads to that of directly mapped threads. A thread performance comparison between Linux and Windows is outside the scope of this paper, let alone the interests of its authors.

4.1 Thread Creation

As described in Section 2.1, the procedure for creating a self-blocking thread requires that the calling thread blocks until the newly created thread initializes its self-blocking mechanism. The thread-creation time parameter is intended to quantify the overhead incurred by self-blocking threads during thread creation.

The execution time of thread creation of self-blocking and directly mapped threads was measured directly using two simple programs written in C. The first program measures the execution time of thread creation of directly mapped threads. It trivially creates a variable number of threads by calling the function `pthread_create`, tracking the wall time elapsed using the function `clock`. The second program measures the execution time of thread creation of self-blocking threads. It has the structure of the first program except that the call to `pthread_create` is embedded in a new function responsible for synchronizing the calling thread with the thread to be created. The new function initializes a temporary synchronization composite comprised of a mutex and condition variable, and calls `pthread_create`, passing a reference to the composite. It then calls `pthread_cond_wait` and blocks waiting for the composite to be signalled by the newly created thread. Meanwhile, the new thread first initializes its self-blocking mechanism, then signals the composite of the calling thread so that the latter may proceed.

As shown in Table 1, self-blocking threads are more expensive to create than directly mapped threads. The average execution time of thread creation of a self-blocking thread is about twice that of a directly mapped thread on both Linux and Windows. On Linux, the execution time of thread creation increases as the number of threads increases, approaching a measurable value when the number of threads equals or exceeds $1,000$. On Windows, the execution time of thread creation is stable, around 200 μs per self-blocking thread and 100 μs per directly mapped thread, regardless of the number of threads.[2]

4.2 Message Passing

The message-passing time parameter was first measured for the case of a single sender/receiver, where neither implementation method has an apparent advantage over the other. Here, passing a message involves sending the message and waking up the receiving thread. The time measurements were obtained using

[2] On Windows, according to spawn-time measurement results obtained from Prototype and SWI-Prolog, the execution time of POSIX thread creation is the dominant component of the execution time of Prolog thread creation.

Table 1. Comparison of average execution time of thread creation (*μs per thread*)

# of threads	Linux		Windows	
	Direct mapping	Self-blocking	Direct mapping	Self-blocking
100	0	0	107	205
200	0	0	106	207
500	0	0	106	206
1000	2	6	107	205
2000	7	12	106	204
4000	10	15	106	204

the program described in [9]. The program involves passing a message between N threads M times. The threads are linked in a ring structure. The message is an integer specifying the number of times the message is to be passed. Upon receiving the integer-message, a thread decrements the integer and passes it to the next thread. The message passing between threads continues until the integer becomes less than zero, at which point a thread simply exits. The program is listed in Figure 5. The message-passing time measurements were estimated for select numbers of threads performing message passing $1,000,000$ times. The results are presented in Table 2.[3]

```
start(N, M) :-
    N1 is N - 1,
    thread_self(Thread),
    setup(N1, Thread, NextThread),
    thread_send_message(NextThread, M),
    catch(process(NextThread), _, true).

process(Thread) :-
    repeat,
        thread_get_message(M),
        M1 is M - 1,
        thread_send_message(Thread, M1),
        M1 < 0,
    !.

setup(0, Thread, Thread) :- !.
setup(N, Thread, NextThread) :-
  Goal = process(Thread),
  thread_create(Goal, NewThread, [detached(true)]),
  N1 is N - 1,
  setup(N1, NewThread, NextThread).
```

Fig. 5. Program for measuring simple message-passing time

Overall, the performance of self-blocking threads and directly mapped threads are comparable on both Linux and Windows. On a closer examination, however, the self-blocking approach is consistently, albeit slightly, faster than the direct mapping approach as implemented in both the prototype and SWI-Prolog. The number of threads that can be created in SWI-Prolog is limited to less than 100 threads, thus the time measurements corresponding to numbers of threads equal or exceeding 100 are unobtainable. The simple message-passing time is relatively stable, around 4 *μs* on Linux, 12 *μs* on Windows, per message, for a range of 10

[3] For assurance and sheer curiosity, the time measurements of Java threads were also obtained and presented. On Linux, Java threads perform simple message passing twice as fast as Prolog threads using either approach. The Java speedup is likely due to Prolog's need to validate, in a mutually exclusive manner, the existence of a thread prior to accessing its message queue. The question as to why Java threads were unable to maintain a similar speedup factor on Windows is outstanding.

Table 2. Comparison of average execution time of threads performing simple message-passing (μs *per message*)

(a) Average execution time on Linux

# of threads	self-blocking	direct mapping	SWI-Prolog 5.6.61	Java 1.6.0_06
10	5.86	5.90	5.99	3.03
20	4.36	5.26	4.73	2.94
40	4.26	4.78	4.58	2.91
80	4.02	4.53	4.94	3.21
100	4.15	4.38	–	3.24
200	4.12	4.38	–	3.35

(b) Average execution time on Windows

# of threads	self-blocking	direct mapping	SWI-Prolog 5.6.61	Java 1.6.0_06
10	11.75	13.21	14.54	11.75
20	11.95	12.20	13.71	11.75
40	11.95	12.73	13.29	11.22
80	11.95	12.48	13.38	11.26
100	12.04	12.83	–	11.39
200	12.78	13.51	–	11.39

to 400 threads. However, this parameter is likely to increase as the number of threads increases due in part to cache exhaustion due, in turn, to the uncommon memory requirements of Prolog threads.

The message-passing time parameter was, second, measured for the case of multiple senders/receivers, where self-blocking threads have a decisive advantage over directly-mapped threads. Here, message passing may involve a series of time-consuming operations, including adding (copying) a sender's message to a message queue, searching a list of waiting receivers for one whose skeletal message matches a newly added message, searching a message queue for a message matching a receiver's skeletal message, waking up potential receivers or just a matching receiver, and adding a new receiver to a list of waiting receivers.

The classic concurrency problem of the dining philosophers was used to illustrate the speed advantage of self-blocking threads in programs that require extensive message passing. The solution found in [10] was adapted to obtain wall time measurements for a variable number of philosophers. The measurements are depicted graphically in Figure 6.

As expected, self-blocking threads outperform directly mapped threads, by a factor of 2 on Linux and by an order of magnitude on Windows. The source of the speedup is transparent. In the self-blocking approach, a new sender signals at most one potential receiver, whereas in the direct-mapping approach, the sender must signal all waiting receivers, even though only one of which might succeed in getting the sender's message while the other receivers will attempt in vain to unify their skeletal messages with the old messages of previous senders. In addition to performing needless unification, the majority of receivers effects needless task-switches performed by the operating system at the behest of unassuming senders.

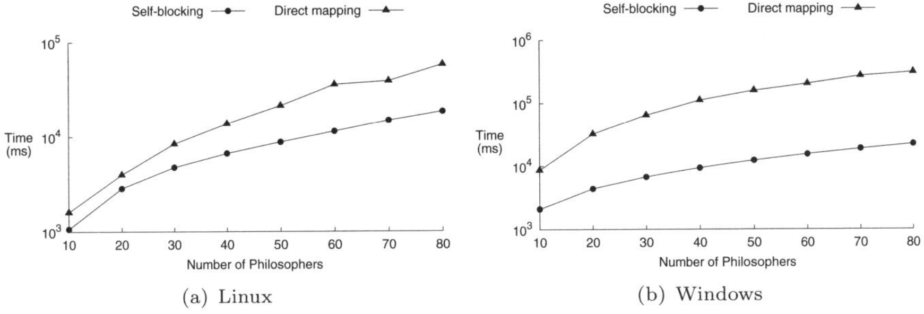

(a) Linux (b) Windows

Fig. 6. The Dining Philosophers benchmark (10,000 eat-think cycle per philosopher)

4.3 Synchronization

The synchronization time parameter was measured using a simple program, which creates a variable number of threads, each of which updates a shared resource 10,000 times. Mutual exclusion is achieved using a global mutex and the synchronization primitives `mutex_lock/1` and `mutex_unlock/1`. The average execution time per mutual exclusion was estimated by subtracting the wall time required to execute an equal number of updates sequentially. The results are presented in Table 3.

The performance of self-blocking and directly mapped threads in programs that require extensive synchronization varies depending on the implementation of Prolog mutex. For implementations potentially compliant with [1], self-blocking threads compare favorably to directly mapped threads on Linux. On Windows, the former (self-blocking) threads outperform the latter threads by a factor as high as 1.7. Moreover, on Windows, the prototype's compliant implementation

Table 3. Comparison of average execution time of threads updating a shared resource (*μs per mutual exclusion*)

(a) Average execution time on Linux

# of threads	self-blocking	direct mapping (compliant)	direct mapping (incompliant)	SWI-Prolog 5.6.61
10	7.53	7.97	0.56	0.86
20	7.90	8.01	0.75	0.95
40	7.47	8.52	0.91	1.02
80	7.53	8.70	0.96	1.08
100	6.88	8.78	0.99	–
200	7.89	8.93	1.01	–

(b) Average execution time on Windows

# of threads	self-blocking	direct mapping (compliant)	direct mapping (incompliant)	SWI-Prolog 5.6.61
10	11.06	16.10	1.53	11.31
20	10.90	17.04	1.49	11.91
40	10.46	17.37	1.51	12.52
80	10.89	17.39	1.49	12.49
100	10.57	17.52	1.49	–
200	10.75	18.18	1.48	–

using self-blocking threads outperforms SWI-Prolog incompliant implementation using directly mapped threads. The criteria for compliance, for the purpose of this comparison, is that a Prolog mutex is indestructible while it is in use, e.g., one or more threads are blocked attempting to acquire the mutex. As shown in Table 3, lifting this requirement of indestructibility can result in a synchronization speed characteristic of low-level programming languages, however, to the negation of the premise of using self-blocking threads, which is to provide a safe and user-friendly Prolog multithreaded environment.

5 Related Work

While Prolog systems agree on how to create threads, they differ widely on how to cancel them.

SWI-Prolog [3] and Yap [5] defer the implementation of `thread_cancel/1` to the programmer with the insight that thread cancellation is best implemented based on the thread model of the application at hand. In the boss/worker thread model, for example, `thread_cancel/1` may be implemented by communicating to the thread to be cancelled a specially coded message instructing the thread to exit or abort. In a computation-intensive application, for another example, cancelling a thread may be achieved by signalling the thread to execute a goal quoting a control primitive, such as `thread_exit(cancelled)`.

In XSB [4], thread cancelation is a joint responsibility of the system and the application. The latter initiates the process of canceling a thread by calling `thread_cancel/1`, giving the thread to be cancelled as an argument. For its part, XSB internally flags the given thread as canceled and waits for the thread execution to reach a call or execute port, at which point XSB throws a cancelation error ending its role in the thread cancelation process. The target thread, henceforth, is expected to catch the error, release any allocated resources and exit voluntarily.

Ciao [2] provides a primitive named `eng_kill/1`, which attempts to cancel the thread associated with a given goal identifier. The attempt may succeed, fail, block or render the system in an unstable state, depending on whether, irrespectively, the thread to be cancelled is trappable at a standard port, the goal identifier is valid, the thread is blocked by a system call, or other noted, however unspecified, situations.

Other Prolog systems, such as BinProlog and Qu-Prolog, provide other variations on the theme of thread cancellation. However, the primitives tasked with cancelling a thread are summarily documented. Attempts to learn of the internals of these primitives, through haphazard queries written with ill intents, showed that thread cancellation in these systems is problematic.

6 Conclusion

This paper presented an experimental implementation approach for creating Prolog threads with the provision of facilitating their destruction at any point during execution. The approach is based on self-blocking threads, a common implementation technique for managing thread interactions in multithreaded applications. The ability to cancel a thread safely and synchronously improves Prolog's standing as a useful programming language, capable of expressing variable solutions to complex concurrent problems for prototyping or production purposes. Additionally, it preserves the integrity of Prolog's traditional top-level loop program and improves Prolog's embeddability into multi-paradigm, multi-language applications.

Thread cancellability with self-blocking threads increases the complexity of system and extension development, as might be expected of features of high-level programming languages. Standard library functions, such as `seek`, `sleep`, `select`, may not be used directly to implement built-in and library predicates. Instead, these functions are reemployed within newly designed, more complex functions which are reentrant, persistent, asynchronous and able to communicate intermediate results. This added complexity may be viewed as a fair price, paid at the right layer in the right currency, C, in exchange for preserving Prolog's dictum of combining simplicity and power at the user level.

Although native in their own right, self-blocking threads exhibit the programmability of green threads,[4] as they are at most one standard port away from relinquishing processor control and one wake-up call from regaining it. As such, they are fit to yield the main benefits of both native and green multithreaded environments, namely parallelism and portability. Used in this capacity, the self-blocking approach constitutes a cost-efficient compromise between using native preemptive threads [11] and nonnative cooperative threads [12].

The performance of self-blocking threads compares favorably to that of directly mapped threads, despite that the time cost of creating a self-blocking thread is twice that of a directly mapped thread, due to the initial cost of the former's self-blocking mechanism. Self-blocking threads support a wide range of algorithms for implementing message passing, a primary means of thread communication and synchronization [1]. For programs that require extensive message passing, experimental results showed that execution times vary by up to an order of magnitude, depending on the operating system and the algorithm used for matching the messages of senders and receivers. Given that directly mapped threads can hardly do without a message queue and message passing, the run time advantage of self-blocking threads should offset the initial cost of their self-blocking mechanisms.

The utility of self-blocking threads extends beyond simplifying thread cancellation to enabling the implementation of high-level features, such as the separation of thread creation and execution, the implementation of suspend and resume primitives, backtracking, multiple executions and execution modes. The ability to separate thread creation from execution, proposed in passing in [13], facilitates the implementation of a high level API, which subsumes the one recommended in [1], which in turn facilitates the implementation of yet higher-level

[4] Green threads are threads that are scheduled by a virtual machine instead of natively by the underlying operating system.

parallel operators analogous to those introduced in [6] and [7]. Experiments are being conducted to evaluate the merits of new multithreading primitives in terms of simplicity and expressiveness, as well as performance.

Acknowledgments. The authors thank Jan Wielemaker and Richard O'Keefe for their insightful, differing views. This research was supported by the Office of Science (BER), U.S. Department of Energy, Grant No. DE-FG02-05ER64105.

References

1. Wielemaker, J., Moura, P., Nunes, P., Robinson, P., Marques, R., Swift, T.: ISO/IEC DTR 13211-5:2007 Prolog Multi-threading Predicates (2007)
2. Bueno, F., Cabeza, D., Carro, M., Hermenegildo, M., Lopez-Garcıa, P., Puebla, G.: The Ciao Prolog System. Reference Manual (v1. 8). The Ciao System Documentation Series–TR CLIP4/2002.1, School of Computer Science, Technical University of Madrid, UPM (May 2002)
3. Wielemaker, J.: SWI Prolog 5.6 Reference Manual. Department of Social Science Informatics, University of Amsterdam, Amsterdam, Marz (2006)
4. Sagonas, K., Swift, T., Warren, D., Freire, J., Rao, P.: XSB Prolog. The XSB System Version 3.1. Programmers Manual, vol. 1 (2007)
5. Santos-Costa, V., Damas, L., Reis, R., Azevedo, R.: The Yap Prolog Users Manual. Universidade do Porto and COPPE Sistemas (2006)
6. Moura, P., Crocker, P., Nunes, P.: High-level multi-threading programming in logtalk. In: Hudak, P., Warren, D.S. (eds.) PADL 2008. LNCS, vol. 4902, pp. 265–281. Springer, Heidelberg (2008)
7. Casas, A., Carro, M., Hermenegildo, M.: Towards a high-level implementation of flexible parallelism primitives for symbolic languages. In: Proceedings of the 2007 International Workshop on Parallel Symbolic Computation, pp. 93–94 (2007)
8. The IEEE and The Open Group: 1003.1 Standard for Information Technology-Portable Operating System Interface (Posix) System Interfaces, Issue 6. IEEE Std 1003.1-2001. System Interfaces, Issue 6 (2001)
9. Halen, J., Karlsson, R., Nilsson, M.: Performance measurements of threads in Java and processes in Erlang. Webpage, Last visit (January 2006)
10. de Bosschere, K., Tarau, P.: Blackboard-based extensions in Prolog. Software—Practice & Experience 26, 49–69 (1996)
11. Wielemaker, J.: Native preemptive threads in SWI-prolog. In: Palamidessi, C. (ed.) ICLP 2003. LNCS, vol. 2916, pp. 331–345. Springer, Heidelberg (2003)
12. Eskilson, J., Carlsson, M., Palamidessi, C., Glaser, H., Meinke, K.: SICStus MT—A Multithreaded Execution Environment for SICStus Prolog. In: Palamidessi, C., Meinke, K., Glaser, H. (eds.) ALP 1998 and PLILP 1998. LNCS, vol. 1490, pp. 36–53. Springer, Heidelberg (1998)
13. Carro, M., Hermenegildo, M.: Concurrency in Prolog Using Threads and a Shared Database. Logic Programming. In: Proceedings of the 1999 International Conference on Logic Programming (1999)

Interoperating Logic Engines

Paul Tarau[1] and Arun Majumdar[2]

[1] Department of Computer Science and Engineering
University of North Texas
Denton, Texas, USA
tarau@cs.unt.edu
[2] Vivomind Intelligence, Inc.
Rockville, Maryland, USA
arun@vivomind.com

Abstract. We introduce a new programming language construct, *Interactors*, supporting the agent-oriented view that programming is a dialog between simple, self-contained, autonomous building blocks.

We define *Interactors* as an abstraction of answer generation and refinement in *Logic Engines* resulting in expressive language extension and metaprogramming patterns.

As a first step toward a declarative semantics, we sketch a pure Prolog specification showing that Interactors can be expressed at source level, in a relatively simple and natural way.

Interactors extend language constructs like Ruby, Python and C#'s multiple coroutining block returns through *yield* statements and they can emulate the action of fold operations and monadic constructs in functional languages.

Using the Interactor API, we describe at source level, language extensions like dynamic databases and algorithms involving generation of infinite answer streams.

Keywords: Prolog language extensions, logic engines, semantics of metaprogramming constructs, generalized iterators, agent oriented programming language constructs.

1 Introduction

Agent programming constructs have influenced design patterns at "macro level", ranging from interactive Web services to mixed initiative computer human interaction. *Performatives* in Agent communication languages [1] have made these constructs reflect explicitly the intentionality, as well as the negotiation process involved in agent interactions. At a more theoretical level, it has been argued that *interactivity*, seen as fundamental computational paradigm, can actually expand computational expressiveness and provide new models of computation [2].

In a logic programming context, the Jinni agent programming language [3] and the BinProlog system [4] have been centered around logic engine constructs providing an API that supported reentrant instances of the language processor.

A. Gill and T. Swift (Eds.): PADL 2009, LNCS 5418, pp. 137–151, 2009.

This has naturally led to a view of logic engines as instances of a generalized family of iterators called *Fluents* [5], that have allowed the separation of the first-order language interpreters from the multi-threading mechanism, while providing a very concise source-level reconstruction of Prolog's built-ins.

Building upon the *Fluents* API described in [5], this paper will focus on bringing interaction-centered, agent oriented constructs from software design frameworks and design patterns to programming language level.

The resulting language constructs, that we shall call *Interactors*, will express control, metaprogramming and interoperation with stateful objects and external services. They complement pure Horn Clause Prolog with a significant boost in expressiveness, to the point where they allow emulating at source level virtually all Prolog builtins, including dynamic database operations.

Interruptible Iterators are a new Java extension described in [6]. The underlying construct is the `yield` statement providing multiple returns and resumption of iterative blocks, i.e. for instance, a `yield` statement in the body of a `for` loop will return a result for each value of the loop's index.

The `yield` statement has been integrated in newer Object Oriented languages like `Ruby` [7,8] `C#` [9] and `Python` [10] but it goes back to the *Coroutine Iterators* introduced in older languages like CLU [11] and ICON [12].

Interactors can be seen as a natural generalization of Interruptible Iterators and Coroutine Iterators. They implement the the more radical idea of allowing clients to communicate to/from inside blocks of arbitrary recursive computations. The challenge is to achieve this without the fairly complex interrupt based communication protocol between the iterator and its client described in [6]. Towards this end, Interactors provide a structured two-way communication between a client and the usually autonomous service the client requires from a given language construct, often encapsulating an independent component.

2 First Class Logic Engines

Our *Interactor API* is a natural extension of the *Logic Engine API* introduced in [5]. An *Engine* is simply a language processor reflected through an API that allows its computations to be controlled interactively from another *Engine* very much the same way a programmer controls Prolog's interactive toplevel loop: launch a new goal, ask for a new answer, interpret it, react to it.

A *Logic Engine* is an *Engine* running a Horn Clause Interpreter with LD-resolution [13] on a given clause database, together with a set of built-in operations. The command

```
new_engine(AnswerPattern,Goal,Interactor)
```

creates a new Horn Clause solver, uniquely identified by `Interactor`, which shares code with the currently running program and is initialized with `Goal` as a starting point. `AnswerPattern` is a term, usually a list of variables occurring in `Goal`, of which answers returned by the engine will be instances. Note however that `new_engine/3` acts like a typical constructor, no computations are performed at this point, except for allocating data areas. In our actual implementation, with all data areas dynamic, engines are lightweight and engine creation is extremely fast.

The `get/2` operation is used to retrieve successive answers generated by an Interactor, on demand. It is also responsible for actually triggering computations in the engine. The query

```
get(Interactor,AnswerInstance)
```

tries to harvest the answer computed from `Goal`, as an instance of `AnswerPattern`. If an answer is found, it is returned as `the(AnswerInstance)`, otherwise the atom `no` is returned. As in the case of the `Maybe` Monad in Haskell, returning distinct functors in the case of success and failure, allows further case analysis in a pure Horn Clause style, without needing Prolog's CUT or if-then-else operation.

Note that bindings are not propagated to the original `Goal` or `AnswerPattern` when `get/2` retrieves an answer, i.e. `AnswerInstance` is obtained by first standardizing apart (renaming) the variables in `Goal` and `AnswerPattern`, and then backtracking over its alternative answers in a separate Prolog interpreter. Therefore, backtracking in the caller interpreter does not interfere with the new Interactor's iteration over answers. Backtracking over the Interactor's creation point, as such, makes it unreachable and therefore subject to garbage collection.

An Interactor is stopped with the `stop/1` operation that might or might not reclaim resources held by the engine. In our actual implementation we are using a fully automated memory management mechanism where unreachable engines are automatically garbage collected.

So far, these operations provide a minimal *Coroutine Iterator API*, powerful enough to switch tasks cooperatively between an engine and its client and emulate key Prolog built-ins like `if-then-else` and `findall` [5], as well as higher order operations like *fold* and *best_of*.

3 From Fluents to Interactors

We will now describe the extension of the *Fluents* API of [5] that provides a minimal bidirectional communication API between interactors and their clients.

The following operations provide a "mixed-initiative" interaction mechanism, allowing more general data exchanges between an engine and its client.

3.1 A Yield/Return Operation

First, like the `yield return` construct of `C#` and the `yield operation` of Ruby and Python, our `return/1` operation

```
return(Term)
```

will save the state of the engine and transfer *control* and a *result* `Term` to its client. The client will receive a copy of `Term` simply by using its `get/2` operation.

Similarly to Ruby's `yield`, our `return` operation suspends and returns data from arbitrary computations (possibly involving recursion) rather than from specific language constructs like a `while` or `for` loop.

Note that an Interactor returns control to its client either by calling `return/1` or when a computed answer becomes available. By using a sequence of `return/get` operations, an engine can provide a stream of *intermediate/final results* to its client, without having to backtrack. This mechanism is powerful enough to implement a complete exception handling mechanism (see [5]) simply by defining

```
throw(E):-return(exception(E)).
```

When combined with a `catch(Goal,Exception,OnException)`, on the client side, the client can decide, upon reading the exception with `get/2`, if it wants to handle it or to throw it to the next level.

3.2 Interactors and Coroutining

The operations described so far allow an engine to return answers from any point in its computation sequence. The next step is to enable an engine's client to *inject* new goals (executable data) to an arbitrary inner context of an engine. Two new primitives are needed:

```
to_engine(Engine,Data)
```

used to send a client's data to an Engine, and

```
from_engine(Data)
```

used by the engine to receive a client's Data.

A typical use case for the *Interactor API* looks as follows:

1. the *client* creates and initializes a new *engine*
2. the client triggers a new computation in the *engine*, parameterized as follows:
   (a) the *client* passes some data and a new goal to the *engine* and issues a `get` operation that passes control to it
   (b) the *engine* starts a computation from its initial goal or the point where it has been suspended and runs (a copy of) the new goal received from its *client*
   (c) the *engine* returns (a copy of) the answer, then suspends and returns control to its *client*
3. the *client* interprets the answer and proceeds with its next computation step
4. the process is fully reentrant and the *client* may repeat it from an arbitrary point in its computation

Using a metacall mechanism like `call/1` (which can also be emulated in terms of engine operations [5]) or directly through a source level transformation [14], one can implement a close equivalent of Ruby's `yield` statement as follows:

```
ask_engine(Engine,Query, Result):-
  to_engine(Engine,Query),
  get(Engine,Result).

engine_yield(Answer):-
  from_engine((Answer:-Goal)),
  call(Goal),return(Answer).
```

The predicate `ask_engine/3` sends a query (possibly built at runtime) to an engine, which in turn, executes it and returns a result with an `engine_yield` operation. The query is typically a goal or a pattern of the form `AnswerPattern:-Goal` in which case the engine interprets it as a request to instantiate `AnswerPattern` by executing `Goal` before returning the answer instance.

As the following example shows, this allows the client to use, from outside, the (infinite) recursive loop of an engine as a form of *updatable persistent state*.

```
sum_loop(S1):-engine_yield(S1=>S2),sum_loop(S2).

inc_test(R1,R2):-
   new_engine(_,sum_loop(0),E),
   ask_engine(E,(S1=>S2:-S2 is S1+2),R1),
   ask_engine(E,(S1=>S2:-S2 is S1+5),R2).

?- inc_test(R1,R2).
R1=the(0 => 2),
R2=the(2 => 7)
```

Note also that after parameters (the increments 2 and 5) are passed to the engine, results dependent on its state (the sums so far 2 and 7) are received back. Moreover, note that an arbitrary goal is injected in the local context of the engine where it is executed. The goal can then access the engine's *state variables* `S1` and `S2`. As engines have separate garbage collectors (or in simple cases as a result of tail recursion), their infinite loops run in constant space, provided that no unbounded size objects are created.

4 A (Mostly) Pure Prolog Specification

At a first look, Interactors deviate from the usual Horn Clause semantics of pure Prolog programs. A legitimate question arises: are they not just another procedural extension, say, like assert/retract, setarg, global variables etc.?

We will show here that the semantic gap between pure Prolog and its extension with Interactors is much narrower than one would expect. The techniques that we will describe can be seen as an executable specification of Interactors within the well understood semantics of logic programs (SLDNF resolution).

Toward this end, we will sketch an emulation, in pure Prolog, of the key constructs involved in defining Interactors.

There are four distinct concepts to be emulated:

1. we need to eliminate backtracking to be able to access multiple answers at a time
2. we need to emulate copy_term as different search branches and multiple uses of a given clause require fresh instances of terms, with variables standardized apart
3. we need to emulate suspending and resuming an engine
4. engines should be able to receive and return Prolog terms

We will focus here on the first two, that are arguably less obvious, by providing actual implementations. After that, we will briefly discuss the feasibility of the last two.

4.1 Metainterpreting Backtracking

First, let's define a clause representation, that can be obtained easily with a source-to-source translator. Clauses in the database are represented with difference-list terms, structurally isomorphic to the binarization transformation described in [14]. The code of a classic Prolog naive reverse + permutation generator program becomes:

```
:-op(1150,xfx,<=).

clauses([
    [app([],A,A)|B]<=B,
    [app([C|D],E,[C|F])|G]<=[app(D,E,F)|G],

    [nrev([],[])|H]<=H,
    [nrev([I|J],K)|L]<=[nrev(J,M),app(M,[I],K)|L],

    [perm([],[])|N]<=N,
    [perm([O|P],Q)|R]<=[perm(P,S),ins(O,S,Q)|R],

    [ins(T,U,[T|U])|V]<=V,
    [ins(W,[X|Y],[X|Z])|X0]<=[ins(W,Y,Z)|X0]
]).
```

Note that we can assume that variables are local to each clause and therefore they have been standardized apart accordingly[1].

First, let's define the basic inference step (equivalent to an LD-resolution step, [13]) as a simple "arrow composition" operation:

```
compose(F1,F2,A<=C):-copy_term(F1,A<=B),copy_term(F2,B<=C).
```

We can now add a new "arrow" to a list of existing arrows, provided that the composition succeeds:

[1] Allowing shared variables would bring a different, but nevertheless interesting semantics, with "inter-clausal variables" seen as write-once global variables.

```
match_one(F1,F2,Fs,[NewF|Fs]):-compose(F1,F2,F3),!,NewF=F3.
match_one(_,_,Fs,Fs).
```

We can see an arrow as representing the current goal. The next step is to let an arrow select from a *list* of clauses the ones that match:

```
match_all([],_,Fs,Fs).
match_all([Clause|Cs],Arrow,Fs1,Fs3):-
  match_one(Arrow,Clause,Fs1,Fs2),
  match_all(Cs,Arrow,Fs2,Fs3).
```

We can add a stopping condition to mark the success of an LD-derivation as matching an arrow of the form `Answer<=[]`

```
derive_one(Answer<=[],_,Fs,Fs,As,[Answer|As]).
derive_one(Answer<=[G|Gs],Cs,Fs,NewFs,As,As):-
  match_all(Cs,Answer<=[G|Gs],Fs,NewFs).
```

With these building blocks in place, the result of the LD-derivations of *all answer instances* of a query can be defined as:

```
all_instances(AnswerPattern,Goal,Clauses,Answers):-
  Gs=[AnswerPattern<=[Goal]],
  derive_all(Gs,Clauses,[],Answers).
```

where `derive_all` lifts the derivation process to progressively solve all existing and newly generated goals:

```
derive_all([],_,As,As).
derive_all([Arrow|Fs],Cs,OldAs,NewAs):-
  derive_one(Arrow,Cs,Fs,NewFs,OldAs,As),
  derive_all(NewFs,Cs,As,NewAs).
```

Finally, we can integrate the clause database:

```
all_answers(X,G,R):-clauses(Cs),all_instances(X,G,Cs,R).
```

and try out a few goals:

```
?- all_answers(Xs+Ys,app(Xs,Ys,[1,2,3]),Rs).
Rs = [[]+[1, 2, 3], [1]+[2, 3], [1, 2]+[3], [1, 2, 3]+[]]

?- all_answers(P,perm([1,2,3],P),Ps).
Ps = [[1, 2, 3], [2, 1, 3], [2, 3, 1], [1, 3, 2], [3, 1, 2], [3, 2, 1]]
```

Note, that for non-ground queries, answers computed this way keep variable equalities as expected:

```
?- List=[A,B,B,A],all_answers(R,nrev(List,R),Rs).
List = [A, B, B, A],
Rs = [[_A, _B, _B, _A]]
```

Note that, except for relying on `copy_term` and a cut that can be replaced with a negation as failure, the metainterpreter is entirely written in pure Prolog.

4.2 Emulating copy_term

We can emulate the effect of copy_term in the previously described metainterpreter by observing that a logical variable can be "split" into two new ones and consequently a Prolog term can be recursively deconstructed and rebuilt as two fresh terms, identical to it up to uniform variable renamings.

```
fork_term('$v'(T1,T2), R1,R2):-R1=T1,R2=T2.
fork_term(T, T1,T2):-
  nonvar(T),functor(T,F,N),(F/N) \== ('$v'/2),
  functor(T1,F,N),functor(T2,F,N),
  fork_args(N,T,T1,T2).

fork_args(0,_,_,_).
fork_args(I,T,T1,T2):-I>0,
  I1 is I-1,arg(I,T,X),
  fork_term(X,A,B),
  arg(I,T1,A),arg(I,T2,B),
  fork_args(I1,T,T1,T2).
```

One can see that this produces indeed two fresh copies of the original term:

```
?- fork_term(f(A,B,g(B,A)),T1,T2).
A = '$v'(_A1, _A2),
B = '$v'(_B1, _B2),
T1 = f(_A1, _B1, g(_B1, _A1)),
T2 = f(_A2, _B2, g(_B2, _A2)).
```

Note that functor and arg can be seen as generic abbreviations for predicates describing the building/decomposition operations for each function symbol occurring in the program and $v/2 can be assumed to be any function symbol not occurring in the program. Along the lines of [15] one can see that this functionality can be also expressed through a simple program transformation provided that nonvar/1 can be expressed using negation as failure as

```
  nonvar(X):- not(X=0),not(X=1).
```

We will obtain a slightly different definition of composition, that would require replacing both the clause and the resolvent with one of the copies while using the other pair of copies for the arrow compositions.

```
compose(F1,F2, A<=C, NewF1,NewF2):-
   fork_term(F1,A<=B,NewF1),
   fork_term(F2,B<=C,NewF2).
```

One can now see that after propagating the extra arguments through the clauses of the metainterpreter described in subsection 4.1, together with the source level transformations we just mentioned, a metainterpreter that does not require copy_term can be derived.

4.3 Implementing Suspend/Resume and Term/Exchanges

The metainterpreter described in subsection 4.1 can be easily modified to return the current goal list when observing a return(X) instruction and then be resumed at will, by adding a clause similar to the one handling the case `Answer<=[]`. At this point, data exchange operations and `to_engine` and `from_engine` can be implemented through an extra argument added to the metainterpreter.

5 Interactors and Higher Order Constructs

As a first glimpse at the expressiveness of the Interactor API, we will implement, in the tradition of higher order functional programming, a *fold* operation [16] connecting results produced by independent branches of a backtracking Prolog engine:

```
efoldl(Engine,F,R1,R2):-
  get(Engine,X),
  efoldl_cont(X,Engine,F,R1,R2).

efoldl_cont(no,_Engine,_F,R,R).
efoldl_cont(the(X),Engine,F,R1,R2):-
  call(F,R1,X,R),
  efoldl(Engine,F,R,R2).
```

Classic functional programming idioms like *reverse as fold* are then implemented simply as:

```
reverse(Xs,Ys):-
  new_engine(X,member(X,Xs),E),
  efoldl(E,reverse_cons,[],Ys).

reverse_cons(Y,X,[X|Y]).
```

Note also the automatic *deforestation* effect [17] of this programming style - no intermediate list structures need to be built, if one wants to aggregate the values retrieved from an arbitrary generator engine with an operation like sum or product.

6 Emulating Dynamic Databases with Interactors

The gain in expressiveness coming directly from the view of logic engines as answer generators is significant. We refer to [5] for source level implementations of virtually all essential Prolog built-ins. The notable exception is Prolog's dynamic database, requiring the bidirectional communication provided by interactors.

The key idea for implementing dynamic database operations with Interactors is to use a logic engine's state in an infinite recursive loop.

First, a simple difference-list based infinite server loop is built:

```
queue_server:-queue_server(Xs,Xs).

queue_server(Hs1,Ts1):-
  from_engine(Q),server_task(Q,Hs1,Ts1,Hs2,Ts2,A),return(A),
  queue_server(Hs2,Ts2).
```

Next we provide the queue operations, needed to maintain the state of the database.

```
server_task(add_element(X),Xs,[X|Ys],Xs,Ys,yes).
server_task(push_element(X),Xs,Ys,[X|Xs],Ys,yes).
server_task(queue,Xs,Ys,Xs,Ys,Xs-Ys).
server_task(delete_element(X),Xs,Ys,NewXs,Ys,YesNo):-
  server_task_delete(X,Xs,NewXs,YesNo).
```

Then we implement the auxiliary predicates supporting various queue operations:

```
server_task_remove(Xs,NewXs,YesNo):-
  nonvar(Xs),Xs=[X|NewXs],!,YesNo=yes(X).
server_task_remove(Xs,Xs,no).

server_task_delete(X,Xs,NewXs,YesNo):-
  select_nonvar(X,Xs,NewXs),!,YesNo=yes(X).
server_task_delete(_,Xs,Xs,no).

select_nonvar(X,XXs,Xs):-nonvar(XXs),XXs=[X|Xs].
select_nonvar(X,YXs,[Y|Ys]):-nonvar(YXs),YXs=[Y|Xs],
  select_nonvar(X,Xs,Ys).
```

Next, we put it all together, as a dynamic database API.

We can create a new engine server providing Prolog database operations:

```
new_edb(Engine):-new_engine(done,queue_server,Engine).
```

We can add new clauses to the database

```
edb_assertz(Engine,Clause):-
  ask_engine(Engine,add_element(Clause),the(yes)).

edb_asserta(Engine,Clause):-
  ask_engine(Engine,push_element(Clause),the(yes)).
```

and we can return fresh instances of asserted clauses

```
edb_clause(Engine,Head,Body):-
  ask_engine(Engine,queue,the(Xs-[])),
  member((Head:-Body),Xs).
```

or remove them from the the database

```
edb_retract1(Engine,Head):-Clause=(Head:-_Body),
  ask_engine(Engine,
    delete_element(Clause),the(yes(Clause))).
```

Finally, the database can be discarded by stopping the engine that hosts it:

```
edb_delete(Engine):-stop(Engine).
```

The following example shows how the database generates the equivalent of `clause/2`, ready to be passed to a Prolog metainterpreter.

```
test_clause(Head,Body):-
  new_edb(Db),
    edb_assertz(Db,(a(2):-true)),
    edb_asserta(Db,(a(1):-true)),
    edb_assertz(Db,(b(X):-a(X))),
  edb_clause(Db,Head,Body).
```

As a side note, combining this emulation with the metainterpreter described in section 4, provides an executable specification of Prolog's dynamic database operations in pure Prolog, worth investigating in depth, as future work.

Externally implemented dynamic databases can also be made visible as Interactors and reflection of the interpreter's own handling of the Prolog database becomes possible. As an additional benefit, multiple databases can be provided. This simplifies adding module, object or agent layers at source level. By combining database and communication Interactors, software abstractions like mobile code and autonomous agents can be built as shown in [18]. Encapsulating external stateful objects like file systems or external database or Web service interfaces as Interactors can provide a uniform interfacing mechanism and reduce programmer learning curves in practical applications of Prolog.

Moreover, Prolog operations traditionally captive to predefined list based implementations (like DCGs) can be made generic and mapped to work directly on Interactors encapsulating file, URL and socket Readers.

7 Simplifying Algorithms: Interactors and Combinatorial Generation

Various combinatorial generation algorithms have elegant backtracking implementations. However, it is notoriously difficult (or inelegant, through the use of impure side effects) to compare answers generated by different OR-branches of Prolog's search tree.

7.1 Comparing Alternative Answers

Optimization problems, selecting the "best" among answers produced on alternative branches can easily be expressed as follows:

- running the generator in a separate logic engine
- collecting and comparing the answers in a client controlling the engine

The second step can actually be automated, provided that the comparison criterion is given as a predicate

```
compare_answers(First,Second,Best)
```

to be applied to the engine with an `efold` operation

```
best_of(Answer,Comparator,Generator):-
  new_engine(Answer,Generator,E),
  efoldl(E,compare_answers(Comparator),no,Best),
  Answer=Best.
```

```
compare_answers(Comparator,A1,A2,Best):-
  if((A1\==no,call(Comparator,A1,A2)),Best=A1,Best=A2).

?-best_of(X,>,member(X,[2,1,4,3])).
X=4
```

Clearly, a similar mechanism can be used to count the number of solutions without having to accumulate them to a list.

7.2 Encapsulating Infinite Computations Streams

An infinite stream of natural numbers is implemented as:

```
loop(N):-return(N),N1 is N+1,loop(N1).
```

The following example shows a simple space efficient generator for the infinite stream of prime numbers:

```
prime(P):-prime_engine(E),element_of(E,P).

prime_engine(E):-new_engine(_,new_prime(1),E).

new_prime(N):-N1 is N+1,
  if(test_prime(N1),true,return(N1)),new_prime(N1).

test_prime(N):-
  M is integer(sqrt(N)),between(2,M,D),N mod D =:=0
```

Note that the program has been wrapped, using the `element_of` predicate defined in [5], to provide one answer at a time through backtracking. Alternatively, a forward recursing client can use the `get(Engine)` operation to extract primes one at a time from the stream.

8 Applications of Interactors and Practical Language Extensions

Interactors and Multi-Threading. As a key difference with typical multi-threaded Prolog implementations like Ciao-Prolog and SWI-Prolog [19,20], our Interactor API is designed up front with a clear separation between *engines* and *threads* as we prefer to see them as orthogonal language constructs.

While one can build a self-contained lightweight multi-threading API solely by switching control among a number of cooperating engines, with the advent of multi-core CPUs as the norm rather than the exception, the need for *native* multi-threading constructs is justified on both performance and expressiveness grounds. Assuming a dynamic implementation of a logic engine's stacks, Interactors provide lightweight independent computation states that can be easily mapped to the underlying native threading API.

A minimal native Interactor based multi-threading API has been implemented in [3] on top of a simple thread launching built-in:

```
run_bg(Engine,ThreadHandle).
```

This runs a new Thread starting from the engine's `run()` predicate and returns a handle to the Thread object. To ensure that access to the Engine's state is safe and synchronized, we hide the engine handle and provide a simple producer/consumer data exchanger object, called a `Hub`. Some key components of the multi-threading API, partly designed to match Java's own threading API are:

- `bg(Goal)`: launches a new Prolog thread on its own engine starting with `Goal`.
- `hub_ms(Timeout,Hub)`: constructs a new `Hub` - a synchronization device on which `N` consumer threads can wait with `collect(Hub,Data)` (similar to a synchronized `from_engine` operation) for data produced by `M` producers providing data with `put(Hub,Data)` (similar to a synchronized `from_engine` operation.

Associative Interactors. The message passing style interaction shown in the previous sections between engines and their clients, can be easily generalized to associative communication through a unification based blackboard interface [21]. Exploring this concept in depth promises more flexible interaction patterns, as out of order `ask_engine` and `engine_yield` operations would become possible, matched by association patterns.

9 Interactors Beyond Logic Programming Languages

We will now compare Interactors with similar constructs in other programming paradigms.

9.1 Interactors in Object Oriented Languages

Extending Interactors to mainstream Object Oriented languages is definitely of practical importance, given the gain in expressiveness. An elegant open source Prolog engine `Yield Prolog` has been recently implemented in terms of Python's *yield* and `C#`'s *yield return* primitives [22]. Extending Yield Prolog to support our Interactor API only requires adding the communication operations `from_engine` and `to_engine`. In older languages like `Java`, `C++` or `Objective C` one needs to implement a more complex API, including a `yield return` emulation.

9.2 Interactors and Similar Constructs in Functional Languages

Interactors based on logic engines encapsulate future computations that can be unrolled on demand. This is similar to lazy evaluation mechanisms in languages like Haskell [23]. Interactors share with Monads [24] the ability to sequentialize functional computations and encapsulate state information. With higher order functions, monadic computations can pass functions to inner blocks. On the other hand, our `ask_engine` / `engine_yield` mechanism, like Ruby's `yield`, is arguably more flexible, as it provides arbitrary switching of control (coroutining) between an Interactor and its client. The ability to define Prolog's `findall` construct as well as `fold` operations in terms of Interactors, is similar to definition of comprehensions [24] in terms of Monads.

10 Conclusion

We have shown that Logic Engines encapsulated as Interactors can be used to build on top of pure Prolog a practical Prolog system, including dynamic database operations, entirely at source level. We have also provided a sketch of an executable semantics for Logic Engine operations in pure Prolog. This shows that, in principle, their exact specification can be expressed declaratively.

In a broader sense, Interactors can be seen as a starting point for rethinking fundamental programming language constructs like Iterators and Coroutining in terms of language constructs inspired by *performatives* in agent oriented programming.

Beyond applications to logic-based language design, we hope that our language constructs will be reusable in the design and implementation of new functional and object oriented languages.

Among real world applications of these ideas, we have been pursuing a new model of natural language understanding [25] where multiple concurrently processing agents, using lightweight interpretation engines implemented as interactors transform text into semantic model structures for reasoning in the Oil and Gas exploration and production domain.

References

1. Mayfield, J., Labrou, Y., Finin, T.W.: Evaluation of KQML as an Agent Communication Language. In: Wooldridge, M., Müller, J.P., Tambe, M. (eds.) IJCAI-WS 1995 and ATAL 1995. LNCS, vol. 1037, pp. 347–360. Springer, Heidelberg (1996)
2. Wegner, P., Eberbach, E.: New Models of Computation. Comput. J. 47(1), 4–9 (2004)
3. Tarau, P.: Orthogonal Language Constructs for Agent Oriented Logic Programming. In: Carro, M., Morales, J.F. (eds.) Proceedings of CICLOPS 2004, Fourth Colloquium on Implementation of Constraint and Logic Programming Systems, Saint-Malo, France (September 2004)
4. Tarau, P.: BinProlog 11.x Professional Edition: Advanced BinProlog Programming and Extensions Guide. Technical report, BinNet Corp. (2006)
5. Tarau, P.: Fluents: A Refactoring of Prolog for Uniform Reflection and Interoperation with External Objects. In: Palamidessi, C., Moniz Pereira, L., Lloyd, J.W., Dahl, V., Furbach, U., Kerber, M., Lau, K.-K., Sagiv, Y., Stuckey, P.J. (eds.) CL 2000. LNCS, vol. 1861. Springer, Heidelberg (2000)
6. Liu, J., Kimball, A., Myers, A.C.: Interruptible iterators. In: Morrisett, J.G., Jones, S.L.P. (eds.) POPL, pp. 283–294. ACM, New York (2006)

7. Matsumoto, Y.: The Ruby Programming Language (June 2000)
8. Sasada, K.: YARV: yet another RubyVM: innovating the ruby interpreter. In: Johnson, R., Gabriel, R.P. (eds.) OOPSLA Companion, pp. 158–159. ACM, New York (2005)
9. Microsoft Corp.: Visual C# . Project, `http://msdn.microsoft.com/vcsharp`
10. van Rossum, G.: A Tour of the Python Language. In: TOOLS (23), p. 370. IEEE Computer Society, Los Alamitos (1997)
11. Liskov, B., Bloom, T., Schaffert, J.C., Snyder, A., Atkinson, R., Moss, E., Scheifler, R.: CLU. LNCS, vol. 114. Springer, Heidelberg (1981)
12. Griswold, R.E., Hanson, D.R., Korb, J.T.: Generators in Icon. ACM Trans. Program. Lang. Syst. 3(2), 144–161 (1981)
13. Tarau, P., Boyer, M.: Nonstandard Answers of Elementary Logic Programs. In: Jacquet, J. (ed.) Constructing Logic Programs, pp. 279–300. J.Wiley, Chichester (1993)
14. Tarau, P., Boyer, M.: Elementary Logic Programs. In: Deransart, P., Małuszyński, J. (eds.) PLILP 1990. LNCS, vol. 456, pp. 159–173. Springer, Heidelberg (1990)
15. Warren, D.H.D.: Higher-order extensions to Prolog – are they needed? In: Michie, D., Hayes, J., Pao, Y.H. (eds.) Machine Intelligence 10. Ellis Horwood (1981)
16. Bird, R.S., de Moor, O.: Solving optimisation problems with catamorphism. In: Bird, R.S., Woodcock, J.C.P., Morgan, C.C. (eds.) MPC 1992. LNCS, vol. 669, pp. 45–66. Springer, Heidelberg (1993)
17. Wadler, P.: Deforestation: Transforming programs to eliminate trees. Theor. Comput. Sci. 73(2), 231–248 (1990)
18. Tarau, P., Dahl, V.: High-Level Networking with Mobile Code and First Order AND-Continuations. Theory and Practice of Logic Programming 1(3), 359–380 (2001)
19. Carro, M., Hermenegildo, M.V.: Concurrency in prolog using threads and a shared database. In: ICLP, pp. 320–334 (1999)
20. Wielemaker, J.: Native preemptive threads in SWI-prolog. In: Palamidessi, C. (ed.) ICLP 2003. LNCS, vol. 2916, pp. 331–345. Springer, Heidelberg (2003)
21. De Bosschere, K., Tarau, P.: Blackboard-based Extensions in Prolog. Software — Practice and Experience 26(1), 49–69 (1996)
22. Jeff Thompson: Yield Prolog. Project, `http://yieldprolog.sourceforge.net`
23. Peyton Jones, S.L. (ed.): Haskell 98 Language and Libraries: The Revised Report (September 2002), `http://haskell.org/definition/haskell98-report.pdf`
24. Wadler, P.: Comprehending monads. In: ACM Conf. Lisp and Functional Programming, Nice, France, pp. 61–78. ACM Press, New York (1990)
25. Majumdar, A.K., Sowa, J.F., Stewart, J.: Pursuing the goal of language understanding. In: Eklund, P., Haemmerlé, O. (eds.) ICCS 2008. LNCS, vol. 5113, pp. 21–42. Springer, Heidelberg (2008)

High-Level Interaction with Relational Databases in Logic Programming

António Porto

Department of Computer Science
Faculty of Sciences, University of Porto*
ap@dcc.fc.up.pt

Abstract. Most real-world applications have come to rely on the mature technology of relational databases for persistent storage, interacting through SQL embedded in the host programming language. Using logic programming we present a higher-level alternative to SQL, close in spirit to natural language, yielding much more concise expressions that are easier to understand and promote better code maintenance. This is achieved using the flexible operator syntax and the deductive capabilities, first to compile a clausal representation of the database scheme from a high-level description, and then to interpret queries and commands, through the compiled scheme, into SQL statements.

1 Introduction

About a decade ago we launched a large project to build an information system development platform, and a full-blown academic management system on top, using almost exclusively logic programming to achieve high levels of abstraction in the code. The goals were met [1] but little reporting was made of the scientific achievements. One of them was a novel database interaction technology, whose overview is the purpose of this paper, allowing a high-level management of a standard relational database from within the logic programming code. The approach is very different from that of deductive databases (see eg. [2,3]), where database tables (the extensional database) are viewed as predicates in logic programs, with joins expressed through variable sharing. We relied instead on natural language principles to design a variable-free structural language for queries and commands of remarkable conciseness and readability, using the atomic terminology for concepts and attributes introduced in a given scheme definition, itself expressed in another concise and readable structural language. The explicit representation in logic programming of a database scheme has been advocated before [4], but with a rather low-level approach to encode basic set-theoretic constructions and using the corresponding encoding of the relational calculus as a query language. We are unaware of other approaches similar in spirit to our own, whose aim is not to impose the logic programming syntax and semantics on the relational model but

* The work reported here was carried out while the author was affiliated with the Faculty of Sciences and Technology, New University of Lisbon.

A. Gill and T. Swift (Eds.): PADL 2009, LNCS 5418, pp. 152–167, 2009.

rather to use its intrinsic deductive power and flexibility to process very high-level database management languages, providing access to the robust relational database technology inside highly maintainable (compact and natural) code.

The framework works as follows. A database scheme definition is written in a language we have designed (itself a novelty in terms of conceptual modelling), and a processor is invoked to compile the scheme into a simple clausal form (just facts). The compiled scheme is used in two ways. One is to feed a Web-based meta-information system that we built as part of our project, allowing developers to navigate the scheme through all relevant conceptual links, and to create, backup, or delete the corresponding database tables. The other use is in the query and command processing machinery, that translates compact conceptual expressions into SQL, typically deducing implicit joins in queries and implicit multiple table operations in commands.

The whole treatment revolves around the simple notion of *concept* with *attributes*, some of which define identity. The natural language phrase "the a of c" turns simply to a/c in our query language, with a either a textual or inherited attribute of c, inheritance involving an implicit join. Chaining and conjunction yield other natural paraphrases, ie. $(a,b)/c/d$ for "the a and b of the c of d.

In this paper we can aim only at a cursory overview of the approach, trying to illustrate with a few examples the declarative nature of the proposed languages and how their processing is implemented. All the examples are taken from the domain of academic management, necessarily simplified for the purpose at hand.

2 The Scheme

We first give an informal overview of the language used to define the scheme, followed by a formal abstract model of the scheme syntax and semantics, and then a brief summary of the compiled form.

2.1 The Scheme Definition Language

For defining a database scheme we devised a corresponding *scheme definition language* (SDL), with a few design principles in mind, namely simplicity and expressiveness.

We consider irrelevant, and detrimental to our simplicity goal, the traditional distinction between entities and relationships. We find it much simpler to have a uniform view of *concepts*, encompassing real-world notions of entities, relationships, situations, events, acts, etc., all amenable to a simple semantics of sets of individuals with an inner structure given by the notion of local *attributes*, some of which determine identity. Concepts and attributes can and should be named systematically with nouns, leading to very natural query expressions based on noun phrases, in contrast to the proliferation of verbal-based properties in the OWL language [5] and the non-uniformity this raises for relational querying.

The basic concepts are the predefined *data types* $\mathcal{T}$ that are usual in relational databases: $\{\,$`int`, `num`, `date`, `time`$\,\} \cup \{\,$`str(`n`)` $\mid n$ is a positive numeral$\}$ with predefined interpretations as the sets of, respectively, integers, numbers, dates, time points and strings of at most n characters, plus a few other data types for large textual and binary objects.

A structured concept has an atomic name and a number of *lexical* attributes also identified by atomic names, each of a given data type. The semantic intuition is that the concept denotes a set of individuals and each of its lexical attributes denotes a total function from that set to the attribute's data type, yielding the elementary pieces of information (values of the given types) characterizing the individual members of the concept in a given database. The individuals themselves are uniquely identified in a standard manner by an *identity* subset of the lexical attributes, the others being called *dependent* because there is a functional dependency from the identity to each one of them.

We illustrate this with a simple example using our SDL syntax:

```
organization_type << abbreviation : str(2)
                  >> name : str(20).
```

The concept `organization_type` has just two lexical attributes, `abbreviation` and `name`, respectively the identity (under `<<`) and a dependent one (under `>>`), both typed as (differently sized) strings. The concept corresponds to a database table with the same name and attributes, `abbreviation` being the primary key.

Both the formal and intuitive understanding of the scheme benefit from considering a total ordering of each concept's lexical attributes, implicitly expressed in the SDL definition. So an individual `organization_type` in a database on this scheme might be eg. the tuple (`dp`, `Department`), whose identity is just its prefix (`dp`).

The choice of concept and attribute names affects the readability of queries. We have a simple guideline, namely using always singular noun phrases such that "the a of the c" makes sense for any attribute a of a concept c.

Let us now consider a simple definition of an organization:

```
organization << code : int  = auto
             >> name : str(60),
                type : organization_type.
```

The comma is used to group more that one attribute under `>>` (in this case) or `<<` (in general). The decision to use integer codes as identifiers, expressed here under `<<`, is a very common practice in databases when we expect a large number of individual members of a concept. The equation to `auto` expresses an implicit value assignment, on the creation of a new tuple, by auto-incrementing the current largest code; this is a handy standard feature in databases. The attribute named `type` is constrained to belong not to a data type but to another concept (`organization_type`), ie. we are defining a *conceptual* attribute giving rise to a foreign key in the corresponding database table. What are the corresponding lexical attributes? Their sequence and data types must match those of the referred concept's identity, in this case the single attribute `abbreviation:str(2)` of `organization_type`. As for the name(s), in the present case of a unary reference the standard choice is to use the conceptual attribute name (`type`) also for its single lexical attribute. In the sequel we'll see how to treat the case of non-unary references . Summing up, the `organization` table has the tuple of lexical attributes (`code:int`, `name:str(40)`, `type:str(2)`), the primary key (`code`) and a foreign key from (`type`) to (`abbreviation`) in `organization_type`.

The previous SDL definition of `organization` can be simplified in several ways. We must point out, first, that in order to have a single-pass SDL compiler we require that a concept definition that refers to other concepts must come after their own definitions, eg. in this case `organization` after `organization_type`. Given the abundance of entities with reference `code:int=auto` and lexical attribute `name` (of multiple sizes), it is very useful to define a corresponding suitable abstraction, which we can do with three mechanisms. First, we simply omit the identity part of a definition to implicitly assume `<< code:int=auto`. Second, we can define *virtual* concepts that do not generate database tables but are blueprints for other concepts or conceptual attributes. Third, we can use terms with logical variables as names of virtual concepts parameterizing eg. string size. Using the '`*`' prefix to mark a concept as virtual, we then present this definition of virtual entities of variable-size name:

```
* entity(N) >> name : str(N).
```

The definition of an organization simply becomes, using sub-concept notation:

```
organization : entity(40) >> type.
```

Comparing with the previous definition of `organization`, the term to the left of `>>` has the effect of the previous first two lines, through instantiated inheritance from the virtual concept, and using just `type` achieves the effect of the previous last line, because when facing such an atomic attribute definition the compiler checks if the possessive composition of attribute and concept names, in this case `organization_type`[1], is a previously defined concept, as indeed we assume here.

Things get more interesting when defining concepts identified by more than one attribute, as shown next for a course edition.

```
year : int.
* type(S,N) << code : str(S) >> name : str(N).
period_type : type(2,20).
* period   << - type, - number : int.
* edition  <<   year,   period.
course : type(6,60) >> credits : int, department : organization.
course_edition << course, edition >> lecturer : employee.
```

The first line defines a data subtype, with no attached semantics but useful for expressiveness. The virtual variable-sizes `type` is used in defining the database concept `period_type`, meant to contain tuples such as eg. (`s`, `semester`). The virtual `period`'s attribute `type`, as explained before, implicitly references `period_type`, this being an already defined concept. The prefixing by '`-`' of both attributes

[1] This is language-dependent. For French we would get `type_de_organization`.

of `period` signals the contextual (rather than global) nature of their names: when a conceptual attribute is a `period`, the corresponding sub-attribute names are constructed using the already mentioned possessive composition with the referring attribute, eg. the lexical attributes of `edition` are `year`, `period_type` and `period_number`. Non-prefixed identity attributes, as those of `edition`, have global names, so `course_edition` has the lexical attributes `course` (it has a unary reference), `year`, `period_type` and `period_number`.

Consider now the enrollment of a student in a course edition, valid only if the student is registered in that year.

```
registration << student, year.
enrollment << registration, course_edition >> ? grade.
```

When expanding the identity attributes of `enrollment` we *merge* the resulting lexical attributes, ending up with `student` (assuming a unary reference), `year`, `course`, `period_type` and `period_number`. The single attribute `year` is present in both foreign keys associated with `registration` and `course_edition`. Conceptual attributes not only allow very compact scheme definitions, as shown, but are also crucial to the power of the query language, as we can use eg. `lecturer/course_edition/enrollment` for "the lecturer of the course edition of the enrollment". The `?` prefix on `grade` signals it as *null*, a common convenience for allowing database states where the value of `grade` is not (yet) defined for certain `enrollment` tuples.

Let us look at sub-concepts. We may wish for example to make persons a subtype of agents (to cater for computational agents):

```
agent  : entity(60) >> common_name: str(30), identifier: str(20).
person : agent      >> sex: str(1).
```

The database concept `agent` gets both its identity attribute `code` and the dependent attribute `name` from the virtual concept `entity`, to which are added `common_name` and `identifier`. When declaring `person` an `agent`, however, since this is a database (rather than virtual) concept we get from it only the identity attributes, ie. `code`, to which is added the non-referential `sex`. Inheritance, eg. of `name` to `person` from `agent`, is in the query language, as shown later.

Another useful feature is sub-attribute inheritance, exemplified below:[2]

```
student >> number, < person, study_program.
```

Each student corresponds to a person in a study program. So `student` is not a sub-concept of `person` and gets its own (implicit) `code` identifier. But a student "is a" person in the sense of corresponding to a unique one (it's an attribute), and we unambiguously say eg. "the name of the student" for the name of the student's person. Indeed, `name/student` will do that in our query language, because the `<` prefix in the above definition allows the inheritance of a `student`'s `person`'s attributes as its own, through the implicit join.

[2] The prefix `<` binds tighter than the comma.

More features are available but not described here for lack of space: predefined values, composite names, comments, concept extension, and patterns for generic sets of concepts (eg. graphs with nodes and arcs/paths).

2.2 The Abstract Scheme Model

In the formal treatment we implicitly assume universal quantification of meta-variables in the appropriate domains, including positive integer indexes on sequences to denote the corresponding element. We use $_{\text{fin}}$ to denote restriction to finite sets, and $^+$ for finite non-empty sequences. We refer to the domains *dom* of functions using implicit currying.

A conceptual scheme has an abstract syntactic structure built from the set of data types $\mathcal{T}$ and a set of names $\mathcal{N}$ disjoint from $\mathcal{T}$ and including $\{*, \texttt{\{\}}\}$.

Definition 1. *A* conceptual scheme *is a 4-tuple* $\langle C, A, T, R\rangle$ *with a* concept *set* $C \subset_{\text{fin}} \mathcal{N}$ *and mappings for* attributes $A : C \to \mathcal{N} \rightharpoonup \mathcal{N}^+$, lexical types $T : C \to \mathcal{N} \rightharpoonup \mathcal{T}$ *and* conceptual references $R : C \rightharpoonup \mathcal{N} \rightharpoonup \wp_{\text{fin}}(C)$, *satisfying the following conditions:*

1. *the* lexical attributes *are* $L(c) = dom(T(c)) = \{\, a \mid A(c, a) = a \,\} \subset_{\text{fin}} \mathcal{N}$*;*
2. $A(c, a)_i \in L(c)$ *and* $A(c, a)_i = A(c, a)_j \Rightarrow i = j$*;*
3. $C \times \{*, \texttt{\{\}}\} \subseteq dom(A)$*, with the* self $A(c, *)$ *a permutation*[3] *of* $L(c)$ *and the* identity $A(c, \texttt{\{\}})$ *a prefix thereof;*
4. $dom(R(c)) \subseteq dom(A(c)) \setminus \{*\}$*;*
5. $c' \in R(c, a) \Rightarrow \tau(c', \texttt{\{\}}) = \tau(c, a)$*, the* tuple type $\tau : dom(A) \to \mathcal{T}^+$ *being defined by* $\tau(c, a)_i = T(c, A(c, a)_i)$*;*
6. $c' \in R(c, \texttt{\{\}}) \Rightarrow A(c', \texttt{\{\}}) = A(c, \texttt{\{\}})$.

We can see that each concept has a non-empty finite set of lexical attributes with corresponding data types, and possibly a disjoint set of non-lexical attributes mapped to tuples of lexical ones. The lexical attributes of c are ordered in its self $A(c, *)$, starting with its identity $A(c, \texttt{\{\}})$. An attribute a of c may reference other concepts $R(c, a)$, its lexical tuple $A(c, a)$ having the same tuple type as the identity of every referred concept. Non-lexical attributes without conceptual references correspond to virtual concepts in the scheme definition language.

The semantics of a conceptual scheme characterize its possible databases, a notion lifted from the semantic domains of values $[\![\,\tau\,]\!]$ for the data types $\tau \in \mathcal{T}$.

Definition 2. *A* database Δ *for a scheme* $\langle C, A, T, R\rangle$ *is a mapping of* C *where:*

1. $\tau(c, *) = \tau_1 \cdots \tau_n \Rightarrow \Delta(c) \subseteq_{\text{fin}} [\![\,\tau_1\,]\!] \times \cdots \times [\![\,\tau_n\,]\!]$*;*
2. $x, y \in \Delta(c),\ x \neq y \Rightarrow \pi(c, \texttt{\{\}}, x) \neq \pi(c, \texttt{\{\}}, y)$*, a* projection π *being defined by* $\pi(c, a, t)_i = t_j \Leftrightarrow A(c, a)_i = A(c, *)_j$*;*
3. $c' \in R(c, a),\ t \in \Delta(c) \Rightarrow \exists t' \in \Delta(c') \,.\, \pi(c, a, t) = \pi(c', \texttt{\{\}}, t')$.

[3] We mean a sequence where each element of $L(c)$ appears exactly once.

Each tuple in $\Delta(c)$ is an individual member (values for self) of the concept c. Condition 1 ensures type correctness for all database tuples. The role of {} as identity (primary key) is enforced by condition 2. Finally, any conceptual reference (foreign key) is satisfied in the database by condition 3.

Non-lexical attributes are not strictly needed for defining keys through projections (their lexical tuples would suffice), but they are essential for writing compact and abstract scheme definitions and queries. Sub-attribute inheritance is not reflected in the scheme model, being irrelevant for the relational database implementation, but is also very useful for the query and command languages.

2.3 The Compiled Scheme

A scheme definition is compiled into a logic program consisting solely of facts for a few predicates expressing the defined scheme model $\langle C, A, T, R\rangle$.

For the database concepts we assert

$$\texttt{dc}(c) \Leftrightarrow c \in C$$

For attributes it pays to pre-compile the distinctions of identity vs. dependent and lexical vs. generic, which we do with these four predicates:

$$\texttt{ila}(c,a,t) \Leftrightarrow T(c,a) = t,\ \exists i\ a = A(c,\{\})_i$$
$$\texttt{dla}(c,a,t) \Leftrightarrow T(c,a) = t,\ \forall i\ A(c,\{\})_i \neq a$$
$$\texttt{iga}(c,a,[a_1,\cdots,a_n]) \Leftrightarrow A(c,a) = a_1 \cdots a_n,\ \forall i \exists j\ a_i = A(c,\{\})_j$$
$$\texttt{dga}(c,a,[a_1,\cdots,a_n]) \Leftrightarrow A(c,a) = a_1 \cdots a_n,\ \exists i \forall j\ a_i \neq A(c,\{\})_j$$

For the concept references we use

$$\texttt{cr}(c,a,c') \Leftrightarrow c' \in R(c,a)$$

Here are a few example clauses for the scheme presented before:

```
dc( agent ).          rc( organization, type, organization_type ).
ila( person, code, int ).                  rc( person, {}, agent ).
iga( person, code, [code] ).            dla( agent, name, str(60) ).
dga( course_edition, edition, [year,period_type,period_number] ).
```

Besides the coding of the abstract model two extra types of information are generated: attributes with a default assignment, whose paradigmatic case is that of auto-increment of codes, eg. `ada(agent,code,auto)`; and sub-attribute inheritance, eg. `sai(student,person)`.

In reality our scheme definition compiler produces two outputs: the clauses mentioned above, which are used for all runtime database management operations in the application(s) built over the scheme, and a variant with more details, eg. virtual concepts, named data types and online comments, used in the automatic Web-based scheme documentation system.

3 Queries

We can launch queries with a backtrackable call (`Query <? Tuple`) or a determinate (`Query <?> Tuple_list`). The `Query` term must be a valid conceptual expression, defining a database view yielding a sequence of value tuples, represented in the answer term as <tuple> ::= <value> | <value>,<tuple>.[4]

The conceptual expressions are built using a variety of infix and prefix operators, taking advantage of the flexible precedence definition mechanism (a standard feature of Prolog) to minimize the use of parenthesis.

As an example, the query for "the name and sex of the students enrolled in courses of the CS department in 2008/09" can be represented by a term whose main operators, besides the usual conjunction and equality, are '/' ("of the") and '$' ("for which"):

```
( name, sex ) / student /
enrollment $ ( acronym/department/course = 'CS', year = 2009 )
```

The form of the expression is close to its natural language counterpart, certainly much closer than the corresponding SQL statement

```
select distinct a1.name, p1.sex
from   enrollment e1, course c1, organization o1,
       student s1, agent a1, person p1,
where  e1.course = c1.code
   and c1.department = o1.code  and o1.acronym = 'CS'
   and e1.year = 2009           and e1.student = s1.code
   and s1.person = a1.code      and s1.person = p1.code
```

where many more concepts have to be made explicit, along with aliases and join equations. Attribute chains like "the acronym of the department of the course" are explicit in our conceptual expression and effective towards its readability, whereas they are scattered and therefore hidden in the SQL syntax.

The default ordering of answers is database-dependent. We can specify ascending or descending order on given selection attributes by prefixing them with `*>` or `*<`, respectively. Prefixing an intermediate attribute in the selection with `?` puts its identity in the selection tuple. So, returning to our example, the alternative selection sub-term `(*< sex, *> name) / ? student` would ask for the descending sex, ascending name and code of the students.

By default the SQL `distinct` qualifier is applied to the selection, yielding distinct tuples (the view of answers as sets). This can be overridden with the `??` prefix, eg. using `?? grade / enrollment $ ( course_edition = CE )` one can retrieve the multiset of grades for a particular course edition, useful for computing a histogram, say.

A very useful feature in most applications is to have parameters under global assignment whose current values are reflected in the queries. For example, the query for the students enrolled in *the* course edition (assumed to be contextually assigned) is `student/enrollment$(@course_edition)`. Its parsing calls `course_edition=@CE` to retrieve the current value, and then compiles the constraint `course_edition=CE`. Usage is very flexible for scheme-defined parameters, eg. `course_edition=@CE` succeeds with `CE=(123,2009,s,1)` after

[4] We can avoid lists because <value>s are themselves not lists.

the assignments year@=2009, course@=123 and period@=(s,2), and conversely year =@ Y succeeds with Y=2008 after course_edition@=(95,2008,s,1).

Constraints under $ can be grouped inside nested conjunctions and disjunctions. A common individual constraint is <attribute-chain> <op> <value>, with <attribute-chain> ::= <attribute> | <attribute-chain> / <attribute-chain> and appropriate <op>s (=, \=, >, etc.) and <value>s (@<parameter> is a value). The common case of identity valuation, {}=V, can simply be written {V}.

Sometimes we need to express constraints using sub-queries instead of explicit values, as in "the current year lecturers that were also students (here)" with lecturer/enrollment$(@year,person/lecturer^person/student). The operator ^ ("is a") assumes an attribute chain on the left but a query on the right, so student is here the database concept and not the attribute of enrollment.

The dual operator of ^ is ~ ("is not a"). Both exist also as prefix (rather than infix) operators (meaning respectively "there is a" and "there isn't a") over query expressions. But if we use eg. A$(···^B$X···) we generally want, inside X, to relate attributes of B to attributes of A. For the latter we use the * prefix to move one level up in the context of attribute interpretation. As an example we can express "the students enrolled this year in only one course" with

```
student / enrollment$( @year, ~enrollment$( @year, *student,
                                             course \= *course )
```

where *student can be read as "the same student" and is just shorthand for student = *student, equating the student of the inner and outer enrollments.

Similar conceptual contexts can appear in the selection part of a query, eg. for "the current courses and the lecturers that ever taught them" we can use

```
( course, lecturer/enrollment$( *course ) ) / enrollment$( @year )
```

Queries such as this, yielding for each course a number of lecturers, suggest the usefulness of packing the answer accordingly. This is achieved by using ";" instead of "," where the grouping is needed. So, each solution of the alternative query (course;lecturer···)/··· <? CL binds CL to a term c: [l_1,···,l_n] with a course c and a list of lecturers l_i of c.

We can use group selections such as sum (+), average (+/) or count (#), eg. (#student,course)/enrollment$··· for "the number of students enrolled in each course···", the grouping being implicit in the remaining selection elements.

4 Commands

The major commands are + <constrained-concept>, - <constrained-concept> and <constrained-concept> -+ <equalities>, standing respectively for the *creation*, *deletion* and *update* of concept members. They are much more powerful than their strict SQL counterparts, which we also make available (essentially for implementing the former) as respectively =+, =- and =-+. We can call for example +person$(sex=f,name=N,common_name=CN,identifier=I), that will start by calling agent$(name=N,common_name=CN,identifier=I)=+C to create a new tuple for `agent`, returning the auto-incremented new self `code C`, and then create the `person` sub-instance with `=+person$({C},sex=f)`.

We can also take advantage of parameters. Imagine the code for a Web service for students to enroll in courses. Upon its invocation the parameters `student`, `year`, etc. have assigned values, and when the student clicks on a course its code gets passed and assigned to `course`, nothing more being needed than to call `+enrollment$(@student,@course_edition)`.

Even more powerful is the update command. We can simply use, for example, `@student-+(identifier=I)` to update the student's identifier in the `agent` tuple whose `code` is that of the `student`'s `code`. The true power comes across when updating an identity attribute. Since this implies a change in the identity, that change has to be propagated all over the database tables where the concept instance is present. In order not to violate foreign keys this has to performed by creation and deletion, instead of immediate update, and in the correct order when chasing dependencies. The compiled scheme clauses have all the information for this reasoning to be performed flawlessly, which in some cases would be a daunting task if done manually. If, for example, there was some reason to change the code of a course, expressing it can be deceptively simple, just `@course-+(code=C)`, and in the end the course code will have changed in `course`, `course_edition`, `enrollment`, etc.

Deletion is similarly powerful, but presents more occasion for ambiguity and inconsistency. Deleting a concept instance implies, much as for identity updates, to chase dependencies in order to eliminate the instance from the database. But while this is sound for sub-concepts and derived concepts (where it is part of the identity), what about super-concepts and dependent concepts (where it is a dependent attribute)? In both cases we may have a strong or weak reading of the deletion, respectively deleting or not the super-instance or derived concept. If for the super-concept it might make sense (delete the individual, not just the fact that it belongs to a node in the hierarchy), for derived concepts it is hard to justify (say, delete enrollments with a peculiar grade that is being deleted). So we opt for the weak reading, resulting in failure if any of the hard cases happens.

Speaking of failure, it should be mentioned that we provide contextual transactions (`in_transaction:Exec`) that can be nested. Actually any command raises an exception if not called under a transaction.

5 Implementation

In the sequel we present code fragments in Prolog, although the actual implementation was made using a compositional alternative dialect. We sometimes omit actual procedure arguments and their treatment, and show unfoldings of actual definitions, to keep the presentation manageable by focusing on the essentials and the cases being illustrated.

The implementation of the query and command processing takes clear advantage of two hallmarks of logic programming: its deductive search capabilities, and its distinctive use of partially instantiated terms.

The heart of the processing is the handling of a <constrained-concept> ::= <concept> [$ <constraints>], an expression that appears both in queries and commands, through a procedure hcc whose clauses are

```
hcc( C$X, K, B$W ) :- !, h_co( C, B ), h_cs( X, [B|K]$W ).
hcc( C,   _, B$W ) :-    h_co( C, B ).
```

The "inputs" are the <constrained-concept> C$X and a context stack K which is the (possibly empty) list of concept bases (see next) under which C$X is interpreted. The "outputs" are the *concept base* B that becomes associated to C, and the *where-list* W derived from handling the constraints X in the context extended with B. In the second clause there are no constraints under C and W is returned free, because the where-list is global and constructed by incremental instantiation always keeping a free tail. We see the sharing of that global structure in the recursive hadling of a conjunction of constraints:

```
h_cs( (A,B), KW ) :- !, h_cs( A, KW ), h_cs( B, KW ).
```

The penalty of having to traverse a partially instantiated where-list to update its tail is low (the lists are short) and compensated by the efficiency of single argument passing in many clauses, as above, rather than using difference-lists.

We handle a concept by first checking it to be such and then performing the initial partial binding of the concept base using a new identifier:

```
h_co( C, b(I*C,_,_) ) :- dc( C ), new_co_id( C, I ).
```

A concept base b(I*C,N,J) corresponds to a particular instance I of the database table C. The variable N, initially free, is a boolean witness that gets bound when it is deemed that the instance is actually needed (not always). The initially free J is meant to collect information on the joins with other concept instances, being always a free-tail list with elements T:B where B is a joined concept base and T the join type, one of s (sub- or super-concept) or a(A) (attribute A). J acts as a cache for joins implicit in attribute resolution, as will become clear next.

Consider as a first example the query name/student${1}. It goes through hcc(student${1},[],BW), calling h_cs({1},[b(s1*student,N,J)]$W) for a new identity s1.[5] This goes on to handle a single constraint through

```
hsc( {V}, KW ) :- !, hrc( =,{},V, KW ).
hrc( Op,L,R, K$W ) :- hra( L,K, A), hrv( R,K, V), brc( Op,A,V, W).
```

We have to handle a relational attribute (hra) and a relational value (hrv), and build the relational constraint (brc). The relational attribute must be local, ie. resolved from the current concept base B at the top of the context K:

```
hra( E, [B|_], LT ) :- ha( E, B, AB ), glt( AB, LT ).
```

We invoke a generic procedure to handle an attribute that returns an *attribute base* AB, from which we get its lexical tuple LT. In our simple case of identity

[5] We use the first letter of the concept name and an associated counter.

`E={}` we get `AB=B=b(s1*student,_,_)` and `LT=(code/s1)`, given the scheme clause `iga(student,{},[code])`. Since the call to `hrv` in this case simply yields `V=1`, the call to `brc` finally constructs the equality constraint and makes sure it belongs to `W` by calling `is_in((code/s1)=1,W)`. Given the clauses

```
is_in( X, [X|_] ) :- !.
is_in( X, [_|L] ) :- is_in( X, L ).
```

called with a free-tail list this either checks the element is already there or puts it at the end with another free tail. So, `hcc(student${1},[],BW)` is solved with `BW=B$W=b(s1*student,_,_)$[(code/s1)=1|_]`. After this it's time for the call `hs(name,[b(s1*student,_,_)],S-[])` to handle the selection part of the query (with a difference-list result). The atomic (attribute) selection case is

```
hs( A, [B|_], SS ) :- iqo( O ), ha( A, B, AB ), as( AB, O, SS ).
```

where `iqo` yields the implicit query order (`0`, `/` or `\`) that goes with the computed attribute base `AB` to add as selection. Handling the attribute goes through

```
ha( A, B, AB ) :- cb_c( B, C ), gal( A,C, L ), hl( L,B, AB ).
```

that starts by extracting the concept from the base—the trivial unit clause is `cb_c( b(_*C,_,_), C )`—to call the major deductive procedure on the scheme to get the attribute location of an attribute (chain) of a concept, finally handling the location relative to the concept base to get the attribute base. The result of `gal(name,student,L)` is `L=@(a(person),person,@(s,agent,name))`, with two indirections. The first expresses the need to join the attribute `person` (of a `student` instance) with the identity of (an instance of) the database concept `person`. The second expresses an identity join (from `person`) to its super-concept (could be sub-) `agent` to arrive at the local attribute `name`. The search for this location is done by implementing a sensible notion of inheritance with overriding: first we check if the attribute `name` is local to `student` (it isn't); then we go recursively *up* the "is-a" hierarchy calling `cr(student,{},S)` (failing); next is the check for local sub-attribute inheritance (`sai(student,X),ga(X,name)` succeeds with `X=person` (`ga` is an abstraction of `iga` or `dga`), and we proceed from there); finally, failing the previous attempts we would go *down* for the sub-concepts.

Handling the location updates the concept base joins, retrieving or creating concept instance identifiers. In our case the joins are new, so we end up with `B= b(s1*student,n,[a(person):b(p1*person,_,[s:b(a1*agent,n,_)|_])|_])`. Notice the deduced need (`n`) for `student` (because of a join on its attribute `person`) and `agent` (to get its attribute `name`) but not for the `person` concept, since the join can be made directly to its super-concept `agent`. The computed attribute base is `AB=(name/b(a1*agent,n,_))`. Adding this selection (eg. with implicit ascending order `O=(/)`) results in `S=[name/a1:(/)]`, using the scheme clause `dga(agent,name,[name])` to connect the generic to lexical attributes.

The next processing stage extracts the from-list of needed concept instances while updating the where-list with the implicit join conditions. In our example we get `F=[s1*student,a1*agent]` and `W=[code/s1=1,person/s1=code/a1]`. Finally we invoke the SQL translator `sql(q(D,S,F,W),SQL)`[6] whose code is rather straightforward.

An SQL query is delivered to a previously set-up database connection via the predicate `db_query(Q,I)`. If successful the call returns in `I` an integer handler for retrieving the answer tuples one at a time, with either the determinate `db_fetch(I,T)` or the backtrackable `db_back(I,T)`. The elements of `T` correspond to their data types, eg. integers and atoms for `int` and `str(_)`, d(y,m,d) for a `date` with year y, month m and day d.

6 Manifold Attributes

Most concepts and attributes in the real world have a temporal nature, ie. their individual values change with time. When this happens with a periodic regularity, as with the course editions in an educational institution, the temporal structure is explicitly ascribed to attributes in the scheme (we've used `year`, `period`). Most of the temporal variability is, however, non-periodic. An agent's identifier should be changeable at any time, as well as its name (eg. through marriage). We may wish to register such changes in the database, to be able to look at the evolution of things, but also wish to retain simplicity in most queries, saying eg. "the student's identifier" to mean the current (real-time) value.

Another prevalent variability is that of names, acronyms, etc. with language (eg. English, French). Again, we ideally want a database scheme accomodating the multi-lingual variability but avoiding explicit mention of language in queries and commands where it can be assumed in context.

We can achieve these goals with special notation in the scheme definition language, and the corresponding treatment in the query and command languages, for what we call *manifold* attributes. Temporal and multi-lingual are (the most common) examples of manifold types.

6.1 Temporal Attributes

For a temporal attribute we have to specify its granularity (date, moment) and existence (continuous, discontinuous). For example, the following definitions

```
name(N)       : str(N).
identifier(N) : str(N).
* entity(N)         >> @- name(N).
agent : entity(60) >> @  identifier(20).
```

declare the `agent`'s `name` continuous (defined at all times) and `identifier` discontinuous, with change (for both) registered by date. Continuity affects the consistency checks on database changes, but not the scheme. The temporal manifold is considered *local*, meaning that independently marked temporal attributes of a

[6] `D` is a boolean "distinct" global flag.

given concept (name and identifier in our example) acquire independent variability (one may change without the other doing so). So, this definition actually gives rise to three concepts, implicitly defined by

```
agent.
agent_with_name       << agent, start: date
                      >> end: date, name(60).
agent_with_identifier << agent, start: date
                      >> end: date, identifier(20).
```

With this scheme the query name/student${1}, in the absence of a value for the contextual parameter temporal_validity, is deduced to be equivalent to

```
name / agent_with_name$( start=<today, end>today, agent= *person )
/ student${1}
```

where today is a conventional global value computed (and cached) in context. We see from the translation that the convention for a temporal interval is that start is included and end excluded.

Regarding commands, the creation + agent$(name=N) is equivalent to

```
agent =+ A,
=+ agent_with_name$(agent=A,start=min_date,end=max_date,name=N)
```

with appropriate conventional values min_date and max_date. Registering the change of a continuous temporal attribute A to a value V at time T typically involves the pattern

```
C$(end=max_date) =-+ (end=T), =+ C$(start=T,end=max_date,A=V).
```

6.2 Multi-lingual Attributes

The multi-lingual manifold type, contrary to the temporal, is *global* rather than local. By this we mean that marked attributes of a given concept are all grouped together for the manifold variation. For example, if we define

```
* entity(N) >> $ name(N).
agent : entity(60) >> $ common_name : str(30).
```

we get two multi-lingual attributes name and common_name of agent that vary together under each language, the translation being equivalent to

```
agent >> language, name(60), common_name : str(30).
ml_agent << agent, language >> name(60), common_name: str(30).
```

The multi-lingual manifold type, besides being global, is *existential*, meaning that at least one variety of the attributes must exist for some value of the manifold type (language in this case). This explains why we keep the attributes in the original concept, along with the extra manifold type, for which we assume there is a scheme definition such as

```
language << acronym : str(2) >> name(20).
```

The `language` attribute in the table `agent` is interpreted as the *default* for its `name` and `common_name`. Tuples in `ml_agent` yield the available translations.

The working of the query `name/student${1}` is more subtle and complex than for the temporal case, and always returns a value (the manifold is existential). If the `language` parameter has no currently assigned value, the selection is from the (default) `agent` table. If assigned, eg. `language=@en`, then `en` (English) is the *choice* language for multi-lingual attribute selection: for the given `agent` identity, if a tuple with `language=en` exists, in either `agent` or `ml_agent`, then its `name` is returned, otherwise the default `name` in the `agent` table. This is achieved through an automatically generated database view.

6.3 Manifold Combination

Manifolds can be combined. A good final definition for temporal and multi-lingual agent attributes is

```
agent : entity(60) >> @ $ ( name(60), common_name : str(30) ),
                      @ identifier(20).
```

This expresses that, as should be expected, the name and common name change together over time, and for each such change we have to provide values in a default language (this itself may change!) plus eventual translations in other languages. The identifier may change independently, and is language-independent.

7 Conclusions and Further Work

We have shown how to interact with relational databases using a vastly more effective language than SQL, following natural language principles of noun phrase composition with implicit conceptual relations and contextual definite references. The language has been implemented with high reliance on the distinguishing features of logic programming, namely structural unification and implicit backtracking, to reason over a compiled version of a database scheme. This compilation is also a deductive task carried out by a logic program, over a scheme description in a language that exploits inheritance and a simple theoretically sound model to achieve also a high level of conciseness and readability. Generic treatment of manifold phenomena such as temporal and multi-lingual attributes is incorporated in the scheme definition and database interaction languages, resulting in very powerful effects with little effort.

The architecture is available to developers of Prolog applications through the scheme compiler, the resulting online scheme documentation, and a few interface predicates for queries and commands. A team of around ten people has used it for years to build a very large real-world academic management system [1].

There are several directions for improving and building on this work. One can offer the query and command languages as a stand-alone database interface

(Web) service, or embed it in other programming languages capable of calling Prolog. One can achieve static optimizations of the code by partial evaluation, which should be a reasonably manageable endeavour since we are using a purely compositional alternative to Prolog. A major challenge is to tackle the problem of scheme change. This is a fact of life for most real-world applications, and generally a nightmare for the software development teams. One would have to jump from a purely static view of a scheme to a much higher-level plane where to express the *process* of scheme change rather than purely its *result*, and use this to deduce the impacts, and proceed with the necessary changes, on both the current relational database structure and the database interaction code.

On the political rather than technical side it would be interesting to promote these languages as complementary to the current dogmatic choice of languages for the semantic Web, as we believe there is a misguided misconception of what is "content", and an approach favouring a question-answering paradigm of how to acquire useful information, tapping on the immense potential of existing relational databases, is no less adequate than the idea of extracting "knowledge" as structured data to be reasoned upon.

References

1. Porto, A.: An integrated information system powered by prolog. In: Dahl, V., Wadler, P. (eds.) PADL 2003. LNCS, vol. 2562, pp. 92–109. Springer, Heidelberg (2002)
2. Ceri, S., Gottlob, G., Tanca, L.: Logic Programming and Databases. Springer, Heidelberg (1990)
3. Liu, M.: Deductive database languages: problems and solutions. ACM Comput. Surv. 31(1), 27–62 (1999)
4. Niemi, T., Järvelin, K.: Prolog-based meta-rules for relational database representation and manipulation. IEEE Transactions on Software Engineering 17(8), 762–788 (1991)
5. Smith, M.K., Welty, C., McGuinness, D.L.: OWL Web Ontology Language Guide (2004), `http://www.w3.org/TR/owl-guide/`

Typed Datalog

David Zook[⋆], Emir Pasalic, and Beata Sarna-Starosta

LogicBlox, Inc.
Atlanta, GA USA
{david.zook,emir.pasalic,bss}@logicblox.com
http://www.logicblox.com

Abstract. Static type safety is an important feature of many commercial programming languages, as has become apparent in our experience developing LogicBlox—a Datalog-based platform for building enterprise-scale systems for corporate planning. Existing approaches to enhancing Datalog (and Prolog) with type safety are problematic for LogicBlox applications because (1) they do not support inclusion constraints, which are crucial for database reasoning, and (2) their worst-case running times are exponential in the size of the programs. In the LogicBlox environment—where clients interactively add and execute programs and queries—efficient compilation and execution are critical, and so a PTIME type-checking algorithm is preferred. Furthermore, one of the central design goals of LogicBlox is to express the compiler itself in Datalog, which in general excludes exponential-time algorithms.

This paper presents a definition of type safety for Datalog which can express inclusion constraints along with an efficient (PTIME) and sound (but not complete) type-checking algorithm, proposes work-arounds for some common limitations of the algorithm, and indicates how the type-checking algorithm itself may be represented in Datalog.

Keywords: Datalog, Type System, Deductive Databases, Meta-compilation.

1 Introduction

LogicBlox is a commercial platform for building enterprise-scale corporate planning and pricing applications, which feature analyses that require aggregation across very large data sets, combined with simulation and modeling techniques. As traditional relational databases are not well-suited for applications of this kind, the LogicBlox environment is founded on proprietary database technology, fronted by a Datalog-like logic programming language. We use the LogicBlox language for three separate purposes: (1) to describe graphical user interfaces and the behavior of the applications, (2) to specify the database schemas and active rules, and (3) to express queries on the interaction between the applications and databases.

⋆ This paper describes work conceived, built, and financed by the entire LogicBlox development team, especially: Molham Aref, Mark Bloemeke, Greg Brooks, Wes Hunter, and Wael Sinno.

A. Gill and T. Swift (Eds.): PADL 2009, LNCS 5418, pp. 168–182, 2009.

Datalog [1,2,3] is a syntactic subset of Prolog introduced in the 1980s for database processing. By supporting a limited, safe form of recursion, Datalog considerably extends the expressive power of traditional database query languages, most notably SQL, at the same time—unlike Prolog—allowing SQL's set-at-a-time evaluation. Also similarly to SQL, the programs in Datalog are guaranteed to terminate, which obviates its need for extra-logical constructs such as Prolog's "cut" operator. As Datalog is not fully Turing-complete, its expressiveness is still limited. However, for ordered databases, Datalog has been shown to capture the complexity class of PTIME [4,5][1], which is a significant improvement over SQL. After its introduction as a smarter version of SQL in the 1990's, Datalog lost the interest of researchers for a time, until recently re-gaining attention in applications falling outside of the realm of traditional database reasoning, which include: program analysis [6,7,8], networks [9,10], security protocols [11], knowledge representation [12], robotics [13] and gaming [14].

The use of Datalog in building applications for commercial customers exposed to us the need to enhance the language in a variety of ways, such as adding support for: negation, aggregation, functional dependencies, update rules, and constraints. Furthermore, we realized that the efficiency of compilation and evaluation is paramount, because queries and programs are often executed between users' actions and software response. We have also found a real need for strong static typing, dictated by at least these reasons:

Increased safety. Datalog programs must be capable of maintaining the integrity of a database with respect to given database schemas. The typing approach we present in this work is a superset of the traditional referential integrity constraints.

Early error reporting. Transactions over large databases may run for several hours or even days. Static detection of type errors can—and does—result in significant time savings for the customers.

Better performance. Information deduced during type checking is used by the low-level database engine to perform a number of optimizations, including run-time code generation, efficient data storage, and elimination of unnecessary run-time checks.

Motivated by these real-world requirements, our paper makes the following contributions:

1. It presents a type system for Datalog which, unlike other known logic programming type systems, (i) naturally represents inclusion constraints, (ii) naturally supports subtyping (although remaining monomorphic), and (iii) is implementable by an algorithm which is PTIME (worst-case) in the size of the program;
2. It indicates how our type-checking algorithm can be expressed in Datalog itself; and
3. It provides a discussion of the incompleteness of the proposed type system.

[1] A programming language L captures a complexity class P if L can express every algorithm in P, and if every algorithm in P is expressible in L.

Our type system has been implemented as a part of the LogicBlox development environment. The type algorithms are written in C++ and compiled on the Linux (both 32- and 64-bit), Windows, and Macintosh platforms.

Roadmap. We begin with an overview of Datalog, including the relevant subset of LogicBlox extensions (Sections 2 and 3). Next, we discuss the notions of type safety in our implementation of Datalog, and present our type system (Sections 4 and 5). Then, we outline how our type checking algorithm can be implemented in Datalog as a part of meta-compilation strategy (Section 6). Before concluding with a discussion of related and future work (Section 8), we discuss the practical limitation of the incompleteness of our type-checking algorithm, and present some thoughts on how to overcome them in practice (Section 7).

2 Datalog (with Extensions)

We use, possibly subscripted, $?x$, $?y$, $?z$ to denote logical variables, a, b, c, to denote arbitrary constant values, k, n, m to denote numerical values, f, g to denote arbitrary function symbols, and p, q to denote logical predicates.

A Datalog program is a collection of clauses specifying a set of logical predicates. A *predicate* of the form $f(?x_1, \ldots, ?x_n)$ defines a n-ary relation f. A *(regular) clause* of the form *Head* `<-` *Body* asserts that, for any assignment of values to the variables, *Head* is true under the condition that *Body* is true. A *unit clause*, or a *fact*, has an empty body, and indicates predicates that are true under all conditions. Datalog supports *recursion* by allowing the same predicates to appear in both heads and bodies of the clauses.

The goal of a Datalog computation is to find the instances of the *intensional predicates*—predicates appearing in the heads of one or more regular program clauses—based on the data provided for the *extensional predicates*—predicates appearing only in the regular clause bodies and the facts. Given an interpretation (in the sense of first-order logic) for each of the extensional predicates (together called the *extensional database*), the computation calculates a satisfying interpretation for each of the intensional predicates.

Example 1. Consider the following Datalog definition of the ancestor relation:

```
ancestor(?x,?y) <- parent(?x,?y).                      (1)
ancestor(?x,?y) <- parent(?x,?z), ancestor(?z,?y).     (2)
```

The logical meaning of the recursive clause (2) is that, for any assignment of values to the variables `?x` $= a$, `?y` $= b$, and `?z` $= c$, if both `parent(`a`,`c`)` and `ancestor(`c`,`b`)` are true, then `ancestor(`a`,`b`)` must also be true. The program computes the intensional predicate `ancestor` based on the facts provided for the extensional predicate `parent`.

2.1 Syntax

The context-free grammar for the extension of Datalog underlying our approach is shown in Figure 1. A *program* consists of zero or more statements. A *statement* is a rule terminated with a '.'. A *rule* is an atom (the *head* of the rule), followed by a '$\leftarrow$', followed by a well-formed formula (the *body* of the rule). A *well-formed formula* is either an empty formula or a conjunction. A *conjunction* is one or more literals, separated by the *conjunction symbol* ','. A *literal* is an atom, possibly preceded by a negation sign '!'. An *atom* is a functor applied to a parenthesized list of terms. A *functor* is an identifier naming a predicate. The *arity* of the atom is the number of its arguments. A *term* is either a constant or a variable. A *constant* is an arbitrary identifier.[2] A *variable* is an identifier preceded by the *variable indicator* '?'.

In addition to complying with the context-free grammar, a program is required to satisfy the following context-sensitive restrictions:

1. All atoms sharing the same functor f must have the same arity $n = |f|$.
2. Every variable occurring in the head of a rule must also occur in its body.

Note that a predicate may appear in the head of more than one rule. For a predicate q, the all set of rules with q in their heads is called the *procedure* of q.

P	$\equiv$	S^*
S	$\equiv$	$R.$
R	$\equiv$	$A \leftarrow W$
W	$\equiv$	$\epsilon \mid C$
C	$\equiv$	$L \mid L, C$
L	$\equiv$	$A \mid !A$
A	$\equiv$	$p(T^*)$
T	$\equiv$	$?x \mid a$

Fig. 1. Extended Datalog Syntax

2.2 Semantics

The *logical semantics* of a Datalog program P is a conjunction of closed well-formed formulas of first-order logic (FOL). Each rule in P is understood as a conditional logical formula, where the (suitably quantified) body is the condition, and the (suitably quantified) head is the consequence. Disjunction, conjunction and negation in the rule are given their standard FOL meanings, as are variables and constants. In addition, every variable is universally quantified over the entire rule.

The *operational semantics* of a Datalog program is dictated by the specific *evaluation algorithm* used to compute a model conforming to the logical semantics. Our presentation remains independent of any particular operational semantics, relying only on the logical semantics. One area where operational semantics may vary is for Datalog extended with negation. It is well known that introducing negation leads to ambiguity concerning which logical model is the "natural" choice for the evaluation algorithm. Numerous operational semantics incorporating negation have been proposed, from disallowing the use of negation in recursion (*global stratification* [2]), to allowing the algorithm to fail to resolve some facts (e.g., the Well-Founded Semantics [15]). In our type-checking approach, we assume that: (1) negation does not occur in the heads of the rules, (2) the computed model is minimal, and (3) the use of negation is *safe*, meaning that every variable occurring inside a negative literal also occurs inside a positive literal in the same rule.

[2] Datalog terms are a subset of Prolog terms in the sense that only nullary function symbols are allowed.

2.3 Syntactic Sugar

According to the grammar in Figure 1, a non-empty body of a rule must be a conjunction of atoms. This restriction is unnecessary, as we can transform any logical formula in a rule body, with atoms arbitrarily nested using negation, conjunction and disjunction, into a set of logically equivalent rules, by (1) translating that formula into Disjunctive Normal Form (DNF), and (2) if the resulting disjunction has more than one alternative, splitting the rule into a separate rule for each alternative, duplicating the original head atom for each new rule. Furthermore, the body of a rule can contain an embedded universal quantification. A rule of the form:

$$A \leftarrow C_1, \texttt{all}(?x^* : W_{\texttt{if}} \rightarrow W_{\texttt{then}}), C_2.$$

is logically equivalent to the following two rules (where the $?y^*$ are all the variables inside the quantification *not* in $?x^*$):

$$A \leftarrow C_1, \texttt{!existsNot}(?y^*), C_2.$$

$$\texttt{existsNot}(?y^*) \leftarrow W_{\texttt{if}}, !W_{\texttt{then}}.$$

$W \equiv \epsilon \mid D$
$D \equiv C \mid D; C$
$C \equiv U \mid U, C$
$U \equiv L \mid (W) \mid !(W) \mid Q$
$Q \equiv \texttt{all}(?x^* : W \rightarrow W)$

Fig. 2. Extended Rule Body Syntax (enhancement to Figure 1)

If the rules resulting from the above transformations are syntactically correct (for example, if negation is safe), then the original rule can be considered correct. Therefore, in the following, we allow unrestricted use of negation, conjunction, disjunction, and universal quantification in rule bodies. Figure 2 formalizes these syntax extensions.

3 Constraints

Most database applications require some form of constraints (e.g., referential integrity constraints [3]). Unlike a rule, which calculates new values for a predicate, a constraint *restricts* the predicate's domain. We support constraints by means of a special nullary predicate `fail()`.

Example 2. A typical referential integrity constraint for the `ancestor` program would require that any value occurring in the first argument of `parent(?x,?y)` also occurs in `person(?x)`. This constraint can be expressed as a rule:

```
fail() <- parent(?x,?y),!person(?x).
```

which defines `fail()` to be true if, for any assignment of values `?x` $= a$, `?y` $= b$, `parent`(a, b) is true, but `person`(a) is false.

Adding support for constraints extends the usual operational semantics of Datalog by allowing programs to *fail.* Failure indicates that no satisfying interpretations *which also assign* `fail()` *false* can be found for the intensional predicates.

$$\begin{array}{lcl} S & \equiv & R. \\ & | & Z. \\ Z & \equiv & \texttt{fail()} \leftarrow W \\ & | & W \rightarrow W \end{array}$$

Fig. 3. Constraint Syntax (enhancement of Figure 1)

Constraints expressed using `fail()` may be difficult to read. Hence—as a notational convenience—we introduce a *positive* form of a constraint, with syntax shown in Figure 3. A positive constraint is a clause in which the '→' is used instead of the the rule's '←'. The body of a positive constraint is to the left of the '→', whereas the head is to the right. In general, the meaning of a positive constraint $W_1 \rightarrow W_2$ is the same as the rule $\texttt{fail()} \leftarrow W_1, !(W_2)$.

Example 3. The positive form of the constraint from Example 2 is:

```
parent(?x,?y) -> person(?x).
```

The simplest form of a constraint is an *arity constraint*: $p(?x_1, ..., ?x_k) \rightarrow .$, used to introduce the predicate p and identify its arity (k).

4 Type Safety

4.1 Background

We view a *type* as a set of values. Therefore, we define types for Datalog as unary predicates. A *type declaration* is a constraint of the form $p(?x_1, ..., ?x_m) \rightarrow t_1(?x_1), ..., t_m(?x_m)$ (with all $?x_i$s distinct), which requires that any value occurring in the ith argument of the predicate p (denoted $p.i$) must also occur in the predicate t_i. We say that *$p.i$ has type t_i* (denoted $p.i \sqsubseteq t_i$). This notion of type declaration corresponds to the notions of *inclusion constraints*[3], and referential integrity constraints in database literature, giving our approach a practical value in Datalog applications in this area.

Since the type declaration is a constraint, it is logically equivalent to a rule with `fail()` in the head. Thus, one way to process such a declaration would be to evaluate the rule along with the rest of the program, and then check whether the `fail()` predicate is true, in which case the evaluation would fail. This strategy corresponds to checking an inclusion constraint at run time, which amounts to *dynamic* type checking.

But we want to check as much statically as possible. Clearly since—by definition—the data supplied for the extensional predicates is arbitrary, any type-checking for an extensional predicate must be dynamic. However, static reasoning is possible for the intensional predicates. For a declaration Z of an intensional predicate q, the compiler can attempt to *logically derive* Z from the rules for q (given the type declarations of the extensional predicates). If the derivation succeeds, Z may be removed from the run-time evaluation of the program. If the derivation fails, the compiler can provide a warning that the rule may cause run-time failure. We formalize this intuition in the following sections.

[3] Stating that whenever values occur in certain columns in a database, then those values must also occur in some other columns.

% Types	% Extensional predicates
person(?x) -> .	parent(?x,?y) -> person(?x), person(?y).
gender(?x) -> .	hasGender(?x,?g) -> person(?x), gender(?g).
% Values	% Intensional predicates
gender(male) <- .	father(?x,?y) <- parent(?x,?y), hasGender(?x,male).
gender(female) <- .	father(?x,?y) -> person(?x), person(?y).

Fig. 4. Example Datalog Program

Example 4. Consider the program in Figure 4. The program defines two types, `person` and `gender`, providing the latter with two predefined values, `male` and `female`. The program also gives type declarations for the extensional predicates `parent(?x,?y)`, and `hasGender(?x,?g)`. Using the types and extensional predicates, the program specifies a rule calculating the `father(?x,?y)` predicate. Finally, a type declaration for `father` requires that both arguments are of type `person`. The goal of the type-checker is to prove, from the extensional declarations (of `parent` and `hasGender`), that the declaration of `father` will hold for any well-typed extensional database. The basic insight for this proof is straightforward: from the rule, it is apparent that any value v ($?x = v$) occurring in the first argument of `father` (denoted $father.1$) must also occur in both $parent.1$ and $gender.1$. From the declarations of these two predicates, it is clear that v must also occur in $person$. The proof for $father.2$ is similar.

4.2 Type System

Figure 5 shows the definition of our type system for Datalog programs. Note that no type environment is needed because Datalog has no nested syntactic structures. We annotate each type rule with an identifier r_n, and enclose the program statements in curly-braces, to differentiate them from type judgments.

A type judgment can be (1) a simple inclusion, (2) a disjunctive inclusion, or (3) a conjunctive inclusion. A *simple inclusion*, written $\tau \sqsubseteq \mu$, asserts that, for any extensional database, every value in τ is also in μ (μ is also called a *type bound* of τ). A *disjunctive inclusion*, written $\tau \sqsubseteq (\mu_1; ...; \mu_m)$ where τ and μ_is are type expressions, asserts that, for any extensional database, every value in τ is also in at least one of the μ_is. A *conjunctive inclusion*, written $(\mu_1, ..., \mu_m) \sqsubseteq \rho$, is complementary to the disjunctive inclusion, and asserts that every value that is in all of the μ_is must be in ρ.

A *type expression* can be (1) a name of a unary predicate, written t, (2) the type of the ith argument of predicate p, written $p.i$, or (3) the type of the variable $?x$ within the rule r, written $r : ?x$.

The type rule GIVEN asserts the initial type judgments that can be obtained from the extensional type declarations. The type rule BODY asserts that the type of a variable $?x$, occurring in the ith position of a predicate p in the body of some program rule, is restricted to the type of $p.i$. The type rule SIMPLETRANS applies transitivity to the subtype relation.

$$\frac{\begin{array}{c}\{p(x_1, ..., x_k) \rightarrow ..., t_i(x_i).\} \\ p \text{ is extensional}\end{array}}{\vdash p.i \sqsubseteq t.i}\ (\text{GIVEN}) \qquad \frac{\text{fail}() \ < -p_1(?x), ..., p_m(?x).}{\vdash (p_1, ..., p_m) \sqsubseteq \text{ fail}()}\ (\text{EXCL})$$

$$\frac{\begin{array}{c}\{r : A \leftarrow ..., p(..., ?x, ...), ...\} \\ x \text{ is the } i\text{-th argument of } p\end{array}}{\vdash r : ?x \sqsubseteq p.i}\ (\text{BODY}) \qquad \frac{\begin{array}{c}\{r_1 : q(..., ?x_j, ...) \leftarrow W_1\} \\ \cdots \\ \{r_m : q(..., ?x_j, ...) \leftarrow W_m\} \\ \text{the } r_i\text{'s form } q\text{'s procedure}\end{array}}{\vdash q.j \sqsubseteq (r_1 : ?x_j; ...; r_m : ?x_j)}\ (\text{HEAD})$$

$$\frac{\vdash \tau \sqsubseteq \mu \quad \vdash \mu \sqsubseteq \rho}{\vdash \tau \sqsubseteq \rho}\ (\text{SIMPLETRANS})$$

$$\frac{\begin{array}{c}\vdash \tau \sqsubseteq (\mu_1; ...; \mu_m) \\ \text{for every } i, \vdash \mu_i \sqsubseteq \rho \text{ or } \vdash \mu_i \sqsubseteq \tau\end{array}}{\vdash \tau \sqsubseteq \rho}\ (\text{DISJTRANS}) \qquad \frac{\begin{array}{c}\vdash (\mu_1, ..., \mu_m) \sqsubseteq \rho \\ \text{for every } i, \vdash \tau \sqsubseteq \mu_i \text{ or } \vdash \rho \sqsubseteq \mu_i\end{array}}{\vdash \tau \sqsubseteq \rho}\ (\text{CONJTRANS})$$

$$\frac{\begin{array}{c}\{q(..., ?x_j, ...) \rightarrow ..., t(?x_j), ...\} \\ \text{not } \vdash q.j \sqsubseteq t\end{array}}{\text{warn}(\text{"}?x_j \text{ is not a subtype of } t\text{"})}\ (\text{UNSAFE}) \qquad \frac{\vdash r : ?x \sqsubseteq \text{ fail}}{\text{warn}(\text{"var } ?x \text{ in rule } r \text{ is contradictory"})}\ (\text{EMPTY})$$

Fig. 5. Type Rules - Unary Inclusion

The type rule HEAD relates the type bound of $q.i$ to the bounds discovered in each of the rules r_j from q's procedure. Every value v in $q.i$ must have been derived by an application of at least one r_j, and so v must obey the type bound of the corresponding variable from that rule. This is true because of the minimality of the computed model requires that q does not contain any values other than those derived by the rules in q's procedure. Thus, the type rule HEAD introduces a disjunctive type judgment (when there is more than one rule in q's procedure), which is then used by the type rule DISJTRANS.

The type rule DISJTRANS makes the general assertion that, for any disjunctive inclusion $\tau \sqsubseteq (\mu_1; ...\mu_m)$, if a type expression ρ is a type bound for every μ_i, then it is also a type bound for τ. In effect, this type rule finds the least common supertype for all μ_is. A subtlety in the type rule DISJTRANS is the "or" condition, covering the case when τ includes itself. This situation can occur in recursive rules, such as rule (2) in Example 1. If a head predicate q is present in the body of a rule, the type rule BODY produces type judgments of the form $r : ?x \sqsubseteq q.i$. However, the type rule HEAD produces a disjunctive inclusion of $?x$: $q.i \sqsubseteq ...; r : ?x; ....$ Thus, since $r : ?x$ provides no information about a type bound for $q.i$, only those disjuncts *not* contained in $q.i$ are included in deducing the type bound.

Finally the type rule UNSAFE verifies what has been proven against the intensional type declarations. If a type declaration required that an argument of an intensional predicate has a particular type, but that type cannot be inferred from the rules, then a warning is issued.

The type rules CONJTRANS and EMPTY are discussed in Section 5.

Example 5. The type rules can be applied to the program in Figure 4 as follows (we refer to the rule `father(?x,?y) <- parent(?x,?y), hasGender(?x,male).` as r_1):

1. Applying GIVEN to the extensional declarations yields the type judgments: $parent.1 \sqsubseteq person$, $parent.2 \sqsubseteq person$, $hasGender.1 \sqsubseteq person$, and $hasGender.2 \sqsubseteq gender$.
2. Applying BODY to rule r_1 yields type judgments: $r_1 : ?x \sqsubseteq parent.1$, $r_1 : ?x \sqsubseteq hasGender.1$, and $r_1 : ?y \sqsubseteq parent.2$
3. Applying HEAD to r_1 yields: $father.1 \sqsubseteq r_1 : ?x$, and $father.2 \sqsubseteq r_1 : ?y$.
4. Applying SIMPLETRANS yields $father.1 \sqsubseteq parent.1$ and $father.2 \sqsubseteq parent.2$.
5. Applying SIMPLETRANS again yields $father.1 \sqsubseteq person$ and $father.2 \sqsubseteq person$.
6. The objective of the proof has been achieved, and applying UNSAFE fails to find any missing inclusions.

Despite the simplicity of our approach to type checking, based on inclusion constraints, presented type system has features comparable to more complex type systems, in particular:

Sub-Typing. A type declaration of a unary predicate in effect defines a subtype relationship. For example, the type declaration `boy(?x) -> person(?x).` states that the type `boy` is a subtype of `person`. Whenever a variable of type `person` is required, the type rules will allow the variable to have type `boy` instead.

Multiple "Inheritance". The type rules allow a predicate argument to be declared with more than one type. For example, the following program will be handled perfectly well by the type system.

```
thing(?x) -> .
big(?x) -> thing(?x).
red(?x) -> thing(?x).
myBalloon(?x) -> big(?x), red(?x).
```

5 Type Consistency

Most type systems assume that the types do not overlap, except that the supertypes contain their subtypes. However, in logic programs such disjointness must be explicitly declared. For example, according to the logical meaning of the following program, the types `man` and `woman` may have common elements:

```
person(?x) ->.
man(?x) -> person(?x).
woman(?x) -> person(?x).
```

A function common in type systems is verifying that the same object is not required to belong to non-overlapping types (we follow Gregor Meyer [16] in calling this *type consistency*, although our approach to checking it differs significantly from his). Hence, it is desirable to allow declarations asserting that types are disjoint. A declaration of this kind can be formulated by means of an *exclusion constraint* of the form `fail()` $\leftarrow p_1(?x), ..., p_m(?x)$. The type rule EXCL turns such a constraint into a conjunctive inclusion with supertype `fail`.

So suppose, for instance, that a program contains the exclusion constraint `fail() <- man(?x), woman(?x).`. If that program were also to contain a rule r with some variable $?x$ occurring as an argument to both `man` and `woman`, then the type rule Body would infer the type judgments $r : ?x \sqsubseteq$ `man` and $r : ?x \sqsubseteq$ `woman`. Consequently, the type rule ConjTrans, working with the exclusion constraint, infers $r : ?x \sqsubseteq$ `fail`, which in turn triggers the type rule Empty to produce a warning.

6 Meta-compilation

Pursuant to our design goal of expressing the LogicBlox compiler in (extended) Datalog, we translate the type system from Section 4.2 into an equivalent Datalog program. The starting point of this translation is the *meta-model*—a set of predicates capturing the syntax of the language (without constraints) from Figure 1. Figure 6 shows the declarations of the meta-model predicates. In the meta-model, the program subject to type checking is represented as a set of facts. Note that each syntactic construct (rule, atom, term, etc.) is associated with a unique constant. Also note that some of the predicate arguments (e.g., the second argument of `name` or `value`) are untyped, as assigning a type to them would serve no useful purpose. The type declarations in the program (both for extensional and intensional predicates) are captured by the `argType` predicate, which associates a predicate/argument-index pair ($?p$, $?i$) with a type ($?t$).

To illustrate the encoding, Figure 7 lists the meta-model facts representing the declaration and rule for the `father` predicate from the program in Figure 4.

The type rules of Figure 5 can now be expressed as shown in Figure 8. The first four rules determine which predicates are intensional (appear in the head of some program rule), and which are extensional (otherwise). The next three rules declare the predicates `simpleInclPred` (representing type judgements of the form $p.i \sqsubseteq q.j$), `simpleInclVar` (representing type judgments of the form $r : x \sqsubseteq p.i$), and `disjIncl` (representing type judgments of the form $p.i \sqsubseteq (r_1 : ?x_1; ...r_m : ?x_m)$).

The translation of the type rules is straightforward except for two cases. Firstly, because of the two forms of "simpleIncl" judgments, the type rule SimpleTrans

```
% Rule Syntax
Rule(?r) -> .
head(?r,?a) -> Rule(?r), Atom(?a).
body(?r,?a) -> Rule(?r), Atom(?a).

Atom(?a) -> .
functor(?a,?p) -> Atom(?a),
                  Predicate(?p).
arg(?a,?i,?t) -> Atom(?a), Term(?t).
negated(?a) -> Atom(?a).
```

```
Term(?t) -> .

Variable(?x) -> Term(?x).
name(?x,?n) -> Variable(?x).

Constant(?c) -> Term(?c).
value(?c,?v) -> Constant(?c).

% Type Declarations
argType(?p,?i,?t) -> Predicate(?p),
                     Predicate(?t).
```

Fig. 6. Meta-Model Predicates

```
% Datalog Syntax.
Rule(r3).
head(r3,a1).
body(r3,a2).
body(r3,a3).

Atom(a1).
functor(a1,father).
arg(a1,1,x1).
arg(a1,2,x1).

Atom(a2).
functor(a2,parent).
arg(a2,1,x1).
arg(a2,2,x2).

Atom(a3).
functor(a3,hasGender).
arg(a3,1,v1).
arg(a3,2,c1).

Term(x1).
Variable(x1).
name(x1,x).

Term(x2).
Variable(x2).
name(x1,y).

Constant(c1).
value(c1,male).

% Type Declarations.
argType(father,1,person).
argType(father,2,person).
```

Fig. 7. Example Meta-Model

must be split into two separate clauses. Secondly, the type rule DISJTRANS requires the use of the `all` quantifier. Despite these differences, this specification of the type system closely follows the formal specification of Figure 5.

Indeed these advanced semantics become important in this case, because—after transforming the `all` construct (as described in Section 2.3)—the type-checking program contains recursion through negation. Intuitively, this is right because evaluation of the type rule DISJTRANS may provide a new type bound for some predicate argument, which in turn might be used by the type rule BODY, and so on. Thus, the type-checking program is not globally stratified. Using the Well-Founded Semantics approach to negation can guarantee termination of the evaluation, but will not guarantee in general that the resulting model will be complete (the truth or falsity of some of the facts may be undetermined). So the translation into (extended) Datalog has at once indicated important information about the type rules.

7 Limitations

Clearly, placing limitations on the running time of the type-checking algorithm results in limitations of the completeness of the type inference. We now present two common cases of valid inferences that cannot be discovered by our algorithm.

Example 1: Cascading Disjunctive Inclusions. The type rule DISJTRANS handles disjunctive inclusions with every immediate supertype having a simple inclusion leading to the common supertype. However, the immediate supertypes may be related to the common supertype by another disjunctive inclusion, in which case the type rule DISJTRANS is not sufficient. For example, consider the following program:

```
Intensional(?p) -> Predicate(?p).
Intensional(?p) <- head(?r,?a), functor(?a,?p).
Extensional(?p) -> Predicate(?p).
Extensional(?p) <- Predicate(?p), !Intensional(?p).
simpleInclPred(?p,?i,?q,?j) -> Predicate(?p), Predicate(?q).
simpleInclVar(?r,?x,?p,?i) -> Rule(?r), Variable(?x), Predicate(?p).
disjIncl(?p,?i,?r,?x) -> Predicate(?p), Rule(?r), Variable(?x).

% Given
simpleInclPred(?p,?i,?q,1) <- argType(?p,?i,?t), Extensional(?p).

% Body
simpleInclVar(?r,?x,?p,?i) <- body(?r,?a), arg(?a,?i,?x), Variable(?x).

% SimpleTrans
simpleInclPred(?p,?i,?r,?k) <- simpleInclPred(?p,?i,?q,?j),
                               simpleInclPred(?q,?j,?r,?k).
simpleInclVar(?r,?x,?q,?j) <- simpleInclVar(?r,?x,?p,?i),
                              simpleInclPred(?p,?i,?q,?j).

% Head
disjIncl(?q,?j,?r,?x) <- head(?r,?a), functor(?a,?q), arg(?a,?j,?x).

% DisjTrans
simpleInclPred(?p,?i,?q,?j) <-
   all(?r,?x : disjIncl(?p,?i,?r,?x)) -> ( simpleInclVar(?r,?x,?q,?j)
                                         ; simpleInclVar(?r,?x,?p,?i) ).

% Unsafe
warn(?q,?j,?t) <- Intensional(?q), argType(?q,?j,?t),
                  !simpleInclPred(?q,?j,?t,1).
```

Fig. 8. Type-Checking Algorithm as an Extended Datalog Program

```
a(?x) <- b1(?x), ... ; b2(?x), ... .
b1(?x) <- c1(?x), ... ; c2(?x), ... .
d(?x) <- c1(?x) ; c2(?x) ; b2(?x) .
% derive the following:
a(?x) -> d(?x).
```

The following type judgments can be deduced from the program rules: $\mathtt{a} \sqsubseteq (\mathtt{b1};\mathtt{b2})$, $\mathtt{b1} \sqsubseteq (\mathtt{c1};\mathtt{c2})$, $\mathtt{c1} \sqsubseteq \mathtt{d}$, $\mathtt{c2} \sqsubseteq \mathtt{d}$, and $\mathtt{b2} \sqsubseteq \mathtt{d}$.

The type rule DisjTrans cannot apply here because the required intermediate supertypes—c1, c2 and b2—are separated into two disjunctions. However, the programmer can guide the compiler by introducing a type defined as the disjunction of c_1 and c_2 using the rule: `t(?x) <- c1(?x) ; c2(?x)`. Based on this rule, the type rules Body and Head enable derivation of the following type judgments: $\mathtt{c1} \sqsubseteq \mathtt{t}$, $\mathtt{c2} \sqsubseteq \mathtt{t}$, and $\mathtt{t} \sqsubseteq (\mathtt{c1};\mathtt{c2})$.

These additional type judgments allow the type rule DisjTrans to make two new deductions: `b1` $\sqsubseteq$ `t`, and `t` $\sqsubseteq$ `d`. By the type rule SimpleTrans, `b1` $\sqsubseteq$ `d`. Finally, the type rule DisjTrans can be applied to connect `a` and `d`: `a` $\sqsubseteq$ `d`, which is the desired inclusion.

Example 2: Mixing Conjunctive and Disjunctive Inclusions. A more complex issue arises when the inference requires combining disjunction and conjunction. For example, the following program sets up a conjunction of disjunctions in the type judgments:

```
% a1, a2, a3, and a4 are extensional.
b1(?x) <- a1(?x) ; a2(?x).
b2(?x) <- a3(?x) ; a4(?x).

c(?x) <- b1(?x), b2(?x), ... .
```

```
d(?x) <- a1(?x),  a3(?x) ;
         a1(?x),  a4(?x) ;
         a2(?x),  a3(?x) ;
         a2(?x),  a4(?x).

% derive the following:
c(?x) -> d(?x).
```

The soundness of the desired inference depends on being able to distribute conjunctions across disjunctions, which our efficient type rules are not strong enough to do.

8 Related and Future Work

Typed Prolog. There is a rich history of research in typing Prolog and Datalog, all of which differ from the work presented here in the following two ways. First, the worst-case running times of the type-checking algorithms is exponential, which prevent expressing them in Datalog. Second, none of the algorithms directly captures the notion of inclusion constraints, which is critical in database applications.

One well-known example is the Mycroft-O'Keefe type system [17,18], which adapts the Hindley-Milner algorithm to Prolog. While allowing a limited form of parametric polymorphism and type inference, it does not support subtyping (the simplest form of an inclusion constraint), making the expression of inclusion constraints inconvenient. Various proposals for supporting polymorphism have been made [19,16]. One avenue for future research would be to introduce parametric polymorphism into the LogicBlox language while maintaining the ability to express inclusion constraints.

Datalog Typing. In their pioneering paper, Fruhwirth et al. [20] present a type system using unary predicates as types – an idea also adopted above. However our approach differs significantly in respect to how Datalog is used to express the types, and also with respect to the already mentioned issue of exponential running time. Recently de Moor et al. [21] have presented a *non-Cartesian* type-checking algorithm for Datalog. The system supports inclusion constraints and subtyping (but not polymorphism), but with an exponential running time. A non-Cartesian type system, instead of validating the type of each argument independently, considers *tuples* of types, capturing correlated values of multiple arguments. An interesting and useful question is whether such notions can be implemented efficiently in Datalog.

Chase Algorithms. In the database community there is a wealth of literature on deducing inclusion dependencies using *chase algorithms* (for a good recent review of chase techniques, see [22]). Chase techniques suffer from exponential-time complexity with the introduction of disjunction. Possibly, the insights garnered in creating the efficient type-checking algorithm for LogicBlox could provide techniques for improvements in this domain.

Meta-Modeling. Finally, the only case of combining Datalog with meta-modeling that we are aware of is Evita Raced [23]), which features a bootstrapped meta-circular compiler implemented in Datalog, and applied to a meta-model similar to the one presented in this paper. That version of Datalog, however, has no type system, and does not support constraints.

References

1. Maier, D., Warren, D.S.: Computing with Logic: Logic Programming with Prolog. Benjamin/Cummings (1988)
2. Colomb, R.M.: Deductive Databases and Their Applications. Taylor & Francis, Inc., Abington (1998)
3. Abiteboul, S., Hull, R., Vianu, V.: Foundations of Databases. Addison-Wesley, Reading (1995)
4. Papadimitriou, C.H.: A note on the expressive power of Prolog. Bulletin of the EATCS 26, 21–23 (1985)
5. Kolaitis, P.G., Vardi, M.Y.: On the expressive power of datalog: tools and a case study. In: PODS. ACM Press, New York (1990)
6. Lam, M.S., Whaley, J., Livshits, V.B., Martin, M.C., Avots, D., Carbin, M., Unkel, C.: Context-sensitive program analysis as database queries. In: PODS 2005, pp. 1–12. ACM, New York (2005)
7. Hajiyev, E., Verbaere, M., de Moor, O.: Codequest: Scalable source code queries with datalog. In: Thomas, D. (ed.) ECOOP 2006. LNCS, vol. 4067, pp. 2–27. Springer, Heidelberg (2006)
8. Hajiyev, E., Ongkingco, N., Avgustinov, P., de Moor, O., Sereni, D., Tibble, J., Verbaere, M.: Datalog as a pointcut language in aspect-oriented programming. In: OOPSLA 2006. ACM Press, New York (2006)
9. Loo, B.T., Condie, T., Garofalakis, M.N., Gay, D.E., Hellerstein, J.M., Maniatis, P., Ramakrishnan, R., Roscoe, T., Stoica, I.: Declarative networking: language, execution and optimization. In: International Conference on Management of Data, pp. 97–108. ACM, New York (2006)
10. Loo, B.T., Condie, T., Hellerstein, J.M., Maniatis, P., Roscoe, T., Stoica, I.: Implementing declarative overlays. SIGOPS Oper. Syst. Rev. 39(5) (2005)
11. Li, N., Mitchell, J.C.: Datalog with constraints: A foundation for trust management languages. In: Dahl, V., Wadler, P. (eds.) PADL 2003. LNCS, vol. 2562, pp. 58–73. Springer, Heidelberg (2002)
12. Leone, N., Pfeifer, G., Faber, W., Eiter, T., Gottlob, G., Perri, S., Scarcello, F.: The dlv system for knowledge representation and reasoning. ACM Trans. Comput. Logic 7(3), 499–562 (2006)

13. Ashley-Rollman, M.P., De Rosa, M., Srinivasa, S.S., Pillai, P., Goldstein, S.C., Campbell, J.D.: Declarative programming for modular robots. In: Workshop on Self-Reconfigurable Robots/Systems and Applications at IROS 2007 (October 2007)
14. White, W., Demers, A., Koch, C., Gehrke, J., Rajagopalan, R.: Scaling games to epic proportions. In: SIGMOD 2007. ACM Press, New York (2007)
15. Gelder, A.V., Ross, K.A., Schlipf, J.S.: The well-founded semantics for general logic programs. Journal of the ACM 38, 620–650 (1991)
16. Beierle, C., Meyer, G.: Using types as approximations for type checking prolog programs. In: Middeldorp, A. (ed.) FLOPS 1999. LNCS, vol. 1722. Springer, Heidelberg (1999)
17. Mycroft, A., O'Keefe, R.A.: A polymorphic type system for prolog. Artif. Intell. 23(3), 295–307 (1984)
18. Lakshman, T.L., Reddy, U.S.: Typed prolog: A semantic reconstruction of the mycroft-o'keefe type system. In: ISLP 1991, pp. 202–217 (1991)
19. Kifer, M., Wu, J.: A first-order theory of types and polymorphism in logic programming. In: LICS, pp. 310–321. IEEE Computer Society, Los Alamitos (1991)
20. Frühwirth, T.W., Shapiro, E.Y., Vardi, M.Y., Yardeni, E.: Logic programs as types for logic programs. Logic in Computer Science, 300–309 (1991)
21. de Moor, O., Sereni, D., Avgustinov, P., Verbaere, M.: Type inference for datalog and its application to query optimisation. In: PODS 2008. ACM Press, New York (2008)
22. Deutsch, A., Nash, A., Remmel, J.B.: The chase revisited. In: Lenzerini, M., Lembo, D. (eds.) PODS 2008, pp. 149–158. ACM Press, New York (2008)
23. Condie, T., Chu, D., Hellerstein, J.M., Maniatis, P.: Evita raced: Metacompilation for declarative networks. In: VLDB 2008 (2008)

Using Bloom Filters for Large Scale Gene Sequence Analysis in Haskell

Ketil Malde[1] and Bryan O'Sullivan[2]

[1] Institute of Marine Research, Bergen, Norway
ketil.malde@imr.no
[2] Serpentine Green Design, San Francisco, USA
bos@serpentine.com

Abstract. Analysis of biological data often involves large data sets and computationally expensive algorithms. Databases of biological data continue to grow, leading to an increasing demand for improved algorithms and data structures. Despite having many advantages over more traditional indexing structures, the Bloom filter is almost unused in bioinformatics. Here we present a robust and efficient Bloom filter implementation in Haskell, and implement a simple bioinformatics application for indexing and matching sequence data. We use this to index the chromosomes that make up the human genome, and map all available gene sequences to it. Our experiences with developing and tuning our application suggest that for bioinformatics applications, Haskell offers a compelling combination of rapid development, quality assurance, and high performance.

1 Introduction

A central part of bioinformatics involves work with biological sequences. These sequences represent molecules of DNA, RNA, and protein, all of which are structured as long chains of smaller building blocks. For computational purposes, these chains are usually represented as strings over fixed alphabets. For instance, the nucleotides of DNA are represented using the alphabet of A (for adenine), C (cytosine), G (guanine), and T (thymine).

Since the introduction of large-scale sequencing in the early 1990s, public sequence databases have doubled in size every 18 months. The U.S. National Center for Biotechnology Information's GenBank database now contains 110 million nucleotide sequences, totaling 200GB of data[1].

Over the past two decades, the cost of generating new sequences has dropped by three orders of magnitude. As this trend is likely to continue, the rate at which biological sequences are produced will increase dramatically. For instance, the newest generations of pyrosequencing technologies produce hundreds of megabytes of sequence data per run [19][23][7].

Much of bioinformatics research involves the development of "throwaway" code that integrates preexisting components to create focused analytic tools that

[1] http://www.nih.gov/news/health/apr2008/nlm-03.htm

A. Gill and T. Swift (Eds.): PADL 2009, LNCS 5418, pp. 183–194, 2009.

have short lifespans. For many tasks, such as accessing and manipulating data from the more than 1 000 known public databases [10], languages like Python and Perl are widely used, with performance-critical analysis delegated to code written in languages such as C and C++.

An ideal situation for bioinformaticians is to be able to develop new analytic tools rapidly, without sacrificing speed or correctness. With these goals in mind, we used Haskell to prototype some novel uses of Bloom filters for sequence analysis.

1.1 Sequence Similarity

The core of sequence analysis is the search for similarity between sequences. Similarity provides the basis for many important tasks, for example:

- Genes are usually identified based on their similarity to known proteins and gene transcripts.
- The sequencing process commonly produces only fragments of the true sequence. These fragments are clustered by similarity, and then assembled by joining fragments whose ends are similar.
- Identifying similar regions of genomes from different organisms can reveal evolutionary relationships between those organisms, and shed light on the mechanisms of evolution.

Applications like these are ubiquitous. They are usually computationally expensive due to the size of the data sets involved.

A commonly used metric for sequence similarity is the edit distance or Levenshtein distance, which is the number of edit operations needed to transform one sequence into another. The edit distance between two sequences n and m can be calculated using dynamic programming in $O(nm)$ time [11][22][20]. This approach quickly becomes impractical for large sequences, and heuristic methods are usually used instead.

1.2 Word-Based Approaches

Heuristic approaches typically start by identifying fixed-size exact matches, called k-words[2]. Once a sufficient number of matches is identified, they are used as a starting point (or *seed*) to construct a more accurate alignment or comparison score.

The choice of k-word size is influenced by several factors. Sequences often contain errors introduced by the sequencing process, or differ due to mutations. Words should therefore be short enough that the number of false negatives is reasonable. For instance, if the data have a (rather severe) error rate of 5%, a word size of less than 20 will ensure that hits can be found. On the other hand, shorter words are less likely to be unique in a data set, which increases the chance of false positives. The inherent non-randomness of genes and genomes amplifies this problem.

[2] These are also known as q-grams, or k-tuples.

An index can store k-words either directly, using tables, or in a sparse data structure. The simplest approach is to use each word as an index in a table of size α^k, where α is the alphabet size. This approach is used by e.g. BLAT [13], which by default indexes words of length 11. To reduce the density of the index, BLAT only indexes non-overlapping words and removes words that occur frequently in the data set. As the table grows exponentially with word size, available memory limits the possible word lengths. Although longer words are often desirable, to make efficient use of memory they require sparse data structures like hash tables or search trees. This incurs additional overheads in space and time.

1.3 Suffix Trees and Arrays

Suffix trees [25] and suffix arrays [18] provide interesting alternatives to word-oriented indexing, as they allow searching for words of arbitrary length. They form the basis of several tools for sequence analysis, e.g. [2][16][12]. While both suffix trees and suffix arrays can be constructed in linear time, and can perform lookups of a length-m string in $O(m)$ time, this comes at a cost of about $12m$ bytes per position with 32-bit pointers [1]. Suffix structures are thus memory intensive. Unlike the word-based approaches, it is not straightforward to reduce memory use by omitting frequent or overlapping words. In addition, while the sensitivity of word-based indexing can be improved using gapped words [24], it is not clear how to apply this approach to suffix structures.

1.4 Bloom Filters

The Bloom filter [4] is a set-like data structure that uses space efficiently. Unlike a normal set data structure, its query operation is probabilistic: it may report false positives. The error rate is tunable: an application that can tolerate a higher error rate will consume less memory than one with stricter needs.

For example, to represent a 400 000-element set with a 1% false positive rate, a Bloom filter will use 0.46MB of memory. If we reduce the false positive rate to 0.01%, the space consumption doubles, to 0.91MB. The size of a Bloom filter does not depend on the sizes of its elements. In our case, this property offers the prospect of efficiently indexing long sequences.

A Bloom filter is implemented as an m-bit array and a family of h distinct hash functions. The empty set is represented as a zeroed bit array. To add an element, we compute h hashes over it. We use each hash value as an offset into the array, and set each corresponding bit to 1. To query the set for membership, we compute h hashes over the input. If any corresponding bit is not 1, the element is not present in the array. False positives arise if distinct values hash to the same offsets for all h hash functions.

Although Bloom filters are widely used in networking [5] and formal methods [9], they are almost unknown in bioinformatics. In the sections that follow, we discuss their use to implement solutions to some typical bioinformatics problems, and investigate how they perform on massive data sets.

2 Methods

2.1 A Fast Bloom Filter in Haskell

We implemented a Bloom filter in Haskell. Our library is general purpose in nature[3], and provides typical Haskell interfaces to construct and query immutable Bloom filters:

```
fromList :: (a -> [Hash])          -- family of hash functions
         -> [a]                    -- elements to add
         -> Bloom a

elem :: a -> Bloom a -> Bool
```

To achieve a false positive rate of 0.1% for an input list of known size, we use a family of 10 hash functions. Building a Bloom filter requires many modifications to a bit array, in this case 10 per element added. We use the ST monad [15] to efficiently make in-place modifications to this bit array, then freeze it to present an immutable interface to consumers of the library.

We avoid developing many independent hash functions by using Dillinger and Manolios's technique of double hashing [9]. We compute two hashes over a value, and combine their results using cheap algebraic operations to produce further hash values on demand. Although the resulting hash values are not independent, analysis has shown them to provide good enough dispersion for practical use [14].

We double our hashing performance by computing both hashes in a single traversal of an element, by using Haskell's foreign function interface (FFI) to invoke Jenkins's `hashlittle2` implementation[4].

We also use a power-of-two table size, so that we can perform cheap bit-manipulation operations to turn a hash value into a valid array index.

2.2 Indexing Sequences with Bloom Filters

We used the Bloom filter to implement a simple indexing scheme for biological sequences. As with other indexing schemes, the sequences are cut into fixed-length overlapping fragments that can be stored in the Bloom filter.

We allow a choice of word length and overlap (the distance between the beginnings of successive words). These parameters can be tuned to optimize the trade-off between sensitivity, specificity, and resulting index size. For instance, given the sequence *GATTACCA*, a word length of 3, and an overlap of 2, the index would store the three words *GAT*, *TTA*, and *ACC*. In our test application, we use a word size of 30 and an overlap of 6. The Bloom filter is configured to give a false positive rate of 0.005. As our implementation limits filter sizes to powers of two for efficiency, the observed false positive rate may be substantially lower in practice.

[3] `http://hackage.haskell.org/cgi-bin/hackage-scripts/package/bloomfilter`

[4] `http://burtleburtle.net/bob/hash/`

To calculate a distance between a *query* sequence and a *target* sequence, we index the target using a Bloom filter, then score the query sequence against it. If the Bloom filter uses an overlap of 1—i.e. every word from the target sequence is used in the Bloom filter—the score is the number of words from the query that match the filter. With larger overlaps, we match every word from the query sequence against the filter, but remove matches that occur closer than the overlap. Typically, such matches arise from spurious similarities to unrelated parts of the target, or highly repetitive sequences.

We can also calculate the expected number of false positives introduced by the Bloom filter, to quantify their effect on result quality. Under the assumption that the probability of a false positive result is word-independent, we can model false positives using a binomial distribution. Given a number of lookups n and false positive rate p, the expected number of false positives is np, with standard deviation $\sqrt{np(1-p)}$.

We implemented a simple application that reads a set of FASTA-formatted files containing target sequences, and builds a Bloom filter for each. Query sequences are then read from standard input, and matched against the Bloom filters, and the best hit is reported.

To compare the efficiency of Bloom filter indexing to other approaches, we also implemented versions of the application that use a balanced binary tree (using the standard Haskell module Data.Set) with ByteString elements. Since comparison of strings requires time proportional to their lengths, this is not an optimal strategy, and we therefore also implemented a version using words encoded as integers [17].

2.3 Applications and Data

We benchmarked our program in two different settings. We began by filtering ESTs for contaminants. We then clustered ESTs by matching them to chromosomes.

Sets of expressed sequence tags, or *EST*s, are an important source of genomic information. These sequences are produced from messenger RNA gene transcripts. ESTs are usually incomplete, and thus represent fragments of genes. In addition, error rates are high—typically about 0.5–1% even in regions of relatively high quality.

The current release of GenBank contains over eight million human ESTs, representing 4.2 gigabytes of data. We downloaded these from the University of California, Santa Cruz web site[5].

The human genome is about 3 billion nucleotides in length, split into 23 chromosomes. We downloaded the set of sequences representing these chromosomes from UCSC[6].

An EST originates from a gene that resides on a chromosome. Knowing the location of each EST helps with a number of tasks, among which are identifying

[5] ftp://hgdownload.cse.ucsc.edu/goldenPath/hg18/bigZips/est.fa.gz

[6] `ftp://hgdownload.cse.ucsc.edu/goldenPath/hg18/bigZips/chromFaMasked.zip`

the gene; identifying its full extent and internal structure; and discovering or identifying surrounding patterns that regulate the expression of the gene. We thus used our application to cluster ESTs by identifying their chromosomes of origin. An EST is assigned to the chromosome with most matching k-words if the number of matches is statistically significant.

Our second application filtered sequences for contamination. As part of the sequencing process, the molecules to be sequenced are inserted into a host organism (typically the bacterium *E. coli*) for mass production. Occasionally, genomic DNA from the host organism is retrieved and sequenced instead of the desired sequence, thus contaminating the resulting sequence data with unwanted sequences. It is therefore necessary to screen sequence data by comparing it to the *E. coli* genome, and remove the offending sequences before further analysis.

While human chromosomes range up to 240 megabases (Mb) in size, the 5Mb *E. coli* genome is relatively small. To provide a smaller test case for comparing different indexing implementations, we also downloaded the genome for one strain of *E. coli* from GenBank[7] .

All tests were performed on a single core of a 2.4GHz Intel Core2 processor, using version 6.8.3 of the GHC Haskell compiler.

3 Results

We randomly selected ESTs in sets of various sizes, and benchmarked the three different indexing implementations by matching the ESTs against the *E. coli* genome. The times are shown in Figure 1, we see that while integer matching is faster than strings, the Bloom filter substantially outperforms both. A linear regression shows that the Bloom filter indexing stage takes only 1.7 seconds, compared to 20.2 for the Integer-encoded and 11.9 for the string-based indexing. Similarly, the Bloom filter matches 1718 sequences per second, compared to 589 and 310 for the Integer and string based indexes, respectively.

Perhaps more important than time spent is memory consumption. Time affects how long we must wait for a result, but excessive memory consumption prevents us from successfully processing large sequences. While the set based implementations allocate 160–190MB of memory (as measured by `top`) for this test, the Bloom filter application runs in a mere 20MB, of which the Bloom filter itself uses only 2MB.

By comparing the outputs from the set-based and the Bloom-filter-based implementations, we can measure the number of actual false positives generated. The results from the 10K data set are displayed in Figure 2. Here, 76.5% of the sequences generated no false matches, and only 370 sequences had two or more false matches.

Figure 2 also shows the expected number of false matches, calculated separately for each sequence. Here, we see clearly that due to the power of two rounding of the Bloom filter size, the observed false positive rate is lower than the requested rate.

[7] `http://www.ncbi.nlm.nih.gov/entrez/viewer.fcgi?db=nuccore\&id=56384585`

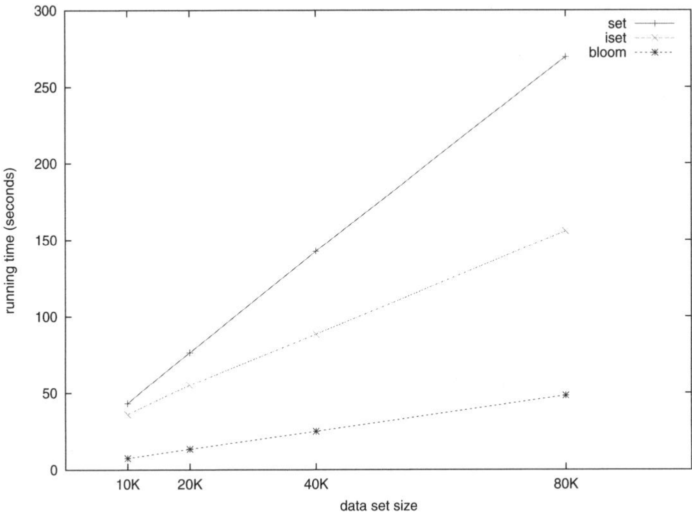

Fig. 1. Times (in seconds) using the Bloom filter, sets of ByteStrings, and sets of integers to index the *E. coli* genome, and match sets of sequences against it

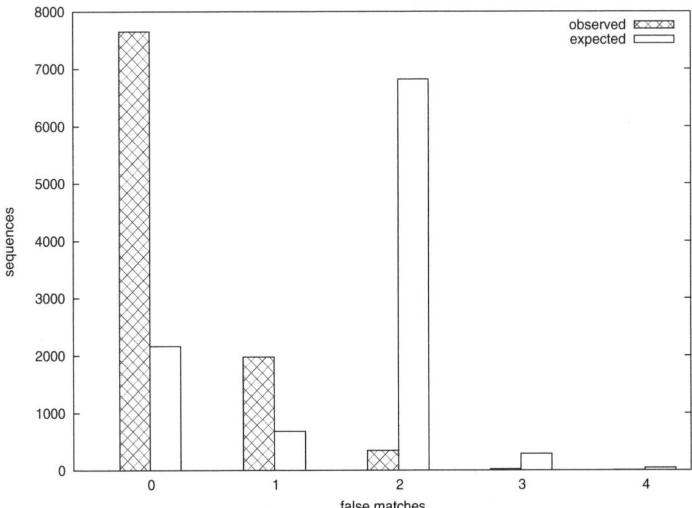

Fig. 2. False positives introduced by the Bloom filter from the 10K data set. 7 652 of the sequences have no false matches, 1 978 have one false match, 345 have two, 22 have three, and 3 sequences have four false matches. Also the expected false positives, calculated as described in Section 2.2.

Finally, we built Bloom filters for the 23 chromosomes constituting the human genome, and matched all ESTs against them. Indexing the chromosomes took 26 minutes, and the resulting Bloom filters consumed from 16 to 64MB of

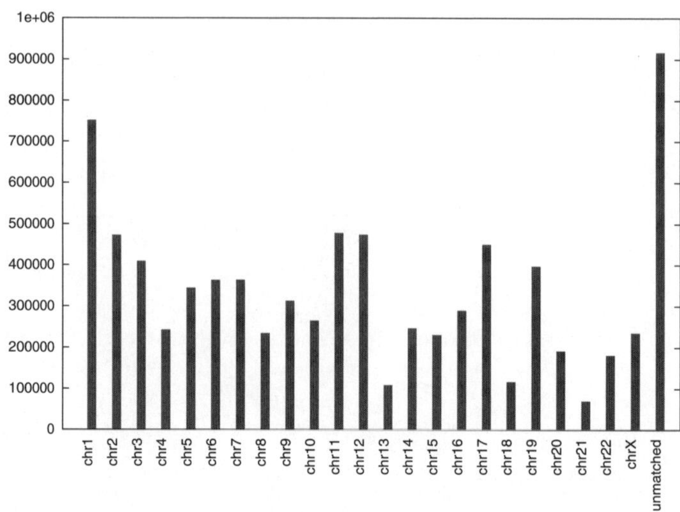

Fig. 3. Matching sequences by chromosome. As the chromosome sequences used have had repetitive regions masked, a large fraction of sequences are left unmatched.

memory, depending on chromosome size. The total memory used for the entire genome was 864MB. Matching the set of eight million ESTs against the Bloom filters took 49 hours. The resulting distribution of sequence locations is shown in Figure 3.

The chromosome sequences used here were masked, where repetitive regions were erased to avoid false positives. Many genes reside in masked regions, which seems to be the most likely explanation for 916 583 sequences that failed to match any of the chromosome. Manual checks have confirmed this for a small sample. Other possible explanations can be low quality sequence causing false negatives, or contamination.

4 Discussion and Conclusion

4.1 Performance Tuning Experiences

Early profiling of our application's performance indicated that the Bloom filter library accounted for over 70% of run time, even though we had addressed performance early on by double hashing in a single pass and using power-of-two sizes for bit arrays. Further investigation caused us to make a number of substantial changes. These all remained internal to the Bloom filter implementation, and did not affect its public interface.

By default, the GHC compiler checks the bounds of array accesses at run time, and we had somehow missed this early on. Switching to the alternative "unsafe" interfaces doubled our performance, by eliminating branches from an inner loop.

The lazy variant of the ByteString data type represents strings in chunked form [8], so a sequence can straddle multiple chunk boundaries. The Jenkins hash functions operate over contiguous C strings. To address this, we began by concatenating chunks into one contiguous string. In addition, the ByteString library by default makes a defensive copy of data that must remain immutable, to protect it from modification by native code. We were thus copying every ByteString at least once, and those that straddled a chunk boundary twice. We reimplemented the Jenkins hash code to operate incrementally over ByteString chunks and eliminated the defensive copying from the ByteString library, thereby doubling our performance.

GHC performs runtime safety checks on the bounds of bit-shifting operations. Even given constant shift values, we were unable to predict the circumstances under which GHC would eliminate those checks from our code. To ensure uniform branch-free performance, we implemented our own bit-shifting functions using GHC's word-level primitives. The branches thereby eliminated netted us a performance gain of perhaps 20%.

Many of our low-level optimizations were motivated by reading dumps from GHC's simplifier phase, using Stewart's `ghc-core` tool[8]. Although simplifier output is challenging to read, with some experience it gives a clear picture of when unnecessary memory allocations, or unboxing and reboxing operations, are occurring.

Faced with a number of potentially unsafe code transformations, we used the QuickCheck testing tool [6] to give ourselves statistical confidence that our code remained correct. We found its ability to provide us with a test case when a test failed to be invaluable in quickly directing us to the sources of bugs. For instance, when we rewrote the Jenkins hashing code to consume chunks incrementally, we wrote a QuickCheck property to ensure that the hash of a contiguous string was the same as the hash of a chunked string. Checking this property over successively larger random inputs exposed three subtle errors in our handling of boundary conditions during chunk traversal.

The final speed of our Bloom filter was approximately five times better than when we began, and came within 8% of a C program that we had written to offer a point of comparison. This experience suggests that low-level Haskell performance tuning can be highly profitable. With extensive use of QuickCheck, we keep the risk of unsafe changes low, and create working code more quickly.

While we have begun writing about the practicalities of Haskell performance analysis and tuning in [21], there remains plenty of scope for further compiler improvements; more experience reports; and better tool support to assist programmers in writing faster (but still safe!) Haskell code.

4.2 Bloom Filters, Bioinformatics and Haskell

The Bloom filter is a tremendously useful data structure: in settings such as ours, it holds substantial advantages over traditional indexing schemes by allowing indexing of large data sets with long word sizes quickly, and with low memory consumption.

---

[8] `http://hackage.haskell.org/cgi-bin/hackage-scripts/package/ghc-core`

The industry-standard alignment tool BLAST [3] aligns approximately 40 sequences per second when aligning the 10K data set against the *E. coli* genome. As BLAST identifies the alignments while our indexing merely detect the *presence* of a similarity, this result is not directly comparable to the results reported above. Nonetheless, it illustrates the potential benefit of using the Bloom filter as a preprocessing stage to eliminate unlikely candidates for a match.

To turn our sample implementation into an industry strength tool, there are many options to be explored: The impact of false positives could be reduced by requiring two or more consecutive (that is, spaced apart by exactly the overlap length) matches. Instead of counting matches along the length of the sequence, we could count matches within a fixed-size region (window). We could improve sensitivity by using gapped word indices [24]. Sequence quality should be taken into account. Our objective here has been to demonstrate the efficacy of Bloom filters in this application, and we therefore defer exploring these possibilities for the future.

We developed our prototype over the course of a few days, using preexisting Haskell libraries to parse sequence data and manipulate Bloom filters. The application-specific code amounted to 75 lines.

The field of bioinformatics is, in a sense, divided in two. On one side are standard algorithms and data structures, which must be highly optimized to deal with large data sets. These are typically implemented in C. On the other side are analysis pipelines, often project-specific, which combining such tools to perform a complete analysis. Here, rapid development is important, and scripting languages are often used.

We have demonstrated that we can address both sides of this divide with Haskell. The efficient implementation of crucial data structures such as ByteStrings and Bloom filters allows the application programmer to implement pipelines of functions, and from there entire tools, in a straightforward, even naïve, way, and still achieve both excellent performance and a high degree of confidence in results.

Acknowledgments

The authors wish to thank Shannon Engelbrecht for her extensive comments on drafts of this manuscript.

KM is supported by grant NFR 183640/S10 from the national Functional Genomics Programme (FUGE) of the Research Council of Norway.

References

1. Abouelhoda, M.I., Kurtz, S., Ohlebusch, E.: Replacing Suffix Trees with Enhanced Suffix Arrays. Journal of Discrete Algorithms 2(1), 53–86 (2004)
2. Abouelhoda, M.I., Ohlebusch, E., Kurtz, S.: Optimal Exact String Matching Based on Suffix Arrays. In: Laender, A.H.F., Oliveira, A.L. (eds.) SPIRE 2002. LNCS, vol. 2476, pp. 31–43. Springer, Heidelberg (2002)
3. Altschul, S., Gish, W., Miller, W., Myers, E., Lipman, D.: A basic local alignment search tool. Journal of Molecular Biology 215(3), 403–410 (1990)

4. Bloom, B.H.: Space/time trade-offs in hash coding with allowable errors. Communications of the ACM 13(7), 422–426 (1970)
5. Broder, A., Mitzenmacher, M.: Network applications of Bloom filters: A survey. Internet Mathematics 1(4), 636–646 (2003)
6. Claessen, K., Hughes, J.: QuickCheck: a lightweight tool for random testing of Haskell programs. In: ACM SIGPLAN Notices, pp. 268–279. ACM Press, New York (2000)
7. Cloonan, N., Forrest, A.R.R., Kolle, G., Gardiner, B.B.A., Faulkner, G.J., Brown, M.K., Taylor, D.F., Steptoe, A.L., Wani, S., Bethel, G., Robertson, A.J., Perkins, A.C., Bruce, S.J., Lee, C.C., Ranade, S.S., Peckham, H.E., Manning, J.M., McKernan, K.J., Grimmond, S.M.: Stem cell transcriptome profiling via massive-scale mRNA sequencing. Nature Methods 5(7), 613–619 (2008)
8. Coutts, D., Stewart, D., Leshchinskiy, R.: Rewriting haskell strings. In: Hanus, M. (ed.) PADL 2007. LNCS, vol. 4354, pp. 50–64. Springer, Heidelberg (2006)
9. Dillinger, P.C., Manolios, P.: Bloom filters in probabilistic verification. In: Hu, A.J., Martin, A.K. (eds.) FMCAD 2004. LNCS, vol. 3312, pp. 367–381. Springer, Heidelberg (2004)
10. Galperin, M.Y.: The molecular biology database collection: 2008 update. Nucleic Acids Research 36, D2–D4 (2008)
11. Gotoh, O.: An improved algorithm for matching biological sequences. Journal of Molecular Biology 162, 705–708 (1982)
12. Kalyanaraman, A., Aluru, S., Brendel, V., Kothari, S.: Space and time efficient parallel algorithms and software for EST clustering. IEEE Transactions on Parallel and Distributed Systems 14(12), 1209–1221 (2003)
13. Kent, W.J.: BLAT—the BLAST-like alignment tool. Genome Research 12(4), 656–664 (2002)
14. Kirsch, A., Mitzenmacher, M.: Less hashing, same performance: Building a better bloom filter. In: Azar, Y., Erlebach, T. (eds.) ESA 2006. LNCS, vol. 4168, pp. 456–467. Springer, Heidelberg (2006)
15. Launchbury, J., Jones, S.L.P.: Lazy functional state threads. In: Programming Languages Design and Implementation, pp. 24–35. ACM Press, New York (1994)
16. Malde, K., Coward, E., Jonassen, I.: Fast sequence clustering using a suffix array algorithm. Bioinformatics 19(10), 1221–1226 (2003)
17. Malde, K., Schneeberger, K., Coward, E., Jonassen, I.: RBR: Library-less repeat detection for ESTs. Bioinformatics 22(18), 2232–2236 (2006)
18. Manber, U., Myers, G.: Suffix arrays: a new method for on-line string searches. SIAM Journal on Computing 22(5), 935–948 (1993)
19. Margulies, M., Egholm, M., Altman, W.E., Attiya, S., Bader, J.S., Berka, L.A.B.J., Braverman, M.S., Chen, Y.-J., Chen, Z., Dewell, S.B., Du, L., Fierro, J.M., Gomes, X.V., Godwin, B.C., He, W., Helgesen, S., Ho, C.H., Irzyk, G.P., Jando, S.C., Alenquer, M.L.I., Jarvie, T.P., Jirage, K.B., Kim, J.-B., Knight, J.R., Lanza, J.R., Leamon, J.H., Lefkowitz, S.M., Lei, M., Li, J., Lohman, K.L., Lu, H., Makhijani, V.B., McDade, K.E., McKenna, M.P., Myers2, E.W., Nickerson, E., Nobile, J.R., Plant, R., Puc, B.P., Ronan, M.T., Roth, G.T., Sarkis, G.J., Simons, J.F., Simpson, J.W., Srinivasan, M., Tartaro, K.R., Tomasz3, A., Vogt, K.A., Volkmer, G.A., Wang, S.H., Wang, Y., Weiner4, M.P., Yu, P., Begley, R.F., Rothberg, J.M.: Genome sequencing in microfabricated high-density picolitre reactors. Nature 437(7057), 376–380 (2005)

20. Needleman, S., Wunsch, C.: A general method applicable to the search for similarities in the amino acid sequence of two proteins. Journal of Molecular Biology 48(3), 443–453 (1970)
21. O'Sullivan, B., Stewart, D., Goerzen, J.: Real World Haskell. In: Profiling and optimization, ch. 25. O'Reilly Media, Sebastopol (2008)
22. Smith, T.F., Waterman, M.S.: Identification of common molecular subsequences. Journal of Molecular Biology 147, 195–197 (1981)
23. Steemers, F.J., Gunderson, K.L.: Illumina profile: technology and assays. Pharmacogenomics 6(7), 777–782 (2005)
24. Valle, G.: Discover 1: a new program to search for unusually represented DNA motifs. Nucleic Acids Research 21(22), 5152–5156 (1993)
25. Weiner, P.: Linear pattern matching algorithms. In: Proceedings of 14th IEEE Symposium on Foundations of Computer Science (FOCS), pp. 1–11 (1973)

One Table Fits All

Jorge Costa and Ricardo Rocha

DCC-FC & CRACS
University of Porto, Portugal
c0607002@alunos.dcc.fc.up.pt, ricroc@dcc.fc.up.pt

Abstract. Tabling is an implementation technique that overcomes some limitations of traditional Prolog systems in dealing with redundant sub-computations and recursion. The performance of tabled evaluation largely depends on the implementation of the table space. Arguably, the most successful data structure for tabling is tries. However, while tries are efficient for variant based tabled evaluation, they are limited in their ability to recognize and represent repeated answers for different calls. In this paper, we propose a new design for the table space where tabled subgoal calls and/or answers are stored only once in a common global trie instead of being spread over several different tries. Our preliminary experiments using the YapTab tabling system show very promising reductions on memory usage.

Keywords: Tabling Logic Programming, Table Space, Implementation.

1 Introduction

Tabling [1,2] is an implementation technique where intermediate answers for subgoals are stored and then reused whenever a repeated call appears. The performance of tabled evaluation largely depends on the implementation of the table space – being called very often, fast lookup and insertion capabilities are mandatory. Applications can make millions of different calls, hence compactness is also required. Arguably, the most successful data structure for tabling is *tries* [3]. Tries meet the previously enumerated criteria of efficiency and compactness.

Used in applications that pose many queries, possibly with a large number of answers, tabling can build arbitrarily many and/or very large tables, quickly filling up memory. A possible solution for this problem is to dynamically abolish some of the tables. This can be done using explicit tabling primitives or using a memory management strategy that automatically recovers space among the least recently used tables when memory runs out [4]. An alternative approach is to store tables externally in a relational database management system and then reload them back only when necessary [5].

A complementary approach to the previous problem is to study how less redundant, more compact and more efficient data structures can be used to better represent the table space. While tries are efficient for variant based tabled

A. Gill and T. Swift (Eds.): PADL 2009, LNCS 5418, pp. 195–208, 2009.

evaluation, they are limited in their ability to recognize and represent repeated answers for different calls. In [6], Rao *et al.* proposed a table organization using *Dynamic Threaded Sequential Automata* (DTSA) which recognizes reusable subcomputations for subsumption based tabling. In [7], Johnson *et al.* proposed an alternative to DTSA, called *Time-Stamped Trie* (TST), which not only maintains the time efficiency of the DTSA but has better space efficiency.

In this paper, we propose a different approach. We propose a new design for the table space where all tabled subgoal calls and/or answers are stored in a *common global trie* instead of being spread over several different trie data structures. Our approach resembles the *hash-consing* technique [8], as it tries to share data that is structurally equal. An obvious goal is to save memory usage by reducing redundancy in the representation of tabled calls/answers to a minimum. We will focus our discussion on a concrete implementation, the YapTab system [9,10], but our proposals can be easy generalized and applied to other tabling systems.

The remainder of the paper is organized as follows. First, we briefly introduce some background concepts about tries and the table space. Next, we describe YapTab's new design for the table space organization using the common global trie and then, we describe how we have extended YapTab to provide engine support for our new design. At last, we present some preliminary experimental results and we end by outlining some conclusions.

2 Table Space

The basic idea behind tabling is straightforward: programs are evaluated by storing answers for tabled subgoals in an appropriate data space, called the *table space*. Repeated calls to tabled subgoals[1] are not re-evaluated against the program clauses, instead they are resolved by consuming the answers already stored in their table entries. During this process, as further new answers are found, they are stored in their tables and later returned to all repeated calls.

Within this model, the table space may be accessed in a number of ways: **(i)** to find out if a subgoal is in the table and, if not, insert it; **(ii)** to verify whether a newly found answer is already in the table and, if not, insert it; and **(iii)** to load answers to repeated subgoals. With these requirements, a correct design of the algorithms to access and manipulate tabled data is critical to achieve an efficient implementation. YapTab uses *tries* which is regarded as a very efficient way to implement the table space [3].

A trie is a tree structure where each different path through the trie data units, the *trie nodes*, corresponds to a term. Each root-to-leaf path represents a term described by the tokens labelling the nodes traversed. Two terms with common prefixes will branch off from each other at the first distinguishing token. For example, the tokenized form of the term $p(X, q(Y, X), Z)$ is the stream of 6 tokens: $p/3, VAR_0, q/2, VAR_1, VAR_0, VAR_2$. Variables are represented using

[1] We say that a subgoal repeats a previous subgoal if they are the same up to variable renaming.

the formalism proposed by Bachmair *et al.* [11], where each variable in a term is represented as a distinct constant. Formally, this corresponds to a function, $numbervar()$, from the set of variables in a term t to the sequence of constants $VAR_0, ..., VAR_N$, such that $numbervar(X) < numbervar(Y)$ if X is encountered before Y in the left-to-right traversal of t.

Internally, the trie nodes are 4-field data structures. The first field stores the node's token, the second field stores a pointer to the node's first child, the third field stores a pointer to the node's parent and the fourth field stores a pointer to the node's next sibling. Each node's outgoing transitions may be determined by following the child pointer to the first child node and, from there, continuing through the list of sibling pointers. To increase performance, YapTab enforces the *substitution factoring* [3] mechanism and implements tables using two levels of tries - one for subgoal calls, the other for computed answers. More specifically, the table space of YapTab is organized in the following way:

- each tabled predicate has a *table entry* data structure assigned to it, acting as the entry point for the predicate's *subgoal trie.*
- each different subgoal call is represented as a unique path in the subgoal trie, starting at the predicate's table entry and ending in a *subgoal frame* data structure, with the argument terms being stored within the path's nodes.
- the subgoal frame data structure acts as an entry point to the *answer trie.*
- each different subgoal answer is represented as a unique path in the answer trie. Oppositely to subgoal tries, answer trie paths hold just the substitution terms for the free variables which exist in the argument terms of the corresponding subgoal call.
- the leaf's child pointer of answers is used to point to the next available answer, a feature that enables answer recovery in insertion order. The subgoal frame has internal pointers that point respectively to the first and last answer on the trie. Whenever a repeated subgoal starts consuming answers, it sets a pointer to the first leaf node. To consume the remaining answers, it must follow the leaf's linked list, setting the pointer as it consumes answers along the way. Answers are loaded by traversing the answer trie nodes bottom-up.

An example for a tabled predicate `t/2` is shown in Figure 1. Initially, the subgoal trie is empty. Then, the subgoal `t(a(1),X)` is called and three trie nodes are inserted: one for the functor `a/1`, a second for the constant `1` and one last for variable `X`. The subgoal frame is inserted as a leaf, waiting for the answers. Next, the subgoal `t(a(2),X)` is also called. It shares one common node with `t(a(1),X)` but, having `a/1` a different argument, two new trie nodes and a new subgoal frame are inserted. At the end, the answers for each subgoal are stored in the corresponding answer trie as their values are computed. Note that, for this particular example, the completed answer trie for both subgoal calls is exactly the same.

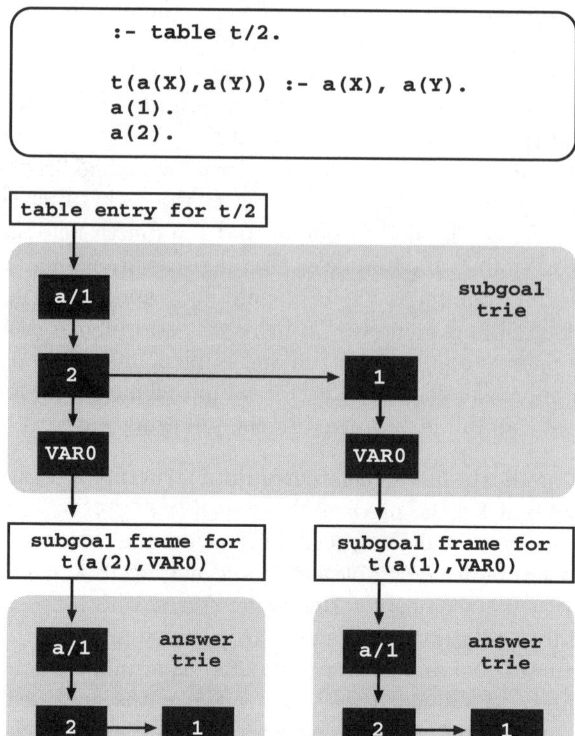

Fig. 1. YapTab's original table design

3 Common Global Trie

We next describe YapTab's new design for the table space organization. In this new design, all tabled subgoal calls and/or answers are now stored in a common global trie (GT) instead of being spread over several different trie data structures. The GT data structure still is a tree structure where each different path through the trie nodes corresponds to a subgoal call and/or answer. However, here a path can end at any internal trie node and not necessarily at a leaf trie node.

The previous subgoal trie and answer trie data structures are now represented by a unique level of trie nodes that point to the corresponding terms in the GT (see Figure 2 for details). For the subgoal tries, each node now represents a different subgoal call where the node's token is the pointer to the unique path in the GT that represents the argument terms for the subgoal call. The organization used in the subgoal tries to maintain the list of sibling nodes and to access the corresponding subgoal frames remains unaltered. For the answer tries, each node now represents a different subgoal answer where the node's token is the pointer to the unique path in the GT that represents the substitution terms for the free variables which exist in the argument terms. The organization used in the

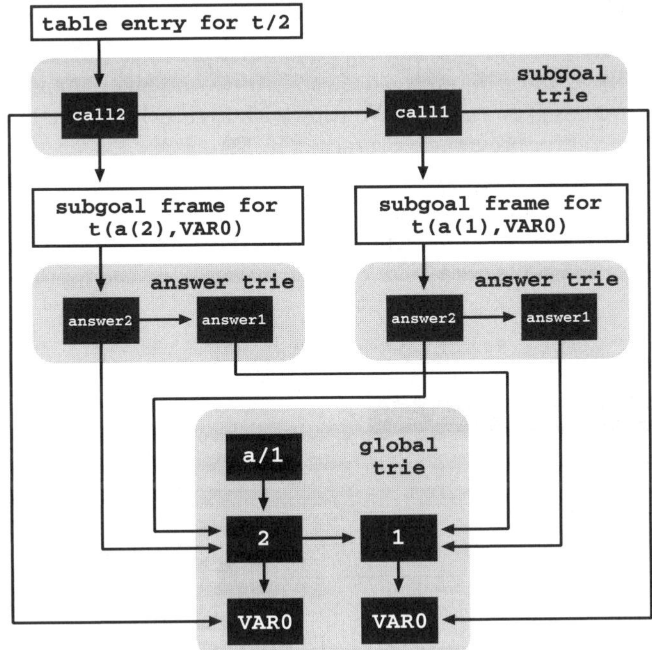

Fig. 2. YapTab's new table design

answer tries to maintain the list of sibling nodes and to enable answer recovery in insertion order remains unaltered. With this organization, answers are now loaded by following the pointer in the node's token and then by traversing the corresponding GT's nodes bottom-up.

Figure 2 uses again the example from Figure 1 to illustrate how the GT's design works. Initially, the subgoal trie and the GT are empty. Then, the first subgoal `t(a(1),X)` is called and three nodes are inserted in the GT: one to represent the functor `a/1`, another for the constant `1` and a last one for variable `X`. Next, a node representing the path inserted in the GT is stored in the subgoal trie (node labeled `call1`). The token field for the `call1` node is made to point to the leaf node of the GT's inserted path and the child field is made to point to a new subgoal frame. For the second subgoal call, `t(a(2),X)`, we start again by inserting the call in the GT and then we store a node in the subgoal trie (node labeled `call2`) to represent the path inserted in the GT.

As we saw in the previous example, for each subgoal call we have two answers: the terms `a(1)` and `a(2)`. However, as these terms are already represented in the GT, we need to store only two nodes, in each answer trie, to represent them (nodes labeled `answer1` and `answer2`). The token field for these answer trie nodes are made to point to the corresponding term representation in the GT. With this example we can see that paths in the GT can end at any internal trie node (and not necessarily at a leaf trie node) and that a common path in the GT can simultaneously represent different subgoal and answer terms.

4 Implementation Details

We then describe in more detail the data structures and algorithms for YapTab's new table design based on the GT. We start with Figure 3 showing in more detail the table organization previously presented in Figure 2.

Internally, tries are represented by a top *root node*, acting as the entry point for the corresponding subgoal, answer or global trie data structure. For the subgoal tries, the root node is stored in the corresponding table entry's `subgoal_trie_root_node` data field. For the answer tries, the root node is stored

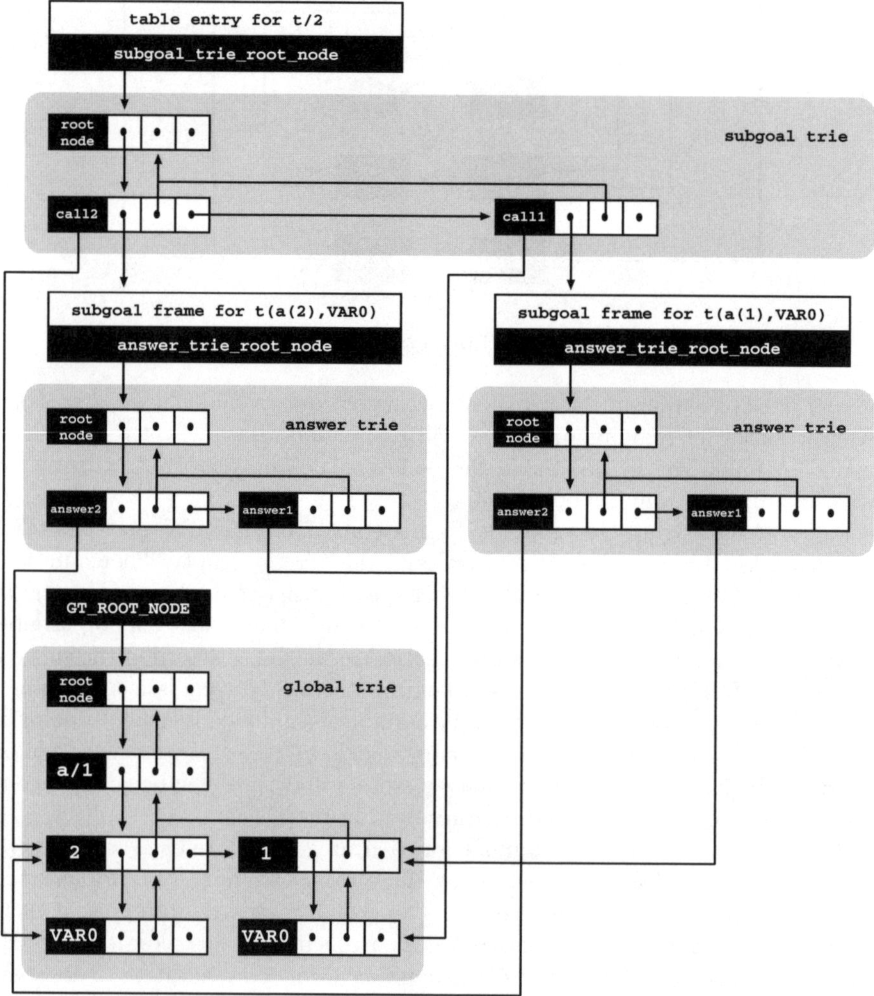

Fig. 3. Implementation details for YapTab's new table design

```
trie_node_check_insert(TRIE_NODE parent, TOKEN t) {
  child = parent->child
  if (child == NULL) {             // the list of sibling nodes is empty
    child = new_trie_node(t, NULL, parent, NULL)
    parent->child = child
  } if (is_not_a_hash_table(child)) {     // sibling nodes without hashing
    sibling_nodes = 0              // to count the number of sibling nodes
    do {           // check if token t is already in the list of siblings
      if (child->token == t)
        return child
      sibling_nodes++
      child = child->sibling
    } while (child)
    child = new_trie_node(t, NULL, parent, parent->child)
    if (sibling_nodes > MAX_SIBLING_NODES_PER_LEVEL) {  // alloc new hash
      hash = new_hash_table(child)
      parent->child = hash
    } else
      parent->child = child
  } else {                                    // sibling nodes with hashing
    hash = child
    bucket = hash_function(hash, t)    // get the hash bucket for token t
    child = bucket
    sibling_nodes = 0
    while (child) {     // check if token t is already in the hash bucket
      if (child->token == t)
        return child
      sibling_nodes++
      child = child->sibling
    }
    child = new_trie_node(t, NULL, parent, bucket)
    if (sibling_nodes > MAX_SIBLING_NODES_PER_BUCKET)      // expand hash
      expand_hash_table(hash)
  }
  return child
}
```

Fig. 4. Pseudo-code for the `trie_node_check_insert()` procedure

in the corresponding subgoal frame's `answer_trie_root_node` data field. For the global trie, the root node is stored in the `GT_ROOT_NODE` global variable.

Regarding the trie nodes, remember that they are internally implemented as 4-field data structures. The first field (`token`) stores the token for the node and the second (`child`), third (`parent`) and fourth (`sibling`) fields store pointers, respectively, to the first child node, to the parent node, and to the sibling node.

Traversing a trie to check/insert for new calls or for new answers is implemented by repeatedly invoking a `trie_node_check_insert()` procedure for each token that represents the call/answer being checked. Given a trie node `parent` and a token `t`, the `trie_node_check_insert()` procedure returns the child node of `parent` that represents the given token `t`. Figure 4 shows the pseudo-code for this procedure.

Initially, the procedure checks if the list of sibling nodes is empty. If this is the case, a new trie node representing the given token `t` is initialized and inserted as the first child of the given `parent` node. To initialize new trie nodes, we use a `new_trie_node()` procedure with four arguments, each one corresponding to the initial values to be stored respectively in the `token`, `child`, `parent` and `sibling` fields of the new trie node.

Otherwise, if the list of sibling nodes is not empty, the procedure checks if they are being indexed through a hash table. Searching through a list of sibling nodes is initially done sequentially. This could be too expensive if we have hundreds of siblings. A threshold value (`MAX_SIBLING_NODES_PER_LEVEL`) controls whether to dynamically index the nodes through a hash table, hence providing direct node access and optimizing search. Further hash collisions are reduced by dynamically expanding the hash tables when a second threshold value (`MAX_SIBLING_NODES_PER_BUCKET`) is reached for a particular hash bucket.

If not using hashing, the procedure then traverses sequentially the list of sibling nodes and checks for one representing the given token `t`. If such a node is found then execution is stopped and the node returned. Otherwise, a new trie node is initialized and inserted in the beginning of the list. If reaching the threshold value `MAX_SIBLING_NODES_PER_LEVEL`, a new hash table is initialized and inserted as the first child of the given `parent` node.

If using hashing, the procedure first calculates the hash bucket for the given token `t` and then, it traverses sequentially the list of sibling nodes in the bucket checking for one representing `t`. Again, if such a node is found then execution is stopped and the node returned. Otherwise, a new trie node is initialized and inserted in the beginning of the bucket list. If reaching the threshold value `MAX_SIBLING_NODES_PER_BUCKET`, the current hash table is expanded.

To manipulate tries we use two interface procedures. For traversing a trie to check/insert for new calls or for new answers we use the

```
trie_check_insert(TRIE_NODE root, SUBGOAL_CALL_ANSWER goal)
```

procedure, where `root` is the root node of the trie to be used and `goal` is the subgoal call/answer to be inserted. The `trie_check_insert()` procedure invokes repeatedly the previous `trie_node_check_insert()` procedure for each token that represents the given `goal` and returns the reference to the leaf node representing its path. Note that inserting a term requires in the worst case allocating as many nodes as necessary to represent its complete path. On the other hand, inserting repeated terms requires traversing the trie structure until reaching the corresponding leaf node, without allocating any new node.

To load a term from a trie back to the Prolog engine we use the

```
trie_load(TRIE_NODE leaf)
```

procedure, where `leaf` is the reference to the leaf node of the term to be returned. When loading a term, the trie nodes are traversed in bottom-up order.

When inserting terms in the table space we need to distinguish two situations: **(i)** inserting tabled calls in a subgoal trie structure; and **(ii)** inserting answers in a particular answer trie structure. The former situation is handled by the `subgoal_check_insert()` procedure as shown in Figure 5 and the latter situation is handled by the `answer_check_insert()` procedure as shown in Figure 6.

```
subgoal_check_insert(TABLE_ENTRY te, SUBGOAL_CALL call) {
  st_root_node = te->subgoal_trie_root_node
  if (GT_ROOT_NODE) {                                  // new table design
    leaf_gt_node = trie_check_insert(GT_ROOT_NODE, call)
    leaf_st_node = trie_node_check_insert(st_root_node, leaf_gt_node)
  } else {                                             // original table design
    leaf_st_node = trie_check_insert(st_root_node, call)
  }
  return leaf_st_node
}
```

Fig. 5. Pseudo-code for the `subgoal_check_insert()` procedure

In the original table design, the `subgoal_check_insert()` procedure simply uses the `trie_check_insert()` procedure to check/insert the given `call` in the subgoal trie corresponding to the given table entry `te`. In the new design based on the GT, the `subgoal_check_insert()` procedure now first checks/inserts the given `call` in the GT. Then, it uses the reference to the GT's leaf node representing `call` (`leaf_gt_node` in Figure 5) as the token to be checked/inserted in the subgoal trie corresponding to the given table entry `te`. Note that this is done by calling the `trie_node_check_insert()` procedure, thus if the list of sibling nodes in the subgoal trie exceeds the `MAX_SIBLING_NODES_PER_LEVEL` threshold value, then a new hash table is initialized as described before.

```
answer_check_insert(SUBGOAL_FRAME sf, ANSWER answer) {
  at_root_node = sf->answer_trie_root_node
  if (GT_ROOT_NODE) {                                  // new table design
    leaf_gt_node = trie_check_insert(GT_ROOT_NODE, answer)
    leaf_at_node = trie_node_check_insert(at_root_node, leaf_gt_node)
  } else {                                             // original table design
    leaf_at_node = trie_check_insert(at_root_node, answer)
  }
  return leaf_at_node
}
```

Fig. 6. Pseudo-code for the `answer_check_insert()` procedure

The `answer_check_insert()` procedure works similarly. In the original table design, it checks/inserts the given `answer` in the answer trie corresponding to the given subgoal frame `sf`. In the new design based on the GT, it first checks/inserts the given `answer` in the GT and, then, it uses the reference to the GT's leaf node representing `answer` (`leaf_at_node` in Figure 6) as the token to be checked/inserted in the answer trie corresponding to the given subgoal frame `sf`. Again, if the list of sibling nodes in the answer trie exceeds the `MAX_SIBLING_NODES_PER_LEVEL` threshold value, a new hash table is initialized.

Finally, the `answer_load()` procedure is used to consume answers. Figure 7 shows the pseudo-code for it. In the original table design, it simply uses the

```
answer_load(ANSWER_TRIE_NODE leaf_at_node) {
  if (GT_ROOT_NODE) {                                   // new table design
    leaf_gt_node = leaf_at_node->token
    answer = trie_load(leaf_gt_node)
  } else {                                          // original table design
    answer = trie_load(leaf_at_node)
  }
  return answer
}
```

Fig. 7. Pseudo-code for the `answer_load()` procedure

`trie_load()` procedure to load from the answer trie the answer given by the trie node `leaf_at_node`. In the new design based on the GT, the `answer_load()` procedure first accesses the GT's leaf node represented in the `token` field of the given trie node `leaf_at_node` (`leaf_gt_node` in Figure 7). Then, it uses the `trie_load()` procedure to load from the GT back to the Prolog engine the answer represented by the obtained GT's leaf node.

On completion of a subgoal, a strategy exists that avoids answer recovery using bottom-up unification and performs instead what is called a *completed table optimization* [3]. This optimization implements answer recovery by top-down traversing the completed answer trie and by executing specific WAM-like code from the answer trie nodes. This is implemented by extending the answer trie nodes with a fifth field where the WAM-like instructions are stored. With our new design, the nodes in the GT can belong to several different subgoal/answer tries, and thus this optimization is no longer possible. In the experimental section that follows, we have thus disabled this optimization, but to be fair when comparing YapTab with and without GT support, in both designs, the answer trie nodes include this fifth field.

Another potential problem of having nodes that can belong to several different subgoal/answer tries occurs when abolishing tables to reclaim space. Currently, YapTab does not support table abolish operations when using GT's design. A possible solution is to have an extra field in GT's trie nodes to count the number of external references to each node and only allow deletion when the number of references reaches zero.

5 Preliminary Experimental Results

We next present some preliminary experimental results comparing YapTab with and without support for the common global trie data structure. The environment for our experiments was an AMD Athlon XP 2800+ with 1 GByte of main memory and running the Linux kernel 2.6.24-19.

To evaluate the impact of our proposal, first we have defined a tabled predicate `t/5` that simply stores in the table space terms defined by `term/1` facts, and then we used a top query goal `test/0` to recursively call `t/5` with all combinations of one and two free variables in the arguments.

An example of such code for functor terms of arity 1 (500 terms in total) is shown next.

```
:- table t/5.
t(A,B,C,D,E) :- term(A), term(B), term(C), term(D), term(E).

term(f(1)).
term(f(2)).
...
term(f(499)).
term(f(500)).

test :- t(A,f(1),f(1),f(1),f(1)), fail.
...
test :- t(f(1),f(1),f(1),f(1),A), fail.
test :- t(A,B,f(1),f(1),f(1)), fail.
...
test :- t(f(1),f(1),f(1),A,B), fail.
test.
```

We experimented the `test/0` predicate with 7 different kinds of 500 `term/1` facts: integers, atoms and functor terms of arity 1 to 5. Table 1 shows the memory usage, in KBytes, and the running times, in milliseconds, to store to the tables (first execution of the program) and to load from the tables (second execution of the program where the tables are already completed) the complete set of subgoals/answers for YapTab with (column ***YapTab+GT***) and without (column ***YapTab***) support for the common global trie data structure.

The results in Table 1 show that GT support can reduce memory usage proportionally to the depth and redundancy of the terms stored in the GT. In particular, for functor terms of arity 2 to 5, the results show an increasing and very significant reduction on memory usage. The results for integer and atoms terms are also very interesting as they show that the cost of representing only atomic terms in the GT (between 7% and 8% in these experiments) can be manageable when we increase redundancy. Note that integers and atoms terms are represented by a single node in the original YapTab design, and by an extra node (therefore requiring two nodes) if using the GT approach.

Table 1. Memory usage (in KBytes) and store/load times (in milliseconds) for YapTab with and without support for the common global trie data structure

Terms	*YapTab (a)*			*YapTab+GT (b)*			*Ratio (b)/(a)*		
	Mem	*Store*	*Load*	*Mem*	*Store*	*Load*	*Mem*	*Store*	*Load*
500 int	49074	490	155	52803	738	164	1.08	1.51	1.06
500 atom	49074	508	158	52803	770	167	1.08	1.52	1.06
500 f/1	49172	693	242	52811	1029	243	1.07	1.48	1.00
500 f/2	98147	842	314	56725	1298	310	**0.58**	1.54	**0.99**
500 f/3	147122	1098	377	60640	1562	378	**0.41**	1.42	1.00
500 f/4	196097	1258	512	64554	1794	435	**0.33**	1.43	**0.85**
500 f/5	245072	1418	691	68469	2051	619	**0.28**	1.45	**0.90**

Table 2. Memory usage (in KBytes) and store/load times (in milliseconds) for YapTab with and without support for the common global trie data structure

Data Set	*YapTab (a)*			*YapTab+GT (b)*			*Ratio (b)/(a)*		
	Mem	*Store*	*Load*	*Mem*	*Store*	*Load*	*Mem*	*Store*	*Load*
carcinogenesis	1020	42290	42211	993	43010	43103	**0.97**	1.02	1.02
mutagenesis	432	116139	7516	314	112443	7308	**0.73**	**0.97**	**0.97**

On the other hand, these results seem to indicate that memory reduction comes at a price in execution time. With GT support, we need to navigate in two tries when checking/inserting a term. Moreover, in some situations, the cost of inserting a new term in an empty/small trie can be less than the cost of navigating in the GT, even when the term is already stored in the GT. However, our results seem to suggest that this cost decreases also proportionally to the depth and redundancy of the terms stored in the GT.

The results obtained for loading terms do not suggest significant differences. However and surprisingly, the GT approach showed to outperform the original YapTab design in some experiments.

Next, we tested our approach with two well-known Inductive Logic Programming (ILP) [12] benchmarks: the *carcinogenesis* and the *mutagenesis* data sets. We chose these two data sets because they are good real-world applications to test the two different situations observed in Table 1: the *carcinogenesis* data set stores more atomic terms and the *mutagenesis* data set stores more diverse terms. We used these data sets in a Prolog program that simulates the test phase of an ILP system. For that, first we ran the April ILP system [13] for the two data sets in order to collect the set of clauses generated for each. The simulator program then uses the corresponding set of generated clauses to run the positive and negative examples defined for each data set against them. Table 2 shows the memory usage, in KBytes, and the running times, in milliseconds, to store to the tables (first execution of the program) and to load from the tables (second execution of the program where the tables are already completed) the complete set of subgoals/answers for YapTab with (column ***YapTab+GT***) and without (column ***YapTab***) support for the common global trie data structure.

In general, the results in Table 2 confirmed the results obtained in Table 1 for memory usage. YapTab's GT support was able to reduce memory usage in both data sets proportionally to the depth and redundancy of the terms stored in the GT. In particular, for the *carcinogenesis* data set, memory usage showed to be slightly less with GT support, thus confirming our belief that the cost of representing atomic terms in the GT can be manageable when we increase redundancy.

For the running times, the results in Table 2 are significantly better than the results obtained in Table 1. The running times, both for storing and loading the complete set of subgoals/answers, are almost the same for YapTab with and without GT support. These results suggest that, at least for some class of applications, GT support has potential to achieve significant reductions on memory usage without compromising running time.

6 Conclusions and Further Work

We have presented a new design for the table space organization that uses a common global trie to store terms in tabled subgoal calls and answers. Our goal is to reduce redundancy in term representation, thus saving memory by sharing data that is structurally equal. Our preliminary experiments using the YapTab tabling system showed that our approach has potential to achieve significant reductions on memory usage without compromising running time.

Further work will include exploring the impact of applying our proposal to other real-world applications that pose many subgoal queries, possibly with a large number of redundant answers, seeking real-world experimental results allowing us to improve and expand our current implementation. In particular, we intend to study how alternative/complementary designs for the table space organization can further reduce redundancy in term representation.

Acknowledgements

This work has been partially supported by the research projects STAMPA (PTDC/EIA/67738/2006) and JEDI (PTDC/ EIA/66924/2006) and by Fundação para a Ciência e Tecnologia.

References

1. Tamaki, H., Sato, T.: OLDT Resolution with Tabulation. In: Shapiro, E. (ed.) ICLP 1986. LNCS, vol. 225, pp. 84–98. Springer, Heidelberg (1986)
2. Chen, W., Warren, D.S.: Tabled Evaluation with Delaying for General Logic Programs. Journal of the ACM 43(1), 20–74 (1996)
3. Ramakrishnan, I.V., Rao, P., Sagonas, K., Swift, T., Warren, D.S.: Efficient Access Mechanisms for Tabled Logic Programs. Journal of Logic Programming 38(1), 31–54 (1999)
4. Rocha, R.: On Improving the Efficiency and Robustness of Table Storage Mechanisms for Tabled Evaluation. In: Hanus, M. (ed.) PADL 2007. LNCS, vol. 4354, pp. 155–169. Springer, Heidelberg (2006)
5. Costa, P., Rocha, R., Ferreira, M.: Tabling Logic Programs in a Database. In: Workshop on (Constraint) Logic Programming, pp. 125–135 (2007)
6. Rao, P., Ramakrishnan, C.R., Ramakrishnan, I.V.: A Thread in Time Saves Tabling Time. In: Joint International Conference and Symposium on Logic Programming, pp. 112–126. MIT Press, Cambridge (1996)
7. Johnson, E., Ramakrishnan, C.R., Ramakrishnan, I.V., Rao, P.: A Space Efficient Engine for Subsumption-Based Tabled Evaluation of Logic Programs. In: Middeldorp, A. (ed.) FLOPS 1999. LNCS, vol. 1722, pp. 284–300. Springer, Heidelberg (1999)
8. Goto, E.: Monocopy and Associative Algorithms in Extended Lisp. Technical Report TR 74-03, University of Tokyo (1974)
9. Rocha, R., Silva, F., Santos Costa, V.: YapTab: A Tabling Engine Designed to Support Parallelism. In: Conference on Tabulation in Parsing and Deduction, pp. 77–87 (2000)

10. Rocha, R., Silva, F., Santos Costa, V.: On applying or-parallelism and tabling to logic programs. Theory and Practice of Logic Programming 5(1&2), 161–205 (2005)
11. Bachmair, L., Chen, T., Ramakrishnan, I.V.: Associative Commutative Discrimination Nets. In: Gaudel, M.-C., Jouannaud, J.-P. (eds.) CAAP 1993, FASE 1993, and TAPSOFT 1993. LNCS, vol. 668, pp. 61–74. Springer, Heidelberg (1993)
12. Muggleton, S.: Inductive Logic Programming. In: Conference on Algorithmic Learning Theory, Ohmsma, pp. 43–62 (1990)
13. Fonseca, N.A., Silva, F., Camacho, R.: April - An Inductive Logic Programming System. In: Fisher, M., van der Hoek, W., Konev, B., Lisitsa, A. (eds.) JELIA 2006. LNCS (LNAI), vol. 4160, pp. 481–484. Springer, Heidelberg (2006)

Recycle Your Arrays!

Roman Leshchinskiy

Programming Languages and Systems, School of Computer Science and Engineering,
University of New South Wales
rl@cse.unsw.edu.au

Abstract. Purely functional arrays are notoriously difficult to implement and use efficiently due to the absence of destructive updates and the resultant frequent copying. Deforestation frameworks such as stream fusion achieve signficant improvements here but fail for a number of important operations which can nevertheless benefit from elimination of temporaries. To mitigate this problem, we extend stream fusion with support for in-place execution of array operations. This optimisation, which we call *recycling*, is easy to implement and can significantly reduce array allocation and copying in purely functional array algorithms.

Keywords: Deforestation, Optimisation, Array Programming, Functional Programming.

1 Introduction

Functional languages such as Haskell are wonderful because they allow programs to be written at a high level of abstraction. However, this places a significant burden on the compiler which must incorporate a large number of sophisticated optimisations to achieve satisfactory performance. One such optimisation, *fusion* or *deforestation* [1], removes temporary data structures and combines traversals when possible. A classical example is the transformation $map\, f \circ map\, g \mapsto map\,(f \circ g)$ which eliminates a temporary list by performing the two maps in lockstep instead of one after the other.

For the most part, research has concentrated on fusion for inductive data structures, in particular lists [2,3,4]. In comparison, fusion of purely functional array operations has received relatively little attention with *functional array fusion* [5] and *stream fusion* [6,7,8] being notable recent exceptions. Unfortunately, even these frameworks treat arrays as list-like sequences, concentrating on regular traversals like *map* or *filter* and completely neglecting operations that rely on efficient indexing, such as updates, sorting etc. But often, these operations are the very reason for choosing arrays over lists!

To understand the problem, consider the bulk update operation (//) which yields an array obtained by updating an existing array with a list of index/value pairs. For instance, $\langle a, b, c, d, e\rangle \;//\; [(0, x), (2, y)] = \langle x, b, y, d, e\rangle$.

Without optimisation, the term $xs \;//\; ps \;//\; qs$ is evaluated by allocating a temporary array $ys = xs \;//\; ps$ and then creating another array $zs = ys \;//\; qs$ which is the final result of the computation. Obviously, we would like to perform

A. Gill and T. Swift (Eds.): PADL 2009, LNCS 5418, pp. 209–223, 2009.

the second update in-place, thus *recycling ys* and eliminating *zs* (we cannot simply update *xs* without losing referential transparency). Existing fusion frameworks are of no help here, though. They only implement loop fusion and these two loops cannot be fused!

This example highlights the difference between loop fusion and the optimisation we call recycling. Although both eliminate temporary arrays, the former does so by reducing the number of loops in a program whereas the latter removes unnecessary array allocation and copying by executing operations in-place. Of course, fusing loops is usually preferable but, as we have seen, not always possible.

In this paper, we extend the stream fusion framework with recycling capabilities with the goal of executing as many array operations as possible in-place even when loop fusion fails. Our approach relies on rewriting and is much less powerful than techniques based on static analysis [9,10,11] or linear types [12] but significantly easier to implement. It applies to all operations that rely on destructive updates. For simplicity, we only consider bulk updates in this paper and base our development on three representative use cases shown below. Note that here and in the rest of the paper, *map*, *filter* etc. denote the corresponding array operations, not standard Haskell list functions.

	Term	Expected evaluation strategy
(1)	*xs* // *ps* // *qs*	Perform the two updates in-place on a copy of *xs*.
(2)	*map* (+1) *xs* // *ps*	Store the result of the *map* in a new array and update it in-place.
(3)	*map* (+1) (*xs* // *ps*)	Update a copy of *xs* and then increment each element in-place.

The rest of the paper is structured as follows. Section 2 describes a simple implementation of arrays in Haskell and introduces stream fusion. In Section 3, we develop a framework capable of optimising the first two use cases by providing a pure interface to destructive array initialisation and integrating it with stream fusion. In Section 4, we tackle the third example which requires more advanced mechanisms for performing array operations in-place. Section 5 demonstrates the feasibility of our approach on a simple algorithm and quantifies the performance gains. Finally, in Section 6 we suggest future research directions and conclude.

2 Setting the Stage

The optimisations introduced in this paper operate on a fairly low-level representation of arrays. This means that they cannot operate directly on the standard Haskell *Array* type. It is too abstract, does not provide access to its underlying implementation and also supports rather sophisticated index spaces which would significantly complicate the development.

Instead, we introduce our own array type *Vector*, a thin wrapper over the low-level array primitives provided by the Glasgow Haskell Compiler (GHC) which supports the mechanisms required by our framework. We also give a quick introduction to stream fusion and show its implementation for *Vector*.

```
                    -- abstract data types
data Vector a
data MutableVector s a
                    -- monadic operations
newMV          :: Int → ST s (MutableVector s a)
readMV         :: MutableVector s a → Int → ST s a
writeMV        :: MutableVector s a → Int → a → ST s ()
unsafeFreezeMV :: MutableVector s a → ST s (Vector a)
                    -- pure operations on mutable vectors
lengthMV       :: MutableVector s a → Int
sliceMV        :: MutableVector s a → Int → Int → MutableVector s a
                    -- pure operations
index          :: Vector a → Int → a
length         :: Vector a → Int
```

Fig. 1. Basic vector operations

2.1 Arrays in Haskell

On the lowest level, arrays as provided by GHC live through two distinct phases. In the first phase, a *mutable* array is allocated and initialised by means of destructive updates. This code is necessarily monadic. Once initialisation is complete, the mutable array is *frozen*, i.e., converted to an *immutable* read-only array which can then be freely used in purely functional code.

Figure 1 shows the basic data types and operations implementing such arrays. Effects are encapsulated by the state transformer monad *ST* [13] which can be embedded in pure code with the operator *runST*:

```
runST :: (forall s. ST s a) → a
```

The state token *s* ties a *MutableVector* to a particular *ST* computation. This is crucial for ensuring referential transparency.

To get a feel for how to use these primitive operations, consider the following implementation of *map* for *Vector*:

```
map :: (a → b) → Vector a → Vector b
map f xs = runST $ do v ← newMV n                    -- allocate
                      mapM_ (put v) [0 .. n − 1]     -- initialise
                      unsafeFreezeMV v               -- freeze
  where
    n       = length xs
    put v i = writeMV v i (f (index xs i))
```

This code illustrates the standard pattern of allocating a *MutableVector*, initialising it and then freezing it to a *Vector*. Freezing is an unsafe operation since for the sake of efficiency, it does not copy the array. Instead, the original *MutableVector* and the frozen *Vector* share the same block of memory. This implies that subsequent destructive writes to the mutable vector would change the value of the immutable one, thus violating referential transparency. It is the programmer's responsibility to ensure that this does not happen. Typically, the mutable vector will not be used after freezing, as in the above example.

Later, we will rely on the support for constant time slicing provided by *MutableVector*. The function *sliceMV* v i n extracts n elements starting from index i from v. Again, the elements are not copied but, rather, aliased by the slice such that updating the slice will also change the original vector and vice versa.

2.2 Stream Fusion

Of course, the primitive vector operations are much too imperative for our taste. We really want to program in terms of familiar combinators such as *map*, *filter*, *zip* etc. As the previous definition of *map* demonstrates, they are easily implemented on top of the primitive interface. However, although correct, this implementation is not very efficient when used in *pipelines* of computations. For instance, when evaluating *map f* (*map g xs*) the result of *map g xs* is stored in a temporary vector and then f is mapped over it in a second traversal. We would like to fuse the two loops, in effect computing *map* ($f \circ g$) *xs* and thus eliminating the temporary.

Stream fusion achieves this by providing a coinductive, functional view of an array, which we call a *stream*:

$$
\begin{aligned}
&\textbf{data}\ \mathit{Step}\ s\ a &&= \mathit{Yield}\ a\ s \mid \mathit{Skip}\ s \mid \mathit{Done} \\
&\textbf{data}\ \mathit{Stream}\ a &&= \exists s.\ \mathit{Stream}\ (s \rightarrow \mathit{Step}\ s\ a)\ s\ \mathit{Int}
\end{aligned}
$$

A stream is made up of three components: a *stepping function*, a *seed* and a *size hint* which gives an upper bound on the number of elements in the stream. Streams are traversed by repeatedly applying the stepping function to the current seed. In each step, the function can yield the next element and a new seed (*Yield*), return just a new seed without producing an element (*Skip*) or signal the end of the stream (*Done*). We can easily provide *Stream* versions of standard combinators such as *map* or *filter*. In the following, we use the suffix S to distinguish them from their vector counterparts. We only show the implementation of *mapS* here and refer the reader to [7] for other stream combinators.

```
mapS :: (a → b) → Stream a → Stream b
mapS f (Stream next s n) = Stream next' s n
  where
    next' s = case next s of
                Yield x s' → Yield (f x) s'
                Skip s'    → Skip s'
                Done       → Done
```

Like all stream producers, *mapS* is not recursive. This is crucial since it allows pipelines of stream transformers, like *mapS f* $\circ$ *mapS g*, to be fused and optimised by general-purpose transformations such as inlining and constructor specialisation which GHC already implements [14,15]. The need to avoid recursion is also the motivation for *Skip* which is necessary for filtering out elements.

Stream fusion itself relies on two functions which convert between streams and vectors. Obtaining a *Stream* from a *Vector* is straightforward:

```
stream :: Vector a → Stream a
stream xs = Stream next 0 n
  where
    n                  = length xs
    next i | i < n     = Yield (index xs i) (i + 1)
           | otherwise = Done
```

The inverse operation constructs a new *Vector* following the usual pattern of allocation, initialisation and freezing identified in the previous section:

```
unstream :: Stream a → Vector a
unstream (Stream next s n) = runST $
   do v  ← newMV n
      n' ← fill v s 0
      unsafeFreezeMV (sliceMV v 0 n')
  where
   fill v s i = case next s of Yield x s' → do writeMV v i x
                                               fill v s' (i + 1)
                               Skip s'    → fill v s' i
                               Done       → return i
```

While enough space for n elements is allocated initially, that is only an upper bound on the actual length of the stream. After consuming the entire stream, the exact number of elements becomes known and only the corresponding slice of the vector is frozen. Note that in contrast to *mapS* and *stream*, *unstream* is recursive. This does not interfere with optimisation since it is a pure consumer, i.e., it does not produce a stream.

Based on the functions introduced in this section, we can implement typical vector operations in terms of operations on streams:

```
map :: (a → b) → Vector a → Vector b
map f = unstream . mapS f . stream
```

The last missing ingredient in the fusion framework is a mechanism for eliminating unnecessary conversions from and to streams. GHC allows this to be implemented as part of the library by specifying a *rewrite rule* which is applied whenever possible during optimisation [16]:

$$\langle \textbf{stream/unstream} \rangle \ \forall s.\ \mathit{stream}\ (\mathit{unstream}\ s) \mapsto s$$

The semantics is straightforward: instead of creating a temporary vector from the stream s and then converting it back to a stream, we can use s directly. The following transformation sequence demonstrates this rule in action:

$$\begin{aligned}
& map\, f\, (map\, g\, xs) \\
= \; & \{\text{inline}\} \\
& unstream\, (mapS\, f\, (stream\, (unstream\, (mapS\, g\, (stream\, xs))))) \\
= \; & \{\text{apply } \textbf{stream/unstream}\} \\
& unstream\, (mapS\, f\, (mapS\, g\, (stream\, xs)))
\end{aligned}$$

The resulting code only has one loop (*unstream*) and does not create any temporary vectors, operating on streams instead. As mentioned above, after another round of inlining GHC's optimiser is capable of completely eliminating any stream-related overheads, producing a tight, efficient loop which executes the two *mapS* in lockstep.

3 Basic Recycling

Stream fusion only works for combinators which can be implemented in terms of streams. Unfortunately, some crucial vector operations cannot be written in this way. For instance, the bulk update operation (//) described in the introduction has no efficient stream counterpart. We can, of course, implement (//) directly by destructively updating a mutable copy of a vector:

```
(//) :: Vector a → [(Int, a)] → Vector a
xs // ps = runST $ do v ← newMV n
                      mapM_ (copy v) [0 .. n − 1]
                      mapM_ (put v) ps
                      unsafeFreezeMV v
  where
    n          = length xs
    copy v i   = writeMV v i (index xs i)
    put v (i, x) = writeMV v i x
```

However, this implementation is, again, not optimal since it introduces superfluous temporary vectors when used in pipelines. In particular, none of the three use cases from the introduction are evaluated as desired. For instance, as discussed previously, *xs* // *ps* // *qs* unnecessarily copies the result of *xs* // *ps* into a new vector before updating it with *qs*. This is a great opportunity for recycling!

3.1 Combining Initialisers

While this particular example can be simply rewritten to *xs* // (*ps* ++ *qs*), we are, of course, interested in a more general solution which is applicable to all array operations that can benefit from recycling. Our approach is based on a data type which encapsulates the allocation and initialisation of a *MutableVector*:

```
data New a = New (∀s. ST s (MutableVector s a))
```

New simply wraps a monadic initialiser which produces a *MutableVector*. Constructing a *Vector* from it is straightforward:

$$
\begin{array}{l}
\mathit{new} :: \mathit{New}\ a \rightarrow \mathit{Vector}\ a \\
\mathit{new}\ (\mathit{New}\ \mathit{init}) = \mathit{runST}\ \$\ \mathbf{do}\ \{\ v \leftarrow \mathit{init};\ \mathit{unsafeFreezeMV}\ v\ \}
\end{array}
$$

We can also define an operation which produces a fresh, mutable copy of a *Vector*:

$$
\begin{array}{l}
\mathit{clone} :: \mathit{Vector}\ a \rightarrow \mathit{New}\ a \\
\mathit{clone}\ \mathit{xs} = \mathit{New}\ \$\ \mathbf{do}\ v \leftarrow \mathit{newMV}\ n \\
\qquad\qquad\qquad\qquad\qquad \mathit{mapM\_}\ (\mathit{copy}\ v)\ [0\, ..\, n-1] \\
\qquad\qquad\qquad\qquad\qquad \mathit{return}\ v \\
\quad \mathbf{where} \\
\qquad n \qquad\quad = \mathit{length}\ \mathit{xs} \\
\qquad \mathit{copy}\ v\ i = \mathit{writeMV}\ v\ i\ (\mathit{index}\ \mathit{xs}\ i)
\end{array}
$$

With these definitions in hand, we are now in the position to introduce the core technique of our approach. First, we define all array operations that can benefit from recycling (e.g. bulk update) as functions on *New*.

$$
\begin{array}{l}
\mathit{update} :: \mathit{New}\ a \rightarrow [(\mathit{Int},\ a)] \rightarrow \mathit{New}\ a \\
\mathit{update}\ (\mathit{New}\ \mathit{init})\ \mathit{ps} = \mathit{New}\ \$\ \mathbf{do}\ v \leftarrow \mathit{init} \\
\qquad\qquad\qquad\qquad\qquad\qquad\qquad \mathit{mapM\_}\ (\mathit{put}\ v)\ \mathit{ps} \\
\qquad\qquad\qquad\qquad\qquad\qquad\qquad \mathit{return}\ v \\
\quad \mathbf{where} \\
\qquad \mathit{put}\ v\ (i, x) = \mathit{writeMV}\ v\ i\ x
\end{array}
$$

The corresponding operations on *Vector* are now easily obtained with the help of *clone* and *new*, as the following definition of (//) shows:

$$
\mathit{xs}\ //\ \mathit{ps} = \mathit{new}\ (\mathit{update}\ (\mathit{clone}\ \mathit{xs})\ \mathit{ps})
$$

The new definition has a crucial advantage: it makes array copying explicit and is much more amenable to rewriting than the original monadic one. In fact, all we need to do is eliminate unnecessary conversions between *Vector* and *New*. This principle is quite similar to stream fusion, as is the rule implementing it:

$$
\langle \mathbf{clone/new} \rangle\ \ \forall p.\ \mathit{clone}\ (\mathit{new}\ p) \mapsto p
$$

The rule encodes the basic idea of recycling: there is no need to copy a mutable vector if it is immediately discarded. This simple mechanism is already sufficient to handle the first use case from the introduction:

$$
\begin{array}{ll}
 & \mathit{xs}\ //\ \mathit{ps}\ //\ \mathit{qs} \\
= & \{\text{inline}\} \\
 & \mathit{new}\ (\mathit{update}\ (\mathit{clone}\ (\mathit{new}\ (\mathit{update}\ (\mathit{clone}\ \mathit{xs})\ \mathit{ps})))\ \mathit{qs}) \\
= & \{\text{apply } \mathbf{clone/new}\} \\
 & \mathit{new}\ (\mathit{update}\ (\mathit{update}\ (\mathit{clone}\ \mathit{xs})\ \mathit{ps})\ \mathit{qs})
\end{array}
$$

The resulting code performs the two updates in-place and does not unnecessarily copy vectors. As with stream fusion, inlining and other standard optimisations further improve its performance.

It is important to realise that the correctness of the rewrite rule crucially depends on the fact that it does *not* operate directly on a vector but rather on a computation which constructs one. This allows the *clone*/*new* pair to be safely eliminated even if the computation is shared since it produces a new vector each time it is executed.

3.2 Integrating Stream Fusion

The framework developed in the previous section is capable of eliminating temporaries from adjacent applications of (//) and similar operations. But what about *map*, *filter* and other combinators which benefit from loop fusion as opposed to just recycling? Fortunately, it turns out that stream fusion can be seamlessly integrated with our approach.

The key observation is that both *unstream* and *clone* can be implemented in terms of a more primitive combinator which initialises a vector from a *Stream*:

$$fill :: Stream\ a \rightarrow New\ a$$

Its definition is easily derived from the implementation of *unstream* given in Section 2.2 – all we need to do is replace *runST* by the constructor *New* and refrain from freezing the *MutableVector*. Of course, there is no need to duplicate this code as we can now use *fill* in the definition of *unstream*:

$$\begin{aligned} &unstream :: Stream\ a \rightarrow Vector\ a \\ &unstream\ s = new\ (fill\ s) \end{aligned}$$

Analogously, *clone* can be easily rewritten to use the new combinator:

$$\begin{aligned} &clone :: Vector\ a \rightarrow New\ a \\ &clone\ xs = fill\ (stream\ xs) \end{aligned}$$

With these definitions, *unstream* and *clone* are no longer primitive with respect to fusion. We need to reformulate our rewrite rules to account for this:

$$\begin{aligned} &\langle\textbf{fusion}\rangle \quad \forall s.\ stream\ (new\ (fill\ s)) \mapsto s \\ &\langle\textbf{recycling}\rangle\ \forall p.\ fill\ (stream\ (new\ p)) \mapsto p \end{aligned}$$

The rules are obtained from **stream/unstream** and **clone/new** simply by expanding the definitions of the respective combinators. It is instructive to contrast the roles played by the two rules:

- **fusion** is derived from the original stream fusion rule and eliminates temporary *immutable* vectors by fusing loops;
- **recycling** eliminates unnecessary copying of *mutable* vectors during the initialisation phase.

The following example shows that the first rule implements stream fusion in the new system:

$$\begin{aligned}
& \mathit{map}\ f\ (\mathit{map}\ g\ \mathit{xs}) \\
= & \ \{\text{inline}\} \\
& \mathit{new}\ (\mathit{fill}\ (\mathit{mapS}\ f\ (\mathit{stream}\ (\mathit{new}\ (\mathit{fill}\ (\mathit{mapS}\ g\ (\mathit{stream}\ \mathit{xs}))))))) \\
= & \ \{\text{apply } \textbf{fusion}\} \\
& \mathit{unstream}\ (\mathit{mapS}\ f\ (\mathit{mapS}\ g\ (\mathit{stream}\ \mathit{xs})))
\end{aligned}$$

It is also intructive to see how the recycling functionality developed in the previous section is still provided by the second rule:

$$\begin{aligned}
& \mathit{xs}\ //\ \mathit{ps}\ //\ \mathit{qs} \\
= & \ \{\text{inline}\} \\
& \mathit{new}\ (\mathit{update}\ (\mathit{fill}\ (\mathit{stream}\ (\mathit{new}\ (\mathit{update}\ (\mathit{fill}\ (\mathit{stream}\ \mathit{xs}))\ \mathit{ps}))))\ \mathit{qs}) \\
= & \ \{\text{apply } \textbf{recycling}\} \\
& \mathit{new}\ (\mathit{update}\ (\mathit{update}\ (\mathit{fill}\ (\mathit{stream}\ \mathit{xs}))\ \mathit{ps})\ \mathit{qs})
\end{aligned}$$

But this is not all! By integrating stream fusion and recycling, the new system is also able to handle the second use case from the introduction, as the following transformation sequence shows:

$$\begin{aligned}
& \mathit{map}\ (+1)\ \mathit{xs}\ //\ \mathit{ps} \\
= & \ \{\text{inline}\} \\
& \mathit{new}\ (\mathit{update}\ (\mathit{fill}\ (\mathit{stream}\ (\mathit{new}\ (\mathit{fill}\ (\mathit{mapS}\ (+1)\ (\mathit{stream}\ \mathit{xs}))))))\ \mathit{ps}) \\
= & \ \{\text{apply } \textbf{fusion} \text{ or } \textbf{recycling}\} \\
& \mathit{new}\ (\mathit{update}\ (\mathit{fill}\ (\mathit{mapS}\ (+1)\ (\mathit{stream}\ \mathit{xs})))\ \mathit{ps})
\end{aligned}$$

In a sense, the last rewriting step performs both fusion and recycling which explains why either of the two rewrite rules can be applied here. It can be seen either as executing the update in-place or as fusing the *map* with the subsequent stream-based copying. In any case, the nondeterminism does not lead to problems since the two rewrite rules are confluent.

4 Recycling for Transformers

The last unsolved problem are computations in which transformers such as *map* cannot be fused with preceding operations but can be executed in-place, as in our third use case. Even with the framework developed in the previous section, $\mathit{map}\ (+1)\ (\mathit{xs}\ //\ \mathit{ps})$ allocates two vectors where one would be sufficient. Here, the elements are incremented *after* updating the array. This can be done in-place but so far, we have not introduced any mechanisms for handling such cases.

Before explaining our solution, it is important to point out that this form of in-place execution is only possible for a restricted set of array operations which meet the following conditions:

- they do not change the type of the elements,
- they process the array sequentially and
- the result fits into the original array.

Fortunately, many important operations such as filtering and scanning fall into this category. Calls to *map* can be optimised in this way (as in our example) as long as they do not violate the first requirement.

4.1 Monadic Streams

In the context of our fusion framework, we can observe that certain stream transformers of type *Stream a* → *Stream a* can be executed in-place, thus recycling mutable vectors. Since such in-place operations are necessarily monadic, we must generalise streams to support monadic computations. Fortunately, this generalisation is straightforward:

$$\textbf{data}\ \mathit{MStream}\ m\ a\ =\ \exists s.\ \mathit{MStream}\ (s\ \rightarrow\ m\ (\mathit{Step}\ s\ a))\ s\ \mathit{Int}$$

Monadic streams are parametrised by a monad m and the stepping function is executed in that monad. *MStream* is strictly more general than *Stream* as the latter can be obtained by instantiating the former at the identity monad *Id*:

$$\textbf{type}\ \mathit{Stream}\ a\ =\ \mathit{MStream}\ \mathit{Id}\ a$$

Most stream operations can be trivially reimplemented to work on monadic streams. Again, we use *mapS* as an example:

```
mapS :: Monad m ⇒ (a → b) → MStream m a → MStream m b
mapS (MStream next s n) = MStream next' s n
  where
    next' s = do r ← next s
                 case r of
                   Yield x s' → return (Yield (f x) s')
                   Skip s'    → return (Skip s')
                   Done       → return Done
```

It is easy to verify that the semantics of *mapS* remains unchanged for *Stream* with the new definitions. In the rest of the paper, we will assume that streams are defined as described above and that all stream operations have been suitably generalised to monadic streams.

The main advantage of monadic streams is their ability to model mutable arrays, whereas pure streams are only restricted to immutable ones. To make use of this functionality, we must provide conversions from *MutableVector* to *MStream* and back. The first direction is straightforward:

```
streamM :: MutableVector s a → MStream (ST s) a
streamM v = MStream next 0 n
  where
    n                 = lengthMVector v
    next i| i < n     = do x ← readMV v i
                           return (Yield x (i + 1))
          | otherwise = return Done
```

Since our goal is to execute stream transformers in-place, the inverse operation should overwrite an existing mutable vector rather than allocating a new one. Unsurprisingly, its implementation is quite similar to *unstream* from Section 2.2:

$$
\begin{aligned}
&\mathit{unstreamM} :: \mathit{MutableVector}\ s\ a \to \mathit{MStream}\ (\mathit{ST}\ s)\ a \\
&\qquad\qquad\qquad\qquad\qquad\qquad\qquad \to \mathit{ST}\ s\ (\mathit{MutableVector}\ s\ a) \\
&\mathit{unstreamM}\ v\ (\mathit{MStream}\ \mathit{next}\ s\ \_) = \textbf{do}\ n \leftarrow \mathit{loop}\ s\ 0 \\
&\qquad\qquad\qquad\qquad\qquad\qquad\qquad\quad \mathit{return}\ (\mathit{sliceMV}\ v\ 0\ n) \\
&\quad \textbf{where} \\
&\qquad \mathit{loop}\ s\ i = \textbf{do}\ r \leftarrow \mathit{next}\ s \\
&\qquad\qquad\qquad\quad \textbf{case}\ r\ \textbf{of} \\
&\qquad\qquad\qquad\qquad \mathit{Yield}\ x\ s' \to \textbf{do}\ \mathit{writeMV}\ v\ i\ x \\
&\qquad\qquad\qquad\qquad\qquad\qquad\qquad \mathit{loop}\ s'\ (i+1) \\
&\qquad\qquad\qquad\qquad \mathit{Skip}\ s' \quad\ \to \mathit{loop}\ s'\ i \\
&\qquad\qquad\qquad\qquad \mathit{Done} \qquad \to \mathit{return}\ i
\end{aligned}
$$

Note that *unstreamM* assumes that the vector is large enough to hold all elements of the stream and correctly adjusts its length if there are fewer elements, as required for in-place filtering.

The two conversions are sufficient to implement stream-based in-place transforers for mutable vectors. This operation is provided as a function on *New* since it will be later used in rewrite rules:

$$
\begin{aligned}
&\mathit{transform} :: (\forall m.\ \mathit{Monad}\ m \Rightarrow \mathit{MStream}\ m\ a \to \mathit{MStream}\ m\ a) \\
&\qquad\qquad\qquad\qquad\qquad\qquad\qquad\qquad \to \mathit{New}\ a \to \mathit{New}\ a \\
&\mathit{transform}\ f\ (\mathit{New}\ \mathit{init}) = \mathit{New}\ \$\ \textbf{do}\ v \leftarrow \mathit{init} \\
&\qquad\qquad\qquad\qquad\qquad\qquad\qquad \mathit{unstreamM}\ v\ (f\ (\mathit{streamM}\ v))
\end{aligned}
$$

Note that f must be polymorphic in the monad as the rewrite system introduced below will instantiate it at the identity monad in addition to ST.

4.2 In-Place Stream Transformers

For the newly gained ability to execute stream transformers in-place to be useful, pure stream operations must be replaced by their monadic counterparts whenever possible. Our fusion framework cannot identify such opportunities automatically. Instead, we introduce a special combinator which allows us to "mark" stream transformers which can benefit from recycling:

$$
\begin{aligned}
&\mathit{inplace} :: (\forall\ m.\ \mathit{Monad}\ m \Rightarrow \mathit{MStream}\ m\ a \to \mathit{MStream}\ m\ a) \\
&\qquad\qquad\qquad\qquad\qquad\qquad\qquad \to \mathit{Stream}\ a \to \mathit{Stream}\ a \\
&\mathit{inplace}\ f = f
\end{aligned}
$$

Semantically, *inplace* simply restricts its polymorphic argument to the identity monad. To the fusion system, however, it identifies the stream transformer as a candidate for in-place execution. This information is used in the following rewrite rule which ties together the mechanisms developed in this section:

$$\langle\textbf{inplace}\rangle\ \ \forall f\ p.\ \mathit{fill}\ (\mathit{inplace}\ f\ (\mathit{stream}\ (\mathit{new}\ p))) \mapsto \mathit{transform}\ f\ p$$

The rule eliminates an unnecessary array allocation (*fill*) by executing the stream transformer f in-place, thus recycling the vector created by p. It highlights the role of *inplace* since this transformation is only valid for some f. Again, it is our reponsibility to identify and mark such transformers.

To handle the last use case, *map* must be marked as *inplace* but only if it does not change the type of the elements. In fact, we can define a special version of *map* which is always a candidate for in-place execution:

$$\begin{array}{l} \mathit{inplace\_map} :: (a \rightarrow a) \rightarrow \mathit{Vector}\ a \rightarrow \mathit{Vector}\ a \\ \mathit{inplace\_map}\ f = \mathit{unstream}\ .\ \mathit{inplace}\ (\mathit{mapS}\ f)\ .\ \mathit{stream} \end{array}$$

Note that *inplace_map* has a more restrictive type than *map* but is semantically equivalent otherwise. All we need to do now is replace *map* by *inplace_map* if and only if the types allow it. Fortunately, rewrite rules yet again provide a solution here:

$$\langle \textbf{inplace\_map} \rangle \quad \mathit{map} \mapsto \mathit{inplace\_map}$$

The type of *inplace_map* constraints the applicability of the rule which is precisely what we want. In fact, this technique, known as specialisation, is so useful that GHC's support for it actually predates the rewrite rule mechanism.

With this piece of the puzzle in place, our framework is finally capable of properly optimising the third use case:

$$\begin{array}{ll} & \mathit{map}\ (+1)\ (\mathit{xs}\ //\ \mathit{ps}) \\ = & \{\text{specialise with } \textbf{inplace\_map}\} \\ & \mathit{inplace\_map}\ (+1)\ (\mathit{xs}\ //\ \mathit{ps}) \\ = & \{\text{inline}\} \\ & \mathit{new}\ (\mathit{fill}\ (\mathit{inplace}\ (\mathit{mapS}\ (+1))\ (\mathit{stream}\ (\mathit{new}\ (\mathit{update}\ (\mathit{clone}\ \mathit{xs})\ \mathit{ps}))))) \\ = & \{\text{apply } \textbf{inplace}\} \\ & \mathit{new}\ (\mathit{transform}\ (\mathit{mapS}\ (+1))\ (\mathit{update}\ (\mathit{clone}\ \mathit{xs})\ \mathit{ps})) \end{array}$$

Expanding the remaining combinators and verifying that the array elements are indeed incremented in-place is left as an exercise to the reader.

4.3 Monadic Stream Fusion

Interestingly, the last example would also be correctly optimised by rewriting *inplace f* (*stream* (*new p*)) to *stream* (*new* (*transform f p*)) and subsequently applying either **fusion** or **recycling**. Although arguably simpler, such a rule would interfere with stream fusion in some slightly more complex cases:

$$\begin{array}{ll} & \mathit{map}\ (>5)\ (\mathit{map}\ (+1)\ (\mathit{xs}\ //\ \mathit{ps})) \\ = & \{\text{specialise, inline and apply } \textbf{fusion}\} \\ & \mathit{new}\ (\mathit{fill}\ (\mathit{mapS}\ (>5) \\ & \qquad (\mathit{inplace}\ (\mathit{mapS}\ (+1))\ (\mathit{stream}\ (\mathit{new}\ (\mathit{update}\ (\mathit{clone}\ \mathit{xs})\ \mathit{ps})))))) \\ = & \{\text{rewrite as described above}\} \\ & \mathit{new}\ (\mathit{fill}\ (\mathit{mapS}\ (>5) \\ & \qquad (\mathit{stream}\ (\mathit{new}\ (\mathit{transform}\ (\mathit{mapS}\ (+1))\ (\mathit{update}\ (\mathit{clone}\ \mathit{xs})\ \mathit{ps})))))) \end{array}$$

Since $mapS\ (> 5)$ cannot be executed in-place, $mapS\ (+1)$ should not be, either! Doing so effectively "unfuses" the two $mapS$, resulting in three loops instead of two. In contrast, **inplace** avoids this pitfall by requiring that the output of the stream transformer is immediately converted to a vector and not passed on to another stream consumer.

Unfortunately, this does not completely solve the problem as demonstrated by the following transformation sequence:

$$
\begin{aligned}
& map\ (> 5)\ (map\ (+1)\ (xs\ //\ ps)) \\
= \ & \{\text{inline}\} \\
& new\ (fill\ (mapS\ (> 5)\ (stream\ (new\ (fill \\
& \qquad (inplace\ (mapS\ (+1))\ (stream\ (new\ (update\ (clone\ xs)\ ps))))))))) \\
= \ & \{\text{apply } \mathbf{inplace}\} \\
& new\ (fill\ (mapS\ (> 5)\ (stream\ (new\ (transform \\
& \qquad (mapS\ (+1))\ (update\ (clone\ xs)\ ps))))))
\end{aligned}
$$

Here, **inplace** was applied *before* **fusion**, thus preventing the two $mapS$ from being fused. There are two ways to avoid this. Firstly, GHC provides a staging mechanism for rewrite rules which would allow us to give precedence to fusion over recycling. A better solution, however, is to undo the effects of **inplace** if the vector is immediately converted back to a stream. The following rule accomplishes this:

$$
\begin{aligned}
&\langle \mathbf{uninplace} \rangle\ \ \forall f\ p. \\
&\qquad\qquad stream\ (new\ (transform\ f\ p)) \mapsto inplace\ f\ (stream\ (new\ p))
\end{aligned}
$$

It is easy to verify that **uninplace** is equivalent to the inverse of **inplace** immediately followed by **fusion**. In the problematic example, applying **uninplace** after the last step restores the desired behaviour.

To ensure that the rewrite system is confluent two additional, fairly obvious, rules are required:

$$
\begin{aligned}
&\langle \mathbf{inplace2} \rangle\ \ \forall f\ g\ s.\ inplace\ f\ (inplace\ g\ s) \mapsto inplace\ (f \circ g)\ s \\
&\langle \mathbf{mfusion} \rangle\ \ \forall f\ g\ p.\ transform\ f\ (transform\ g\ p) \mapsto transform\ (f \circ g)\ p
\end{aligned}
$$

To see why they are necessary, consider all possible rewriting steps for the term $map\ (+1)\ (map\ (+1)\ (xs\ //\ ps))$ where both maps can be executed in-place.

5 Benchmarks

To test our approach we have implemented the Rootfix algorithm [17] which, given a tree labelled by numbers, computes the sum of labels on the path from the root for each node. Thus, by labelling all nodes with 1 the algorithm can be used to determine the depth of each node. It operates on a special array-based encoding of a tree derived from its parenthetical representation. For instance, the complete binary tree of depth 3 can be written as `"((()())(()()))"`, i.e., each node is represented by a pair of parentheses enclosing the parenthetical representations of its children. The array encoding is obtained by storing the indices of the left and right parentheses of all nodes in two separate arrays, indexed by the preorder number of the nodes. For the complete binary tree, this results in the two arrays $\langle 0,1,2,4,7,8,10\rangle$ and $\langle 13,6,3,5,12,9,11\rangle$.

Rootfix is a data parallel algorithm which is of particular importance to us since we intend to employ the framework developed in this paper in the Data Parallel Haskell project [6]. Its implementation is quite simple:

$$
\begin{array}{l}
\mathit{rootfix} :: \mathit{Num}\ a \Rightarrow \mathit{Vector}\ a \rightarrow \mathit{Vector}\ \mathit{Int} \rightarrow \mathit{Vector}\ \mathit{Int} \rightarrow \mathit{Vector}\ a \\
\mathit{rootfix}\ \mathit{xs}\ \mathit{ls}\ \mathit{rs} = \mathbf{let}\ \mathit{zs} \quad = \mathit{replicate}\ (\mathit{length}\ \mathit{xs} * 2)\ 0 \\
\qquad\qquad\qquad\qquad\quad \mathit{vs} \quad = \mathit{zs}\ /\!/\!/\ \mathit{zip}\ \mathit{ls}\ \mathit{xs}\ /\!/\!/\ \mathit{zip}\ \mathit{rs}\ (\mathit{map}\ \mathit{negate}\ \mathit{xs}) \\
\qquad\qquad\qquad\qquad\quad \mathit{sums} = \mathit{prescanl}'\ (+)\ 0\ \mathit{vs} \\
\qquad\qquad\qquad\quad \mathbf{in} \\
\qquad\qquad\qquad\quad \mathit{map}\ (\mathit{index}\ \mathit{sums})\ \mathit{ls}
\end{array}
$$

Here, (///) is similar to (//) but takes a vector of value/index pairs instead of a list and *prescanl′* computes the prefix sum of an array with a strict accumulator. The numerous fusion and recycling opportunities are easy to spot and GHC does a good job here, applying **fusion** three times, **recycling** twice and **inplace** once.

The performance improvements are encouraging. Recycling reduces the number of array allocations from 5 to 2 compared to stream fusion alone. For a perfect binary tree of depth 23, the algorithm runs in 3517ms on a 2.6GHz Intel Core 2 Duo, as opposed to 5040ms with only stream fusion, a speedup of roughly 1.4. The results are similar for other tree sizes (the shape of the tree does not affect the performance). It remains to be seen how useful recycling will be for larger algorithms but we expect it to provide significant benefits in many cases.

6 Conclusion

We have described an optimisation framework for array programs which extends stream fusion with advanced recycling mechanisms for situation in which loop fusion is not possible. The new system is able to optimise more programs than stream fusion alone while remaining manageable with only 6 core rewrite rules. Thanks to GHC's excellent optimisation capabilities, it can be implemented as a library and does not require changes to the compiler. The initial performance gains are encouraging although the framework is yet to be tested in large real-world programs.

While we have restricted ourselves to arrays and stream fusion, we believe that the concepts developed in this paper are easily transferrable to other data structures and fusion systems. Moreover, it would be interesting to see if our approach can be extended to work across function boundaries and in particular to recursive functions with single-threaded uses of arrays. Here, we envision a system similar to constructor specialisation [14]. In the near future, we intend to integrate recycling into the Data Parallel Haskell project which provided the original motivation for this work.

References

1. Wadler, P.: Deforestation: transforming programs to eliminate trees. Theoretical Computer Science (Special issue of selected papers from 2nd European Symposium on Programming) 73(2), 231–248 (1990)
2. Gill, A., Launchbury, J., Peyton Jones, S.: A short cut to deforestation. In: Conference on Functional Programming Languages and Computer Architecture, pp. 223–232 (1993)
3. Johann, P.: Short cut fusion: Proved and improved. In: Taha, W. (ed.) SAIG 2001. LNCS, vol. 2196, pp. 47–71. Springer, Heidelberg (2001)
4. Svenningsson, J.: Shortcut fusion for accumulating parameters & zip-like functions. In: Proceedings of the 7th ACM SIGPLAN International Conference on Functional programming, pp. 124–132. ACM Press, New York (2002)
5. Chakravarty, M.M.T., Keller, G.: Functional array fusion. In: Leroy, X. (ed.) Proceedings of the Sixth ACM SIGPLAN International Conference on Functional Programming, pp. 205–216. ACM Press, New York (2001)
6. Chakravarty, M.M.T., Leshchinskiy, R., Peyton Jones, S., Keller, G., Marlow, S.: Data Parallel Haskell: a status report. In: DAMP 2007: Proceedings of the 2007 workshop on Declarative aspects of multicore programming, pp. 10–18. ACM, New York (2007)
7. Coutts, D., Leshchinskiy, R., Stewart, D.: Stream fusion: from lists to streams to nothing at all. In: Proceedings of the 2007 ACM SIGPLAN International Conference on Functional programming, pp. 315–326. ACM Press, New York (2007)
8. Coutts, D., Stewart, D., Leshchinskiy, R.: Rewriting Haskell strings. In: Hanus, M. (ed.) PADL 2007. LNCS, vol. 4354, pp. 50–64. Springer, Heidelberg (2006)
9. Bloss, A.: Update analysis and the efficient implementation of functional aggregates. In: Proceedings of the 4th international conference on Functional programming languages and computer architecture, pp. 26–38. ACM, New York (1989)
10. Odersky, M.: How to make destructive updates less destructive. In: Proc. 18th ACM Symp. on Principles of Programming Languages, pp. 25–36. ACM Press, New York (1991)
11. Sastry, A.V.S., Clinger, W., Ariola, Z.: Order-of-evaluation analysis for destructive updates in strict functional languages with flat aggregates. In: Conference on Functional Programming Languages and Computer Architecture, pp. 266–275. ACM Press, New York (1993)
12. Wadler, P.: Linear types can change the world. In: Programming Concepts and Methods, North, 347–359 (1990)
13. Launchbury, J., Peyton Jones, S.L.: Lazy functional state threads. In: SIGPLAN Conference on Programming Language Design and Implementation, pp. 24–35 (1994)
14. Peyton Jones, S.: Call-pattern specialisation for Haskell programs. In: Proceedings of the 2007 ACM SIGPLAN International Conference on Functional programming, pp. 327–337. ACM, New York (2007)
15. Peyton Jones, S., Santos, A.L.M.: A transformation-based optimiser for Haskell. Sci. Comput. Program. 32(1-3), 3–47 (1998)
16. Peyton Jones, S., Tolmach, A., Hoare, T.: Playing by the rules: rewriting as a practical optimisation technique in GHC. In: Hinze, R. (ed.) 2001 Haskell Workshop. ACM, New York (2001)
17. Leiserson, C.E., Maggs, B.M.: Communication-efficient parallel algorithms for distributed random-access machines. Algorithmica 3, 53–77 (1988)

Towards a Complete Scheme for Tabled Execution Based on Program Transformation*

Pablo Chico de Guzman[1], Manuel Carro[1], and Manuel V. Hermenegildo[1,2]

[1] School of Computer Science, Univ. Politécnica de Madrid, Spain
[2] IMDEA Software, Spain
pchico@clip.dia.fi.upm.es, {mcarro,herme}@fi.upm.es

Abstract. The advantages of tabled evaluation regarding program termination and reduction of complexity are well known —as are the significant implementation, portability, and maintenance efforts that some proposals (especially those based on suspension) require. This implementation effort is reduced by program transformation-based continuation call techniques, at some efficiency cost. However, the traditional formulation of this proposal [1] limits the interleaving of tabled and non-tabled predicates and thus cannot be used as-is for arbitrary programs. In this paper we present a complete translation for the continuation call technique which, while requiring the same runtime support as the traditional approach, solves these problems and makes it possible to execute arbitrary tabled programs. We also present performance results which show that the resulting `CCall` approach offers a useful tradeoff that can be competitive with other state-of-the-art implementations.

Keywords: Tabled logic programming, Continuation-call tabling, Implementation, Performance, Program transformation.

1 Introduction

Tabling [2,3,4] is a strategy for executing logic programs which uses *memoization* of already processed calls and their answers to improve several of the limitations of SLD resolution. It brings termination for bounded term-size programs and improves efficiency in programs which perform repeated computations. It has been successfully applied to deductive databases [5], program analysis [6,7], reasoning in the semantic Web [8], model checking [9], etc.

However, tabling also has certain drawbacks, including that predicates to be tabled have to be carefully selected[1] in order not to incur in undesired slowdowns and, specially relevant to our discussion, that its efficient implementation

* This work was funded in part by EU FET project IST-15905 *MOBIUS*, and FP7 grant agreement 215483 *S-Cube*, Spanish MEC project TIN2008-05624 DOVES, ITEA2/PROFIT FIT-340005-2007-14 *ES_PASS*, and by Madrid Regional Government program S-0505/TIC/0407 *PROMESAS*.

[1] Note that XSB includes an `auto_table` declaration to automatically select which predicates are to be tabled in order to ensure termination. This declaration triggers a conservative analysis which may mark more predicates than strictly needed.

A. Gill and T. Swift (Eds.): PADL 2009, LNCS 5418, pp. 224–238, 2009.

is generally complex. In *suspension-based tabling* the computation state of suspended tabled subgoals has to be preserved to avoid backtracking over them. This is done either by *freezing* the stacks, as in the SLG-WAM [10], by copying to another area, as in CAT [11], or by using an intermediate solution as in CHAT [12]. *Linear tabling* maintains instead a single execution tree without requiring suspension and resumption of sub-computations. The computation of the (local) fixpoint is performed by making subgoals "loop" in their alternatives until no more solutions are found. This may force some computations to be repeated. Examples of this method are the linear tabling of B-Prolog [13,14] and the DRA scheme [15]. Suspension-based mechanisms achieve very good performance but, in general, require deeper changes to the underlying implementation. Linear mechanisms, on the other hand, can usually be implemented on top of existing sequential engines without major modifications.

The Continuation Call (`CCall`) approach to tabling [1] tries to combine the best of both worlds: it is a suspension-based mechanism (and, therefore, it does not need recomputation) which requires relatively simple additions to the Prolog implementation / compiler,[2] thus making maintenance and porting much easier. In [16] we proposed a number of optimizations to the `CCall` approach and showed that with such optimizations performance could be competitive with traditional implementations. However, this was only partially satisfactory since the `CCall` tabling approach is restricted to programs with no interleaving of tabled and non-tabled predicate calls, and thus cannot execute general tabled programs.

In this paper we present an extension of the `CCall` translation which, while requiring the same runtime support of the traditional proposal, overcomes the problem pointed out above. We also present a complexity comparison with CHAT and performance results comparing with state-of-the-art implementations.

2 The Continuation Call Technique

We sketch now how tabled evaluation [4,10] works from a user point of view and we briefly describe the Continuation Call technique, on which we base our work.

2.1 Tabling Basics

We will use as example the program in Figure 1, whose purpose is to determine the reachability of nodes in a graph. Since the graph contains a cycle, the query `path(1,Z)` will make the program loop forever under the standard SLD resolution strategy, regardless of the order of the clauses. In this case, tabling changes the operational semantics of the `path/2` predicate to distinguish the first occurrence of a `path/2` goal (the *generator*) and subsequent calls which are identical up to variable renaming (the *consumers*). The generator applies resolution using the program clauses to derive answers for the goal. The consumer (the first recursive call in our example) *suspends* the current execution path (using implementation-dependent means) and starts execution on the second clause of predicate `path/2`. When this branch finally succeeds, the answer generated for the initial query, `path(1,1)`, is

[2] As an example, no modification to the underlying engine is needed.

```
:- table path/2.

path(X, Z):-
    edge(X, Y),
    path(Y, Z).
path(X, Z):-
    edge(X, Z).

edge(1,1).
```

Fig. 1. A sample program

```
path(X, Y):- slg(path(X, Y)).
slg_path(path(X, Z), Id):-
    edge(X, Y),
     slgcall(path_cont(Id, [X], path(Y, Z))).
slg_path(path(X, Z), Id):-
    edge(X, Z),
    answer(Id, path(X, Z)).
path_cont(Id, [X], path(Y, Z)):-
    answer(Id, path(X, Z)).
```

Fig. 2. The program in Figure 1 after being transformed for tabled execution

inserted in the table entry associated with its generator. This makes it possible to reactivate the consumer and to continue execution at the point where it was stopped. Thus, consumers do not use SLD resolution, but obtain instead the answers from the table where they were previously inserted by the generator. Predicates not marked as tabled are executed according to SLD resolution, hopefully with minimal overhead due to the availability of tabling.

2.2 `CCall` by Example

`CCall` implements tabling by a combination of program transformation and side effects in the form of insertions into and retrievals from a table which relates calls, answers, and the continuation code to be executed after consumers read answers from the table. We will now sketch how the mechanism works using the path/2 example (Figure 1). The original code is transformed into the program in Figure 2, whose execution is shown in Figure 3.

Roughly speaking, the transformation for tabling is as follows: the predicate to be actually tabled is a variation (slg_path/2) of the initial predicate (path/2). In order to preserve the previous interface, path/2 calls slg_path/2 through a primitive, slg/1, which keeps track of which invocation is a generator or a consumer and makes sure that its argument is executed to completion. After completion, it will return, on backtracking, all the solutions found for the tabled predicate. To this end, slg/1 checks if the call has already been executed. If so, all of its answers are returned on backtracking. Otherwise, slg/1 passes control to the transformed version of its argument, slg_path/2 (step 2).[3] slg_path/2 receives in its first argument the original call to path/2 and in the second argument the identifier of its generator, which is used to relate operations on the table with this initial call. Each clause of slg_path/2 is derived from a clause of the original path/2 predicate by:

- Adding an answer/2 primitive at the end of each clause of the original tabled predicate. answer/2 inserts answers in the entry of the table identified by its first argument (step 7) after checking for redundant answers (i.e., step 10 does not insert the redundant answer) and fails.

[3] A unique name has been created by simply prepending slg_ to the original predicate name. Any means of constructing a unique predicate name can be used.

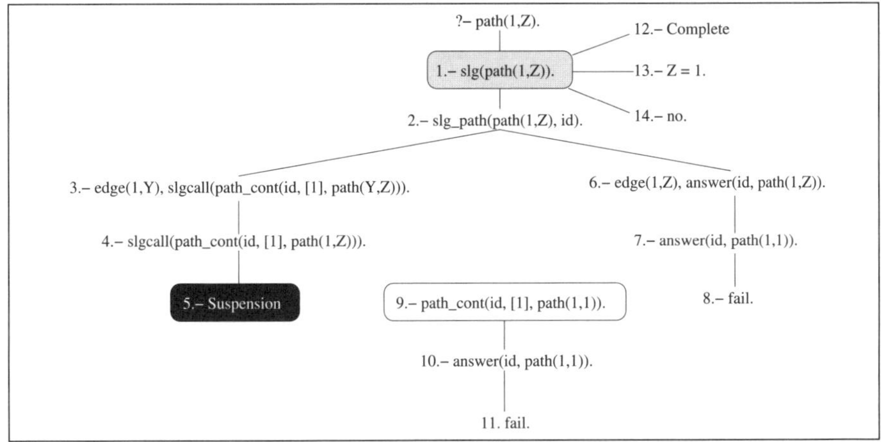

Fig. 3. Tabling execution of Figure 1

- Instrumenting calls to tabled predicates using the slgcall /1 primitive (step 4). If this tabled call is a consumer, path_cont/3, along with its arguments, is recorded as (one of) the continuation(s) of its generator and execution suspends (step 5). If the tabled call is a generator, it is associated with a new call identifier and execution follows using slg_path /2 to derive new answers (as done by slg /1 (step 1)). Besides, path_cont/3 will be recorded as a continuation of the generator identified by Id if the tabled call cannot be completed (because there may be dependencies on previous generators). The path_cont/3 continuation will be called to consume found answers (step 9) or erased upon completion of its generator.
- Encoding the remaining of the clause body of path/2 after the recursive call using path_cont/3. This is constructed in a similar way to slg_path /2, i.e., applying the same transformation as for the initial clauses and calling slgcall /1 if this clause contains another call to the tabled predicate.

The second argument of path_cont/3 is a list of bindings needed to recover the environment of the continuation call; in other words, the variables which are reachable before a consumer is suspended and which can be necessary when the consumer is resumed. In our example, when the execution suspends (step 5), the value of X has to be saved since it will be used by the answer/2 primitive when the consumer is resumed (step 10).

A safe approximation of the variables which should appear in this list is the set of variables which appear in the clause before the tabled goal and which are used in the continuation, including the answer/2 primitive. Variables appearing in the tabled call itself do not need to be included, as they will be passed along anyway.

Key Contribution of `CCall`: A new predicate name is created for all points where suspension can happen. Suspension is performed by saving this predicate name (equivalent to saving a program counter), a list of bindings (equivalent to protecting the environment from backtracking), and a generator identifier (to

```
:- table t/1.

t(A):-
    p(B),
    A is B + 1.
t(0).

p(B):- t(B), B < 1.
```

Fig. 4. A program for which the original CCall transformation fails

```
t(A):- slg(t(A)).
slg_t(t(A), Id):-
    p(B), A is B + 1,
    answer(Id, t(A)).

slg_t(t(0), Id):-
    answer(Id, t(0)).

p(B):- t(B), B < 1.
```

Fig. 5. The program in Figure 4 after being wrongly transformed for tabled execution

relate answers in the table with the generator). Resumption is performed by constructing a Prolog goal with the information saved on suspension plus the answer which raised the resumption. This mechanism is significantly simpler to implement than other approaches such as SLG-WAM or CHAT, where non-trivial extensions to the SLD abstract machine had to be introduced. Consequently, porting and maintainability are simpler too, since `CCall` is independent of the compiler. Creating a Prolog term on the heap is the only low-level operation to be implemented.

3 Mixing Tabled and Non-tabled Predicates

The `CCall` approach to tabling, as originally proposed, has a serious limitation which shows up when non-tabled predicates appear between a generator and its consumers: the variables created during the execution of these non-tabled predicates may be needed to correctly suspend and resume consumers. However, `CCall` just saves the environment of the parent call.

3.1 Problems in the Original Transformation

As an example of the problem, Figure 4 shows a tabled program where tabled and non-tabled execution (t/1 and p/1) are mixed. The translation of the program is shown in Figure 5, following the rules in Section 2.2.

The execution of the program for query t(A) is shown in Figure 6. Execution proceeds correctly until slg/1 is called again from p/1. At that point, execution should suspend (and later resume), but slg/1 does not have any associated continuation, and it does not have any pointer to the code to be executed on resumption (partially in p/1 and partially in slg_t/2): B < 1, A **is** B + 1, answer(Id,t(A)) is lost on backtracking and it is not reachable when resuming. Consequently, the second answer to the query, t(1), is lost.

The call to t(B) made by p(B) could have been translated using the slgcall/1 primitive, generating a continuation for the remaining code of p/1, but, even in that case, the code segment "A **is** B + 1, answer(Id, t(A))" in the first clause of slg_t/1 would be lost anyway. This is an example of why all the frames between

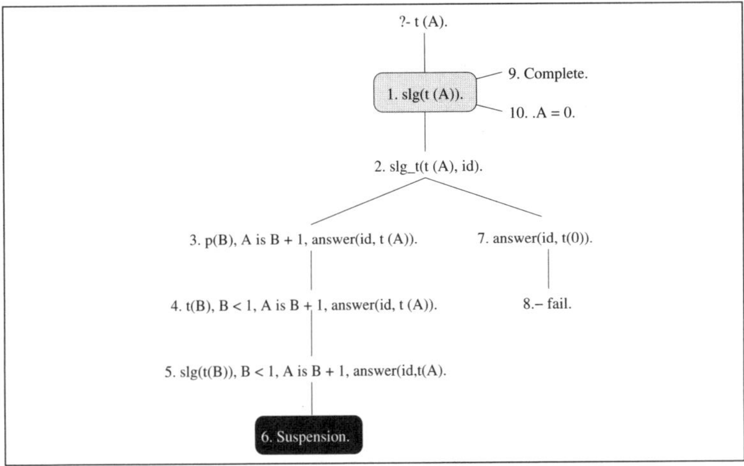

Fig. 6. Tabling execution of example of Figure 1

a consumer and its nearest generator have to be saved when suspending, and it is not enough to save just the last one, as in the original `CCall` proposal.[4]

3.2 Marking Predicates as Bridges

To solve this problem, we have extended the translation to take into account a new kind of predicates, named *bridges*. A bridge predicate is a non-tabled predicate whose clauses generate frames which have to be saved in the continuation of a consumer. In the example of Figure 4, `p/1` would be a bridge predicate.

Bridge predicates are all the non-tabled predicates which can appear in the execution tree of a query between a generator and each of its consumers, i.e., the predicates whose environments lie in the local stack between the environment of the generator and that of each of its consumers. Note that tabled predicates do not need to be included as bridge predicates as their environment will be saved already by the translation.

Thus, in order to determine a minimal set of bridge predicates, B_{min}, we need to locate the points where a consumer will appear. Detecting that a call will definitely be a consumer is an undecidable problem (because it would need identifying where infinite failures happen). Therefore, generating B_{min} is also undecidable and a *safe approximation*, which may mark as bridges some predicates which do not need to be marked, has to be applied.

As we will see in Section 4, the disadvantages of such an over-approximation are minor. Bridge predicates (with an extra argument) can be called when not needed, incurring a small overhead, and some code may be duplicated (to accept a new argument for the case where a bridge predicate is called from a tabled execution). The algorithm we have implemented (Figure 7) only detects

[4] Which does work, however, when all the calls to the tabled predicates appear in the body of a clause of a tabled predicate.

Make a graph G with an edge $(p1/n1,\ p2/n2) \Leftrightarrow p2/n2$ **is** called from $p1/n1$
$Bridges = \emptyset$
FOR each predicate T in TABLED PREDICATES
  $Forward =$ All predicates reached from T in G
  $Backward =$ All predicates from which T **is** reached in G
  $Bridges = Bridges \cup (Forward \cap Backward)$
$Bridges = Bridges -$ TABLED PREDICATES

Fig. 7. Safe approximation to mark bridge predicates

tabled predicates which can recursively call themselves. For the examples used for performance evaluation in Section 6, using the safe approximation algorithm produces, on average, a slowdown of only 3% with respect to a perfect (manual) characterization of bridge predicates.

4 A General Translation for Tabled Programs

In this section we present program transformation rules which take into account bridge predicates. This transformation assumes that all the bridge predicates (and possibly some more) have been marked by adding :– bridge P/N declarations in the program.

As seen in Section 2.2, a continuation saves all the information needed to resume a consumer, including environment variables and continuation code. Consequently, the goal of the new translation is to associate a continuation with each of the bridge calls within the scope of tabled execution (Figure 9). Continuations for tabling will have a new argument (the continuation to be executed) and new continuations are pushed onto this argument as they appear, in much the same way as environments are pushed onto the local stack.

4.1 Translation Rules

The new translation rules are shown in the metaprogram in Figure 8, where we have used a sugared Prolog-like language. We use for conciseness functional syntax where needed [17]. Infix '∘' is a generic concatenation function which joins either atoms or (linear) structures. It may appear in an output head position with the expected semantics.

The trans/2 predicate receives in its first argument the program clauses one by one and returns in its second argument a list of clauses resulting from the translation of the input clause. The first clause of trans/2 ensures that predicates which are neither tabled nor bridges are not transformed.[5] The second one generates, for each tabled predicate, a single-clause predicate to maintain the interface of the new predicate with the rest of the code (i.e., the first predicate in Figure 9, left). The third clause of trans/2 translates clauses of tabled predicates, and the fourth one translates clauses of bridge predicates, keeping the original clauses as well so that they can be called from non-tabled predicates.

[5] Predicates table/1 and bridge/1 (generated by the compiler from the corresponding declarations) are used to check if their argument is a predicate head or a clause of a tabled or bridge predicate, respectively.

```
trans(C, C) :- \+ table(C), \+ bridge(C).
trans(( :- table P/N ), ( P(X1..Xn) :- slg(P(X1..Xn)) )).
trans(( Head :- Body ), LC) :-
    table(Head),
    Head_tr =.. ['slg_' ∘ Head, Head, Id],
    End = answer(Id, Head),
    transBody(Head_tr, Body, Id, [], End, LC).
trans(( Head :- Body ), [( Head :- Body ) | LC]) :-
    bridge(Head),
    Head_tr =.. [Head ∘ '_bridge', Head, Id, Cont],
    End = call(Cont),
    transBody(Head_tr, Body, Id, Cont, End, LC).

transBody([], [], _, _, [], []).
transBody(Head, Body, Id, ContPrev, End, [( Head :- Body_tr ) | RestBody_tr]) :-
    following(Body, Pref, Pred, Suff),
    getLBinds(Pref, Suff, LBinds),
    updateBody(Pred, End, Id, Pref, LBinds, ContPrev, Cont, Body_tr),
    transBody(Cont, Suff, Id, ContPrev, End, RestBody_tr).

following(Body, Pref, Pred, Suff) :-
    member(Body, Pred),
    (table(Pred); bridge(Pred)), !,
    Body = Pref ∘ Pred ∘ Suff.

updateBody([], End, _Id, Pref, _LBinds, _ContPrev, [], Pref ∘ End).
updateBody(Pred, _End, Id, Pref, LBinds, ContPrev, Cont, Pref ∘ EndClause) :-
    getNameCont(NameCont),
    Cont = NameCont(Id, LBinds, Pred, ContPrev),
    ( bridge(Pred) ->
          EndClause =.. [Pred ∘ '_bridge', Pred, Id, Cont]
     ;
          EndClause = Call(Cont)
    ).
```

Fig. 8. The Prolog code of the translation rules

A new predicate head (Head_tr) is generated, and its body will result from transforming the body literals appearing after a call to a tabled or a bridge predicate. The variable End holds the code to appear as last goal of the body corresponding to Head_tr. This code can be answer/2, for clauses of tabled predicates, or **call**(Cont), for clauses of bridge predicates. The latter will be used to call a continuation which will be received as fourth argument of the generated bridge predicate.

transBody/6 generates, in its last argument, the translation of the body of a clause by processing, in each iteration, the code remaining until either the next tabled / bridge call or the end the clause. In order to do that, following/4 splits a clause body into three parts: a *prefix*, from the beginning of the body up to the first occurrence of a tabled or bridge call, the tabled / bridge call itself, and the rest of the clause (the *suffix*).

```
t(A) :- slg(t(A)).
slg_t (t(A), Id) :-
   p_bridge(p(B), Id,
            slg_t0(Id, [A], p(B), [])).

slg_t (t(0), Id) :- answer(Id, t(0)).

slg_t0(Id, [A], p(B), []) :-
   A is B + 1,
   answer(Id, t(A)).

p(B) :- t(B), B < 1.

p_bridge(p(B), Id, Cont) :-
   slgcall (p_bridge0(Id, [], t(B), Cont)).

p_bridge0(Id, [], t(B), Cont) :-
   B < 1,
   call(Cont).
```

Fig. 9. The program in Figure 4 after being transformed for tabled execution

The updateBody/8 predicate returns, in its last argument, the translation for the prefix identified by following/4; the list of variables which have to be saved in order to recover the environment of the consumer was already obtained by getLBinds/3. The suffix will be transformed into a continuation to be associated with a new predicate symbol, generated by getNameCont/1. The body of this new predicate is generated by recursively calling transBody/6.

The first clause of updateBody/8 takes care of the base case, when there are no calls to bridge or tabled predicates left, and the End of the clause, generated by trans/2, is appended at the end of the body. Its second clause has two cases which, respectively, generate code for a call to a bridge and a table predicate.

We will now refer to the example in Figure 4, assuming that a :- bridge p/1 declaration has been added to show how a translation would take place.

4.2 Correct Transformation of the Example

The translation of the first clause of t/1 is performed by the third clause of trans/2, which makes the head of the translated clause, Head_tr, to be slg_t (t(A), Id) and states that the final call of that clause has to be answer(Id, t(A)) —i.e., when the clause successfully finishes, it adds the answer to the table.

transBody/6 then takes care of the rest of the body. It identifies the variables which have to be saved (A, in this case) and classifies the body literals as follows:

Pref	Pred	Suff
(none)	p(B)	A **is** B + 1

updateBody/8 generates the body for the predicate associated with Head_tr to give the first clause of slg_t /2, and generates the head (slg_t0 /4) of the clause which corresponds to the translation of Suff. The body of Suff is generated in the recursive call to the trans/6 predicate.

The translation of the second clause of t/1 is simpler, as it only has to add answer(Id, t(0)) at the end of the body of the new predicate.

The original clause for the bridge predicate p/1 is kept to maintain its interface. The translation for the single clause of p/1 is made by the fourth clause of trans/2 where Head_tr is unified with p_bridge(p(B), Id, Cont) and End is unified with **call**(Cont) to resume the pushed continuation. transBody/6 finds an empty list of environment variables and unifies Pref, Pred and Suff with [],

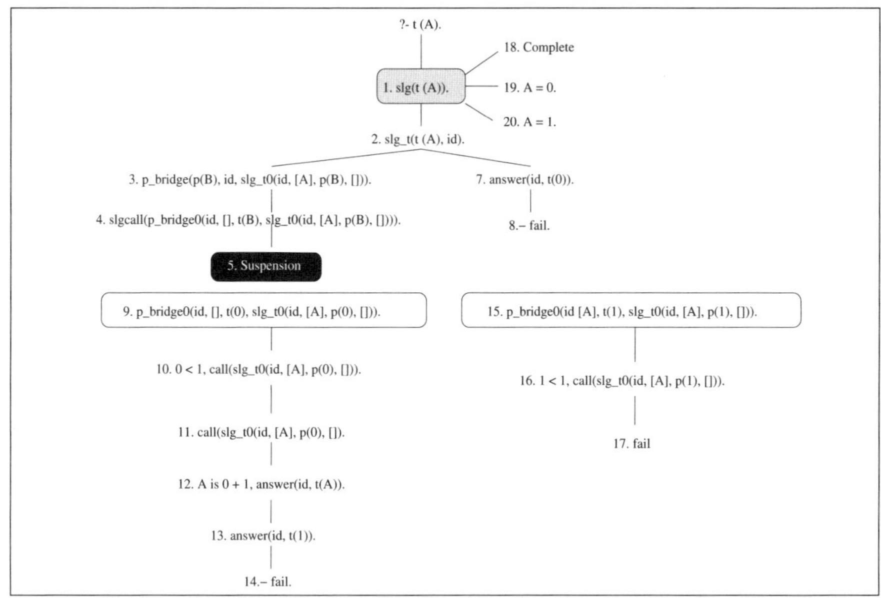

Fig. 10. New `CCall` tabling execution

t(B) and B $<$ 1, respectively. The second clause of updateBody/8 generates the body for the head Head_tr and also the head of the continuation clause which translates Suff (p_bridge0/3). Its body is generated in the recursive call to the trans/6 predicate by the first clause of updateBody/8, after appending Suff and End, generated by trans/2.

4.3 Execution of the Transformed Program

The execution tree for the transformed program is shown in Figure 10. It is similar to that in Figure 6, but a continuation slg_t0(id, [A], p(B), []) is passed to the bridge call to p/1 (step 3). This continuation contains the code to be executed after the execution of p(B) and the list [A] needed to recover the environment of this remaining code. Consequently, there are two nested continuations associated with the suspension (step 4): one continuation to execute the rest of the code of p(B), p_bridge0/4, and another one to execute the rest of the code of t(A), slg_t0/4. As we can see, bridge predicates push continuations which are called when a consumer is resumed.

After the first answer is found (step 7), this nested continuation is resumed (step 9). After executing the remaining code of p(B) (step 10), the next pushed continuation (fourth argument of p_bridge0/4) is called to execute the remaining code of t(A), and the second answer, t(1), is found (step 13). Again, the (nested) continuation is resumed, but it fails at step 16. Finally, the tabled call can be completed (step 18), and each of its answers are returned by backtracking (steps 19 and 20).

5 Θ(CHAT) Is Not Comparable with Θ(`CCall`)

In this section we present a comparative analysis of the complexity of `CCall` and CHAT, which is an efficient implementation of tabling with a comparatively simple machinery. Since it is known that Θ(CHAT) is Θ(SLG-WAM) [18], the final conclusion applies to the SLG-WAM as well.

The complexity analysis focuses on the operations of suspension and resumption. The environment of a consumer has to be protected when suspending to reinstall it when resuming. `CCall` achieves that by copying the continuation associated with the consumer in a special memory area to be protected on backtracking. In the original implementation [1] this continuation is copied from the heap to a separate table (when suspending) and back (when resuming). Alternatively, continuations can be saved in a special memory area with the same data format as the heap [16]. This makes it possible to use WAM code directly on them and, when resuming, they can be directly used as normal Prolog data, without having to copy them each time a consumer is resumed.

On the other hand, CHAT freezes the heap and the frame stack when suspending. These areas are frozen by traversing the choice point stack. For all choice points between the consumer choice point and its generator, their pointers to the end of the heap and frame stack are changed the consumer choice point values. By doing that, heap and frame stack are preserved on backtracking. However, the consumer choice point and the trail segment between consumer and generator (with its associated values) have to be copied onto a special memory area. This makes it possible to reinstall the values of the variables which were bound when suspending (and which backtracking will unbind) when resuming.

Each consumer is suspended only once, and it can be resumed several times. The rest of the operations, i.e., checking if a tabled call is a generator or a consumer, are not analyzed, because they are common to both systems. In addition, we will ignore the cost of working at the Prolog level, since this is an orthogonal issue: `CCall` primitives could be compiled to WAM instructions and working at Prolog level does not increase the complexity. Finally, for simplicity, we assume that both systems use the same scheduling strategy and that the *leader*[6] does not change between the suspension and the resumptions of a consumer.

Θ(`CCall`): When suspending, `CCall` has to copy all the environments until the last generator and the structures in the heap which hang from them. Let E be the size of all the environments and H the size of the structures in the heap. The time consumption when suspending is $\Theta(E + H)$. When resuming, `CCall` only needs to perform pattern matching of the continuation against its clause. The time taken by this matching depends on the size of the list of bindings, which is known to be $\Theta(E)$. Since each consumer can be resumed N times, the time consumption of resuming consumers is $\Theta(N \times E)$.

Θ(CHAT): When suspending, CHAT has to traverse the frame and choicepoint stacks, but with the improvements presented in [18], this time can be neglected because a choice point is only traversed once for all the consumers, and only

[6] The leader of a given consumer, C, is the generator which execute the completion algorithm of the generator of C.

the trail and the last choice point have to be copied. Let T be the trail size and C the choice point size, which is bound by a constant for a given program. The time consumption when suspending is: $\Theta(T)$. When resuming, CHAT has to reinstall the values of the frame and the choice point. Since each consumer can be resumed N times, the time consumption of resuming is $\Theta(N\times T)$.

Analyzing the worst cases of both systems: We can conclude $E + H \geq T$, because each variable can be only once in the trail, and then `CCall` is worse than CHAT when suspending. On the other hand, if $E < T$, than `CCall` is better than CHAT when resuming. Consequently, for a plausible general case, the more resumptions there are, the better `CCall` behaves in comparison with CHAT, and conversely. In any case, the worst and best cases for each implementation are different, which makes them difficult to compare. For example, if there is a very large structure pointed to from the environments, and none of its elements are pointed to from the trail, `CCall` is slower than CHAT, since it has to copy all the structure in a different memory area when suspending and CHAT does nothing both when suspending and when resuming.

On the other hand, if all the elements of the structure are pointed to from the trail, `CCall` has to copy all the structure on suspension in a different memory area to protect it on backtracking, but it is ready to be resumed without any other operation (just a unification with the pointer to the structure). CHAT has to copy all the structure on suspension too, because all the structure is in the trail. In addition, each time the consumer is resumed, all the elements of the structure have to be reinstalled using the trail, and CHAT has to perform more operations than `CCall`, and then, the more resumptions there are, the worse CHAT would be in comparison with `CCall`. Anyway, as the trail is usually smaller than the heap, we expect CHAT to outperform `CCall` in most cases.

6 Performance Evaluation

We have implemented the proposed technique as an extension of the Ciao system [19], using the improvements presented in [16]. Tabled evaluation is provided to the user as a loadable *package* [20] that implements the new directives and user-level predicates, performs the program transformations, and links in the low-level support for tabling.

Table 1 compares the proposed implementation of tabling with the latest versions of state-of-the-art systems, namely, XSB 3.1 (SLG-WAM), YapTab 5.1.3 (SLG-WAM) [21], and B-Prolog 7.1 on benchmarks also used in other similar performance evaluations. We provide the raw time (in milliseconds) taken to execute these benchmarks and the number of bridge predicates which appear in the new translation. Measurements have been made with Ciao-1.13, using the standard, unoptimized bytecode-based compilation, and with the `CCall` extensions loaded. Note that we did not compare with CHAT, which was available as a configuration option in the XSB system but which was removed in recent XSB versions, since it was experimentally found to be overall slower than the SLG-WAM [22]. All the executions were performed using local scheduling and disabling garbage collection; in the end this did not impact execution times very

Table 1. Comparing Ciao+`CCall` with XSB, YapTab, and B-Prolog

Program	`CCall`	XSB	YapTab	BProlog	# Bridges
path	517.92	231.4	151.12	206.26	0
tcl	96.93	59.91	39.16	51.60	0
tcr	315.44	106.91	90.13	96.21	0
tcn	485.77	123.21	85.87	117.70	0
sgm	3151.8	1733.1	1110.1	1474.0	0
atr2	689.86	602.03	262.44	320.07	0
pg	15.240	13.435	8.5482	36.448	6
kalah	23.152	19.187	13.156	28.333	20
gabriel	23.500	19.633	12.384	40.753	12
disj	18.095	15.762	9.2131	29.095	15
cs_o	34.176	27.644	18.169	85.719	14
cs_r	66.699	55.087	34.873	170.25	15
peep	68.757	58.161	37.124	150.14	10

much. We used `gcc 4.1.1` to compile all systems (when necessary), and executed on Fedora Core Linux, kernel 2.6.9, on an Intel Xeon *Deschutes* processor.

The first benchmark is `path`, the same as Figure 1, which has been executed with a linear (each node follows, and is followed by, only one node, as in a chain) graph. Since this is a tabling-intensive program with no consumers in its execution, the difference with other systems is mainly due to large parts of the execution being done at Prolog level. The following five benchmarks, until `atr2`, are also tabling intensive. As their associated environments are very small, `CCall` is far from its worst case (see Section 5), and the difference with other systems is similar to that in `path` and for a similar reason. The worst case in this set is `tcn` because there are two calls to `slgcall/1` per generator, and the overhead of working at the Prolog level is duplicated.

B-Prolog, which uses linear tabling, suffers from performance problems when costly predicates have to be recomputed: this is what happens in benchmarks from `pg` until `peep`, where tabled and non-tabled execution is mixed. This is a well-known disadvantage of linear tabling techniques which does not affect suspension-based approaches. It has to be noted, however, that the latest versions of B-Prolog implement an optimized variant of its original linear tabling mechanism [14] which tries to avoid reevaluation of looping subgoals.

The difference in speed for SLD execution, at least in those cases where the program execution is large enough to be really significant, must also be taken into account in order to compare the efficiency of our implementation. XSB was shown to be between 1.8 and 2 times slower than Ciao (partially due to being always prepared for tabling execution) and YapTab was about 1.5 times faster.[7]

In non-trivial benchmarks, from `pg` until `peep`, which at least in principle should reflect more accurately what one might expect in larger applications using tabling, execution times are in the end competitive with XSB or YapTab. This is probably due to the fact that the raw speed of the basic engine in Ciao is higher

[7] Note that the tabling-enabled version of Yap is somewhat slower than regular Yap.

than in XSB and closer to YapTab, rather than to factors related to tabling execution, but it also implies that the overhead of the approach to tabling used is reasonable after the optimizations in [16]. In this context it should be noted that in these experiments we have used the baseline, bytecode-based compilation and abstract machine. Turning on global analysis and using optimizing compilers and abstract machines [23,24,25] can improve the speed of both the SLD part of the computation and (the Prolog part of) tabling.

7 Conclusions

We have presented an extension of the continuation call technique which eliminates its limitations when interleaving tabled and non-tabled predicates. Our approach has the advantage of being easier to implement and maintain than other techniques, which usually require non-trivial modifications to low-level machinery. We expect the overhead caused by executing at Prolog level to be reduced as the speed of the source language improves by using global analysis, optimizing compilers, and better abstract machines. Accordingly, we expect the performance of `CCall` to improve in the future and thus gradually gain ground in the comparisons.

Although a non-optimal tabled execution is obviously a disadvantage, it is worth noting that, since our implementation does not (or only very slightly [16]) changes the WAM or the Prolog compiler, the speed at which regular Prolog is executed remains unchanged. In our case, executables which do not need tabling have very little tabling-related code, as the data structures (for tries, etc.) are handled by dynamic libraries loaded on demand, and only stubs are needed in the regular engine. Additionally, the modular design of our approach gives better chances of making it easier to port to other systems.

References

1. Ramesh, R., Chen, W.: Implementation of tabled evaluation with delaying in prolog. IEEE Trans. Knowl. Data Eng. 9(4), 559–574 (1997)
2. Tamaki, H., Sato, M.: OLD resolution with tabulation. In: Shapiro, E. (ed.) ICLP 1986. LNCS, vol. 225, pp. 84–98. Springer, Heidelberg (1986)
3. Warren, D.: Memoing for logic programs. Communications of the ACM 35(3), 93–111 (1992)
4. Chen, W., Warren, D.S.: Tabled Evaluation with Delaying for General Logic Programs. Journal of the ACM 43(1), 20–74 (1996)
5. Ramakrishnan, R., Ullman, J.D.: A survey of research on deductive database systems. Journal of Logic Programming 23(2), 125–149 (1993)
6. Warren, R., Hermenegildo, M., Debray, S.K.: On the Practicality of Global Flow Analysis of Logic Programs. In: Fifth International Conference and Symposium on Logic Programming, pp. 684–699. MIT Press, Cambridge (1988)
7. Dawson, S., Ramakrishnan, C., Warren, D.: Practical Program Analysis Using General Purpose Logic Programming Systems – A Case Study. In: Proceedings of PLDI 1996, pp. 117–126. ACM Press, New York (1996)
8. Zou, Y., Finin, T., Chen, H.: F-OWL: An Inference Engine for Semantic Web. In: Hinchey, M.G., Rash, J.L., Truszkowski, W.F., Rouff, C.A. (eds.) FAABS 2004. LNCS, vol. 3228, pp. 238–248. Springer, Heidelberg (2004)

9. Ramakrishna, Y., Ramakrishnan, C., Ramakrishnan, I., Smolka, S., Swift, T., Warren, D.: Efficient Model Checking Using Tabled Resolution. In: Grumberg, O. (ed.) CAV 1997. LNCS, vol. 1254, pp. 143–154. Springer, Heidelberg (1997)
10. Sagonas, K., Swift, T.: An Abstract Machine for Tabled Execution of Fixed-Order Stratified Logic Programs. ACM Transactions on Programming Languages and Systems 20(3), 586–634 (1998)
11. Demoen, B., Sagonas, K.: CAT: The Copying Approach to Tabling. In: Palamidessi, C., Meinke, K., Glaser, H. (eds.) ALP 1998 and PLILP 1998. LNCS, vol. 1490, pp. 21–35. Springer, Heidelberg (1998)
12. Demoen, B., Sagonas, K.F.: Chat: The copy-hybrid approach to tabling. In: Practical Applications of Declarative Languages, pp. 106–121 (1999)
13. Zhou, N.F., Shen, Y.D., Yuan, L.Y., You, J.H.: Implementation of a linear tabling mechanism. Journal of Functional and Logic Programming 2001(10) (October 2001)
14. Zhou, N.F., Sato, T., Shen, Y.D.: Linear Tabling Strategies and Optimizations. Theory and Practice of Logic Programming 8(1), 81–109 (2008)
15. Guo, H.-F., Gupta, G.: A simple scheme for implementing tabled logic programming systems based on dynamic reordering of alternatives. In: Codognet, P. (ed.) ICLP 2001. LNCS, vol. 2237, pp. 181–196. Springer, Heidelberg (2001)
16. de Guzmán, P.C., Carro, M., Hermenegildo, M., Silva, C., Rocha, R.: An Improved Continuation Call-Based Implementation of Tabling. In: Hudak, P., Warren, D.S. (eds.) PADL 2008. LNCS, vol. 4902, pp. 198–213. Springer, Heidelberg (2008)
17. Casas, A., Cabeza, D., Hermenegildo, M.: A Syntactic Approach to Combining Functional Notation, Lazy Evaluation and Higher-Order in LP Systems. In: FLOPS 2006, Fuji Susono (Japan) (April 2006)
18. Demoen, B., Sagonas, K.: CHAT is θ(SLG-WAM). In: Ganzinger, H., McAllester, D., Voronkov, A. (eds.) LPAR 1999. LNCS, vol. 1705, pp. 337–357. Springer, Heidelberg (1999)
19. Bueno, F., Cabeza, D., Carro, M., Hermenegildo, M., López-García, P. (eds.): G.P.: The Ciao System. Ref. Manual (v1.13). Technical report, C. S. School, UPM (2006)
20. Cabeza, D., Hermenegildo, M.: The Ciao Modular, Standalone Compiler and Its Generic Program Processing Library. Special Issue on Parallelism and Implementation of (C)LP Systems. Electronic Notes in Theoretical Computer Science 30(3) (March 2000)
21. Rocha, R., Silva, F., Costa, V.S.: YapTab: A Tabling Engine Designed to Support Parallelism. In: Conference on Tabulation in Parsing and Deduction. pp. 77–87 (2000)
22. Castro, L., Swift, T., Warren, D.: Suspending and Resuming Computations in Engines for SLG Evaluation. In: Krishnamurthi, S., Ramakrishnan, C.R. (eds.) PADL 2002. LNCS, vol. 2257, pp. 332–346. Springer, Heidelberg (2002)
23. Carro, M., Morales, J., Muller, H., Puebla, G., Hermenegildo, M.: High-Level Languages for Small Devices: A Case Study. In: Flautner, K., Kim, T. (eds.) Compilers, Architecture, and Synthesis for Embedded Systems, pp. 271–281. ACM Press / Sheridan (October 2006)
24. Morales, J., Carro, M., Hermenegildo, M.: Improving the Compilation of Prolog to C Using Moded Types and Determinism Information. In: Jayaraman, B. (ed.) PADL 2004. LNCS, vol. 3057, pp. 86–103. Springer, Heidelberg (2004)
25. Morales, J., Carro, M., Hermenegildo, M.: Comparing Tag Scheme Variations Using an Abstract Machine Generator. In: 10th Int'l. ACM SIGPLAN Symposium on Principles and Practice of Declarative Programming (PPDP 2008), pp. 32–43. ACM Press, New York (2008)

Improving Performance of Conformant Planners: Static Analysis of Declarative Planning Domain Specifications

Dang-Vien Tran, Hoang-Khoi Nguyen, Enrico Pontelli, and Tran Cao Son

Dept. Computer Science
New Mexico State University
{vtran,knguyen,epontell,tson}@cs.nmsu.edu

Abstract. The paper presents novel techniques to process planning problem specifications, expressed in a declarative description language, which enables the description of planning problems with incomplete knowledge. The outcome is improved performance and scalability of conformant planners. The paper proposes two transformations of a planning problem specification, aimed at reducing the size of the initial belief state and the number of actions to be dealt with. The two transformations have been implemented in a static analyzer and in a companion heuristic search conformant planner (CPA+). The performance of the resulting system is compared with other state-of-the-art conformant planners.

Keywords: Planning, Reasoning about Actions, Conformant Planning.

1 Introduction

Declarative languages have been extensively used in the field of reasoning about actions and change (RAC), both as *domain-specific languages* to describe planning domains (e.g., the popular Planning Domain Definition Language (PDDL) [11] and the action languages of Gelfond and Lifschitz [10]) as well as ideal paradigms to manipulate planning domains and compute solutions (e.g., the use of logic programming [9]).

A problem in RAC that has attracted the interest of several researchers is the *conformant planning* problem. Conformant planning is the problem of finding a sequence of actions that achieves the goal from every possible initial state of the world [17]—assuming that we have incomplete knowledge about the properties of the initial state. One of the main difficulties encountered in the process of determining a conformant plan is the high degree of uncertainty. In PDDL, the incompleteness of information about the initial state is specified by special classes of statements, i.e., disjunctive and/or mutual-exclusive statements, referred to as `or`- and `oneof`-clauses, respectively. Often, `oneof`-clauses are used to specify the possible initial states and `or`-clauses are used to eliminate infeasible states. As such, the number of possible initial states depends mainly on the number and the size of the `oneof`-clauses—and these are often exponential in the number of constants present in the problem instances. In fact, three out of six domains in the last planning competition [3] have this property (Table 1).

Effective methodologies are required to deal with the large number of possible initial states. Some conformant planners, such as POND [6] and KACMBP [8], employ a BDD representation of initial states, while others, such as CFF [4], adopt a CNF

A. Gill and T. Swift (Eds.): PADL 2009, LNCS 5418, pp. 239–253, 2009.

Table 1. Number of Constants/Possible Initial States

Instance	# Cons/States	Instance	# Cons/States	Instance	# Cons/States	Instance	# Cons/States
comm-10	$25/2^{11}$	comm-15	$35/2^{16}$	comm-20	$85/2^{21}$	comm-25	$140/2^{26}$
coins-15	$16/4 \times 8^6$	coins-20	$17/9 \times 8^6$	coins-25	$39/10^{20}$	coins-30	$45/10^{25}$
sortnet-10	$11/2^{11}$					sortnet-15	$2^{16}/16$

representation. These types of encodings allow one to avoid dealing directly with the exponential number of states, but they require extra work in determining the truth value of a fluent after the execution of a sequence of actions. For instance, CFF needs to make a call to a SAT-solver with the initial state and the sequence of actions; other planners need to recompute the BDD representation, which could be quite expensive. This is no surprise, since the problem of determining the truth value of a proposition after the execution of a single action in an incomplete initial state is co-NP complete [1].

Another approach has been adopted in the planners `cf2cs(ff)` and CPA [15,20], and further investigated in their successors `t0` and CPA+ [16,19]. This approach relies on an *approximation semantics* in reasoning with incomplete information [18]. The planners `cf2cs(ff)` and `t0` reduce the number of initial states to one, by transforming the original problem to a classical planning problem and using FF, a state-of-the-art classical planner [12], to find solutions. On the other hand, CPA and CPA+ reduce the number of initial states by dividing them into groups and by using the intersection of each group as its representative in the plan computation.

Although the idea of using approximation underlies both CPA+ and `t0`, the major difference between them lies in their implementations. CPA+ could be seen as a standard heuristic search forward planner. `t0` follows a translational approach. The performance of CPA+ depends on its heuristic function and its ability to approximate the initial belief state to a more manageable size. The performance of `t0` largely depends on the performance of FF. `t0` was the winner of the last planning competition[1].

The success of `t0` demonstrates that approximation-based conformant planners can be competitive with heuristic search conformant planners. On the other hand, the competitiveness of CPA+ shows that approximation can make up for the uninformativeness of its heuristic function. The list of challenging problems proposed by `t0` raises the question of whether more informative heuristics and other techniques could enable heuristic search conformant planners to be more efficient and scalable. In particular, we are interested in making planners like CPA+ competitive with `t0`.

In this paper, we investigate different techniques to improve performance and scalability of conformant planners. The main contributions can be summarized as follows:

- We develop techniques for reducing the degree of uncertainty in the initial state. In particular, we develop two transformations of a planning problem specification; one transformation combines the `oneof`-clauses, while the other splits a planning problem into a sequence of smaller problems. The first transformation is sound and complete while the second one is sound and weakly-complete. These transformations are driven by the semantics of the underlying domain description language.

[1] `http://www.ldc.usb.ve/~bonet/ipc5/`

- We experimentally demonstrate that these transformations improve the performance of CPA+ as well as other heuristic search planners. The transformations are implemented as part of a static analyzer of PDDL specifications. The static analyzer is implemented in Prolog—the features of Prolog are vital to this development.
- We experimentally demonstrate that a combination of these transformations and of three well-known heuristics—i.e., the number of fulfilled subgoals, the cardinality, and the graph distance—can be employed effectively in an approximation-based planner to produce significant performance improvements.

2 Background: Declarative Planning Domain Specification

Following the notation in [15], we describe a problem specification as a tuple $P = \langle F, O, I, G\rangle$, where F is the set of propositions, O is a set of actions, I is a set of clauses describing the initial state, and G is a set of clauses describing the goal state. A literal is either a proposition $p \in F$ or its negation $\neg p$. The complement of a literal ℓ, denoted by $\bar{\ell}$, is defined as usual: if $\ell = p \in F$ then $\bar{\ell} = \neg p$, and if $\ell = \neg p$ for some $p \in F$, then $\bar{\ell} = p$. We say that ℓ and $\bar{\ell}$ are complementary literals. For a set of literals L, $\overline{L} = \{\bar{\ell} \mid \ell \in L\}$. A conjunction of literals is often used interchangeably with a set of its conjuncts. Each action a in O is associated with a precondition ϕ and a set of conditional effects of the form $\psi \to \ell$, where ϕ and ψ are sets of literals and ℓ is a literal. We often write $pre(a)$ to denote the precondition ϕ of a, and $a : \psi \to \ell$ to denote an effect $\psi \to \ell$ of a. In PDDL, this is declaratively described as a collection of statements that compose the *domain* specification; for example, the declaration

```
(:action step-in
  :parameters (?e - elevator ?f - floor ?p - pos)
  :precondition (and (at ?f ?p) (shaft ?e ?p))
  :effect (when (in ?e ?f) (and (inside ?e) (not (at ?f ?p)))))
```

describe an action `step-in`, listing its executability conditions (`precondition`) and its conditional effects (`effect`).

The initial state is described as $I = I^d \cup I^o \cup I^r$ where I^d is a set of literals, I^o is a set of `oneof`-clauses, and I^r is a set of `or`-clauses of the form $\texttt{oneof}(\phi_1, \ldots, \phi_n)$ and $\texttt{or}(\phi_1, \ldots, \phi_n)$, where each ϕ_i is a set of literals. A `oneof`-clause indicates that the ϕ_i's are mutually exclusive, while an `or`-clauses is a DNF representation of a formula. G can contain literals or `or`-clauses. Given a `oneof`-clause or an `or`-clause o, we write $L \in o$ to denote that L is an element of o. $lit(o) = \bigcup_{L \in o}(L \cup \bar{L})$.

A set of literals is *consistent* if it does not contain two complementary literals. A *state* s is a consistent and *complete* set of literals, i.e., s is consistent, and for each $p \in F$, either $p \in s$ or $\neg p \in s$. A *partial state* is a consistent set of literals. Given a state s and an action a, a is executable in s if its precondition ϕ is a subset of s. The set of effects of a in s, denoted by $e_a(s)$, is defined by: $e_a(s) = \{l \mid \psi \to l \text{ is an effect of } a, \psi \subseteq s\}$. The execution of a in a state s results in a successor state, denoted by $succ(a, s)$, which is defined by: $succ(a, s) = s \cup e_a(s) \setminus \overline{e_a(s)}$ if a is executable in s; and $succ(a, s) = failed$, otherwise.

In presence of incomplete information about the initial state, I describes a *set of states* (a.k.a. a *belief state*). For example, $I = \{g, \texttt{oneof}(f, \neg f)\}$, or in PDDL:

```
(:init (and g (oneof f (not f))))
```

represents the belief state $\{\{g, f\}, \{g, \neg f\}\}$. The function $succ$ can be extended to define the result of the execution of an action in a belief state, denoted by $succ^*$:

$$succ^*(a, S) = \begin{cases} \{succ(a, s) \mid s \in S\} & \text{if } a \text{ is executable in every } s \in S \\ failed & \text{otherwise} \end{cases} \quad (1)$$

This function can be extended to compute the final belief state resulting from the execution of a plan as follows:

- $\widehat{succ}([a_1, \ldots, a_n], S) = S$ if $n = 0$, and
- $\widehat{succ}([a_1, \ldots, a_n], S) = succ^*(a_n, \widehat{succ}([a_1, \ldots, a_{n-1}], S))$ if $n > 0$.

Search-based conformant planners, such as CFF, employ $\widehat{succ}$ in plan computation.

Approximations: The notion of approximation used in CPA+, `cf2cs(ff)`, and `t0` has been originally proposed in [18]. It is characterized by a function ($succ_A$) that maps an action and a *partial state* to a partial state. Given a partial state δ, the effects of a in δ is defined by: $e_a(\delta) = \{l \mid \psi \to l \text{ is an effect of } a, \psi \subseteq \delta\}$. The possible effects of a in δ are given by: $pc_a(\delta) = \{l \mid \psi \to l \text{ is an effect of } a, \overline{\psi} \cap \delta = \emptyset\}$. The successor partial state from the execution of a in δ is defined by $succ_A(a, \delta) = (\delta \cup e_a(\delta)) \setminus \overline{pc_a(\delta)}$ if a is executable in δ; and $succ_A(a, \delta) = failed$, otherwise.

Similarly to $succ^*$ and $\widehat{succ}$, $succ_A$ can be extended to define $succ_A^*$ and $\widehat{succ}_A$ for computing the result of the execution of an action sequence starting from a *cs-state* (i.e., a set of partial states), as implemented in CPA+.

Approximation-based Conformant Planners: CPA+ implements a best-first search algorithm, whose nodes are sets of partial states. It uses $succ_A$ to compute successor nodes and the number of fulfilled subgoals as its heuristic function. CPA+ automatically identifies an initial set of partial states that guarantees completeness. The performance of CPA+ depends heavily on the size of the initial cs-state ([19]).

`cf2cs(ff)` uses the approximation in a different way. It translates a conformant planning problem P into a classical planning problem $K(P)$ whose solutions can be computed by a classical planner such as FF and are solutions of P. The transformation $K(P)$ is polynomial in the size of P, but incomplete. This issue has been recently addressed by a new translation ($K_{T,M}(P)$), which adds an extra parameter, called *conformant width* to the $K(P)$ translation process. $K_{T,M}(P)$ is complete for T greater than or equal to the width of the problem, but is exponential in it. A particular instance of $K_{T,M}(P)$, denoted by $K_{S_0}(P)$, is complete. `t0` is a combination of $K_{S_0}(P)$ and FF. Thus, both `cf2cs(ff)` and `t0` deal with the incomplete information in the initial situation by compiling it away. The trade-off is a new problem with a larger size.

3 Techniques and Solutions

We describe a number of techniques aimed at enhancing the performance and scalability of heuristic search conformant planners, especially those that implement an explicit representation of the belief states or of the cs-states, like CPA+. The main objective is to reduce the size of cs-states considered during the construction of a plan and remove unnecessary or non-promising alternatives during search.

We will also introduce adaptations of different heuristics for conformant planning, such as the total sum and the cardinality heuristics.

The proposed system is organized as in Fig. 1. The first component is a front-end, that acts as a *static analyzer*. The static analyzer is in charge of performing a semantic analysis of the domain specification and derive semantic-preserving transformations (w.r.t. the possible world semantics). The transformed specification produced by the static analyzer is then fed to the actual planner (CPA+ or another planner, e.g., `t0`).

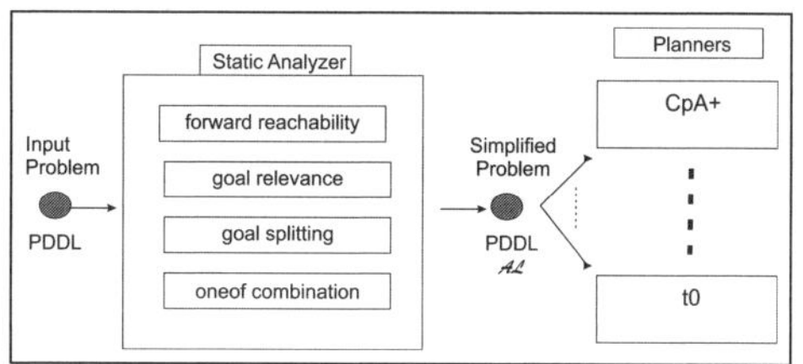

Fig. 1. Overall System

3.1 The Static Analyzer

Preliminary Definitions. Key to our analysis is the notion of *dependence* between actions and propositions. Unless otherwise specified, we denote with P a specification in the declarative domain specification language (PDDL in our case).

Definition 1. *An action* a depends *on a literal* ℓ *if* **(1)** $\ell \in pre(a)$*, or* **(2)** *there exists an effect* $a : \phi \rightarrow h$ *in* P *and* $\ell \in \phi$*, or* **(3)** *there exits an action* b *that depends on* ℓ *and* a *depends on some of the effects of* b*, i.e.,* b *depends on* ℓ *and there exists* $b : \phi \rightarrow h$ *such that* a *depends on* h*. By* $preact(\ell)$ *we denote the set of actions depending on* ℓ*.*

Intuitively, the fact that a depends on ℓ indicates that the truth value of ℓ is going to impact the execution of the action a. For a set of literals L, $preact(L) = \bigcup_{\ell \in L} preact(\ell)$.

Definition 2. *Two literals* ℓ *and* ℓ' *are* distinguishable *if* $\ell \neq \ell'$ *and there is no action that depends on both* ℓ *and* ℓ'*, i.e.,* $preact(\ell) \cap preact(\ell') = \emptyset$*.*

Obviously, the distinguishable relation is symmetric and irreflexive. Two set of literals L_1 and L_2 are distinguishable if $preact(L_1) \cap preact(L_2) = \emptyset$. The dependence between a literal and an action, often used in *reachability analysis*, is defined next.

Definition 3. *A literal* ℓ depends *on an action* a *if* **(1)** $a : \psi \rightarrow \ell$ *is in* P*, and* **(2)** *there exists an action* b *such that* $b : \psi \rightarrow \ell$ *is in* P*, the literal* ℓ' *appears in* ψ *or in* $pre(b)$*, and* ℓ' *depends on* a*. We denote with* $deps(a)$ *the set of literals that depend on* a*.*

Intuitively, ℓ depends on a implies that ℓ may be achieved by executing a. $postact(\ell)$ denotes the set of actions which ℓ depends on, i.e., $postact(\ell)=\{a \mid \ell \in deps(a)\}$.

Definition 4. *Two literals* ℓ *and* ℓ' *are* independent *if* $\ell \neq \ell'$ *and there exists no action that both* ℓ *and* ℓ' *depend on, i.e.,* $postact(\ell) \cap postact(\ell') = \emptyset$*.*

Basic Simplifications. The static analyzer starts its operations with a number of basic normalization steps, aimed at reducing the number of propositions and the number of actions present in the problem specification. We consider two basic steps: *forward reachability* and *goal relevance*. Several planners implement these two steps.

Forward reachability is used to detect *(i)* propositions whose truth value cannot be affected by the actions in the problem specification (w.r.t. the initial state); *(ii)* actions whose execution cannot be triggered w.r.t. the initial state. This process can be modeled as a fixpoint computation.

Let $I_0 = I^d \cup \bigcup_{o \in I^o} lit(o) \cup \bigcup_{o \in I^r} lit(o)$. The set of forward applicable actions is given by $fw_a(I_0) = \{a \mid a \in preact(\ell), \ell \in I_0\}$ and the relevant propositions is $fw_p(I_0) = I_0 \cup \{\ell \mid a \in fw_a(I_0), a : \psi \rightarrow \ell \in P\}$.

Goal relevance proceeds in a similar manner, by detecting actions that are relevant to the achievement of the goal. Let us denote with G_0 the collection of propositions present in the goal G. Then the backward applicable actions are $bw_a(G_0) = \{a \mid \ell \in G_0, a \in fw_p(I_0) \cap postact(\ell)\}$.

Combination of `oneof`**-Clauses.** The idea is based on the *non*-interaction between actions and propositions in different sub-problems of a conformant planning problem.

Example 1. Let $P = \langle \{f, g, h, p, i, j\}, O, I, G \rangle$ where $I = \{$ $\texttt{oneof}(f, g), \texttt{oneof}(h, p), \neg i, \neg j\}$, $G = i \wedge j$, and $O = \{a : f \rightarrow i,\ c : h \rightarrow j,\ b : g \rightarrow i,\ d : p \rightarrow j\}$. It is easy to see that the sequence $\alpha = [a, b, c, d]$ is a solution of P. Furthermore, the search should start from the cs-state consisting of the four states: **(a)** $\{f, \neg g, h, \neg p, \neg i, \neg j\}$, **(b)** $\{\neg f, g, h, \neg p, \neg i, \neg j\}$, **(c)** $\{f, \neg g, \neg h, p, \neg i, \neg j\}$, and **(d)** $\{\neg f, g, \neg h, p, \neg i, \neg j\}$.

Let P' be the problem obtained from P by replacing I with I', where $I' = \{\texttt{oneof}(f \wedge h, g \wedge p), \neg i, \neg j\}$. We can see that α is also a solution of P'. Furthermore, each solution of P' is a solution of P.

This transformation in interesting since the initial cs-state now consists only of two states: $\{f, \neg g, h, \neg p, \neg i, \neg j\}$ and $\{\neg f, g, \neg h, p, \neg i, \neg j\}$. In other words, the number of states in the initial cs-state that a conformant planner has to consider in P' is 2, while it is 4 in P. This transformation is possible because the set of actions that are "activated" by f and g is disjoint from the set of actions that are "activated" by h and p, i.e., $preact(\{f, g\}) \cap preact(\{h, p\}) = \emptyset$. □

The above example shows that different `oneof`-clause can be combined into a single `oneof`-clause, which effectively reduces the size of the initial state that a planner needs to consider in its search for a solution. Theoretically, if the size of the two `oneof`-clauses in consideration is m and n, then it is possible to achieve a reduction in the number of possible partial states from $m \times n$ to $m + n$. Since in many problems the size of the `oneof`-clauses increases with the number of objects, being able to combine the `oneof`-clauses could provide a significant advantage for the planner.

Definition 5. *Let P be a planning problem. Two* `oneof`*-clauses o_1 and o_2 are* combinable *if* **(i)** $lit(o_1) \cap lit(o_2) = \emptyset$*; and* **(ii)** $lit(o_1)$ *is distinguishable from* $lit(o_2)$.

For example, the two `oneof`-clauses in P (Example 1) are combinable. Let $o_1 = \texttt{oneof}(L_1, \ldots, L_n)$ and $o_2 = \texttt{oneof}(S_1, \ldots, S_m)$. Assume that $n \geq m$. A *combination* of o_1 and o_2, denoted by $o_1 \oplus o_2$ (or $o_2 \oplus o_1$) is the clause

$$\texttt{oneof}(L_1 \wedge S_1, \ldots, L_m \wedge S_m, L_{m+1} \wedge S_1, \ldots, L_n \wedge S_1)$$

Intuitively, a combination of o_1 and o_2 is a `oneof`-clause whose elements are pairs obtained by composing one element of o_1 with exactly one element of o_2. It is possible to prove the following result.

Proposition 1. *Let $P = \langle F, O, I, G\rangle$ be a planning problem, where G is a conjunction of literals and o_1 and o_2 are two combinable* `oneof`*-clauses in P. Let $P' = \langle F, O, I', G\rangle$, where I' is obtained from I by replacing o_1 and o_2 by $o_1 \oplus o_2$. Then, every solution of P' is also a solution of P and vice versa.*

Observe that the above proposition may not hold if P contains disjunctive goals.

Example 2. Let $P = \langle\{q, g, h, p, i, j\}, O, I, G\rangle$ where $G = \texttt{or}(i, j)$, $I = \{\texttt{oneof}(h, g), \texttt{oneof}(p, q), \neg i, \neg j\}$, and O consists of $a : p, \neg q \rightarrow i$, $c : p, q \rightarrow i$, $b : g, \neg h \rightarrow j$, and $d : g, \neg h \rightarrow j$. It is easy to check that $\texttt{oneof}(h, g)$ and $\texttt{oneof}(q, p)$ are combinable. Let P' be the problem obtained from P by replacing I with $I' = \{\texttt{oneof}(g \wedge q, h \wedge p), \neg i, \neg j\}$. Then, $[a, b]$ is a solution of P' but not a solution of P. □

The *combinable* notion can be generalized as follows.

Definition 6. *A set of* `oneof`*-clauses $\{o_1, \ldots, o_k\}$ is combinable if for each $1 \leq i \neq j \leq k$ we have that o_i and o_j are combinable.*

Let $\oplus(o_1, \ldots, o_k)$ be the shorthand for $(((o_1 \oplus o_2) \oplus \ldots) \oplus o_k)$. Proposition 1 can be generalized as follows.

Proposition 2. *Let $P = \langle F, O, I, G\rangle$ be a planning problem, where G is a conjunction of literals. Let $\{o_1, \ldots, o_k\}$ be a combinable set of* `oneof`*-clauses in P. Let $P' = \langle F, O, I', G\rangle$, where I' is obtained from I by replacing $\{o_1, \ldots, o_k\}$ with $\oplus(o_1, \ldots, o_k)$. We have that each solution of P' is a solution of P and vice versa.*

Algorithm 1. COMBINABLE(P: planning problem)

Require: $\{o_1, \ldots, o_n\}$: `oneof`-clauses in P

$S = \{o_1, \ldots, o_n\}$
$Q = \emptyset$
while ($S \neq \emptyset$) **do**
  pick $o \in S$ and set s=$\{o\}$
  for all ($o' \in S \wedge o' \notin s$) **do**
    if (o' is combinable with every $r \in s$) **then**
      $s = s \cup \{o'\}$
    end if
  end for
  $S = S \setminus s$
  $Q = Q \cup \{s\}$
end while
return Q

These results allow us to develop an algorithm for reducing the size of the initial state by composing combinable sets of `oneof`-clauses in a planning problem P. We implemented a greedy algorithm, whose running time is polynomial in the size of P, for detecting sets of combinable `oneof`-clauses and replacing them with their corresponding combination. This is possible since testing whether ℓ and ℓ' are distinguishable can be done in polynomial time in the size of P, and the number of pairs of literals that need this test is quadratic in the number of propositions in P.[2] Algorithms 1 and 2 show the procedures to detect combinable groups of `oneof`-clauses and combine them.

[2] The test for combinable can be improved using, e.g., union-find techniques.

Algorithm 2. Composition of `oneof`-clauses

Require: $\{o(L^i_1, \ldots, L^i_{n_i})\}_{i=1}^k$ combinable `oneof`s

```
o = ∅
d[1, ..., k] = [1, ..., 1]
for (i=1 TO max(n_1, ..., n_k)) do
    c = true
    for (j=1 TO k) do
        c = c ∧ L^j_{d[j]}
        if (j < n_j) then
            j = j + 1
        end if
    end for
    o = o ∪ {c}
end for
return o
```

Goal Splitting. Reducing the size of the initial state only helps the planner to start the search. It does not necessarily imply that the planner can find a solution. Furthermore, Table 2 also shows that the technique is helpful only in three out of six domains of the IPC-05. In this section, we present another technique, called *goal-splitting*, which can be used in conjunction with the combination of `oneof` to deal with large planning problems. This technique can be seen as a variation of the goal ordering technique in [13] and it relies on the notion of dependence proposed in Def. 4. The key idea is that if a problem P contains a subgoal whose truth value cannot be negated by the actions used to reach the other goals, then the problem can be decomposed into smaller problems with different goals, whose solutions can be combined to create a solution of the original problem. This is illustrated in the following example.

Example 3. Consider the problem P of Example 1. It is easy to see that the two goals i and j are independent and P can be decomposed into two sub-theories $P_1 = \langle F, O_1, I, i\rangle$ and $P_2 = \langle F, O_2, I_2, j\rangle$ where $O_1 = \{a : f \rightarrow i,\ b : g \rightarrow i\}$ and $O_2 = \{c : h \rightarrow j,\ d : p \rightarrow j\}$ with the following property: if α is a solution of P_1 and β is a solution of P_2 where $I_2 = \widehat{succ}_A(\alpha, I_1)$, then $\alpha; \beta$ is a solution of P.[3] □

Let us start with a definition capturing the condition that allows the splitting of goals.

Definition 7. *Let $P = \langle F, O, I, G\rangle$ be a planning problem and let $\ell \in G$. We say that ℓ is G-separable if, for each $\ell' \in G \setminus \{\ell\}$ we have that $\overline{\ell}$ and ℓ' are independent.*

The proof of the next above proposition is trivial, thanks to the fact that $postact(G \setminus \{\ell\})$ does not contain any action that can make $\overline{\ell}$ true.

Proposition 3. *Let $P = \langle F, O, I, G\rangle$ be a planning problem and let ℓ be G-separable. Let $P_\ell = \langle F, postact(\ell), I, \ell\rangle$ and α be a solution of P_ℓ. Let $P_{G\setminus\{\ell\}} = \langle F, postact(G \setminus \{\ell\}), I', G \setminus \{\ell\}\rangle$, where $I' = \widehat{succ}_A(\alpha, I)$, and β be a solution of $P_{G\setminus\{\ell\}}$. Then, $\alpha; \beta$ is a solution of P.*

[3] $\alpha; \beta$ denotes the concatenation of two sequences of actions.

```
(:action go-up
 :parameters (?e - elevator
              ?f ?nf - floor)
 :precondition (dec_f ?nf ?f)
 :effect (when (in ?e ?f)
     (and (in ?e ?nf)
          (not (in ?e ?f)))) )
```

```
action(go_up(E,F,NF)):-
   elevator(E), floor(F),
   floor(NF).
executable(go_up(E,F,NF),
           [dec_f(NF,F)]):-
   elevator(E),
   floor(F), floor(NF).
causes(go_up(E,F,NF),
       [in(E,NF),neg(in(E,F))],
                         [in(E,F)]) :-
  elevator(E), floor(F), floor(NF).
```

Fig. 2. PDDL action and Prolog representation

On the other hand, it is easy to see that not every plan of P can be split into two parts α and β such that α is a solution of P_ℓ and β is a solution of $P_{G\setminus\{\ell\}}$. We can prove, however, that for each plan γ of P, there is a plan α for P_ℓ and a plan β for $P_{G\setminus\{\ell\}}$ such that γ is a permutation of $\alpha;\beta$. This provides a weak form of completeness.

We note that the splitting proposed in Prop. 3 can be improved by also splitting the propositions and initial states into different theories. We have implemented a generalized version of Prop. 3 to split a problem into a sequence of problems. This implementation also runs in polynomial time in the size of P.

Implementation of the Static Analyzer. The static analyzer is implemented in Prolog (specifically, SICStus Prolog[4]). The choice of Prolog was natural, as it provides several features needed by the problem at hand:

- The components of a problem specification have an obvious representation as Prolog terms and clauses; PDDL actions and fluents have parameters and they can be encoded as complex terms, e.g., the action `go_up` with parameters elevator, floor, floor, is naturally represented by the term `go_up(Elev,Floor1,Floor2)`.
- PDDL statements can be readily mapped to a collection of Prolog rules; in particular, it allows us to keep a non-ground representation, and offers a quick access to the various components of the domain specification. For example, the PDDL action specification of the action `go_up` is translated to the Prolog rules in Fig. 2. Grounding can be obtained for free by simply collecting all valid instances of an action (e.g., using `setof`). Unification allows us to easily select components of the problem specification that meet desired requirements—e.g., a simple goal like `executable(go_up(e0,X,Y),L)` gives us access to the executability conditions of any instance of the action `go_up` targeting elevator `e0`.
- Most of the proposed transformations described are fixpoint computations, and these can be elegantly encoded in Prolog.
- Viewing action specifications as Prolog clauses, allows us to write elegant meta-interpreters to perform abstract executions; for example, if we represent an approximate state as an ordered list `L` of terms (representing the fluent literals that hold in that partial state), then determining the executable actions and the derived

[4] An implementation in SWI Prolog is also available at `http://www.cs.nmsu.edu/~tson/CpA/`

consequences from applying such actions can be reduced to simple Prolog statements, a `findall` applied to the goal `executable(A,C)`, `ord_subset (C,L)`, `causes(A,Cons,_)`. Meta-interpreters allow us to simulate both progression (i.e., if action is applicable, applied it and repeat) and regression (i.e., from the goal find actions that produce the goal and replace goal with their preconditions). Note that abstractions of progressions and regression are needed to compute forward reachability and goal relevance.

4 Experimental Results

We report on the effectiveness of the techniques and the heuristics described in the previous section in improving the performance and scalability of the planner CPA+. We also report on our experiment which shows that the `oneof`-combination can improve the performance of other systems.

4.1 Static Analyzer

The analyzer implements the forward/backward simplifications, the `oneof`-combination, and the goal-splitting algorithm. Its output is a sequence of simplified problems which serve as input to the planners CPA(C) and CPA(2) (described next). The impact of different simplifications on domains from the IPC-05 is shown in Table 2. Results from simplifications in other domains are omitted due to lack of space.

The first two columns show the reduction in the number of actions and propositions obtained by the forward/backward analysis. Each column contains the number of action (resp. propositions) before and after the simplifications are made. The third column details the number of subgoals in the original problem and the number of subtheories obtained through the goal-splitting algorithm. Domains with disjunctive goals are marked with '/D' in this column. The last column shows the reduction of the size of the initial state by applying the `oneof`-combination, the original number of states (as the product of the size of the `oneof`-clauses) and the new number of states. As it can be seen, the number of actions (resp. propositions) reduces sometimes significantly,

Table 2. Size Reduction by Static Analyzer (IPC-05 Domains)

Problem	# Actions	# Prop.	# Goal	`oneof`
comm-20	5710/1968	4070/189	40/40	$2^{21}/2$
comm-25	15515/5153	10900/214	65/65	$2^{26}/2$
coins-25	5500/1870	1920/320	15/15	$10^{20}/10^5$
coins-30	6000/2370	2425/376	20/20	$10^{25}/10^5$
uts-25	110/110	121/21	10/10	10/10
uts-30	420/420	441/41	20/20	20/20
sortnet-10	121/55	132/11	10/1/D	$2^{11}/2^{11}$
sortnet-15	256/12	272/16	15/1/D	$2^{16}/2^{16}$
adder-2	8428/4810	42/28	31/1/D	16/16
adder-3	17820/9996	54/36	45/1/D	64/64
blw-2	24/24	19/19	3/1	18/18
blw-3	40/40	29/29	4/1	125/125

especially in `comm-25` and `coins-30`. However, the reduction ratio in the number of the initial states is much more remarkable, in some cases in the order of several orders of magnitude (e.g., `comm` and `coins` problems). The goals in these domains are also independent and can be split.

4.2 Benchmarks

We use three test suites in our evaluation.

The IPC-05 domains [3]: This test suite consists of six domains used in the last planning competition. The `adder` domain is the synthesis of an adder Boolean circuit. The `coins` domain has the goal of collecting coins from different, initially unknown, positions. The `sortnet` domain is a synthesis of sorting networks which has disjunctive goals and a large number of possible initial states. The `comm` domain encodes a communication protocol whose difficulty lies in the huge size of the initial state. The `uts` domain is the computation of universal transversal sequence for graphs whose number of actions and uncertainty are more manageable comparing to other domains. The suite also contains some problems in the `block-world` domain.

Challenging domains [16]: This test suite consists of the domains that seem to be challenging for conformant planners, as suggested in [16]. They are variations of the grid problems. `dispose` is about retrieving objects whose initial location is unknown and placing them in a trash can at a given location. `push-to` is a variation where objects can be picked up only at two designated positions to which all objects have to be pushed to. `1-dispose` is a variation of `dispose`. `look-n-grab` is about picking up the objects that are sufficiently close, and dumping them in the trash can before continuing.

Other IPC domains: The third test suite contains some domains from the distribution of CFF and `t0`, such as the `ring`, `safe`, and `logistics` domains. In the `ring` domain, one can move in a cyclic fashion (either forward or backward) around a n-room building to lock windows. Each room has a window and the window can be locked only if it is closed. The uncertainty is that the initial state of windows is unknown. The goal is to have all windows locked. In the `safe` domain, a safe has one out of n possible combinations, and one must try all combinations in order to open the safe. The `logistics` domain is the 'incomplete version' of the well-known logistics domain. The uncertainty is in the initial position of each package within its origin city.

4.3 Planners

We experimented with two systems, CPA(C) and CPA(2), which are two modified versions of CPA+. CPA+ is a best-first heuristic search planner that relies on the notion of approximation described earlier. CPA(2) makes use of the heuristic $h_{cs}(\Sigma) = (h_{card}(\Sigma), h_{sub}(\Sigma))$, where (given a cs-state Σ)

- $h_{card}(\Sigma)$ is the *cardinality heuristic*, defined as $h_{card}(\Sigma) = |\Sigma|$.
- $h_{sub}(\Sigma)$ counts how many of the components of the goal are satisfied in Σ.

CPA(C) uses the heuristic function $h_{css}(\Sigma) = (h_{card}(\Sigma), h_{sub}(\Sigma), h_{sum}(\Sigma))$, where

- $h_{sum}(\Sigma)$ is the *total sum heuristic*, defined as $h_{sum}(\Sigma) = \sum_{\delta \in \Sigma} d(\delta)$, where $d(\delta)$ is the well-known sum heuristic value of the problem given that the initial state is $\delta \cup \{\neg p \mid p \in F,\ p \notin \delta,\ \neg p \notin \delta\}$ [14].

The systems uses the transformed problem specification produced by the static analyzer. We compare these systems with `t0` (a total new implementation, obtained from the authors of `t0`), CFF (linux version, downloaded from `http://members.deri.at/~joergh/cff.html`), and POND (version 1.1.1). We do not compare our systems with other planners as they have been compared to `t0` and CFF by others (e.g., [4,16]). These systems were run with the default setting. All experiments have been performed on a Linux Intel 3.06GHz chipset with 1GB of RAM.

4.4 Experiments

We report some key results (the others are omitted due to lack of space). *All timings are expressed in seconds.*

IPC-05 Domains. Table 3 shows the results of our experiments with the IPC-05 domains. The execution time for CPA(C)/CPA(2)/CPA+ is reported in two columns: the time used by the static analyzer (t_S) and the time to compute the solution (each corresponding column). We report next to the time the length of the plan found.

The effects of the `oneof`-combination and goal-splitting techniques can be seen clearly in the three domains `comm`, `coins`, and `uts` where CPA(C)/CPA(2) can solve more problems and are much faster than CPA+. `t0` is more consistent and has better performance in most of the domains applicable to it. CPA(C) is comparable to CFF in most problems except `comm-25`. POND tends to be faster in smaller problems but it does not seem to scale up well in larger problems comparing to CPA(C) or CPA(2). It should be mentioned that the combined heuristics h_{css} (resp. h_{cs}) is not admissible and

Table 3. IPC05 (Time in *sec.*, TO-Time out (30 min), NA-Not Applic., AB-Out of Memory)

Problem	t_S	CPA(C)	CPA(2)	CPA+	t0	CFF	POND
adder-01	10.35	109.91/1134	/TO	47.995/8	NA	NA	/ TO
adder-02	86.76	/TO	/TO	/TO	NA	NA	/ TO
blw-01	0.12	0.006/9	0.007/8	0.018/4	NA	NA	0.01/6
bwl-02	0.13	0.124/64	0.162/26	1016.21/107	NA	NA	0.12/34
bwl-03	0.18	6.876/1338	11.036/198	/TO	NA	NA	7.69/80
coins-10	0.18	0.065/52	0.204/65	180/56	0.088/26	1.02/38	1.07/46
coins-15	0.49	2.26/279	8.148/425	/AB	0.26/81	7.35/79	21.1/124
coins-20	0.66	13.279/928	26.428/580	/AB	0.32/108	38.19/143	211.19/153
comm-15	3.64	0.085/95	0.369/95	/TO	0.192/110	0.22/95	23.34/98
comm-20	141.45	0.731/239	5.108/239	/TO	0.864/278	13.33/239	/ TO
comm-25	1081.35	/TO	716.264/672	/TO	3.996/453	109.49/389	/ TO
sortnet-05	0.11	0.023/12	0.025/12	3.573/15	NA	NA	0.01/12
sortnet-10	0.24	4.205/39	4.135/39	/ TO	NA	NA	0.05/38
sortnet-15	0.52	427.473/65	419.885/65	/TO	NA	NA	0.28/65
uts-05	0.22	0.193/30	0.75/43	50.308/39	0.348/29	0.34/28	0.74/33
uts-10	0.93	4.531/61	30.007/87	/TO	3.536/59	55.49/58	26.16/68
uts-15	0.2	0.416/88	1.776/80	101.461/66	0.168/47	0.04/29	1.19/46
uts-20	0.89	15.375/156	52.003/138	/TO	4.832/85	1.64/59	111.54/88
uts-25	0.23	0.326/52	1.479/34	81.604/50	0.256/34	1.51/33	0.72/32
uts-30	0.86	6.144/76	26.452/74	/TO	2.632/67	25.65/66	39.88/68

Table 4. Challenging Domains (d:dispose/lng:look-n-grab)

Prob.	`oneof`	t_S	CPA(C)	`t0`	Prob.	`oneof`	t_S	CPA(C)	`t0`
d-4-1	16/16	.39	.091/76	.276/57	d-4-2	$16^2/16$	.32	.260/90	.324/86
d-4-3	$16^3/16$	.39	.908/107	.588/139	d-8-1	64/64	3.18	7.848/695	27.849/291
d-8-2	$64^2/64$	5.77	36.359/800	113.459/422	d-8-3	$64^3/64$	8.66	2195.733/951	352.946/457
push-4-1	16/16	.2	.17/148	.520/64	push-4-2	$16^2/16$	.39	.704/288	.992/87
push-4-3	$16^3/16$	.46	2.176/448	3.056/118	push-8-1	64/64	3.36	9.091/991	2536.62/473
push-8-2	$64^2/64$	6.41	61.634/2634	/AB	push-8-3	$64^3/64$	9.77	160.528/3462	/AB
1-d-4-1	16/16	.23	.640/309	0.444/70	1-d-4-2	$16^2/16^2$	.3	17.491/239	/AB
1-d-4-3	$16^3/16^3$	.48	/AB	/AB	1-d-8-1	64/64	2.69	246.569/3617	672.306/468
lng-4-1-1	16/16	.29	0.149/279	0.504/12	lng-4-2-1	16/16	.39	0.004/8	0.824/4
lng-4-3-1	16/16	.47	0.035/8	0.988/4	lng-8-1-1	64/64	3.29	11.73/2216	680.206/140

this is reflected in the length of the solutions found by CPA(C) or CPA(2). They are often longer than those found by other planners. It is also interesting to note that only CPA+ and CPA(C) can solve the `adder-01` problem. This domain has a very large number of actions, whose preconditions are empty—the cardinality heuristic does not help since the number of states is constant in every step of the computation. The number of satisfied subgoals seems to guide the search better than the total sum heuristic.

Challenging Domains. Table 4 contains the results of our experiments with the challenging problems from [16]. They are generated by the scripts that come with `t0`. The other planners are unable to deal with these domains. It should be noted that the performance of `t0` on these problems is different than the results presented in [16]. We learned from the authors of `t0` that the version of `t0` that we obtained is a new implementation, and hence its performance is occasionally different. We report only the performance of CPA(C), since it is almost identical to CPA(2), while CPA+ is capable of solving only a few of these problems. The `oneof`-column gives the number of initial states before and after the `oneof`-combination. The results indicate that CPA(C) is faster than `t0` in most of these domains. It can also solve more problem instances compared to `t0`. Also in this case, we observed that the lengths of the solutions are often longer than those returned by `t0`, sometimes up to 30 times longer. Since CPA(2) and CPA(C) yield similar results, we believe that the better performance of these planners is due to both the `oneof`-combination and the cardinality heuristic.

Domains from Other IPCs. Table 5 reports the results of our experiment with well-known domains from previous IPCs. In these domains, CFF seems to perform best. However, CFF times out when solving `safe-50`, while both `t0` and CPA(C) can solve this instance. CPA(C) and POND seem to be comparable, even though CPA(C) can solve more instances. `t0` is better than CPA(C) and POND in larger problems but slower in smaller ones.

Impact of `oneof`-Combination and Goal-Splitting on POND **and** CFF. We tested the effectiveness of the two simplifications on POND and CFF. Since a combination of several `oneof`-clauses is a `oneof`-clause whose elements are conjunctions of literals, we can only test this optimization with another planner—POND—being the only one that accepts this type of inputs. Table 6 shows the results of our experiment in the `comm` and `coins` domains. As we can see, the performance of POND improves in these problems, and the improvement is more significant when the size of the problem is

Table 5. Domains from Previous IPCs

Prob.	t_S	CPA(C)	t0	CFF	POND	Prob.	t_S	CPA(C)	t0	CFF	POND
ring-2	.07	.004/7	.068/5	.0/7	.01/6	ring-3	.11	.02/8	.052/8	.11/15	.12/13
ring-4	.08	.138/13	.072/13	2.0/25	4.56/16	ring-5	.16	.832/22	.068/17	46/45	282/20
safe-05	.08	.002/5	.052/5	.0/5	.02/10	safe-10	.09	.013/10	.052/10	.01/10	/TO
safe-30	.11	.608/30	.112/30	4.26/30	/TO	safe-50	.16	4.591/50	72.28/50	/TO	/TO
1-2-2-2	.25	.071/49	.056/16	.0/16	4.23/17	1-2-2-4	.34	15.66/526	.076/26	.01/26	/ TO
1-2-3-2	.35	2.23/159	.056/17	.01/17	/ TO	1-2-3-3	.46	/ TO	.116/24	.0/24	/ TO

Table 6. oneof-Combination in POND (Time for solving the original/modified problem)

Problem	Orig/Modified	Problem	Orig/Modified	Problem	Orig/Modified
comm-15	23.34/12.68	comm-16	221.86/147.29	comm-17	>1h
comm-17-1	275/206.88	coins-5	0.04/0.03	coins-10	1.07/0.84
coins-15	21.1/22.19	coins-20	211.19/178.26		

large. However, this technique does not help POND to scale up: it stops with `coins-17` and `comm-21` (`comm-17-1` is smaller than `comm-17` but larger than `comm-16`).

The goal-splitting technique is useful in other planners. Table 7 shows some results of our experiments with CFF in the `coins` domain. All problems in this table cannot be solved by CFF if they were not subject to goal-splitting. The difficulty in these problems lies in the large number of elevators and coins. The goal-splitting technique divides each problem into a sequence of sub-problems, each dealing with one coin but still keeping all elevators. This proved to be difficult for POND and `t0` (cut-off after 5 minutes). On the other hand, CFF can deal with it and goes on solving all subsequent problems. We observed that CFF spends most of the time finding the solution for the first problem. This is reasonable since the location of the elevators is unknown in the first problem and some of these locations will be known at the end of the first solution.

Table 7. Impact of Goal-Splitting on CFF in the `coins` Domain

coins	p21	p23	p25	p27	p30
	24.48	103.14	2.13	6.37	68.09

5 Conclusions and Future Work

In this paper, we investigated semantic analysis and transformations for a traditional declarative specification language used in reasoning about actions and change. The transformations, implemented by a static analyzer, enabled significant gains in performance and scalability of a conformant planner. We demonstrated the usefulness of the simplifications and the heuristics by implementing them in the planners CPA(C) and CPA(2). These planners are competitive with state-of-the-art conformant planners in several domains, and they outperform `t0` in several challenging domains. These results provide a good indication in support of the proposed techniques.

One of our main goals in the near future is to continue this line of research, to address the problems related to the number of actions in the planning problems. This problem can be seen in the adder domain, in which the actions are fairly simple but the number of actions is rather large; in particular, the number of actions that can be executed in each iteration of the search is also large, as the preconditions of every action are always satisfied. It appears that none of the techniques discussed in this manuscript is accurate enough to guide the search in these situations. We would also like to investigate methods to improve the quality of the solutions.

References

1. Baral, C., Kreinovich, V., Trejo, R.: Computational complexity of planning and approximate planning in the presence of incompleteness. Artificial Intelligence 122, 241–267 (2000)
2. Bertoli, P., Cimatti, A., Roveri, M.: Heuristic search + symbolic model checking = efficient conformant planning. In: IJCAI, pp. 467–472. Morgan Kaufmann, San Francisco (2001)
3. Bonet, B., Givan, B.: Results of the conformant track of the 5th planning competition (2006), http://www.ldc.usb.ve/~bonet/
4. Brafman, R., Hoffmann, J.: Conformant planning via heuristic forward search: A new approach. In: ICAPS, pp. 355–364. Morgan Kaufmann, San Francisco (2004)
5. Bryce, D.: POND: The Partially-Observable and Non-Deterministic Planner. In: Notes from the 5th International Planning Competition (2006)
6. Bryce, D., Kambhampati, S., Smith, D.: Planning Graph Heuristics for Belief Space Search. Journal of Artificial Intelligence Research 26, 35–99 (2006)
7. Bryce, D., Kambhampati, S.: Heuristic Guidance Measures for Conformant Planning. In: ICAPS, pp. 365–375. AAAI, Menlo Park (2004)
8. Cimatti, A., Roveri, M., Bertoli, P.: Conformant Planning via Symbolic Model Checking and Heuristic Search. Artificial Intelligence Journal 159, 127–206 (2004)
9. Gelfond, M., Lifschitz, V.: Representing actions in extended logic programs. In: JICSLP. MIT Press, Cambridge (1992)
10. Gelfond, M., Lifschitz, V.: Action Languages. ETAI 3(6) (1998)
11. Ghallab, M., et al.: PDDL: The Planning Domain Definition Language. Yale Center for Comp., Vis. and Ctrl (1998)
12. Hoffmann, J., Nebel, B.: The FF Planning System: Fast Plan Generation Through Heuristic Search. Journal of Artificial Intelligence Research 14, 253–302 (2001)
13. Hoffmann, J., Porteous, J., Sebastia, L.: Ordered landmarks in planning. J. Artif. Intell. Res. 22, 215–278 (2004)
14. Nguyen, X.L., Kambhampati, S., Nigenda, R.: Planning graph as the basis for deriving heuristics for plan synthesis by state space and CSP search. AIJ 135(1-2), 73–123 (2002)
15. Palacios, H., Geffner, H.: Compiling Uncertainty Away: Solving Conformant Planning Problems Using a Classical Planner (Sometimes). In: AAAI (2006)
16. Palacios, H., Geffner, H.: From Conformant into Classical Planning: Efficient Translations that may be Complete Too. In: ICAPS (2007)
17. Smith, D.E., Weld, D.S.: Conformant graphplan. In: AAAI, pp. 889–896 (1998)
18. Son, T.C., Baral, C.: Formalizing sensing actions - a transition function based approach. Artificial Intelligence 125(1-2), 19–91 (2001)
19. Son, T.C., Tu, P.H.: On the Completeness of Approximation Based Reasoning and Planning in Action Theories with Incomplete Information. In: KRR, pp. 481–491 (2006)
20. Son, T.C., Tu, P.H., Gelfond, M., Morales, R.: Conformant Planning for Domains with Constraints — A New Approach. In: AAAI, pp. 1211–1216 (2005)

Layered Models Top-Down Querying of Normal Logic Programs

Luís Moniz Pereira and Alexandre Miguel Pinto

Centro de Inteligência Artificial (CENTRIA)
Universidade Nova de Lisboa
2829-516 Caparica, Portugal
{lmp,amp}@di.fct.unl.pt

Abstract. For practical applications, the use of top-down query-driven proof-procedures is essential for an efficient use and computation of answers using Logic Programs as knowledge bases. Additionally, abductive reasoning on demand is intrinsically a top-down search method. A query-solving engine is thus highly desirable.

The current standard 2-valued semantics for Normal Logic Programs (NLPs), the Stable Models (SMs) semantics, does not allow for top-down query-solving because it does not enjoy the relevance property — and moreover, it does not guarantee the existence of a model for every NLP. To overcome these current limitations we introduce here a new 2-valued semantics for NLPs — the Layered Models semantics — which conservatively extends the SMs, enjoys relevance and guarantees model existence among other useful properties. Moreover, for existential query answering there is no need to compute total models, but just the partial models that sustain the answer to the query, or one might simply know a model one exists without producing it; relevance ensures these can be extended to total models.

A first implementation of a query-solving engine based on this new semantics is presented and described here. It uses the XSB-Prolog engine and its XASP interface to Smodels, thereby providing a useful tool built as a hybrid of the two systems and taking advantage of the best of each.

Conclusions and further work end the paper.

Keywords: Smodels, XSB-XASP, Relevance, Semantics.

1 Introduction

The semantics of Stable Models (SM) is a cornerstone for the definition of some of the most important results in logic programming of the past two decades, providing an increase in logic programming declarativity and a new paradigm for program evaluation. When we need to know the 2-valued truth value of all the literals in a logic program for the problem we are modeling and solving, the only solution is to produce complete models. In such a case, tools like *SModels* [13] or *DLV* [5] can be adequate because they can indeed compute whole models. However, the lack of some important properties of language semantics, like relevance, cumulativity and guarantee of model existence (enjoyed by, say, Well-Founded Semantics [10] (WFS)), somewhat reduces its applicability

A. Gill and T. Swift (Eds.): PADL 2009, LNCS 5418, pp. 254–268, 2009.

in practice, namely regarding abduction, creating difficulties in required pre- and post-processing. But WFS in turn does not produce 2-valued models, though these are often desired, nor guarantees 2-valued model existence.

Furthermore, in SM semantics, in an abductive reasoning situation, computing the whole model entails pronouncement about each of the abducibles whether or not they are relevant to the problem at hand, and subsequently filtering the irrelevant ones. When we just want to find an existential answer to a query, we either compute a whole model and check if it entails the query (the way SM semantics does), or, if the underlying semantics we are using enjoys the *relevance* property — which SM semantics do not— we can simply use a top-down proof-procedure (*à la* Prolog), and abduce by need. In this second case, the user does not pay the price of computing a whole model, nor the price of abducing all possible abducibles or their negations, and then filtering irrelevant ones, because the only abducibles considered will be those needed for answering the query.

The current standard 2-valued semantics for NLPs, the Stable Models [11] semantics, does not allow for top-down query-solving precisely because it does not enjoy the relevance property — and moreover, does not guarantee the existence of a model. Furthermore, frequently there is no need to compute whole models, like its implementations do, but just the partial models that sustain the answer to a query. Relevance ensures these can be extended to whole models.

To overcome these inherent limitations we developed a new 2-valued semantics for NLPs— the Layered Models (LM) semantics— which conservatively extends the SMs, and enjoys relevance and guarantee of model existence and other useful properties.

The core reason SM semantics fails to guarantee model existence for every NLP is that it does not provide a semantics to Odd Loops Over Negation (OLONs)[1]. In fact, the SM semantics community uses its inability to handle odd loops as a means to write Integrity Constraints (ICs).

Example 1. **Odd Loop Over Negation as Integrity Constraint.** Indeed, using Stable Models, one would write an IC in order to prevent X being in any model with the single rule for some atom 'a': $a \leftarrow not\ a, X$. Since the SM semantics cannot provide a semantics to this rule whenever X holds, this type of OLON is used as IC.

The LM semantics provides a semantics to all NLPs. ICs are implemented with rules for reserved atom $falsum$, of the form $falsum \leftarrow X$, where X is the body of the IC we wish to prevent being true. This does not prevent $falsum$ from being in some models. To avoid them the user must either conjoin goals with $not\ falsum$ or, if inconsistency examination is desired, *a posteriori* discard such models. LM semantics separates OLON semantics from IC compliance.

After a brief note on notation and background definitions, we present the formal definition of LM semantics and overview its useful properties. A section describing the current implementation follows and the directions in the development of the next version of our query-solving engine. Conclusions and future work close the paper.

---

[1] OLON is a loop with an odd number of default negations in its circular call dependency path.

2 Background Notation and Definitions

Definition 1. ***Logic Rule.*** *A Logic Rule r has the general form*
$A \leftarrow B_1, \ldots, B_n, not\ C_1, \ldots, not\ C_m$ *where A, the B_i and the C_j are atoms.*

We call A the head of the rule — also denoted by $head(r)$. And $body(r)$ denotes the set $\{B_1, \ldots, B_n, not\ C_1, \ldots, not\ C_m\}$ of all the literals in the body of r. Throughout this paper we will use 'not ' to denote default negation. When the body of the rule is empty, we say the head of rule is a fact and we write the rule just as h.

Definition 2. ***Logic Program.*** *A Logic Program (LP for short) P is a (possibly infinite) set of ground Logic Rules of the form in Definition 1.*

In this paper we focus solely on NLPs, those whose heads of rules are positive literals, i.e., simple atoms; and there is default negation just in the bodies of the rules. Hence, when we write simply "program" or "logic program" we mean a NLP.

3 Layering of Normal Logic Programs

The well-known notion of stratification of LPs has been studied and used for decades now. But the common notion of stratification does not cover all LPs, i.e., there are some LPs which are non-stratified.

Example 2. **Stratified vs Non-Stratified Programs.** Consider the following two programs P_1 and P_2. P_1 is stratified, according to the usual notion of stratification, whereas P_2 is not.

$$P_1:\ x \leftarrow a \quad a \leftarrow not\ b \quad b \leftarrow not\ c \qquad P_2:\ x \leftarrow a \quad a \leftarrow not\ b \quad b \leftarrow not\ a$$

Informally, in P_1, we say atom 'a' is in a stratum above of that of 'b', because there is a rule for 'a' with 'b' in its body; we say 'a' depends on 'b'. But in P_2 that dependency is symmetrical: 'b' also depends on 'a', and we cannot say if 'a' is in a stratum above of that of 'b' or vice-versa.

Definition 3. ***Layering of a Logic Program*** P. *Given a normal logic program P build a dependency graph $G(P)$ such that the atoms of P are the nodes of $G(P)$, and there is an arc from a node A to a node B iff there is a rule in P with head B such that A appears in its body.*

A layering function $l/1$ is just any function defined over the atoms of a program P, assigning each atom an integer, such that:

- *If there is a path in $G(P)$ from A to B, and there is a path in $G(P)$ from B to A then $l(A) = l(B)$.*
- *If there is a path in $G(P)$ from A to B, and there is no path in $G(P)$ from B to A then $l(A) < l(B)$.*

A layering of program P is a partition $P_1, \ldots, P_n$ of P such that P_i contains all rules whose head is an atom A such that $l(A) = i$.

Amongst the several possible layerings of a given program P we can always find the least one, i.e., the layering with the least number of layers. Throughout the rest of the paper when we refer to the program's layering we will always mean such least layering (easily seen to be unique).

Definition 4. ***Direct Dependency.*** *We say an atom A directly depends on an atom B in P iff there is at least one rule of P with head A and with B or $not\ B$ in the body.*

Definition 5. ***Dependency.*** *We say an atom A depends on an atom B in P iff there is a path in $G(P)$ from A to B.*

Definition 6. ***Relevant part of*** P ***for*** A. *The Relevant part of P for some atom A is the subset of rules of P with head A plus the set of rules of P whose heads A depends on, cf [6].*

In example 2 above, although P_2 has no stratification, it has a layering: its bottom layer $L^1_{P_2}$ is comprised of rules $a \leftarrow not\ b$, and $b \leftarrow not\ a$; and its second layer $L^2_{P_2}$ contains only the rule $x \leftarrow a$.

Due to the definition of dependency, this definition of layer does not coincide with that of stratum for usual stratification [2], nor does it coincide with the layer definition of [17]. The original definition of stratification [2] was made on predicate names rather than atoms. By abandoning the restriction of a finite number of strata of [2], the definition of Local Stratification (that now applies to atoms) of Przymusinski [17] is obtained. It copes with infinite ground programs, such as:

$$a(X) \leftarrow not\ b(s(X)) \qquad b(s(X)) \leftarrow not\ a(X)$$

Still, whereas the ground instance of this program (assuming at least one unary constant symbol) is not locally stratified, its ground version comprises just one layer.

The layering of P is said to be depth-bound iff there is one "bottom" layer comprised of rules whose heads are not above any other literal, i.e., iff $L^1_P = \emptyset$.

In practice, all useful programs have a depth-bound layering, but for theoretical completeness we show that the Layered Models semantics — defined in the sequel — also deals with programs with depth-unbound layering.

A typical case of a program with a depth-unbound layering (actually the only one with real theoretical interest, to the best of our knowledge) was presented by François Fages in [9]. We repeat it here for illustration and explanation.

Example 3. **Program with depth-unbound layering.**

$$p(X) \leftarrow p(s(X)) \qquad p(X) \leftarrow not\ p(s(X))$$

Ground (layered) version of this program, assuming there only one constant 0 (zero):

$$\begin{array}{rlrl}
p(0) \leftarrow & p(s(0)) & p(0) \leftarrow & not\ p(s(0)) \\
p(s(0)) \leftarrow & p(s(s(0))) & p(s(0)) \leftarrow & not\ p(s(s(0))) \\
p(s(s(0))) \leftarrow & p(s(s(s(0)))) & p(s(s(0))) \leftarrow & not\ p(s(s(s(0)))) \\
\vdots \leftarrow & \vdots & \vdots \leftarrow & \vdots
\end{array}$$

The only layered model of this program is $\{p(0), p(s(0)), p(s(s(0)))\ldots\}$ or, in a non-ground form, $\{p(X)\}$. The theoretical interest of this program lies in that, although it has no OLONs it still has no SMs either because no rule is supported (under the usual notion of support), thereby showing there is a whole other class of NLPs to which the SMs semantics provides no model.

4 Layered Models Semantics

Definition 7. ***Layered Model of*** P. *Let* $P_1, \ldots, P_n$ *be the least layering of program* P. *An interpretation* M *is a Layered Model of* P *iff*

$$\forall_{1 \leq i \leq n} M|_{\leq i} \textit{ is a minimal model of } \bigcup_{1 \leq j \leq i} P_j$$

where $M|_{\leq i}$ *denotes the restriction of* M *to atoms in layer* i *or a layer before* i. *I.e.*

$$M|_{\leq i} = M \cap \{A : l(A) \leq i\}$$

Intuitively, each minimal model up to and including some layer i must extend a minimal model of the layers below i.

Mark that, by definition, the minimal models up to and including a given layer respect the minimal models up to the layers preceding it. This ensures that the truth assignment to atoms in loops in higher layers are consistent with the truth assignments in loops in lower layers and that these take precedence in their truth labeling.

Note that this is a more general definition than that of perfect models [18], which improves on it, but with similar structure. Perfect model semantics talks about "least models" rather than "minimal models" because in strata there can be no loops and so there is always a unique least model which is also the minimal model. Now layers, as opposed to strata, may contain loops and thus there is not always a least model, so layers resort to minimal models, and these are guaranteed to exist (it is well known, every normal program has minimal models).

It is worth noting that atoms with no rules and appearing in the bodies of some rule are necessarily "placed" in the lowest layer. Any minimal model of this layer will consider these atoms (with no rules) to be false. This ensures compliance with the Closed World Assumption (CWA).

Example 4. **Atom with no rules.** Consider program $P = \{a \leftarrow not\ b\}$. In this case the least layering of P assigns $l(b) = 1$ and $l(a) = 2$, and therefore $P_1 = \{\}$ and $P_2 = \{a \leftarrow not\ b\}$. Necessarily, $M_1 = \{\}$ (which means b is false, and says nothing about a), and $M_2 = \{a\}$. Notice that, although $\{b\}$ is a minimal model of P, it is a non-minimal model of layer 1 and, hence, it is rejected by our Layered Models definition.

Example 5. **Layered Models versus Stable Models.** Consider program P:

$$a \leftarrow not\ b \qquad b \leftarrow not\ c \qquad c \leftarrow not\ a, x$$
$$x \leftarrow not\ y \qquad y \leftarrow not\ x$$

The rules for x and y are in the same layer which is immediately below the layer containing the rules for a, b and c. This program has only one Stable Model: $SM = \{y, b\}$ but, besides that one, it has also other LMs: $M_1 = \{x, a, b\}$, $M_2 = \{x, a, c\}$ and $M_3 = \{x, b, c\}$. As proven in Theorem 4 in section 5, all SMs of a given program are also LMs of it, thereby showing that the Layered Models semantics is a conservative generalization of the Stable Models semantics. In this example, the $SM = \{y, b\}$ is no exception: it is a minimal model of the program, and $\{y\}$ is also a minimal model of layer 1. All other LMs in the example are not SMs.

Besides the lower layer atoms they depend on (if any), atoms involved in loops have no particular *raison d'être* in a model other than being part of a minimal model solution for the respective loop(s), i.e., their only support lies on lower layers. This is true for ELONs as well as OLONs. Thus, loops are just a way to write arbitrary disjunctive choices (viz. shifting rule of [7]). In this example there is no particular reason to choose x or y; we cannot say any of them to be supported for some reason. The same reasoning applies to the top layer where the OLON over a, b, and c resides, provided that in the lower layer the truth of x has been adopted. The apparent lack of support of a in model $\{a, b, x\}$ is due to adopting the usual (classical) notion of support (where every atom true in a model must be supported by all the literals of a body of one of its rules), instead of adopting the new layered support (every atom true in a model must be classically supported just on the lower layers literals of a body of its rules).

The principle used by LMs to provide semantics to any NLP — whether is has OLONs or not, whether it is depth-bound or not — is to accept all, and only, the minimal models that respect the layers of the program. The principle used by SMs to provide semantics to some NLPs is just a "stability" (fixed-point) condition imposed on the SMs by the Gelfond-Lifschitz operator. This stability condition is too restrictive and it even gives rise to some incongruences.

Example 6. **Even Loop Over Negation[2] vs Odd Loop Over Negation.** Consider P_1: $a \leftarrow not\ b \quad b \leftarrow not\ a$. It has two SMs: $SM_1 = \{a\}$, $SM_2 = \{b\}$. Now add the rules $a \leftarrow b$ and $b \leftarrow a$. The ELON is kept, but two OLONs appear now. The program now has no SMs, but it still has one $LM = \{a, b\}$.

The example shows the incongruence in the SMs semantics when dealing with loops: it treats OLONs differently from ELONs and this incongruence stems from the stability requirement which, in our opinion, is too restrictive. The intended semantics of a loop over default negation, be it either an ELON or an OLON, be it written on purpose or be it produced by a series of updates or merges of different NLPs, is a disjunction. In example 6 above, the intended semantics of the ELON $a \leftarrow not\ b \quad b \leftarrow not\ a$ is, usually, $a \vee b$, and that is actually achieved by the SM semantics in this case. But in the same manner of thinking, the intended semantics of program $a \leftarrow not\ b \quad b \leftarrow not\ c$ $c \leftarrow not\ a$ would be $(a \vee b) \wedge (b \vee c) \wedge (c \vee a)$; that is not achieved by the SM semantics. LM semantics succeeds in doing so, while at the same time having upper layers' choices respect their lower layers' choices.

[2] An Even Loop Over Negation (ELON), analogously to an OLON, is a loop in the dependency call graph with an intervening even number of default negations.

5 Properties of the Layered Models Semantics

5.1 Existence

Theorem 1. ***Existence.*** *Every Normal Logic Program has a Layered Model.*

Proof. By construction, it is always possible to find a layering for P and, therefore, its least layering. It is always possible to find a minimal model for layer 1 and, moreover, for each layer above it is always possible to find a minimal model for it which includes a minimal model of the previous layer. □

5.2 Relevance

[6] presents definitions of the Relevance and Cumulativity properties of a semantics of logic programs. We recall them here for self containment.

Definition 8. ***Relevance.*** *A semantics for logic programs is said to be Relevant iff for every program P $a \in Sem(P) \Leftrightarrow a \in Sem(Rel_P(a))$.*

Theorem 2. ***Relevance of Layered Models semantics.*** *The LM semantics is relevant.*

Proof. According to definition 7, the LM semantics of a program P is the intersection of its LMs. So, $a \in LM(P) \Leftrightarrow \forall_{LM_P(M)} a \in M$. For the LM semantics the relevance property is expressed by $a \in LM(P) \Leftrightarrow a \in LM(Rel_P(a))$.

$\Rightarrow$: We assume $a \in LM(P)$, so we can take any M such that $LM_P(M)$ holds, and conclude that $a \in M$. Assuming, by absurd, that $a \notin LM(Rel_P(a))$ this means that there is at least one LM of $Rel_P(a)$ where a is false, i.e., where $not\ a$ is true. Since every LM of P satisfies its subsets we conclude there must be at least one LM of P containing the LM of $Rel_P(a)$ where a is false. But this means that $a \notin LM(P)$ which is an absurd contradicting the initial assumption $a \in LM(P)$.

$\Leftarrow$: Assume $a \in LM(Rel_P(a))$. Take the whole $P \supseteq Rel_P(a)$. Again, a will be in every LM of P because a is in all LMs of $Rel_P(a)$, and every LM of P always contains one LM of $Rel_P(a)$. □

Relevance is the property that makes it possible to implement a top-down call-directed query-derivation proof-procedure — a highly desirable feature if one wants an efficient theorem-proving system that does not need to compute a whole model to answer a query. These methods are designed to try and identify whether a query literal belongs to some LM, and to partially produce a LM supporting a positive answer. The partial solution is guaranteed extendable to a full LM because of relevance.

5.3 Cumulativity

Definition 9. ***Cumulativity.*** *A semantics is Cumulative iff for every program P*

$$\forall_{a,b}(a \in Sem(P) \wedge b \in Sem(P)) \Rightarrow a \in Sem(P \cup \{b\})$$

Theorem 3. ***Cumulativity of Layered Models semantics.*** *LM semantics is cumulative.*

Proof. By definition 7, the semantics of a program P is the intersection of its LMs. So, $a \in LM(P) \Leftrightarrow \forall_{LM_P(M)} a \in M$. For the LM semantics cumulativity becomes expressed by

$$\forall_{a,b}(a \in LM(P) \wedge b \in LM(P)) \Rightarrow a \in LM(P \cup \{b\})$$

Let us assume $a \in LM(P) \wedge b \in LM(P)$. If there is a path from b to a in P, then a depends on b and there exist $i \geq j$ such that $b \in M_j$ and $a \in M_i$, and $M \supseteq M_i \supseteq M_j$. It comes trivially that adding b as a fact to P does not change a's truth-value since every M_i including a already included b.

If there is no path from b to a it means that a does not depend on b's truth-value, and since the LM semantics is relevant, a's truth-value will remain unchanged just by adding b as a fact to P. □

5.4 Stable Models Extension

Theorem 4. ***Stable Models Extension.*** *Any Stable Model is a Layered Model of P.*

Proof. Assume M is a SM of P. It is well known that every SM is also a minimal model. By definition of SM we know M is the least model of P/M (which results from deleting from P all the rules with $not\ a$ in the body where $a \in M$, and then deleting all remaining $not\ x$). The least model can be calculated by iterating the well-known T_P operator [8]. This operator gives as a result an interpretation that differs from the interpretation it takes only by some atoms which are heads of rules whose bodies were true in the input interpretation. This means the atoms in $J \setminus I$, where $J = T_P(I)$, are in a layer above those of I. At each iteration of T_P the previous interpretation atoms are kept. Hence we can conclude $T_P^i(\{\}) = M_i$, and, therefore, M is a LM. □

In example 5 we present a program with a SM — show it to be a LM as well — and other non-SMs LMs.

Some NLPs have no SMs but, by Theorem 1, all have at least one LM. The relation between the Layered Models and the Revised Stable Models ([14,16]) is not yet fully studied, but, at first glance, they seem equivalent. The thorough analysis of the relation between these two semantics remains as future work, for now.

Due to lack of space, the complexity analysis of this semantics is left out of this paper. Nonetheless, a brief note is due. Theorem 1 guarantees every NLP has at least one LM, hence the complexity of finding if one LM exists is trivial, when compared to SMs semantics. The whole point of having a new semantics enjoying relevance is to be able to do brave reasoning (finding if there is any model of the program where some atom a is true) without necessarily computing a whole model, just the relevant subset of the program for a and computing the respective submodel, guaranteed extendable to a whole one. Cautious reasoning (finding out if some atom a is in all models) boils down to finding if a is unconditionally true given its dependency graph.

6 Examples

Example 7. **A joint vacation problem.** Three friends are planning a joint vacation. First friend says "I want to go to the mountains, but if that's not possible then I'd rather go to the beach". The second friend says "I want to go traveling, but if that's not possible then I'd rather go to the mountains". The third friend says "I want to go to the beach, but if that's not possible then I'd rather go traveling". However, traveling is only possible if the passports are OK. They are OK if they are not expired, and they are expired if they are not OK. We code this information as the following NLP:

$$\begin{array}{ll} beach & \leftarrow not\ mountain \\ mountain & \leftarrow not\ travel \\ travel & \leftarrow not\ beach, passport\_ok \\ & \\ passport\_ok & \leftarrow not\ expired\_passport \\ expired\_passport & \leftarrow not\ passport\_ok \end{array}$$

It is easy to see that the first three rules forming an OLON over $beach$, $mountain$, and $travel$ are in layer 2; and the rules for $passport\_ok$ and $expired\_passport$ are in layer 1. This program has only one SM: $\{expired\_passport, mountain\}$. But, looking at the rules relevant for $passport\_ok$ we find no irrefutable reason to assume $expired\_passport$ to be true. The LM semantics allows $passport\_ok$ to be true yielding three other models besides the SM; those are:

$LM_1 = \{beach, mountain, passport\_ok\}$, $LM_2 = \{beach, travel, passport\_ok\}$, and $LM_3 = \{travel, mountain, passport\_ok\}$.

The first layer has two minimal models: $\{passport\_ok\}$ and $\{expired\_passport\}$. Assuming the first minimal model, the second layer has three minimal models which correspond to LM_1, LM_2, and LM_3 above. Assuming the second minimal model (where $expired\_passport$ is true), the second layer has only one minimal model: the SM mentioned above $\{expired\_passport, mountain\}$ (which also a LM).

Example 8. **N-Queens.** When considering the SM semantics, the classical example of the N-Queens problem (apart from diagonal attack prevention) can be expressed as the following NLP (where we assume there are some facts for the rows and for the columns):

$$\begin{array}{ll} hasQueen(X,Y) & \leftarrow row(X), column(Y), not\ noQueen(X,Y) \\ noQueen(X,Y) & \leftarrow row(X), column(Y), column(YY), not\ eq(Y,YY), \\ & \quad hasQueen(X,YY) \\ noQueen(X,Y) & \leftarrow column(Y), row(X), row(XX), not\ eq(X,XX), \\ & \quad hasQueen(XX,Y) \end{array}$$

In this program there are, apparently, two OLONs via both rules for $noQueen/2$: $hasQueen/2$ depends on $not\ noQueen/2$ which, in turn, depends on $hasQueen/2$. We can think of these OLONs, under SM semantics, as providing ICs to eliminate models where we have two mutually attacking queens. However, the rules for $noQueen/2$ are applicable (have the remaining context literals of their bodies true) only when $not\ eq(X,XX)$ (or $not\ eq(Y,YY)$) hold. This means the two queens are not attacking each other and so, the OLONs never get a chance to act as ICs to eliminate models. The undesired models with mutually attacking queens are eliminated by the $not\ eq(X,XX)$ and $not\ eq(Y,YY)$ literals. In this particular case, the LMs coincide with the SMs. If we delete the $not\ eq/2$ occurrences, LM still computes the correct models because a queen cannot attack itself, which is solved by the minimal model. Not so for the SM.

Example 9. **Map coloring.** Again, considering the SM semantics, the rules for any individual node of the classical problem of map coloring can be expressed as the following NLP (where we assume there are some facts for nodes and for the edges):

$$col(C, red) \leftarrow node(C), not\ col(C, blue), not\ col(C, green)$$
$$col(C, blue) \leftarrow node(C), not\ col(C, red), not\ col(C, green)$$
$$col(C, green) \leftarrow node(C), not\ col(C, blue), not\ col(C, red)$$

One can argue that there are OLONs here which, under the SM semantics, work as ICs preventing some undesired models. That is actually not the case in this situation: no OLON acts as an IC under SM semantics because every OLON has a symmetrical one (e.g, the OLON $col(C, red) \leftarrow not\ col(C, blue) \leftarrow not\ col(C, green) \leftarrow not\ col(C, red)$ is symmetrical to OLON $col(C, red) \leftarrow not\ col(C, green) \leftarrow not\ col(C, blue) \leftarrow not\ col(C, red)$) and both together form an ELON which is solvable by SM semantics.

In this example, since every SM is also a LM, and there are no more minimal models besides the SMs, we conclude the LM and SM semantics coincide.

7 Implementation

7.1 XSB-XASP Interface

The Prolog language has been for quite some time one of the most accepted means to codify and execute logic programs, and as such has become a useful tool for research and application development in logic programming. Several stable/production stage implementations have been developed and refined over the years, with plenty of working solutions to pragmatic issues ranging from efficiency and portability to explorations of language extensions. The XSB Prolog system[3] is one of the most sophisticated, powerful, efficient and versatile among these implementations, with a focus on execution efficiency and interaction with external systems, implementing program evaluation following the WFS for NLPs. The XASP interface [3,4] (standing for XSB Answer Set Programming), is included in XSB Prolog as a practical programming interface to Smodels [13], one of the most successful and efficient implementations of the SMs over generalized LPs. The XASP system allows one not only to compute the models of a given NLP, but also to effectively combine 3-valued with 2-valued reasoning. The latter is achieved by using Smodels to compute the SMs of the so-called residual program, the one that results from a query evaluated in XSB using tabling [20]. A residual program is represented by delay lists, that is, the set of undefined literals for which the program could not find a complete proof, due to mutual dependencies or loops over default negation for that set of literals, detected by the XSB tabling mechanism. This method allows to obtain any two-valued semantics in completion to the three-valued semantics the XSB system produces.

Such integration allows to make use of relevance for queries. In SMs it is necessary to compute all complete models for the whole program. In our implementation framework, we sidestep this issue, by using XASP to compute the query relevant residual program on demand. After some degree of transformation, the resulting residual program is sent to Smodels for computation of stable models of the relevant sub-program. The top-down computation, to boot, helps in partly or totally grounding the residual program.

[3] Both the XSB Logic Programming system and Smodels are freely available at: `http://xsb.sourceforge.net` and `http://www.tcs.hut.fi/Software/smodels`.

7.2 Top-Down Query-Solving Implementation Using the Layered Models Semantics

The intended use of LM semantics implementation is to provide a tool for existential querying — much like Prolog — but dealing effectively, and in a 2-valued fashion, with all kinds of loops over negation.

In top-down querying, layers are inherently found by a loop-detection mechanism in the call-graph descending search, this being facilitated by the implementation of XSB Prolog [19]. In practice top-down querying using the LMs semantics corresponds to finding and solving the OLONs (through the minimal choices of which atoms to assume *true*), making sure minimal models found to solve an OLON respect the WFM of the layers below it. This is guaranteed because XSB's residual program computation mechanism simplifies the original program, preserving its layering and semantics, and reducing it according to its WFM. OLON detection and reduction is performed on the residual program.

This first implementation of the LMs semantics is mainly intended to be a proof-of-concept, more than a high-end efficient and optimized final one. By their very nature, depth-unbound programs cannot be solved in full generality. We leave them unsolved, for now, and will consider solvable cases in the next implementation. This implementation is moreover limited to call-consistent programs, i.e., those where the top-down querying ensures the groundness of the queried literal in each step in the derivation tree. Also reserved for the future, is the employing of constructive negation as a way to constrain free variables under default negation, without having to fully ground them.

The present meta-interpreter allows the user to consult a Knowledge Base (KB) — in the form of a finite grounded NLP — and then to pose queries which are solved in a top-down fashion, obtaining as a result a partial LM — if there is one inclusive of the query. Upon backtracking other partial models are returned. The meta-interpreter is comprised of two components: one takes care of the OLONs and the other solves ELONs in a manner compatible with the ICs.

Residual Program. After launching a query in a top-down fashion we must obtain the relevant residual part of the program for the query. This is achieved in XSB Prolog using the `get_residual/2` predicate. According to the XSB Prolog's manual " the predicate `get_residual/2` unifies its first argument with a tabled subgoal and its second argument with the (possibly empty) delay list of that subgoal. The truth of the subgoal is taken to be conditional on the truth of the elements in the delay list". The delay list is the list of literals whose truth value could not be determined to be *true* nor *false*, i.e., their truth value is *undefined* in the WFM of the program.

It is possible to obtain the *residual* clause of a solution for a query literal, and in turn the *residual* clauses for the literals in its body, and so on. This way we can reconstruct the complete relevant residual part of the KB for the literal — we call this a *residual program* or *reduct* for that solution to the query.

More than one such *residual program* can be obtained for the query, on backtracking. Each *reduct* consists only of partially evaluated rules, with respect to the WFM, whose heads are atoms relevant for the initial query literal, and whose bodies are just the *residual* part of the bodies of the original KB's rules. This way, not only do we get just the relevant part of the KB for the literal, we also get precisely the part of those rules bodies still *undefined*, i.e., that are involved in Loops Over Negation.

Example 10. **Solving OLONs.** Consider the program:

$$a \leftarrow not\ a, b \qquad b \leftarrow c \qquad c \leftarrow not\ b, not\ a$$

which coincides with its residual. Solving a query for a, we use its rule and immediately detect the OLON on a. The leaf $not\ a$ is removed; the rest of the body $\{b\}$ is kept as the Context under which the OLON on a is "active" — if b were to be false there would be no need to solve the OLON on a's rule. After all OLONs have been solved, we use the Contexts to create new rules that preserve the meaning of the original ones, except these new ones have no dependency on OLONs. The current Context for a is now just $\{b\}$ instead of the original $\{not\ a, b\}$.

Solving now a query for b, we go on to solve c — $\{c\}$ is b's current Context. Solving c we find leaf $not\ b$. We remove c from b's Context, and add c's body $\{not\ b, not\ a\}$ to it. The OLON on b is detected and the $not\ b$ is removed from b's Context which finally is just $\{not\ a\}$. As it can be seen so far, updating Contexts is similar to performing a Partial Evaluation plus OLON detection and resolution by removing the dependency on the OLON. The new rule for b has its final Context $\{not\ a\}$ as body. I.e., the new rule for b is $b \leftarrow not\ a$. Again, continuing a's final Context calculation, we remove b from a's Context and add $\{not\ a\}$ to it. This additional OLON is detected and $not\ a$ is removed from a's Context which now becomes empty. Since we already exhausted a's dependency call-graph, the final body for the new rule for a is now empty: a will be added as a fact. Moreover, a new rule for b will be added: $b \leftarrow not\ a$. Final program sent to Smodels:

$$a \leftarrow not\ a, b \qquad a \qquad b \leftarrow c \qquad b \leftarrow not\ a \qquad c \leftarrow not\ b, not\ a$$

it has only one $SM = \{a\}$ the only LM of the program. Mark layering is respected when solving OLONs: a's final rule depends on the answer to b's final rule.

Dealing with Integrity Constraints. ICs are written as just $falsum \leftarrow IC\_Body$. $not\ falsum$ is conjoined to the user's query causing the ICs to be included in the residual program which is then sent to Smodels.

Interaction with Smodels. When the meta-interpreter reaches the point where all the relevant OLONs have been successfully and consistently solved, all OLONs resolutions are incorporated in the *residual program* as new rules which do not depend on any OLONs.

Another two rules are added to the Smodels clause store: one creates an auxiliary rule for the initially posed query; with the form: `lmGoal :- Query`, where `Query` is the query conjunct posed by the user. The second rule just prevents Smodels from having any model where the `lmGoal` does not hold, having the form:

```
falsum :- not falsum, not lmGoal
```

This time, we deliberately create an OLON and send it to Smodels as a way of creating an IC that prevents our top goal from being false. It is thence the Smodels implementation the one responsible for solving the ELONs. Notice that since all the

OLONs resolutions have added new alternative rules that do not depend on any OLONs to the *residual program*, all the OLONs become now "harmless" in what the SMs are concerned. The OLONs became *inactive*, already solved in favour of their positive head — cf. [14]. XSB's XASP communication with Smodels permits the programmer to use a "Smodels clause store" to which several rules can be added. This clause store is then sent to Smodels which will consider only those rules when computing a model. After adding all the original residual relevant rules, and also the newly created rules (with the OLON-dependency-free-Contexts as bodies) to the Smodels clause store, the SMs of the stored program are obtained by asking Smodels to compute one model (and on backtracking to compute others, if we so wish). All of this is encapsulated by predicate `getOneSM(-Clauses,+SM)`. The SM obtained is a partial LM of the original program containing only the literals relevant for the query.

Pseudo-Code for the Query-Solving Engine. Next we present, in a succinct way, the pseudo-code for the main procedure of our query-solving engine.

```
lmquery(+QueryList, -RelevantPartialLM) :-
  1. Compute the residual part of the program relevant for
     the query
  2. Select and remove the first literal from query and add
     it to the ancestors list
  3. If an OLON is detected in the ancestors list
     3.1. Subtract the ancestors from the current Context
     3.2. Create a new rule for the head of the OLON
            whose body is the current Context
     else
     3.3. Pick one rule for the selected literal and add
            its body to the current Context
     endif
  4. Send the residual relevant part of the program, plus
     the newly created rule to Smodels
  5. Get one Stable Model as the RelevantPartialLM
```

The source code for this implementation of the LM meta-interpreter can be found at `http://centria.di.fct.unl.pt/~amp/software/ software.html`. Examples and usage instructions are also available on this web page.

8 Conclusions and Future Work

Having defined a more general 2-valued semantics for NLPs much remains to be explored, in the way of properties, complexity, comparisons (namely with the likely equivalent Revised Stable Models[14], where more examples, including practical ones, can be found), implementations, and applications, contrasting its use to other semantics employed heretofore for KRR, though SM has been compared often enough.

That the LM semantics includes the SM semantics and that it always exists and admits top-down querying is a novelty making us look anew at 2-valued semantics use in KRR. LMs' implementation, because of its relevance property, can avoid the need to compute whole models and all models, and hence SM's apodictic need for complete groundness and the difficulties it begets for problem representation. Moreover, abstract partial models, instead of ground ones, may be produced directly by the residual, a subject for further investigation. An efficient engine level implementation is underway at XSB-engine level, that we intend to make a practical and usable alternative to Smodels [13] or DLV [5], where these can be replaced with advantage. This second implementation will include abduction [1], as well as constructive negation mechanisms [12].

The above reported convivial hybrid implementation of LMs and SMs, demonstrates the usefulness and praticality of a NLP semantics, and attending mechanisms, promoting a best of both worlds stance, and attract closer together the LP communities. The applications afforded by LMs are all those of SMs, which it extends, plus those requiring OLONs for model existance, and those where OLONs actually are employed for problem representation. The guarantee of model existance is essential in applications where knowledge sources are diverse (like in the semantic web), and where the bringing together of such knowledge (automatically or not) can give rise to OLONs that would otherwise prevent the resulting program from having a semantics, thereby brusquely terminating the application. A similar situation can be brought about by self- and mutually-updating programs, including in the learning setting, where unforeseen OLONs would stop short an ongoing process if the SM semantics were in use. Finally, codings of ICs via odd loops in SM semantcs found in the literature can be readily transposed to IC coding in LM semantics.Hence, apparently there is only to gain in exploring the adept move from SMs to their more general extension of LMs.

Another topic for future work is exploring the definition of a Well-Founded Layered Model (WFLM). In a nutshell, the WFLM is a partial model which, at each layer, is the intersection of the all LMs. Floating conclusions are disallowed by this definition. Incidental to this topic is the relationship of the WFLM to O-semantics [15]. It is readily apparent that the former extends the latter.

Yet another topic consists in defining partial model schemas, that can provide answers to queries in terms of abstract non-ground model schemas encompassing several instances of ground partial models. This is closely related to consistent abduction of non-ground literals.

Acknowledgements

We thank José Júlio Alferes for his much lighter version of our definition of LMs, and Robert Kowalski for his helpful comments on our previous characterizations of LMs.

References

1. Alferes, J.J., Pereira, L.M., Swift, T.: Abduction in well-founded semantics and generalized stable models via tabled dual programs. Theory and Practice of Logic Programming 4(4), 383–428 (2004)
2. Apt, K.R., Blair, H.A.: Arithmetic classification of perfect models of stratified programs. Fundam. Inform. 14(3), 339–343 (1991)
3. Castro, L., Swift, T., Warren, D.S.: XASP: Answer Set Programming with XSB and Smodels, `http://xsb.sourceforge.net/packages/xasp.pdf`

4. Castro, L.F., Warren, D.S.: An environment for the exploration of non monotonic logic programs. In: Kusalik, A. (ed.) Proc. of the 11th Intl. Workshop on Logic Programming Environments (WLPE 2001) (2001)
5. Citrigno, S., Eiter, T., Faber, W., Gottlob, G., Koch, C., Leone, N., Mateis, C., Pfeifer, G., Scarcello, F.: The dlv system: Model generator and advanced frontends (system description). In: Workshop Logische Programmierung (1997)
6. Dix, J.: A Classification-Theory of Semantics of Normal Logic Programs: I, II. Fundamenta Informaticae XXII(3), 227–255, 257–288 (1995)
7. Dix, J., Gottlob, G., Marek, V.W., Rauszer, C.: Reducing disjunctive to non-disjunctive semantics by shift-operations. Fundamenta Informaticae 28, 87–100 (1996)
8. Van Emden, M.H., Kowalski, R.A.: The semantics of predicate logic as a programming language. J. ACM 23(4), 733–742 (1976)
9. Fages, F.: Consistency of Clark's completion and existence of stable models. Methods of Logic in Computer Science 1, 51–60 (1994)
10. Van Gelder, A., Ross, K.A., Schlipf, J.S.: The well-founded semantics for general logic programs. J. of ACM 38(3), 620–650 (1991)
11. Gelfond, M., Lifschitz, V.: The stable model semantics for logic programming. In: ICLP/SLP, pp. 1070–1080. MIT Press, Cambridge (1988)
12. Liu, J.Y., Adams, L., Chen, W.: Constructive negation under the well-founded semantics. Journal of Logic Programming 38(3), 295–330 (1999)
13. Niemelä, I., Simons, P.: Smodels - an implementation of the stable model and well-founded semantics for normal logic programs. In: Fuhrbach, U., Dix, J., Nerode, A. (eds.) LPNMR 1997. LNCS, vol. 1265, pp. 420–429. Springer, Heidelberg (1997)
14. Pereira, L.M., Pinto, A.M.: Revised stable models - a semantics for logic programs. In: Bento, C., Cardoso, A., Dias, G. (eds.) EPIA 2005. LNCS, vol. 3808, pp. 29–42. Springer, Heidelberg (2005)
15. Pereira, L.M., Alferes, J.J., Aparíco, J.N.: Adding closed world assumptions to well-founded semantics. Theor. Comput. Sci. 122(1-2), 49–68 (1994)
16. Pinto, A.M.: Explorations in revised stable models — a new semantics for logic programs. Master's thesis, Universidade Nova de Lisboa (February 2005)
17. Przymusinski, T.C.: Every logic program has a natural stratification and an iterated least fixed point model. In: PODS, pp. 11–21. ACM Press, New York (1989)
18. Przymusinski, T.C.: Perfect model semantics. In: ICLP/SLP, pp. 1081–1096 (1988)
19. Sagonas, K.F., Swift, T., Warren, D.S.: The xsb programming system. In: Workshop on Programming with Logic Databases (Informal Proceedings), ILPS, p. 164 (1993)
20. Swift, T.: Tabling for non-monotonic programming. Annals of Mathematics and Artificial Intelligence 25(3-4), 201–240 (1999)

Secure Implementation of Meta-predicates*

Paulo Moura

Dep. of Computer Science, University of Beira Interior, Portugal
Center for Research in Advanced Computing Systems, INESC–Porto, Portugal
pmoura@di.ubi.pt

Abstract. This paper identifies potential security loopholes in the implementation of support for meta-predicates. Closing these loopholes depends on three conditions: a clear distinction between closures and goals, support for an extended meta-predicate directive that allows the specification of closures, and the availability of the `call/2-N` family of built-in meta-predicates. These conditions provide the basis for a set of simple safety rules that allows meta-predicates to be securely supported. These safety rules are currently implemented by Logtalk, an object-oriented logic programming language, and may also be applied in the context of Prolog predicate-based module systems. Experimental results illustrate how these rules can prevent several security problems, including accidental or malicious changes to the original meta-predicate arguments and bypassing of predicate scope rules and predicate scope directives.

Keywords: Logic-programming, meta-predicates, security.

1 Introduction

Prolog and Logtalk [1,2] meta-predicates are predicates with one or more arguments that are called as goals on the body of a predicate clause. A typical example is the `findall/3` predicate whose second argument is used for generating solutions that are collected into a list. Meta-arguments may also be closures. In the context of this paper, a closure is defined as a callable term used to construct a goal by appending one or more arguments. The archetypal example is a list mapping predicate that succeeds when a closure can be successfully applied to each element in the list. Meta-predicates are particularly useful in the presence of an encapsulation mechanism such as a module system or an object-oriented extension. Defining an exported or public meta-predicate within a module or an object allows client modules and objects to reuse predicates customized by calls to local predicates.

Meta-predicates require special care in the context of Prolog module systems and object-oriented extensions as meta-calls must be executed in the meta-predicate *calling context* and not in the meta-predicate *definition context*.

* This work is partially supported by the FCT research project MOGGY (PTDC/EIA/70830/2006).

A. Gill and T. Swift (Eds.): PADL 2009, LNCS 5418, pp. 269–283, 2009.

A recent paper [3] showed that the implementation of meta-predicates found in most Prolog *predicate-based* module systems allows a module to call non-exported predicates of another module, thus breaking encapsulation. This problem is usually absent from *atom-based* module systems such as XSB [4] where atoms, including predicate functors, are internally tagged with the definition module. The lack of enforcement of module encapsulation can, however, be thought as a consequence of the original design goals of module systems. Traditional Prolog module systems never aimed to fulfill any security role, being designed instead as a simple solution for partitioning code in different namespaces. Moreover, in most Prolog module systems, any module predicate can be called by using explicit module qualification (Ciao [5,6] and ECLiPSe [7] are notable exceptions, only allowing calls to exported module predicates). Prolog extensions such as Logtalk, however, are designed to enforce encapsulation and predicate scope rules. In this case, meta-predicates must be properly supported without the danger of providing the means of accidental or malicious bypassing of predicate scope directives. The same paper also exposed flaws in the Logtalk support of meta-predicates which allowed bypassing of predicate scope directives. These flaws resulted from clever use of closures and from unsafe handling of goal execution context in the presence of meta-calls. During our research to correct these problems, we uncovered other meta-predicate implementation flaws that are not necessarily related to bypassing of predicate scope directives. In fact, potential loopholes exist that may allow accidental or carefully crafted meta-predicate definitions to change the original meta-predicate call. These changes may allow calling a different predicate in the calling context or calling the intended predicate with corrupted arguments. Calling a predicate different from the one specified in the original meta-predicate call is always a flaw, even when the called predicate is public or exported. Corrupting the original meta-predicate arguments can be done conditionally, resulting in hard to find problems as only specific usage patterns will lead to compromised results.

Correcting these flaws can be accomplished by finding and implementing a set of safety rules that ensures secure compilation and use of meta-predicates. Although our research takes place in the context of the Logtalk programming language, these safety rules are equally relevant in the context of predicate-based Prolog module systems (the proposed safety rules are not tied to the semantic differences between objects and modules). These safety rules are useful even in the context of module systems that allow the `:/2` control construct to bypass predicate scope rules, promoting better coding standards for meta-predicate definitions.

This paper is organized as follows. Section 2 describes an extended meta-predicate declaration directive, which supports the specification of both goals and closures as meta-arguments. Section 3 discusses how meta-calls can be constructed from closures. Section 4 enumerates potential loopholes in the implementation of meta-predicate support. Section 5 presents and discusses the safety rules applied by Logtalk to compile and execute meta-predicates. Section 6 identifies limitations imposed by our safety rules on meta-predicate definitions.

Section 7 presents experimental results in testing common Prolog module systems for the loopholes discussed in this paper. Section 8 presents our conclusions on safe compilation and use of meta-predicates, together with some remarks on the importance of increasing the awareness of security issues among the Logic Programming community.

2 Extended Meta-predicate Directive

User meta-predicates are declared using *meta-predicate directives*. These directives use a meta-predicate template to specify which arguments are *meta-arguments*, i.e. which arguments will be used as goals or closures in the body of the meta-predicate clauses. In plain Prolog, meta-predicate directives are optional and primarily useful for cross-reference tools. When module or object systems are present, meta-predicates directives are required for proper compilation of meta-predicates. An example of a Logtalk meta-predicate directive where the meta-arguments are goals is:

```
:- meta_predicate(findall(*, ::, *)).
```

In meta-predicate templates, the atom :: represents a meta-argument that will be called as a goal. Normal arguments are represented by the atom `*`. This is similar to the declaration of meta-predicates found in most Prolog compilers and in the ISO Prolog standard for modules [8] (the atom :: is used instead of the atom : for consistency with the Logtalk message sending operators). A positive integer, `N`, specifies a closure that will be used to construct a call by appending `N` arguments. For example:

```
| ?- map(double, [1, 2, 3], L).
L = [2, 4, 6]
yes
```

The corresponding `meta_predicate/1` directive would be:

```
:- meta_predicate(map(2, *, *)).
```

The first argument in the `map/3` template specifies that the meta-argument is a closure that will be used to construct a meta-call by appending two arguments. In the example above, this requires the existence of a `double/2` predicate in the calling context of the meta-predicate.

The use of non-negative integers to specify closures was first introduced in Quintus Prolog [9] for providing information to predicate cross-reference tools. A description of this usage can also be found on a recent Prolog standardization proposal [10]. Other Prolog compilers, such as SICStus Prolog [11] and YAP [12], also accept this notation for compatibility with existing code. As discussed later in this paper, the support for specifying closures in meta-predicate directives is essential to ensure safe compilation and use of meta-predicates. The Ciao Prolog system defines an alternative but equivalent syntax for specifying closures, using a compound term `pred(I)` where `I` is the number of extra arguments.

3 From Closures to Meta-calls

Given a closure and its additional arguments, the corresponding meta-call is constructed by appending the extra arguments to the existing ones. Although it is always possible to use the standard predicate `=../2` and a list append predicate to construct the meta-call, the preferable and simpler solution is to use the `call/N` family of built-in meta-predicates found in Logtalk and in most Prolog compilers. The first argument of these predicates must be a closure, with the remaining arguments being interpreted as the closure extra arguments. For example, the query `call(integer, 3)` is equivalent to the query `integer(3)`. These predicates provide improved performance when compared with the explicit construction of meta-calls (which requires building temporary lists).

As discussed later in the paper, the use of the `call/N` family of built-in meta-predicates is mandatory when working with closures as they avoid the introduction of new variables to explicitly represent the constructed meta-calls.

4 Potential Meta-predicate Loopholes

When reasoning about meta-predicate semantics, it is helpful to define a set of terms which helps us visualize how and where meta-calls take place:

Definition context. This is the object or module containing the meta-predicate definition.

Calling context. This is the object or module from which a meta-predicate is called. This can be the object or module where the meta-predicate is defined in the case of a local call or another object or module assuming that the meta-predicate is within scope.

Execution context. This comprises both the calling context and the definition context. It includes all the information needed for the language runtime to execute a meta-predicate call.

Our research is focused on three potential loopholes when implementing meta-predicate support. The first loophole can be exploited to corrupt the original meta-arguments when a meta-predicate is executed:

Making malicious changes to meta-arguments. Using unification with the meta-arguments may allow a meta-predicate to test for specific goals and closures and modify them before making the corresponding meta-calls. This potential loophole can be exploited by testing only for some very specific usage patterns, thus making its detection harder.

The two following loopholes can be exploited to bypass predicate scope directives or to break predicate scope rules. In the case of Logtalk, predicate scope rules are supported using predicate scope directives (object predicates are private by default). In the case of Prolog module systems, it should not be possible to call non-exported predicates from client modules.

Hijacking of the predicate execution context. Hijacking a predicate execution context may allow a meta-predicate to gain access to predicates within the calling context other than the ones specified in the meta-predicate call.

Using closures for constructing unintended meta-calls. A potential loophole exists when appending additional arguments to a closure in order to construct a meta-call. This loophole can be exploited by constructing a call to a predicate with the same functor of the closure but with an arity different to that intended by the caller of the meta-predicate.

5 Compiling Meta-predicates for Safety

This section describes four safety rules, illustrated with examples,[1] intended to close the loopholes discussed above in the context of predicate-based encapsulation module and object systems. The ideal rules would allow catching all problems at compile time. Unfortunately, as we will illustrate in this section, this is not always possible. Some deceiving meta-predicates definitions constitute perfectly valid code; the potential for trouble resulting only from the use of such definitions. For these cases, the compiler can still print a warning. At runtime, our safety rules ensure that any inappropriate use of a meta-predicate definition is caught by generating an appropriate exception.

The first two rules check for the context for meta-predicate calls. The last two rules check for the consistency of meta-predicate directives and the consistency between meta-predicate directives and meta-calls. The rules presentation is conceptual: actual implementations may choose to combine the first and second rules and combine the third and fourth rules. The first three rules are expected to be implemented at the compiler level. The fourth rule may be implemented instead in a programming code style or policy checker.

(a) The meta-arguments on a meta-predicate clause head must be variables.

This simple rule helps to prevent a meta-predicate from modifying the original arguments of a meta-call. By testing and acting upon the actual meta-arguments, a meta-predicate could try to make a meta-call different from the original one to be executed in the calling context. Consider the following example (a):

```
:- object(library).

    :- public(map/3).
    :- meta_predicate(map(*, 2, *)).
    map(In, scale(_), Out) :-
        !, map_(In, scale(3), Out).
    map(In, Closure, Out) :-
        map_(In, Closure, Out).
```

[1] These examples use Logtalk objects. Converting them to Prolog modules requires replacing object directives with module directives, removing the explicit predicate scope directives, and rewriting the meta-predicate directives.

```
    :- meta_predicate(map_(*, 2, *)).
    map_([], _, []).
    map_([X| Xs], Closure, [Y| Ys]) :-
        call(Closure, X, Y),
        map_(Xs, Closure, Ys).

:- end_object.
```

The map/3 meta-predicate in this library object behaves as expected except when the closure argument unifies with the term scale(_). In this case, the original predicate argument is simply ignored and replaced by a fixed value. Assume now that we define the following client object:

```
:- object(client).

    :- public(double/2).
    double(Ints, Doubles) :-
        library::map(Ints, scale(2), Doubles).

    scale(Scale, X, Xscaled) :-
        Xscaled is X*Scale.

:- end_object.
```

In the absence of this safety rule, the compromised behavior of the map/3 meta-predicate could be illustrated by the following goal:

```
| ?- client::double([1,2,3], Doubles).
Doubles = [3,6,9]
yes
```

By implementing this safety rule, Logtalk generates a compile time error[2] for the first clause of the map/3 predicate in the library object:

```
type_error(variable, scale(_))
```

This rule is, however, easy to circumvent by simply moving the unification from the meta-predicate clause head into the clause body. The meta-predicate map/3 in the example above can be easily rewritten as:

```
map(In, Closure, Out) :-
    (   Closure = scale(_) ->
        map_(In, scale(3), Out)
    ;   map_(In, Closure, Out)
    ).
```

Despite this weakness, there are three reasons to include this rule. First, it provides a necessary condition for the second safety rule, described next. Second, rule violations result in compile time errors, which are always preferable to runtime errors. Third, it is trivial to implement: the compiler can apply it before any other rule by simply checking the meta-arguments in the clause heads.

[2] Arguably, this error is more of a representation error than a type error; nevertheless, we decided to follow the practice established by the current ISO Prolog standard.

(b) Meta-calls whose arguments are not variables appearing in meta-argument positions in the clause head must be compiled as calls to local predicates.

This rule applies to the compilation of both meta-predicates and normal predicates. It prevents hijacking of the execution context, which could otherwise be used to call predicates in the calling context not passed as meta-arguments. This problem can occur with e.g. a naive implementation of execution context passing from a clause head to the goals in the clause body.

This rule is trivial to implement when compiling clauses of normal predicates: any meta-call in a clause body must be compiled as a local meta-call. This rule is also easy to implement when compiling clauses of meta-predicates since the corresponding meta-predicate directive is mandatory.

As a consequence of this rule, when a meta-predicate calls a second meta-predicate, the meta-arguments executed in the calling context will be strictly the ones coming from the call to the first meta-predicate. That is, the programmer cannot use a second meta-predicate to construct a meta-call different from the one intended by the original caller of the meta-predicate. Consider the following example (`b1`):

```
:- object(library).

    :- public(meta/2).
    :- meta_predicate(meta(::, ::)).
    meta(Goal1, Goal2) :-
        call(Goal1), call(Goal2).

    :- public(meta/1).
    :- meta_predicate(meta(::)).
    meta(Goal1) :-
        meta(Goal1, local).

    local :-
        write('local predicate in object library'), nl.

:- end_object.
```

The rule requires that client calls to the `meta/1` predicate must result in the interpretation of `local/0` as a call to a local predicate, thus executed in the context of the object `library`. We use the following client object to illustrate the correct behavior:

```
:- object(client).

    :- public(test/0).
    test :-
        library::meta(goal).

    goal :-
        write('goal meta-argument in object client'), nl.
```

```
    local :-
        write('local predicate in object client'), nl.

:- end_object.
```

This safety rule will ensure the following result:

```
| ?- client::test.
goal meta-argument in object client
local predicate in object library
yes
```

Meta-calls can also appear in the body of normal predicates. This rule ensures that an object cannot hijack the execution context of the original, non meta-predicate call and use it through a local meta-predicate to construct arbitrary calls to predicates in the calling context. Therefore, we cannot convert a normal argument into a meta-argument by calling a local meta-predicate. Consider the following simplified version of an example found in [3] (`b2`):

```
:- object(library).

    :- meta_predicate(meta(::)).
    meta(Goal) :-
        call(Goal).

    :- public(normal/1).
    normal(Arg) :-
        meta(Arg).

:- end_object.
```

In this case, the argument in the meta-predicate call, `Arg`, must be interpreted as a local meta-call. Consider now the following client object:

```
:- object(client).

    :- public(test/0).
    test :-
        library::normal(term).

    term :-
        write('Some local, private predicate.').

:- end_object.
```

This safety rule will ensure the following result:

```
| ?- catch(client::test, E, write(E)).
E = error(existence_error(procedure,term), context(object,library,_))
yes
```

Therefore, the predicate `term/0` in the object `client` (which is the calling context for the `normal/1` predicate) will not be called.

Although the two examples above make use of additional user-defined meta-predicates whose meta-arguments are goals, the rule also applies when working with closures and when calling built-in meta-predicates. For example, consider the following tentative exploit (`b3`) using the `call/1` built-in meta-predicate and a meta-predicate definition that does not comply with the corresponding directive (as two arguments are appended to the closure instead of one):

```
:- object(library).

    :- public(m/2).
    :- meta_predicate(m(1, *)).
    m(Closure, Arg) :-
        Closure =.. List,
        list::append(List, [Arg, _], NewList),
        Call =.. NewList,
        call(Call).

:- end_object.
```

With this safety rule in place, the meta-call `call(Call)` above is compiled as a local meta-call since the variable `Call` does not occur in the head of the meta-predicate clause in a meta-argument position. The following definition of a simple client object illustrates the consequences of the meta-predicate definition above:

```
:- object(client).

:- public(test/1).
    test(X) :-
        library::m(a, X).

    a(1). a(2).

    a(3, three). a(4, four).

:- end_object.
```

After compiling and loading these two objects, an example test query would be:

```
?- catch(client::test(X), E, true).
E = error(existence_error(procedure, a/2), context(object, library,_))
yes
```

As the exception term shows, the meta-call is compiled and executed as a local call in the context of the `library` object. Without this safety rule in place, a faulty implementation would wrongly call the predicate `a/2` defined in the object `client`:

```
?- catch(client::test(X), E, true).
X = 3 ;
X = 4
yes
```

The above example shows that meta-predicates with meta-arguments that are closures cannot be defined using `call/1` calls as explicitly constructing the meta-call from the closure results in a new variable not occurring in the clause head. It follows that the use of the `call/2-N` built-in predicates is mandatory for defining meta-predicates that work with closures. This is subsumed by the third rule:

(c) Meta-predicate closures must be used within a `call/2-N` built-in predicate call that complies with the corresponding meta-predicate directive.

The number of additional arguments appended to a closure in a `call/2-N` call must comply with the meta-predicate declaration; simply ensuring that a closure is a variable occurring in a meta-argument position is not a sufficient condition. This rule ensures that a meta-predicate cannot construct a predicate call with the same functor but with a different arity of the original meta-argument. For example, a meta-predicate definition `(c)` such as:

```
:- meta_predicate(map(1, *)).
map(Closure, [Element| Rest]) :-
    ..., call(Closure, Element, Result), ...
```

would result in the following compile time error:

```
arity_mismatch(closure, call(map, Element, Result), map(1, *))
```

The `call/3` meta-call in this example does not comply with the meta-predicate specification, which requires a single additional argument. In fact, the actual meta-call would not be the one that the programmer intended when calling the meta-predicate. Moreover, the call could correspond either to a predicate in the calling context that is not within scope of the meta-predicate definition context or to a non-existing predicate (which would result in a runtime existence error).

(d) The meta-predicate arity should be equal to the sum of the extra arguments specified by each closure plus the number of normal, non meta-arguments.

Assume that we correct the meta-predicate directive used to illustrate the previous rule in order to be consistent with the `call/2-N` call by writing `(d)`:

```
:- meta_predicate(map(2, *)).
```

Trying to compile the updated code would result in the following error:

```
arity_mismatch(closure, map(Closure, [Element| Rest]), map(2, *))
```

This error results from the meta-predicate directive specifying a closure requiring two extra arguments while only one normal argument is declared. This is potentially misleading for a client that may expect the library meta-predicate to call a unary predicate based on the meta-predicate arity.

6 Known Limitations

6.1 Closures with a Variable Number of Arguments

The proposed safety rules and the extended meta-predicate directive do not support the specification of meta-predicates that allow a *variable* number of arguments to be appended to a closure. This restriction makes some common meta-predicates such as `apply/2` useless as a public or exported predicate. The usual definition of this predicate is:

```
apply(Closure, Args) :-
    Closure =.. List,
    append(List, Args, NewList),
    Call =.. NewList,
    call(Goal).
```

As the variable `Goal` is not a meta-argument in the clause head, the meta-call `call(Goal)` is compiled as a call to a local predicate (as per the second safety rule) and not as a call to a predicate in the calling context of the meta-predicate. This restriction is not considered, however, a serious limitation as the number of extra closure arguments is usually known *a priori*, therefore allowing the use of the `call/2-N` built-in meta-predicates.

6.2 Meta-predicates Implemented in Foreign Code

Prolog compilers often include libraries with predicates implemented using a foreign language interface. It is also possible to implement meta-predicates this way. A common example is the implementation of callbacks to Prolog code in the context of GUI extensions (see e.g. the SWI-Prolog XPCE package [13]). In this case, the verification of the safety rules described in the previous section would require manual verification of the source code in the foreign language. It should be noted, however, that the use of foreign language resources rises its own set of security issues that goes well beyond meta-predicates issues.

7 Prolog Module Systems

In this section, we test five Prolog compilers for the potential meta-predicates loopholes described earlier: Ciao 1.10#8, ECLiPSe 5.10#141, SICStus Prolog 4.0.2, SWI-Prolog 5.6.59, and YAP 5.1.3. Although there are other Prolog compilers supporting predicate-based module systems, we believe this is a representative set of module implementation solutions.

Our experiments are complicated by two problems. First, the details of the module versions of the examples in Section 4 differ for each compiler due to the lack of a de-facto standard for Prolog module systems.[3] In particular, the five

[3] The full source code used in the examples for both Logtalk and the tested Prolog compilers is available at `http://logtalk.org/papers/simp/mptests.tar.gz`

tested systems provide three different materializations of a meta-predicate declaration directive. Second, the documentation of the Prolog module systems often forces us to resort to experimentation in order to find out the exact operational semantics of modules, meta-predicate directives, and meta-calls.

The experimental results are presented in Table 1. In this table, a value of `N/A` means that the `meta_predicate/1` directive or its equivalent does not support the specification of meta-predicate templates. The results for the example `(d)` indicate if a Prolog compiler checks for the consistency between meta-predicate directives and the number of extra arguments required by the declared closures. This consistency check should result, at least, in a compilation warning but it is not performed by any of the tested Prolog compilers.

Table 1. Experimental results for the safety rule examples

Examples	Ciao	ECLiPSe	SICStus	SWI (mp)	SWI (mt)	YAP
(a1)	ok	wrong	ok	wrong	wrong	ok
(a2)	ok	ok	wrong	ok	ok	wrong
(b1)	ok	wrong	ok	wrong	wrong	ok
(b1)	ok	wrong	ok	wrong	wrong	ok
(b2)	ok	ok	ok	wrong	ok	ok
(b3)	ok	wrong	wrong	wrong	wrong	wrong
(c)	ok	N/A	wrong	wrong	N/A	wrong
(d)	wrong	wrong	wrong	wrong	wrong	wrong

The conversion of the Logtalk example `(a)` into Prolog module code rises an interesting issue with the module systems of SICStus Prolog and YAP. These systems expand meta-arguments in goals appearing in the body of meta-predicate clauses but not in the head of meta-predicate clauses. As a consequence, the first clause of the `map/3` is never used, making the test result for these Prolog compilers misleading. One workaround is to rewrite this clause using explicit module qualification, which allows all the clauses to be used. Although this rewrite defeats the purpose of the meta-predicate directive, it is also a possible exploit vector. Therefore, we chose to split the example `(a)` in two tests. Test `(a1)` uses the same exact clauses as in example `(a)`. Test `(a2)` uses explicit module qualification for the `scale/1` arguments in the first clause of the meta-predicate `map/3`.

The results for test `(a2)` are interesting and a bit surprising. While the results for SICStus Prolog and YAP are expected, the changes in test `(a2)` allow both ECLiPSe and SWI-Prolog to return correct results, reversing the bad score in test `(a1)` (it is worth noting that the module systems of ECLiPSe and SWI-Prolog are distinct). The Ciao compiler is not fooled by these tricks.

Another interesting result concerns the `(b2)` and `(b3)` examples of our second security rule, `(b)`. All compilers behaved correctly in example `(b2)`. However, with the exception of Ciao, all compilers provided a wrong answer for example `(b3)`, allowing access to a private predicate, `a/2`, in the client module, instead of restricting the access to the predicate `a/1` used as argument in the meta-predicate call. In this case, these Prolog compilers acted properly when meta-arguments are goals but not when the meta-arguments are closures.

Some brief, Prolog compiler-specific comments about the results follow:

Ciao. This is the only tested Prolog compiler that disallows writing meta-predicate directives inconsistent with the meta-predicate definitions. It is also the Prolog compiler that scored the best test results (as expected, giving the emphasis by Ciao developers in static code analysis). The test results for the third example of our second security rule (`b3`) are particularly interesting. The Ciao compiler correctly catches our attempts to specify a closure with a single extra argument while, at the same time, defining the meta-predicate to call the closure with two extra arguments.[4] Correcting the meta-predicate directive to specify a closure with two extra arguments, however, results in the definition of a meta-predicate that only allows a single extra argument to be passed. The Ciao compiler fails to warn the user of this potential problem when compiling the example (`d`).

ECLiPSE. This compiler does not provide a `meta_predicate/1` directive, relying instead on a proprietary `tool/2` directive whose arguments are predicate indicators. Thus, this directive does not allow the programmer to define meta-predicate templates. The test examples are modified to use the `tool/2` directive and the built-in predicate `@/2` as suggested in the ECLiPSe documentation.

SICStus Prolog. This compiler allows the specification of closures in the directive `meta_predicate/1` but only for compatibility with existing code. Correcting the directive in the test example (`b3`) to make it consistent with the meta-predicate definition does not lead to a correct answer.

SWI-Prolog. We present two sets of results for SWI-Prolog. The first set, *mp*, uses an emulation of the `meta_predicate/1` directive provided in the compatibility libraries distributed with SWI-Prolog. The second set, *mt*, uses the SWI-Prolog native directive `module_transparent/1` whose argument is a predicate indicator. Therefore, it does not allow the programmer to define meta-predicate templates. We are discussing with the main SWI-Prolog developer the possible implementation of our safety rules as a component of a general style or policy checker, integrated with the current cross-referencer tool. This would allow existing code to be checked for possible violations without the danger of breaking it.

YAP. Similarly to SICStus Prolog, YAP accepts the specification of closures in the `meta_predicate/1` directive but only for compatibility with existing code. Correcting the directive in the example (`b3`) to match the meta-predicate definition does not result in a correct answer. The safety rules described in this paper are expected to be implemented in a forthcoming version of YAP. Their use is expected to be optional, enabled by a Prolog compiler flag.

---

[4] There is a typo in the Ciao documentation of the meta-predicate specification for closures. The notation `pred(N)` indicates the number of extra arguments, with the closure being used within a `call/N+1` predicate, not within a `call/N` predicate as described in the documentation.

8 Discussion and Conclusions

The safety rules described in this paper fix all known flaws on the Logtalk support for meta-predicates.[5] These rules may also be adapted and applied in the context of predicate-based Prolog module systems in order to correct the flaws uncovered by our experiments. However, given the syntactic and semantic differences among the implementations of Prolog modules systems, the existence of other loopholes is to be expected. Nevertheless, the lack of a formal guarantee that the proposed rules close all loopholes in current implementations should not excuse not fixing the known loopholes.

The safety rules are easy to implement and computationally inexpensive, as exemplified in the current Logtalk compiler implementation. These rules enjoy the nice property of all the required computations being performed at compile time. In the worst case, some of the rules imply that the use of a flawed meta-predicate definition results in a runtime exception due to the meta-calls being compiled as calls to local predicates and not as calls in the meta-predicate calling context. This is an unfortunate consequence of the fact that some safety violations only occur when using meta-predicate definitions that, per se, constitute perfectly valid code. It follows that the worst case cannot be improved by finding stronger compiler checking rules. At best, the compiler could issue a warning when compiling a public meta-predicate whose meta-calls are compiled as a local calls for safety reasons.

The extended `meta_predicate/1` directive described in this paper provides essential information for preventing misuse of closures. We show that specifying closures using positive integers is not just an optional feature, useful for cross-reference and documenting tools or for compatibility reasons, but a necessary feature for safe compilation and use of meta-predicates.

Calls constructed from closures must be made by using the `call/2-N` built-in predicates. This allows the consistency between the meta-predicate directives and definitions to be checked at compile time, preventing loopholes when appending arguments to a closure in order to construct a meta-call. The `call/2-N` family of built-in predicates is already provided by most Prolog compilers and is included in the current draft of the ISO Prolog Core revision standardization proposal.[6]

There is currently no formal proof that the described safety rules are sufficient to prevent highjacking of predicate execution context and the misuse of closures in the context of Logtalk. In the case of Prolog module systems each module system needs a proof, as there is no de-facto standard. These proofs would need to be based on formal descriptions of the module systems, to be provided by their authors; these descriptions are beyond the scope of this paper.

---

[5] All the safety rules are implemented by the Logtalk compiler since version 2.30.6.

[6] In the case of Logtalk, although its current version uses a Prolog system as a back-end compiler, its implementation of the `call/2-N` built-in predicate does not depend on the availability of the `call/2-N` Prolog built-in predicates.

The problems described in this paper are representative of what can go wrong when using meta-predicates in field applications where security is a basic requirement. It is worth noting that the flaws described in this paper are not always evident from a quick inspection of compromised source code (which, by itself, assumes its availability). Despite existing research on improving module systems (see e.g. [3,6]), security concerns are often overlooked by Prolog implementors and programmers. Secure implementation of meta-predicates is just one of the topics where compilers and language runtimes must perform securely. In a scenario of increasing industrial use of Prolog-based solutions, either in embedded form or as stand-alone applications, preemptive thinking about security issues is necessary. In this regard, the Prolog community is still far from the security mindset found in other programing communities.

Acknowledgements. We are grateful to Rémy Haemmerlé and François Fages for bringing to our attention flaws on the implementation of meta-predicates in earlier versions of Logtalk. We thank also Jan Wielemaker and Sara Madeira for their comments and help in revising this paper.

References

1. Moura, P.: Logtalk 2.33.0 User Manual (September 2008)
2. Moura, P.: Logtalk – Design of an Object-Oriented Logic Programming Language. PhD thesis, Department of Computer Science, University of Beira Interior, Portugal (September 2003)
3. Haemmerlé, R., Fages, F.: Modules for Prolog Revisited. In: Etalle, S., Truszczyński, M. (eds.) ICLP 2006. LNCS, vol. 4079, pp. 41–55. Springer, Heidelberg (2006)
4. Group, T.X.R.: The XSB Programmer's Manual: version 3.1 (2007)
5. Bueno, F., Cabeza, D., Carro, M., Hermenegildo, M., López, P., Puebla, G.: The Ciao Prolog System. Technical Report CLIP 3/97.1, The CLIP Group, School of Computer Science, Technical University of Madrid (December 2002)
6. Gras, D.C., Hermenegildo, M.V.: A New Module System for Prolog. In: Palamidessi, C., Moniz Pereira, L., Lloyd, J.W., Dahl, V., Furbach, U., Kerber, M., Lau, K.-K., Sagiv, Y., Stuckey, P.J. (eds.) CL 2000. LNCS, vol. 1861, pp. 131–148. Springer, Heidelberg (2000)
7. Cheadle, A.M., Harvey, W., Sadler, A.J., Schimpf, J., Shen, K., Wallace, M.G.: ECLiPSe: A tutorial introduction. Technical Report IC-Parc-03-1, IC-Parc, Imperial College, London (2003)
8. ISO/IEC: International Standard ISO/IEC 13211-2 Information Technology — Programming Languages — Prolog — Part II: Modules. ISO/IEC (2000)
9. for Computer Science, S.I.: Quintus Prolog 3.5 User's Manual (2003)
10. O'Keefe, R.: An Elementary Prolog Library, `http://www.cs.otago.ac.nz/staffpriv/ok/pllib.htm`
11. for Computer Science, S.I.: SICStus Prolog 4.0.2 User Manual (2007)
12. Costa, V.S.: The YAP User's Manual: version 5.1.3 (2008)
13. Wielemaker, J., Anjewierden, A.: An Architecture for Making Object-Oriented Systems Available from Prolog. In: Proceedings of the 12th International Workshop on Logic Programming Environments, pp. 97–110 (2002)

Author Index